Jon Steele was born in the American Northwest and raised in Great Falls, Montana. He left home at the age of sixteen and worked in an assortment of legal and illegal jobs before joining Independent Television News of London in 1982. He established a reputation as one of the world's top cameramen in dangerous environments. He currently lives in Arab East Jerusalem where he continues to cover the Middle East for ITN. He lives with a stray cat named Killer.

www.booksattransworld.co.uk

WAR JUNKIE

JON STEELE

BANTAM PRESS

LONDON · NEW YORK · TORONTO · SYDNEY · AUCKLAND

TRANSWORLD PUBLISHERS
61–63 Uxbridge Road, London W5 5SA
a division of The Random House Group Ltd

RANDOM HOUSE AUSTRALIA (PTY) LTD
20 Alfred Street, Milsons Point, Sydney,
New South Wales 2061, Australia

RANDOM HOUSE NEW ZEALAND LTD
18 Poland Road, Glenfield, Auckland 10, New Zealand

RANDOM HOUSE SOUTH AFRICA (PTY) LTD
Endulini, 5a Jubilee Road, Parktown 2193, South Africa

Published 2002 by Bantam Press
a division of Transworld Publishers

Copyright © Jon Steele 2002

The right of Jon Steele to be identified as the author of this work has been asserted in accordance
with sections 77 and 78 of the Copyright, Designs and Patents Act 1988.

A catalogue record for this book is available from the British Library.
ISBN 0593 049985

'What A Long Strange Trip It's Been' quoted from *Truckin'* by Robert Hunter,
copyright © Ice Nine Publishing Company. Used with permission.
Permission to reproduce the lines from Buffalo Springfield's 'For What It's
Worth' on pages 107 and 108, written by Stephen Stills, applied for.

Typeset in 10/14pt Palatino by Falcon Oast Graphic Art Ltd.

Printed in Great Britain by
Mackay of Chatham, Chatham, Kent.

1 3 5 7 9 10 8 6 4 2

For Harold Atherton Steele

CONTENTS

1	Crash Zoom	1
2	Big Fun in Sokhumi	4
3	Back in the USSR	60
4	Three Days in October	109
5	Nowhere Roads	166
6	Postcards from a Train	193
7	Christmas Eve	231
8	Nearly Africa	234
9	I Came to Casablanca for the Waters	290
10	Two Cups of Tea	367
11	Goma	370
12	Flash Frame	411
13	Last Shot	413
14	The Colour Temperature of Light	424
	Epilogue: The Way of Sorrows	435

By our own act we were drained of morality, of volition, of responsibility, like dead leaves in the wind.

T.E. Lawrence
Seven Pillars of Wisdom

1

CRASH ZOOM

This is how it happened.

Early morning. Saturday, 21 August 1994. The world fell out from under my feet. I knelt, shattered, on the floor of Heathrow's Terminal Four. My eyes were burning with tears and I was babbling words that made no sense and strangers were looking through my pockets to find out who I was. I couldn't tell them a fuckin' thing.

There were faces and voices and sounds and noise and blurs of bodies speeding past me too fast and too loud. Shapes and sizes warping into a maze with no way out. Bullets and blasts exploding in my brain. Baggage and legs surrounding me like a prison, my heart pounding and screaming, *Run, goddammit! Run!* Nightmares closing in for the kill and another voice chirping over the public-address system about all the fun places to go. Paris, Berlin, Sydney, Mars and . . .

'Attention, Club World and World Traveller passengers. British Airways is happy to announce the nervous breakdown of Jon Denis Steele at check-in counter twenty. Of course, "Jon" isn't his real name, it's "Denis". But he thought a name with a poncy spelling would make him special. Can you imagine? Stupid Denis. Stupid Jon. He should have listened to his father: "You're weak, you're useless, you'll never be anything! I'm ashamed to have you as a son!" And thank you for flying British Airways.'

. . . Madrid, Rio, Hong Kong.

Moments earlier I'd telephoned my wife and driven one more stake through her heart. I wouldn't come to that family wedding after all. Third time I'd changed my mind in twelve hours. We'd been separated for six months. She was hoping we'd get back together. Have a baby. Start over.

And somewhere else in the world a woman I loved or thought I loved or never did. I could still hear her crying over a world of smashed dreams. Her and me and a thousand other broken promises. Rage and tears.

And my son from a long time ago waiting for me to see his play in New York. One more abandonment. 'You've never been there anyway, Dad.'

And all around were bodies and souls I couldn't help, and children bleeding to death, and old men watching their toothless wives choke and vomit and waste away, begging me to save them. And dusty roads lined with bodies and more bodies . . . and shells exploding again and again and bullets zinging across my face and the dark fear of all the nightmares in my life roaring and squeezing the air from my lungs. And when I gagged for breath, all I could smell were dead bodies . . . thousands and thousands of black-purple blobs rotting in the African sun.

Where's the air? Where's the fuckin' air? I CAN'T BREATHE!

'You work for ITN?'

I focused on an unknown face and panned down to his hands. There was a passport and tickets and press credentials with a face and a name. It was me or used to be or never was. I wanted to explain everything. I wanted to show him the small plastic windproof match container that didn't have any matches in it but a wedding ring I hadn't worn in over a year.

'You see my wife is back in the States and I don't know what's happenin' to me and people are going to kill me soon and I deserve it because . . .' But there were no words. Just lumps of dust and death in my throat.

'Do you want me to call ITN?'

I found a business card with my fancy-spelled name.

'This is a Moscow number. You're in London.'

Who was this guy? Why wasn't he hiding? Couldn't he hear the blasts? Whistles and screams and blasts. Listen! Shells rip apart the air and slam and crash anywhere they want and these metal shards, jagged and burning and hungry, fly across the ground looking for flesh. Listen! Closer and closer! We're going to die with all the others. We have to hide – we have to run. Listen, goddammit!

'Jon, do you know the number of ITN in London?'

I closed my eyes against the fear and remembered the number of the Foreign Desk. The unknown man helped me off the floor and sat me on my duffel bag near the phone box. He dropped a pound coin into the phone. I watched his hands dial the number and I wondered what the hell I was doing in London. How the fuck did I get here? He handed me the receiver. 'You'll be fine here. I must go see about my family but I'll come back and check on you.'

And he walked into a crowd of faces. All of them staring at me like a pack of zombies. Any second now the fuckers were going to grab me and rip me to shreds. Coming closer and closer.

Click, click.

'Foreign Desk.'

'Hello . . . Vicky . . . please.'

My voice as shaky as my hands.

'Is that Jon?'

'I need Vicky . . . I need . . .'

'Jon, what is it? Where are you?'

'I'm in trouble. I can't get on this fuckin' plane. I can't do it. I just can't fuckin' do it. I don't even know where the fuck I was goin'. I've hit the wall.'

'Jon, listen to me. I'll send a car for you. Don't move. You'll be fine. Listen to me.'

ITN would book me into a hotel and call the doctor from the Charter Nightingale clinic, one of the best psychiatric hospitals in London.

Christ. Everyone's gonna know.

Jon Steele. ITN cameraman. His pictures were splashed through a string of award ceremonies that year. Cameraman of the Year. Story of the Year. Royal Television Society. BAFTA. Monte Carlo Film Festival. Scoop Awards. A commendation for bravery from Le Press Club de France.

Jon Steele was cracking up. Live and in colour.

2

BIG FUN IN SOKHUMI

17 September 1993

Taganka Square sits just off the banks of the Moscow river . . . two kilometres from the Kremlin. The name comes from the word *tagan*,
meaning the fire irons, skillets and other useful items for the sixteenth-
century kitchen once on offer from the craftsmen who lived and
worked there.

Once upon a time, Catherine the Great booted out the *tagantsy* and
built a prison for criminals and anyone else silly enough to piss her off,
which took on the stuff of legend. Taganka wasn't just a jail for thugs
and thieves, it was Moscow's Bridge of Sighs where men would
suffer and women would weep outside cold stone walls. Even now
you can stumble into any crummy Russian bar and hear some drunken
Russian band wailing away . . . '*Tahgaaaaaaahnka!*' That's when you
know the vodka's been flowing and sooner or later a fight will break
out over a woman, an insult, or both.

A bit later Stalin decided it was a better idea to shovel the criminals
off to Siberian gulags. That way the local residents wouldn't be dis-
turbed by the sound of bullets blasting into skulls. Unlike Catherine,
Stalin liked his inmates dead. Taganka Prison disappeared in
Khrushchev's last days.

Then the People's Soviet Committee for Somethingorother built a complex of ugly grey boxes for the grateful Soviet workers to enjoy as homes. One of those boxes sits atop Taganka Gastronome Supermarket. Barren shelves and all. That was Building Marksistskaya Dom 1. A sixteen- or seventeen-floor firetrap with bad plumbing. I never could figure out how many floors there were exactly: the numbers on the elevators and stairwells were never the same. The People's Committee for Somethingorother made MD1 the home of diplomats from unimportant countries and the Moscow Bureau of Independent Television News. From the fourteenth- (or thirteenth-) floor offices of ITN, I could watch Russia through her seasons of change, or so I liked to think.

What I actually saw was the Moscow sprawl of even more ugly grey boxes and sick trees winding their way along dreary streets looking for a way out of town. Towering above the ugly grey boxes and sick trees were the pale brown towers of Stalin's skyscrapers known as the Seven Sisters. Monuments to the spirit of the New Soviet Man. Grotesque stacks of shit-brown stone designed by someone on bad acid.

And above it all, steam and smoke and diesel fumes filling the air and stirring round and round in a thick, poisonous soup that made for spectacular sunsets during the long summer light of a Moscow evening. Then the blues and greens and yellows of the city's crumbling buildings jumped out from the grey like an impressionist's canvas.

And in the middle of the magic was the Kremlin. Red-brick ramparts soaring over the Moscow river like giant garden walls almost hiding the white cathedral spires and golden domes within. A treasure of mortar and light and dreams.

It all finds perfection in September when leaves turn brown and autumn creeps into the Russian soul. Tram drivers and artists and politicians and street sweepers. They all come back to the city from their tiny dachas in the country. Automobiles and trains are stuffed with potatoes and apples, home-made vodka and tanned faces. Babushkas bottle fruit, men dust off their boots, children go back to school. The last warm days before long weeks of rain dragged them into another Russian winter.

That was my Moscow back then.

I loved the place.

It was my forty-third birthday and I was passing time watching the effect of Yuriev Brain Stretch on Julian Manyon. Julian was the new set of lips in ITN's Moscow bureau. He had everything TV wants in a news correspondent. Tall, handsome, smart as hell, arrogantly confident. A lifetime ago he dropped out of Oxford and fell into the last days of the Vietnam War. He rode through the badlands of the Mekong on a Czechoslovakian-made motorcycle. Beast of a thing called a Jawa. Suited Julian just fine: he rode tall in the saddle. He filed reports for Brit Radio. The Yanks deserted the place and the Viet Cong marched in and Julian hung on for the laughs. He went on to become one of Britain's top news and current-affairs film-makers. His reports were known as well-crafted pieces of television dynamite. Mrs Thatcher despised him. Julian was proud of that.

But nothing could have prepared him for Oleg Nikolaevich Yuriev. Five foot six inches and fiftyish with thinning hair and thick glasses barely hanging on to the tip of his nose. He looked like a guy who couldn't remember his name. Sometimes he couldn't. But ask Oleg anything about Russia and he'll tell you more than is possible to hold in a single brain. He was the Russian fixer in the bureau. Oleg was known and respected by every important politician and journalist in Moscow.

For the last hour, Oleg had been explaining the situation in the former Soviet Republic of Georgia to our most eager Comrade Correspondent. It was obvious Julian wasn't ready for the rollercoaster ride through Oleg's brain where there's no such thing as a straight line.

'Uh, well. It is not that simple. First, Stalin signed a decree and then, well, crop production was down fifty-seven per cent and so, it is like the Russian proverb, "When the lazy dog has nothing to do he licks his balls."'

Julian's head was spinning. I wanted to tell him to keep up. Oleg was the key to everything in Russia but it took world-class training to stay in his league.

We were waiting to hear about a charter flight to T'bilisi, Georgia. From there we'd make our way to the coastal town of Sokhumi in search of Eduard Shevardnadze. He was the last foreign minister of the Soviet Union before the empire melted. He helped Gorbachev find the courage and wisdom to end the Cold War. The man was a hero. These days, Shevardnadze was holed up in Sokhumi's parliament building under heavy shell fire. The Cold War warrior was fighting an old-fashioned hot war. He was losing badly.

Oleg explained to Julian how Shevardnadze had returned to his native Georgia to save the country from civil war. It seemed that Georgia's first non-Soviet president – a professor named Zviad Gamzekhurdia – was not only ineffectual but barking mad. T'bilisi exploded with violence. Gamzekhurdia fled and Shevardnadze flew in to heal the nation. He was baptized in the Orthodox faith. He prayed for the future of Georgia while the guns raged round him.

His small country sat high in the Caucasus mountains. A brooding, jealous Russia to the north and east, the glorious coastline of the Black Sea to the west. In good times the green land was fat with olives and bread and wine. The people had dark hair and dark eyes. Warm hearts and warm smiles. But these were not good times. Bread was scarce. Hearts were full of hate and vengeance. Bullets and Kalashnikovs were plentiful.

The blood in T'bilisi's streets was not yet dry when rebels in the north-west province of Abkhazia made their own strike for independence. The Abkhazians fought like demons and the Georgian army withered under fire. Shevardnadze's troops soon found themselves surrounded with their backs to the sea in Sokhumi.

Shevardnadze was convinced the Russians were behind it. The rebels had too many weapons and their shells were endless and far too accurate for a bunch of drunken Abkhazians. His own troops had the same weapons and were just as drunk as the Abkhazians, but they couldn't hit the broad side of a barn from ten yards.

Yes, he thought. The Russians have come to pay me back for destroying their precious Soviet Union.

He told the world his country was bleeding and he begged for help from anywhere. Nobody listened. It was just another silly war in some faraway place with one of those funny names. So the sixty-seven-year-old Shevardnadze went to stand with his broken army in Sokhumi. He was ready to die. Now he was news.

RIINNNGGG!

Oleg grabbed the phone in mid-sentence. 'So now, Julian, you understand that Georgia needs . . . ALLO!'

Julian's head was saved from information explosion. He turned to me. Glazed eyes, red ears. I was proud of him. It was a brave attempt.

'*DA! . . . DA! . . . DA!*'

7

Oleg's phone voice was a few mega-decibels louder than a steam locomotive from years of bad Russian phone lines. It was impossible to have another conversation within a thousand feet. You had to jump in during the listening bits. Julian's glazed eyes went from me to Oleg then back to me.

'What's going on, Jon?'

'Think we're on our way.'

'*DA! . . . DA!*'

'How can you tell? All he's saying is *"Da!"*'

I shrugged my shoulders. The phone went down and Oleg peered over the rims of his glasses.

'Uh, well . . . he says, well, the man there, that there is a commercial flight – of course there will not be if the shelling resumes, but that is in a different place.'

'Oleg.'

Time to reel him in.

'Oh . . . *da.*'

He understood. He would come down to our level.

'There is a flight to T'bilisi in two hours.'

'Aeroflot?' asked Julian.

'Uh, well . . . no. There is a new airline called Chance.'

Julian let go with one of his laughs. The kind that rattled windows in the next county. Neighbours complained. Kitty cats ran for their lives.

'Chance Airlines!' Julian sputtered. 'This will be fun!'

Oleg laughed nervously and shot me a look . . . Fun?

I picked up my beat-up Sony 200 camera. The 18X1 Fujinon lens was secure. The battery was hot and a clean tape sat in the recorder good to go.

'Yup. Big fun in Sokhumi.'

The usual scene at Moscow's Sheremetevo airport. Stranded passengers and stranded luggage and no seats to anywhere. Oleg tuned in his radar and spotted a tallish man with a pointed nose and a brown suit. A stylish briefcase in a firm grip.

'Hmmm,' said Oleg.

Two minutes later he was back.

'Uh, well. This man is the manager, president, pilot, sometimes baggage-handler and ticketing agent of Chance Airlines. He has borrowed a Tupolev 134 jet from Aeroflot.'

'Borrowed?'

Seemed the guy had taken a pile of nuts with ten million miles on it, scrubbed off the Soviet flag and Aeroflot logo, then plastered huge red letters along the side and *voilà*. Chance Airlines.

Oleg went into a corner with Comrade Entrepreneur. They exchanged pleasantries and wads of cash. Three tickets were pulled from the briefcase, which was stuffed with US dollars.

'Uh, well . . . he thanks us for taking a Chance.'

It did make one wonder about the wisdom of a free-market economy in Russia. But onboard the plane was clean and the flight attendants were not the usual Soviet prison-camp guards but charming and polite. They offered salami, cheese and champagne. Fresh bread and juicy apples. We checked our tickets to make sure we were in the right place.

Julian sat a few rows ahead of us, imbibing and dining away the two hours to T'bilisi. He and a drunken Russian engaged in animated conversation. It looked like neither of 'em understood a word of what the other was saying. Me and Oleg sipped champagne and looked at our lunch.

Mmmm. As Pavlov's effect took hold we ran through our list of supplies. Flak-jackets, helmets, camera batteries and charger, tripod, medical kit, six bottles of water, and . . . no food.

Oops.

'I'm starvin'.'

'Uh, well.'

'Amazin' to see this food on a Russian plane.'

'I, too, cannot believe it.'

We smacked our lips as the pilot told us about airspeed and wind direction and how happy he was we were taking his plane to T'bilisi, and of course . . .

'*Priyatnovo appetita!*'

'What's he sayin'?'

'He says, "Enjoy your lunch." ' And Oleg grabbed the food an inch from my mouth. 'But we cannot eat.'

'Huh?'

'We must save this food.'

'Huh?'

He scooped bits of lunch off my tray and stuffed them into his backpack.

'But—'

'Perhaps we can get bread in T'bilisi.'

'But—'

'I will tell Julian to save his food as well.'

Oleg jumped up the aisles and peeked over Julian's head. He was back with a grin on his face. 'Not a crumb on his plate . . .'

Few things stood between Julian and lunch.

'. . . and he's demanding more champagne.'

'That's one Brit who never got the memo on the End of Empire.'

The jet touched down under a blazing Georgian sun. We walked across the tarmac towards the terminal in search of the luggage. The vision of a soldier came out of the heat. Green battle fatigues and sneakers and Ray-Ban shades. A bottle of brandy in one hand and a Kalashnikov automatic rifle in the other. One of the Georgian army's finest. Julian went off to find the camera kit and I grabbed Oleg. 'Let's go see our friend over there.'

'Uh, well . . . yes, over there.'

Oleg always repeated things he'd just heard. Something to do with the way words filtered into his brain.

We caught up with the Georgian soldier under the wings of yet another borrowed Tupolev jet and another free-market conversion. This time big blue words spelling ORBI. An eagle drawn in arty lines on the tail.

'Uh, well . . . the new Georgian national airline.'

More men in fatigues, climbing the steps of the jet. Arms resting on the black metal and wood stocks of automatic rifles. Brandy all round. The jet whined to life.

'Sokhumi, *da*?'

The soldier stopped and looked us over. His eyes caught the camera hanging from my shoulder. He thought it was swell.

'*Da!* Sokhumi!'

Oleg stepped in to save me from my Russian skills. More than once he'd been forced to explain to some important Russian that Comrade Cameraman did not really mean to express a 'hunger for sleeping dogs' while trying to say 'Hello'.

Oleg told the soldier we were from Kompaniya Televideniya Britanskaya and asked if we could travel with them to Sokhumi because we wanted to tell their story to the world.

The soldier pulled off his Ray-Bans to show the surprise in his eyes. 'You want to go to Sokhumi?'

'*Da!*'

The jet's engines whined higher. The soldier shouted to his comrades on the plane's steps and the sky instantly filled with fists and Kalashnikovs and drowned-out cheers. I couldn't hear the voices but I knew the signs. Every soldier in every army in the world wants his picture taken as he marches off to war. If he dies his picture will say, 'I was alive! I was brave! I was on TV!' The soldier pointed to a shack at the end of the runway. Georgian Army Airport Command. We needed permission to get on the plane.

'Will the pilot wait?'

'*Da!*' He waved his rifle and smiled. 'Or I will shoot him in the brain!' He stopped smiling.

'Oleg, he wouldn't really shoot the fuckin' pilot, would he?'

'Jonka, he is a Georgian!'

'We'd better hurry.'

'Uh, well . . . yes, hurry.'

We ran across the runway. He huffed and puffed about the poor state of post-Soviet aviation just to keep his mind up with his legs.

'Uh, well . . . you see, everybody now wants their own airline and Boris lets all these dinky new countries grab whatever jets were on the ground when the Soviet Union collapsed and the newly freed comrades paint them and call them names like Orbi. No planning, no fuel, no properly trained pilots. It's like the Russian joke . . . this apparatchik calls the party leader in Smolensk . . .'

The airport commander sat at his desk looking down at two telephones and a hand-held radio. None of them in working condition. His hands spinning a well-oiled Tokarov pistol in little merry-go-round circles on the desktop. He looked up and invited us to coffee. It was that kind of war. A jetful of reinforcements waiting to fly off and get killed, and we get coffee. Oleg explained we were in a hurry to get to Sokhumi. The commander raised his hand.

A soldier walked into the room. A small copper tray in his hands and an AK47 slung over his back. OK . . . coffee time. One of those mind-twisters that divide East and West. A small cup of coffee shows an acceptance of the culture and customs. To refuse would be an insult. I sipped while Oleg chatted with the commander.

'We send in two flights each day,' he said. 'In with guns and men, and out with the dead and wounded.'

His hands moved from the black Tokarov to the cup. More little merry-go-round circles. He didn't know how long the Georgian army could last. 'The situation is very bad.' Tasting the coffee. Searching for words. 'I must tell you it is very dangerous.'

A little bell sounded in my head. A cameraman in a war zone likes to think the camera offers him immunity from getting his balls blown off. Fantasyville . . . people die. Adrenaline and fear coming on like a speedball. It felt good.

The commander said the jet would leave in ten minutes. He thanked us for going to Sokhumi and wished us well. Oleg led the charge for the door. Eight soldiers with rifles jumped into our path. Now what? Quick Russian back and forth. Oleg's disbelieving smile.

'They would like a photograph with us.'

One of the soldiers holding up a happy-snap camera.

'I don't believe this.'

We jumped on a bench with some of the lads. Camera ready, chests puffed, rifles like cocks. FLASH!

'*Urah!*'

We ran out the door.

Slash-and-burn TV. Rip apart the gear. Water-bottles in one bag. Spare batteries in another. Bandages in flap pockets of flak-jackets. Repack it all again.

'We'll wear our body armour on to the jet. Everyone carries their own helmet.'

'Jon, would you have space for these?'

Julian laid out a clean pair of jeans, one proper English shirt and a pair of socks. He thought it important to take a change of clothes. Funny what seems important at times.

'Sure, Julian.'

A German TV outfit had a sat truck pitched on the runway near the ORBI jet. The operator agreed to take the rest of our kit to the Metichi Palace Hotel in T'bilisi.

'You should not go to Sokhumi. Our team just got out yesterday. They say there is blood everywhere. The city is going to fall very soon!'

Gong! More bells in my brain.

'No kiddin'. Can we use your satphone?'

A handful of airport workers gathered round Julian as he dialled London. All over the world, locals thought satphones were the bees' knees.

'We're going in now . . . Not sure exactly when we'll get out.'

'Where does this foreign man speak?'

Oleg loved this game. 'Uh, well . . . to England.'

Wide eyes.

'How does it work?'

'Here we go,' I mumbled.

Oleg cleared his throat. 'The voice goes up twenty-two thousand miles into space . . .'

Wider eyes.

'. . . it bounces off a sputnik . . .'

Mmmmms of understanding approval.

'. . . and then it falls twenty-two thousand miles into London.'

Oleg always saved the best till last. He cleared his throat once more. 'And it costs fifty American dollars each minute.'

That called for a cigarette. Two months' wages for a fucking phone call? Over at the jet, the last of the soldiers were climbing aboard. Women on the tarmac stood nearby looking up at the small round windows full of dark eyes. Oleg spotted it while telling his satphone class that, no, it would not be possible to call a cousin in Tajikistan and ask how the goats were doing.

'Uh, well . . . yes . . . leaving.'

'Time to go, Julian!'

It takes a surgeon's skill to remove a telephone from a reporter's face. Gentle coaxing and calm body language followed by . . .

'THE PLANE IS LEAVING!'

Little-known secret: television reporters live in fear of Pissed-off Cameramen. We ran to the jet. The satellite operator called after us, 'You are crazy to go there!'

'Thank you for sharin'!'

His attitude was not the best of send-offs. He shouted again, but I couldn't hear the words. My brain was spinning with the sound of bells, the roar of Illyushun jets and a rush of warm adrenaline. The war drug kicking in. The soldiers cheering.

'*Urah!*'

SLAM!

The door was pressure-locked, and the jet moved down the runway. We'd made it. And the Georgian irregulars smiled, ready to become TV stars. I staggered over men and rifles and rocket grenade launchers looking for an inch of space. Everyone on the floor, seats and carpets torn away, like a flying pick-up truck.

'It makes more room for the bodies on the way back!' a soldier confided.

'You don't say.'

Oleg plopped down on ammunition cases. Julian settled next to a guy in a Russian navy-issue blue-stripe shirt. Two soldiers with grizzled faces shuffled their rifles and made room for me between them.

'Allo! Welcome!'

Their breath smelt of onions and booze, and they shoved a half-drunk bottle of plum brandy in my face. 'Drink!'

I wondered at the wisdom of being on a jet full of drunken Georgians waving Kalashnikovs locked and loaded and ready to fire. On second thoughts . . . I reached for the bottle. Brandy spilled down my face as the Tupolev jet growled and threw us into the sky.

'Eat!'

A loaf of filthy bread in my face. I was hungry and somewhere in my kit were Imodium tablets for what would surely follow, so I ate.

'Drink again!'

OK, fine. Drink again.

'Good!'

And the soldiers slapped me on the back and gave me their hands. I'd passed the test, I was one of them. The bottle went to Oleg and Julian. Full marks for them too.

I looked round at the faces. Sun-brown and wind-carved. Like telling the age of a tree from the number of rings. Soft lines on a pale brown face, maybe twenty years old. Deep crags crunched round dark eyes, late fifties. They were all dressed in shades of green. Not a complete uniform among them. These were the men answering

Eduard Shevardnadze's plea to save Sokhumi. An armed mob sailing through the air at 580 miles per hour.

I reached down between a stack of rifles and grabbed my camera. Flip the power switch and electricity rushes through the circuits and the tape winds round the drum head and light pours through the lens and hits the CCD chip and bits of magic transform the light into 750 lines of video. It was time to work. To be in the world of colour and somehow slip out of it and look back through the viewfinder where electronic images of black and white tell a story.

Soldiers began to smile and pose. Happy-snap time again. I stood with the camera on my shoulder and braced myself against the bulkhead. I framed a wide shot and panned slowly from side to side. I gave it time. Each man wanted to feel the lens looking into his eyes. Cheering and laughing, waving rifles and brandy, victory signs in abundance. I lowered the viewfinder and made a thumbs-up. The men cheered again. I walked to the back of the jet and tried to disappear. Scrunched down and looking for something ... anything, my eyes filtering away reality. Where was the picture? Where was the image?

Over there. Two men holding hands. Between the hands, the black barrel of an AK47. They watched me with big smiles. My mind threw out the men and their smiles. In my eyes there were only the hands and the business end of an automatic rifle. I zoomed in and focused. Pull out ... not too much ... there. My thumb felt for the small button on the back of the lens. A gentle press and roll. There it was. Brothers in arms.

Across from me, an old Orthodox priest. Curls of long grey hair falling from under his black priest hat and down on to the shoulders of his black priest robes. Black beads of a touch-worn rosary moving through his priest fingers.

Roll.

The lens panned from the black beads to his priest face. Lips praying for the soldiers of Georgia. And then his priest eyes look into the lens and into my eyes. Lips still praying and head now nodding as if he knows some terrible secret. As if praying for me.

I lowered the camera. 'Not me, Father. Just along for the ride, but thanks.' Back into the lens.

A helmet balances and turns on the barrel of a gun. Boots with holes in the soles. Two men standing along the bulkhead, arms draped over each other. Rocket shells at their feet. Another soldier alone with his thoughts and a cigarette. He takes long pulls of smoke and holds it deep. He lowers his head and closes his eyes, and smoke slips from his mouth. Afternoon light pours through the windows and small clouds of steel-grey smoke swirl in round tubes of sun hanging in the air.

'Jon!' blurted Julian.

He was pointing at the fellow in the striped shirt next to him. That's when I first saw Eddie Parker.

'He's from Manchester!'

Eddie Parker. Unemployed British Yob and War Tourist. Skinny body and skinny face topped with a blond Hitler Youth haircut. His skinny legs covered with Croatian army-issue trousers. 'Croats! Bunch of assholes! Can't fight their way out of a paper bag!'

Seems Eddie went to Bosnia to fight Serbs and Muslims. He got fed up with whatever discipline there was and wandered off to Armenia to see the war in Nagorno Karabach.

'Jon, what a fucking shithole!'

Then a bit of ethnic strife in Chechnya.

'They should just gas the whole fucking place!'

Now Eddie Parker lived in T'bilisi. Desperate to get laid.

'I'm looking for a girl with a moustache. Someone grateful anyone cared enough to fuck her. KnowhatImean?'

Twenty-five years of life had given Eddie a hard-knocked no-shit philosophy as a guiding force. The flower of British youth, wandering war zones looking to get laid.

'I've hired Eddie for a hundred dollars a day!' yelled Julian.

Made sense. Another set of hands to help with the gear and help us out of any bad boogie-woogie. Eddie had his own still camera. He hoped he could take a few shots for himself and maybe we could help get them published.

'Why not?' I said.

The engines kicked back and the jet began to sink through the sky. The soldiers hushed as older voices began to sing. Deep voices and slow Orthodox tones filling the plane with lament and sadness. I watched the faces of boys and men on the edge of war. Tomorrow many of them would be dead.

Oleg crouched next to me.

'Uh, well . . . we will go to the cockpit now.'

'Right.'

He led me through the sound of rifles clicking and snapping and checking out one more time. Up in the cockpit the mood was serious. The pilots had only one narrow approach into Sokhumi. Fly west out of T'bilisi through the mountains and out over the Black Sea and turn round and land. Columns of smoke rose from a small city on the shoreline.

'Och'amch'ire. The town just south of Sokhumi,' said Oleg. 'The rebels took it this morning.'

The approach into Sokhumi was shrinking by the hour. The pilots looked down at the smoke and now-dead friends. A sharp bank lined us up with the runway. More pillars of smoke and fire on the horizon. The Abkhazians had reached the gates of Sokhumi. For some reason I looked at my watch: 4.47 p.m. I was touching down in a war on the losing side.

Another rush of the war drug through my blood.

Warm buzz.

The pilot hit hard on the tarmac and raced down the taxiway. It looked like any airport in the Soviet Union. Uncut grass along crumbling asphalt, broken-down Aeroflot jets scattered here and there. I slid into the jump-seat by the right hatch door and switched on the camera. The jet slowed near the terminal and two men threw open the hatch. Harsh light and moist air whooshed in with the crack of rapid automatic-rifle fire.

Soldiers ran alongside the jet as it pulled to a stop. I leaned out of the side with the camera rolling. Thousands of desperate souls pushing against a thin green line of Georgian soldiers. Women with babies, old men with young boys, widows with no one. The engines whined down under screams and cries and panic, as the mob pushed closer to the jet. A couple of soldiers rushed towards the mob and let off eight rounds inches over their heads. The terrified human wave settled back for a moment, only to surge forward again.

Crack! Crack! Crack!

More cries and outstretched hands begging to escape. Julian leaned over me to see what the hell was going on. 'Jesus wept.'

I looked up from the eyepiece. He was wearing his flak-jacket and helmet. Smart, very smart.

'Julian, you realize if we get off this plane, we may not get back again.'

Crack! Crack!

'What do you think?'

Another warm buzz.

'Let's go have some fun.'

Julian, Oleg and Eddie gathered up the gear. I threw on my flak-jacket and pushed my way down the steps and into the panic. A few yards away, another gangway. I ran up the steps and focused the lens wide. The terrified wave broke through the thin green line and surrounded the jet like a swamp.

Soldiers backed on to the stairs up to the jet, rifles ready. Tense eyes and twitchy fingers on triggers. Just below me, two stretchers held high in the crush of bodies. One man with bandaged legs, the other shot in the chest. No effort was made to help them through the crowd. In Sokhumi the wounded were just more pieces of baggage along with all the other tattered cases and overstuffed burlap bags.

Crack! Crack! Crack!

A young girl climbs up the stairs and loses her footing. She hangs in the air. Desperate hands pulling at legs like pieces of rope. One of the soldiers on the gangway reaches down and hauls her up. The mob goes mad and crushes harder. Bodies lifted up and washed away in the current. Screaming children, screaming women . . . the whole world screaming. And me wondering what it would be like when we tried to leave.

'Fuckin' hell.'

'Jon!'

Julian calling from down under the nose of the jet and fighting his way through the mob. I ran down into the begging faces, all crying and pleading and reaching to the lens.

'Help us! Help us!'

I reached out and touched one shoulder . . .

'Sorry.'

. . . then I pushed my way through the beggars.

Oleg and Eddie had joined Julian.

'Welcome to Sokhumi,' said Oleg.

A crowd gathering round us. Desperate fear and sweat. A young woman with a baby across her breasts. 'We have no bread! I have been here for three days, look! My child is sick!'

And another. 'My husband went to the front. There is no one to help me!'

Then a din of voices.

'The soldiers will only let their friends on the plane! We will die here!'

'My son was crying all night under the bed, "Don't shoot us! Don't shoot us!" '

And still the hands reaching for the lens and pleading more and more.

'Listen to us! Help us!'

'Look at us! They have turned us into animals!'

Into the terminal. Shadows in dark corners hiding from the madness. No water, no food, no electricity, no way out, no hope. Shadows waiting to die.

Outside the terminal. A steady parade of refugees pushing through the doors not knowing the hopelessness waiting inside. And I wondered again, how the hell were we gonna get out of here?

A jeep pulled up and out stepped Thomas Roth from German Television. If he was here it meant we were in the right place. He'd been in Russia for ever and was one of the best on the scene. Find a tape from the August '91 coup in Moscow. Yeltsin walks out of the Soviet Parliament, the big marble monolith Russians call the White House, steps on to a tank and into history. Look in the lower left frame of the picture . . . there's Thomas scribbling away in his notebook.

From the other side of the jeep Rory Peck. Former officer of Her Majesty's Guards Regiment, now full-time video cowboy. Years ago he picked up a camera in Afghanistan and went as close to the action as he could. Others would sit back and whisper, 'That guy is *bonkers*.' He was a character out of Evelyn Waugh. Came from one of those families with the right accent. Went to all the right schools. You loved him or hated him.

I liked him from that first moment in Azerbaijan. We were running with the rebels down the coast road to Baku. Rory barked lots of things like 'Good God, man!' and 'Do tell!' He held his cigarette in perfect British fashion.

Last out of the jeep was Juliet, Rory's beautiful wife. They'd met in Pakistan during the Afghan War, both their lives shattered with heartbreak. In time they married and moved into a dacha outside Moscow. They surrounded themselves with horses and the children of previous lives. A Very British Couple of the Country Life who enjoyed nothing more than winging off to some nice little war.

We talked about the battle in the city. Thomas said it was getting very bad. As usual Rory was in the thick of it.

'It was very, very scary,' said Thomas.

None of us knew it then but in a few days Rory Peck would be dead. Different battle, different war. His picture on the front pages of Russian papers. His body in a pool of blood. His camera smashed on the ground next to him . . . still running.

'Well, we must be off!' said Rory. 'Good luck!'

They threw themselves into the mob to fight for a place on the jet back to T'bilisi. We piled into a bus full of Georgian troops and headed off to Sokhumi.

The sun was low and filled the sky with soft amber light. Sokhumi was once the Côte d'Azur of the Soviet Union. Brilliant weather. Warm water, warm winds. Now the roads were lined with desperate souls and silent steps, dust and fear. Down in my guts the fear monster hammered at his cage. I needed another hit of the war drug. Something to keep me going. We pulled into Sokhumi just before sundown. Streets strewn with rubbish. Houses and buildings bombed and burning. There didn't seem to be any pattern to the shelling. Just death from the skies to scare the shit out of the Georgian civilians. Every incoming shell a screaming terror.

Whoosh . . . Crash! 'Get out!'

And just to make their point, the Abkhazians were killing every Georgian husband and father they could find at the front. The rebels wanted more than Shevardnadze's death. They wanted to purify their land of Georgian scum. Only then could Abkhazia fulfil its destiny. Ethnic cleansing. Pure and simple.

The parliament stood in a wide square. A fifteen-floored target of pale Caucasus stone, one wing smashed and burned. The rest of the stone was shrapnel-scarred and fire-scorched. Down in the square a teetering flagpole flew what was left of the Georgian flag. It was full of bullet holes.

'Uh, well . . . it seems the rebels are close.'

'Damn close, Oleg.'

Booms echoed from the hills around the city. Heavy artillery and Katyusha rockets three or four kilometres away. Julian and Oleg wandered inside the parliament looking for Eduard Shevardnadze. Eddie minded the gear and told a group of Georgian soldiers that they should get out there and kick some serious ass. I walked off to find a few pictures.

Round the corner behind the parliament. A long row of abandoned Soviet-style flats. A narrow alley in between and an old man struggling with two heavy buckets of water. He stops to rest a moment, wiping his brow and hands, then the sound of incoming rockets.

Whoosh . . . Slam! Crash!

A siren wailed as another shell smashed nearby. I dropped to the dirt and covered my head. Compression waves, dust and bits of stone flew overhead. The old man watched me pull myself up off the ground. He folded his handkerchief, collected his buckets and walked on.

I ran round to the front of the parliament. Soldiers and civilians were dashing through shattered glass into the dark lobby. Seemed like a swell idea to me so I dashed in behind them. Julian, Oleg and Eddie were against a back wall far from the glass. Another swell idea.

'Shevardnadze is upstairs,' said Julian. 'He'll see us but we must wait.'

'Any other press around?'

'They're all down at the Russian barracks. Three kilometres away.'

Quick sums in my mind. If the Russians were behind the shelling then the Russian barracks was the safest place in town. And as we carried Russian press credentials they might just let us in. But there was no way to get there and nasty things were falling out of the sky. It added up to being stuck. Three more shells crashed in the streets. The building shook.

'Hmmm,' said Julian.

'Uh, well,' commented Oleg.

'Yup,' I replied.

Through the shattered glass, the fading light of day. Maybe twenty minutes left. The Sony 200 didn't work well in low light and I didn't have a night-vision lens. The bean-counters controlling ITN's purse strings seemed not to grasp that a bureau surrounded by four wars might be in need of a decent camera kit. The idea made Eddie Parker fume with rage. 'Shit, Jon! Let's shoot the fucking accountants! Those bastards! Let's see their tight asses out here! Bastards! They'd be shitting themselves up to their fucking ears.'

'I suppose that's one way of lookin' at it.'

'Perhaps Eddie should negotiate your next contract, Jon.'

'Maybe so.'

Booms rattled through the halls. Chunks of glass fell on to the pavement. Standing around made me nervous. I looked at Oleg. 'Oleg . . .'

'Uh, well . . .'

'. . . the roof.'

'. . . roof.'

He found a Georgian officer to lead us up endless flights of dark stairs. He wouldn't let us on to the roof. Direct hits had killed seven of his men already. We found a blown-out window on the top floor.

Great view. The city rolling on gentle hills down to the coast. Pale light and crimson clouds and a fat sun sinking into black waves. Automatic rifles crackling like crickets and plumes of smoke and fire rising from the streets where dogs howled with madness and fear. I switched on the camera and sucked it in. The officer peered round the edge of the window.

'Evening is always a good time for terror, *da*?'

'S'pose it is.'

He thought it dangerous to stay much longer. Big-ass camera on a tripod makes a tempting target for a sniper.

'OK. Just one more shot.'

'Why not? If it is our time to die then it is our time to die.' Big smile. Smoke-stained teeth.

I eased back from the window and waited for that small moment when daylight turns soft and the colour temperature fades and you can play with the light. Flip the filters from daylight to tungsten and lock the colour balance into preset. Roll.

Sunset in Sokhumi. Deep blue sky, smoke and clouds, gloriously ablaze above a burning city. Red tracers of anti-aircraft artillery ripping across the sky like firebirds. And me counting thirty slow seconds in my head. Letting the picture run. The war drug hit me again and I let it rush hard.

'OK . . . got it. Let's go.'

Oleg helped me with the tripod and we ran down the dark hall to the stairs. Somewhere in my pounding brain more sums. Anti-aircraft tracers meant ten-inch shells. But aircraft weren't the target. These firebirds hungered for flesh and blood. And when they found them there would be nothing left.

'Help us! Help us!'

A few flights down to Shevardnadze's bunker. A small generator pumping out a trickle of electricity and soldiers walking through pools of dim light. Blacked-out windows stuffed with sandbags. Damp sweat smells. In the outer office twenty men settled in for another long night of waiting. An old fan cranked from side to side, moving the sweat smells from face to face. A crumpled pack of L&M cigarettes on the floor. Stale smoke drifted round like a ghost. Kalashnikovs on knees and bandanas wrapped round heads.

'Looks like a fuckin' casting call for *Rambo VII*.'

'Uh, well . . . now is not the time to engage in your movie fetish,' grunted Oleg.

Maybe not. These were Eduard Shevardnadze's bodyguards, his last line of defence. A two-tonne giant stood against black upholstered doors, belts of bullets wrapped around his chest and a well-used AK47 in his massive hands. The Last Man in the Last Line. He would die to protect that man behind those doors and everyone was suspect. That included television cameramen. We waited out in the hall. Heavy artillery rumbled closer.

The black doors opened and the twenty soldiers stood. A few senior officers emerged with casual salutes and 'at ease'. Then the slow steps of Eduard Shevardnadze, still looking the senior superpower diplomat of the Soviet Union. Neatly pressed blue suit, striped shirt, tasteful red tie. That same shock of white hair flowing across his head.

Rewind, 1981. Washington, D.C. Soviet Foreign Minister Shevardnadze was on his way to a meeting with US Secretary of State James Baker. A gaggle of cameras stood outside the Russian embassy on Sixteenth Street to grab a shot of 'The Shev' on his way to the nearby Madison Hotel. I got tired of waiting and wanted a beer. I grabbed my camera and left. Rounding the corner of the embassy I bumped into a pack of suits talking into their sleeves. State Department security detail with the famous white-haired man in the middle of the pack. The Shev had decided to forget the motorcade and walk through a back alley of Washington for his superpower chat.

On went the camera. I worked my way to the front of the pack and focused on Shevardnadze. They kept walking and I kept back-pedalling, trying not to fall on my ass. He looked at me through the lens and mumbled something in Russian to his translator.

'The Soviet foreign minister wishes to know why you are taking his photograph!'

'Uh . . . because he's an interesting man.'

More mumbled Russian as The Shev considered the stupidity of my observation. One of the security detail pushed me up against a wall and Eduard Shevardnadze walked by, laughing to himself. And now, years later across a smoky room, that same face, through another lens. The laughter gone. A portrait of sadness and pain.

Julian was twitchy. 'Should we go in for the interview?'

'Nope. Not yet.'

I'd been rolling since the doors opened. Black and white images of a great man forgotten by the world, talking to his dispirited soldiers, giving them courage and strength. And looking into their faces like he was searching for something too. He shuffled his feet and looked into the lens as he slipped back behind the upholstered doors and the two-tonne giant with the bullets across his chest sealed Shevardnadze from the world once more. A small clock chimed midnight. Outside the booms and crashes had gone quiet.

'Shit!'

'His war, Julian. Let's eat.'

'Excuse me?'

Oleg talked the soldiers into letting us have a room for the night. Two doors down from Shevardnadze's bunker. We offered the cot to Julian, knowing he would lay claim to it anyway. The small couch smelling like a wet dog went to Eddie because he liked the way wet dogs smelt. Left just enough floor space for me and Oleg.

'Uh, well . . . like any good Soviet hotel.'

'So, what's on the menu, comrade?'

He opened his backpack and laid out the aeroplane leftovers. He sliced up two apples and bits of cheese. I found what was left of the salami. A bottle of mineral water passed around dry mouths. Julian cleared his throat and spoke in resolute addressing-the-staff tones.

'So, Jon. At present we have the airport and a bit of shelling and we shall soon have my interview with Shevardnadze. Then I think we're done.'

'I think we gotta get to the front.'

Julian's hand waved with 'now, now' authority. 'London is only interested in Eduard Shevardnadze.'

'We need to show what the hell's happenin' here. Fuckin' place is gonna fall. We should stay till the end.'

'I am not prepared to spend the next few weeks in this shithole with no way of feeding out material!'

Fuck it, he was right. I hated it when reporters were right. No use collecting a million shots if we couldn't get them on the air. But the war drug was fading again and the fear monster was breaking loose in my guts. I needed to get to the front.

'Now, Jon, please pay attention. I want to do a proper sit-down interview. So, film me in two shot with Shevardnadze, shaking hands.'

'Nope.'

'Excuse me?'

A silent moment for Oleg to clear his throat. Time for reporter—cameraman mud-wrestling.

'We do it on the run.'

'Jon, I have been doing this for twenty years.'

'Julian, this is a story about a war. Let's keep the goddam pictures movin'.'

'I think the viewer will find it interesting to see me with Eduard Shevardnadze.'

'Since when are you the fuckin' story? And another thing, take off that tie!'

Oleg and Eddie's heads bounced back and forth like they were tennis fans. Oleg wishing there was more food to stuff in my mouth and Eddie wishing for blood. A Georgian officer appeared in the doorway, yelling louder than the rest of us. 'What are you doing?'

Instant repentant children.

'Uhhhh.'

'Eduard Shevardnadze is waiting!'

Out the door, down the hall, camera on. The usual Marx Brothers routine. Oleg jumping in front of the camera with the microphone. 'Uh, well . . . testing, one, two, three.' And Julian telling the soldiers with guns surrounding Shevardnadze to 'Shut up!' while fussing about a 'more visual background'. And me standing there grinding my teeth.

'Rollin'.'

'Are you ready, Jon?'

'Yup.'

'Are you quite sure?'

Oh, for Christ's sake.

'Rollin', dammit!'

Shevardnadze's face fills the black and white frame of the eyepiece. Dark circles under lonely eyes. His voice slow and deep like the soldiers' songs on the flight into Sokhumi.

'The situation is dangerous. The enemy is now fighting into the city. People are panicked.'

'Why did you come?'

Shevardnadze shuffles from side to side and mumbles, 'I promised I would protect Sokhumi. I will not abandon the city. Even if the worst happens.'

He walks back to his private office and the camera follows. He sits at his desk of seven yellow telephones. A general stands nearby trying to raise someone on the line. Above Shevardnadze's white head, the carved Great Seal of his crumbling Georgian Republic. The general gives the telephone to Shevardnadze. More bad news. The rebels have broken through the north end of the city. Shevardnadze rubs his chin and covers his eyes.

I backed out of the room still rolling tape. I pulled my eye from the world of black and white images and looked into the room. Cold blue fluorescent light falling down on Shevardnadze like a bitter chill, like in a morgue. The two-tonne giant slammed the doors in my face. Out beyond the sandbagged windows, the shelling began again.

'Sounds a whole lot closer than before, don't it?'

'Uh, well . . . it seems the front has come to us.'

We woke to the sound of outgoing artillery. The Georgians cranking up the last of their heavy guns to chase away the Abkhazians. Other than that it was fairly quiet. We found our shoes and flak-jackets in grumpy fashion. A little precious water was allowed to clean our grubby teeth. Three litres left. The gear was packed and dragged down ten flights of stairs. Outside . . . clear sky and hot sun. The Black Sea sparkled.

Julian and Oleg went off to find transport. Me and Eddie waited on the front steps of the parliament building. The plan was to find wheels and grab a few bang-bang shots then get out on the next plane. Night before, in one of those screwy Russian quirks, Julian managed to get a call out to London over a ragged Soviet phone line. No, they did not want him to stay, and Oleg and Jon should come out as well.

'Remember, we are only interested in Shevardnadze. It's a war nobody cares about,' said a voice from London.

I watched people on the streets of a war nobody cared about. A woman stacked four or five metal jugs on to a pram and made her way through the shelling to the only working water-tap in Sokhumi. How long could she last? Who cared?

A long line of men and women marching in the distance. Suitcases and children dragging alongside, winding down the street and into the square. Shuffles of feet on broken glass. Murmurs and prayers and tears. Who cared? Maybe nobody. Bit of luck and I'd soon be back in T'bilisi swilling beer over a fat-boy dinner.

Across the road an Armoured Personnel Carrier pulls up in front of the hospital. A Georgian soldier pops the rear hatch as two men in white coats rush out with a stretcher. A bloodied soldier hauled from the hatch and on to the stretcher. The doctors carry him towards the surgery. A lifeless hand falls and swings. Too late.

'Bunch of fucking cunts!'

Julian was back, Oleg smiling behind him. Comrade Correspondent was outraged that the Georgian army would not provide a car. Even more outraged that they were not suitably impressed by Julian Manyon's presence among them.

'They say there is no petrol in the entire city!'

Seems Oleg had led Julian to Brigade HQ where some mad dog named General Adamia was about to lead a charge to the front. We were welcome to tag along.

'We just have to fucking get there! Fucking cunts!'

'Bring out the fuckin' cash.'

A stack of American greenbacks found fuel and wheels. Julian, Oleg and Eddie climbed into a clapped-out Lada. I jumped into the side-car of an old Russian motorcycle. We sped through the rubble of Sokhumi's shelled streets.

Brigade HQ was more smashed to hell than the parliament. Still . . . out front a babushka was sweeping up shards of glass with a scratchy broom. The doorman was happy to look after the kit we didn't need.

A bus full of Georgian volunteers sputtered up to headquarters and we piled on. Laughter and smiles.

'Hiya! Anyone here know any camp songs?'

They didn't understand me but they cheered anyway.

'Jon! There's the general.'

Stomping out of the building was Brigade Commander General Adamia, 240 pounds of squat pug-nosed pit-bull wrapped in a white flak-jacket. I hopped off the bus and ran over for a picture. I got too close. He growled, 'Arrrgghh!' and waved his Kalashnikov in my face.

'Brggrrup grzzlski!'

Soldiers ran to his heels.

Mad Dog Adamia was giving orders and somehow the soldiers understood him.

'Arrrgghh! Rggle arrrgghh!'

'*Da, moi general!*'

The general ripped open the door of a grey BMW and climbed in. He waved and growled at the driver. A foot slammed to the floor and the car tore away, Mad Dog's Kalashnikov barrel swinging out the window like a cavalry officer's sword. The bus sputtered and creaked and chased close behind. The Great Georgian Army Counter-offensive was on.

'*Urah!*'

We zipped round corners and up a hill towards the north end of the city. Empty tree-lined roads, warm sun through green leaves. I sat just behind an officer at the front of the bus. He slapped a long banana clip of bullets into his Kalashnikov. Click, snap . . . lock and load. Fingers tapped my shoulder from behind. A young soldier smiled through missing teeth. 'Are you not afraid?'

I tried to think of Russian words for 'Damn straight! Wish I'd had a piss 'cause I'm about to wet myself, that's how fuckin' afraid I am! But riding the edge is the fun part. Right, comrade?'

But I saw his skinny fingers kneading the stock of his rifle. Worn-out Adidas sneakers and no socks. Too-big trousers torn at the knee. He wasn't much over sixteen. I kept my mouth shut and held out my hand. He grabbed it and squeezed hard. General Adamia and the magic bus crossed paths with a Georgian APC. Soldiers in the armoured vehicle pointed up the road. Mad Dog waved his rifle and shouted more orders. 'Rggle arrrgghh!'

Charge!

The bus strained against the gears to keep up. I turned back to Oleg, his metal helmet bouncing on his head.

'Sure are gettin' far from town,' I said.

He nodded like a drunken mushroom.

The parade screeched to a halt. The bus emptied in a flash. I kicked on the camera and ran alongside the mad-dog general. Focus and roll. A rabid look in his eyes. Spittle drooling from his lips. He tears across the road to a group of soldiers running back to town. The gold-star pit-bull snarls and snaps and foams at the mouth. The retreating soldiers stop dead in their tracks begging to explain. The general howls, 'Cowards! You fucking cowards!' and growls and leaps, his fat paw ripping away the commander's AK47. The commander trying to hold on for a second. Big mistake.

'Arrrgghh!'

The general slams his huge boot into the side of the commander. The commander drops the weapon. Stunned and shamed.

'Fuckin' hell. *Patton, the Sequel*.'

The commander's rifle handed to another soldier, and the general screams and orders him back to the front with no weapon. 'You fucking coward!'

Rapid gunfire sounded yards up the street and incoming mortar shells signalled bad news coming our way. General Adamia rallied his soldiers. He would save their brother Georgians and reinforce the front line.

'Don't be afraid, men! I am with you!'

'*Urah!*'

Sounds of battle roaring closer. The line of soldiers moved up to the trees and scurried across the road.

'You going to follow them, Jon?' called Julian.

'Yup.'

The camera fell in and rolled with images of boots and legs and dusty rifles. Over a small hill and into the line of fire. Bullets ripping through the air at 1200 metres per second. Zing–zing. A sound that sucks the air out of your lungs. The soldiers moved ahead ducking behind wide trees along the road. I held back for a shot . . .

Zing, zing. Whoopwhoopwhack!

. . . bits of tree bark blowing up in my face.

'Down!

Zing, zing. Behind me. Julian and Oleg in the dirt . . . thumbs-up. They were OK. Eddie crawled up beside me.

'Getting good, eh?'

A truck rounded the corner. The Georgians had slapped a huge anti-tank gun on to the flatbed. Hit the brakes, reverse round and two long barrels took aim down Abkhazian throats. Eddie screamed with delight. 'Fucking unreal!'

'No shit.'

I ran up to the drainage ditch next to the guns and jumped in on top of two Georgian soldiers.

'Howdy!'

They grunted.

The air exploded as thirty anti-tank rounds blasted into the front, smoke and cordite drifting over us. The gunner shouted to the driver and the truck took off before Abkhaz mortars could find their range. The two Georgian soldiers leaped up to rejoin the line and I crawled up behind them. A heavy machine-gun opened up from God knew where. We fell back into the ditch checking ourselves for hits – nothing but bits of leaves and twigs tumbling down on our heads.

'What a rush!' I laughed.

They grunted again.

Then a shell raced across the sky . . . closer . . . closer, over our heads towards the front . . . then slamming on to the road. Georgian artillery backing up the counter-punch. The Abkhaz machine-gun went quiet and the soldiers crawled out of the ditch towards their comrades. I dashed back to the rest of the ITN squad. Eddie jumped in behind. We fell in a huddle, our four faces in the dirt.

'Think we should go on?' asked Julian.

I watched the soldiers thirty yards ahead. To catch up meant exposing ourselves to machine-gun fire with no cover.

'Ain't sure.'

'We should stay together from here on,' said Julian.

'You're right.'

Sums in my head. Not enough pictures in the can yet. Few more and we'd be OK for a story. Go forward, risky . . . fall back and . . . ah, fuck it.

'Let's go forward just a hair and see what happens. We'll back off if it gets too spooky.'

Four heads nodding.

I picked up the camera and we trotted ahead.

Zing . . . zing . . . zing . . . zing.

Whooooosh . . .

'Shit!'

'Down!'

Slam! Crash!

Abkhazian mortars returning fire. Swell. Two more, then another. Smoke filling the street. A stone house across the pavement. It was like a decision between ants. We raced for cover. Julian across and in . . . Eddie and Oleg across and in . . . I jumped up and ran.

Zing, zing!

That time I felt it. Two steel feathers brushing my face – oh, God – down, fucker! Down! I curled up behind a fat tree. Oleg's voice calling from inside the stone house.

'Jonka! Are you all right?'

'Yeah. Everyone safe?'

'*Da!*'

'Listen, Jon,' yelled Julian, 'I really don't think this is worth it.'

'Nope.'

Abkhazian bullets cutting down the street along the garden fences. Had to be stray fire from the front, right? Or did some stoned machine-gunner have me in his sights? Didn't matter. End up just as dead, either way. Overhead another round of Georgian shells hitting the Abkhazians. The rifles quiet. Sums again. Seconds between the artillery report . . . overhead whistle . . . the hit . . . one, two, three. At every artillery report, the machine-guns went silent for cover. Distance to shelter, three maybe four seconds. Good enough. I got to my knees. Hands on the camera and waited.

Zing, zing.

Boom – go! Through the fence – shooosh – down now! KACRASH! Crawl up the porch and into the dark with the rest of the gang. I rolled on my back and looked around. Place was solid with another floor of concrete above us. Safe for now.

Abkhazian mortars rained down in the street. The rebels had finally figured the range of the anti-tank gun. Except now it was gone and we were the leftovers. We twiddled our thumbs and waited for the storm to pass. Georgian voices drifted in from the road. Oleg crawled out of the hall and peeked around the corner of the glass-lined porch.

'Uh, well . . . it is definitely them.'

'Who?'

'The brave Georgian soldiers. They are heading back to the city.'

Not a good sign. Still we could piggy-back under cover of their rifles if we had to. Oleg yelled through the smoke: 'Allo!'

'*Urah!*'

And they kept running. We crawled to the porch and ducked behind the small concrete wall under the windows. The plan: dash across the street and join the Georgian soldiers back to town. The problem: snipers and machine-guns controlling the street. OK. It was worth the dash. Julian and Oleg first then me and Eddie would follow. I lay in the doorway with the camera and the first team jumped out of the door. Then, from out of nowhere, a deep-throated howl. Fiery metal ripping apart the sky. Jesus! It's on top of us! Julian hit the ground, covering his head. Oleg fell back into the porch. The incoming shell roaring and screaming and reaching into our chests and squeezing our hearts. The ground shakes. Hot metal and shattered glass slicing the air inches above our heads.

'Holy shit! They've got us!'

A little dog from the next garden ran up to the fence near Julian and stuck its snout through the fence yapping away with a hysterical little-dog bark and all I could think of was how much I hated little dogs with hysterical little-dog barks. Julian and Oleg crawled back into the hide-out. I lay under the concrete wall with the camera lens out of the doorway hoping for a shot of the Georgian army shooting back towards the front. Anything to give us some breathing room. No luck. All I saw was an army running away. Swell, just swell.

Then the air ripping apart again – WHOOSH – KACRASH!

The house next door took the hit. Rocks and dust and tree branches fell in front of the lens. The day was not turning out the way we'd planned. I heard Julian's voice behind me.

'The rebels must be trying to cut off the road from reinforcements.'

'Got me, mate. Just seems very fucked out there.'

'I suppose we could wait it out. What do you think?'

And turned round and saw Julian standing, his full six and some inches. 'I think you should get down.'

His eyes darted from side to side as if he'd just remembered he'd left the kettle on. 'Oh . . . right.' And he ducked back into the hall.

The next second, shattered glass above my head as a high-powered bullet ripped by and slammed into the wall behind me. Fuckin' bullet had Julian's name all over it. Someone had us in his sights and was not going to let go. My heart pounded. The fear monster eating at my guts. The war drug gone and crashing fast and me feeling like a fucking junkie. I crawled back into the hallway. We sat in silence, listening to the booms and whistles and crashes outside. A car engine racing through the explosions. Julian peeked round the corner and broke into laughter.

'There goes the general in his BMW!'

I looked at Oleg. I trusted him more than anyone in the world. 'What do you think, comrade?'

He lay on the floor. Hands tucked under his chin like a schoolboy listening to a story. He thought for a moment, then peered over the rims of his glasses. 'I think we should get the fuck out of here.'

Oleg never said 'fuck'. This was serious. We tossed round ideas.

'Wait it out?'

'I suggest we go over the fence and through the next house and as many as we have to till we get back to town.'

'Good idea to stay clear of rifle fire.'

Another shell slammed into the street. And us holding on to our nerves with spiky claws. Then two more.

'Uh, well . . . that could be our only problem.'

Eddie started to work out trajectories and explosive weights of mortar rounds. Oleg still listening like a schoolboy. It was important we all agreed. We were getting hammered and targeted by unseen guns. Two hundred yards back and we'd be out of the line of fire. But it was a long fucking two hundred yards. Then again if Mad Dog Adamia and his boys had split, well, we were in the middle for damn sure and, frankly, there were just too many fucking guns going off in every direction.

'Right, we're fucked.'

'Let's get out of here.'

Out the door and over the fence and into the land of the hysterical dog.

'I wish someone would shoot that fuckin' dog!'

Whoosh. 'Get down!' . . . KACRASH!

Oleg's reproving eyes met mine in the dirt.

'Forget I said that.'

'Not me, Jonka, but perhaps you should apologize to the little doggy.'

Up again and around the back of the house. Looked like the owners had abandoned the place days ago. The little food left in a dish had gone rotten with maggots. The dog shrieked and snapped like a mad-woman. I turned round to kick the fucking thing and saw her puppies. Four of them. Three dead and one barely alive trying to wag its puppy tail and yelping for help. The bitch howled wild-eyed, jumping between me and her dead pups. The shells and bombs had terrorized her. She couldn't give milk and her pups had starved to death.

Julian and Eddie looked over the stone fence. Cover on both sides. They hustled up and over. Me and Oleg ran to the fence and stopped. A big jug of water hanging from the stones. We looked back at the hysterical dog. Then at each other.

'Jonka, you're not thinking—'

'Yup.'

'Of course you are.'

Oleg pulled down the jug and I found a huge metal pan. Filled it with water and set it on the ground. Searched our pockets for food. Just a half-eaten candy bar. I dropped it on the ground. 'Good luck, Momma.'

And we jumped over the wall.

Three or four houses and gardens and we were beyond the hill. We ran out to the street and looked down the long road back to the city. We were in the clear.

Whoosh . . .

'Shit!'

'Down!'

. . . CRASH!

'I don't fuckin' believe this!'

'Uh, well . . . it's like they are chasing us.'

Whoosh . . . CRASH!

'Was it something we said?'

Across the street a man sat between two trees. Black suit. Black hat. Black cane. He watched us get up and hit the dirt over and over again with the incoming shells. He didn't say a word. He was long gone to Loony Tune Land.

'How far to the city, Oleg?'

'Uh, well . . . five miles.'

'Well, the shells have eased off. Let's go.'

We ran fast and low along the garden walls. The flak-jackets felt heavy and slow. My muscles hurt like hell and my mouth was tinder-box dry. No water with us. Just keep going! Julian and Eddie were well ahead on their long legs. Julian's voice called back to us. 'Come on, men!'

Me and Oleg running and huffing and puffing side by side.

'Did he just say . . . "Come on, men"?'

'Uh, well . . . sometimes . . . reporters can be a real . . . pain in the ass!'

'No shit.'

Whoosshhh! And is if by magic a ditch opened under our feet. CRASH! Shredded leaves and branches tumbling down on our heads. For some reason we started laughing.

'You don't suppose Julian heard us, do you?'

'Uh, well . . . it is like the Russian joke. Brezhnev is sitting on the toilet having a crap when the telephone rings—'

Whoosh . . . CRASH!

We caught up with Eddie and Julian. All of us sucking air, drained of strength. We were out of sight of Abkhaz rifles but the shells were still marching after us. 'We have to keep moving.'

'How far now, Oleg? Two miles?'

'Uh, no . . . four and three quarters.'

'Shit.'

Then, from out of the smoke, a big yellow bus rounding the corner on to the main road. We looked at each other for a reality check. Then four voices at once.

'Hey!'

The big yellow mirage stopped. We ran over and piled aboard. The driver barely waited before stepping on the gas. We fell into seats, sweat pouring down our faces.

'So far it's been an interesting day.'

'Uh, well.'

'Fuck me.'

Eddie was trying to talk a soldier out of his rifle. He wanted to blast off a few rounds for laughs.

The bus screeched to a hard stop next to an APC off the side of the road. Men and smoke. Julian and Eddie pulled at the bus windows for the camera. I focused through their hands and rolled. Five or six soldiers dragging two badly wounded comrades. A trail of blood in the dirt. Rear doors fly open and a wounded man tossed on to the deck. The soldiers climb over him and on to the bus. A body dangling between them, bleeding from the hips. I followed them with the lens. Pictures want action not some guy lying on the floor.

My eyes caught the back of the APC. The rear hatch open and bodies stacked six or seven high, all dead. I tried to get the picture in the lens but the bus lunged away and the shot was gone, so I spun round for another.

A bleeding soldier tossed in a seat. Contorted faces and screams, pain and agony. Bandages round his waist soaking through with purple blood. Hands pull up a sleeve and wrap a rubber tube round a bloodied arm. Slapping and hunting for a vein. A filthy needle draws morphine into a syringe. The road rocks and the bus rolls. The needle shakes above a swollen blue vein. Voices scream and the bus grinds to a halt.

I heard the rear doors open again. Two civilians came aboard and stepped over the body on the deck. They looked around, shopping bags in hand, then found seats. They looked out the window to enjoy the view. Just another day on the 3.47 p.m. bus to downtown Sokhumi. Behind us two shells crashed into the road and the bus sped away.

I focused on the body on the deck. A black and white image in the frame. The face ghostly pale, a thick pool of blood flowing from under his legs; the guy was bleeding to death. I pulled my eyes from the lens and tossed the camera into Julian's lap. 'It's rollin', Julian! Keep it going out the window just in case!'

' "In case" what?'

I knelt in the blood and touched his neck. Weak pulse but still ticking. I tried to remember the words from a battlefield medical course with a bunch of British journos. It was all fun and games back then, followed by lots of booze in the evening. Shit! What do I do now? Think! *Open the airway* . . . yeah. I angled his face up from his chest. *Comfort the injured* . . . Right. I looked in his eyes. 'Hi. How goes it?'

'Ahhhh!'

'OK, then, you're still breathin'. This is a good thing.'

Christsake . . . the guy's going into shock and he doesn't speak English and I'm asking stupid questions – what next? *Check bleeding . . .* Right! I grabbed his shoulders and rolled him on to his belly.

'Ahhhh!'

Jesus, his legs. Both calves torn to shreds. Left leg pumping blood in pulsing streams. Right leg with a huge chunk of shrapnel sticking out of the muscle like a mislaid hammer. Black jelly-blood curdling round jagged metal. Ugly, but at least the artery was plugged. An instructor's voice yelling in my head . . . *'You must stop the bleeding!'* I pulled a field bandage from my battle vest and ripped it open. Oleg leaned down, a Swiss Army knife in his hands.

'Don't you use that thing on our food?'

'Uh, well . . . yes. But I will wipe it on my jeans like always.'

'Swell.'

We cut open the leggings and the blood pumped faster. I called a soldier in the next seat. He sat there dazed. I grabbed his sleeve and pulled him to the floor. I shoved his hand into the wounded soldier's crotch and pushed as hard as I could. Where was the arterial pressure point, for Godsake? I pushed harder. The wounded man screamed. Good, still conscious. The dazed soldier pulled away his hand.

'*Nyet!*' I yelled, and I rammed his hand back into place.

'Ahhhhh!'

'I'm sure you think this is all very rude, pal, but we gotta stop the fuckin' blood in your pal's leg or he dies!'

Oleg yelled the words in Russian and the dazed soldier caught on. He pressed down on the artery. The pumping slowed. I covered the wound with two bandages and tied the tails round the leg, pull and squeeze. I stuffed cloth around the edges of the jagged metal in the other leg. The steel shrapnel was looking like bandage enough. Eddie was holding the wounded soldier's head.

'How's his breathin'?'

'He's having a fucking cigarette.'

I looked at my hands for a moment. They were covered in blood. Lots of it. I wiped them across my trousers and grabbed the camera. The bus gunned through Parliament Square and raced to the hospital. Screeching brakes once more and cries and screams. Women in black, frightened men, chaos and panic. Pictures . . . lots of pictures.

A nurse leads a blinded soldier into the hospital, blood trickling down his face. Men on stretchers beg for water. An exhausted doctor runs from litter to litter touching the wounded. Wasn't much else he could do. Too many, way too many. Cars squeal round the corner bringing more wounded, more dead. And all over the hospital garden, bodies draped in white shrouds stained with dark blood, more cries and screams.

I stepped over the bodies and rolled through the panic, cramming as many shots as I could into the lens. I wasn't interested in any dignity for the dead, I just wanted pictures. An old woman in a black scarf, thick tears rolling down her face. A young girl with her hands over her mouth, her young eyes not wanting to understand what was happening, her entire world dying.

Roll.

Soldiers crumbling with grief near bloodied shrouds. Where was the best angle? My eyes caught one soldier stumbling over bodies and holding on to the side of an APC. I jumped like a rabbit and leaped through the tears and pain and stuck the lens in his face. The glass sucked at his terror and it poured into my eyes.

Roll . . . roll.

A shattered man, ready to keel over, his head lowered and staring at the ground. A few hours ago he'd jumped on a bus ready for war. He'd tied a bandana round his head. He would drive away the enemy and save his land. He would live in glory. Now rising to the lens . . . full with horrible truth . . . red and swollen eyes. The counter-assault has failed. Sokhumi was lost. Everyone would die. A warm buzz running through my blood.

'Jon!' yelled Julian. 'Piece to camera.'

I handed him the microphone. Bodies and wounded loading on to a bus bound for the airport.

'Over there by the bus! Gotcha . . . rollin'!'

'. . With many of his soldiers panicking it's only Shevardnadze's presence here, his strength of will, his encouragement to his own soldiers that is keeping this city in Georgian hands. But right now not even he can say how much longer they can hold out.'

Julian's voice capturing this moment of fear. The Georgians' and our own as well. I did sums in my head . . . stand up, interview with The

Shev, kick-ass shots from the front, lots of bodies, teary-eyed civilians
... added up to a story. Now all we had to do was get out of town. We
grabbed a lift to HQ. The shelling went quiet. Civilians and soldiers
running from here to there in the lull.

'I think we could use some shots of shelled buildings.'

'Yeah?'

'And the sea is just around the corner.'

'Yeah?'

'It will help with my script.'

'Oh?'

It was totally unconvincing but what the hell? Another hit of the war
drug might feel good.

'Let's go, then.'

We took off. Beauty shot of the Black Sea coastline. Close-ups of
shelled-out homes. Refugees walking through a smoky frame. An air-
raid siren cutting through the wind. Mortars whistling down fast ...

'Hit the ground!'

... and shells exploding all around then fading away.

'That's it!' said Julian, picking himself up off the pavement.

'Me too.'

We ran through the streets back to HQ. Shells had us in the dirt
every few yards. I could hear the faint round boom of the launch then
whistles screaming closer and closer and wham! Slam! CRASH! Then
up and running till the next outgoing booms.

'You know, Jon, you're getting quite good at this!'

'I'd like to thank my coach and my personal saviour
Jesusfuckin'Christ.'

'Pardon me?'

Boom ...

'Hit it!'

... CRASH!

Civilians crammed into the foyer of HQ. A woman weeping and
squeezing a child in her arms, the child just staring at her mother's
tears. Oleg collected the gear. The old doorman wouldn't take any
money. He only wished to hold out a wrinkled hand.

'Thank you for coming. Please help us!'

A refrigerator truck sat outside and the driver, too, was grateful we
had come. But instead of a handshake he wanted a few hundred

dollars to take us to the airport. Sounded good. We said our goodbyes to Eddie Parker. He wanted to stick around and take a few still shots. The Moustachioed Girls of T'bilisi would have to wait. Eddie Parker was a nutter warped from too many wars. But he was at our side the whole time. I gave him a big hug.

'You be careful. Keep your fuckin' head down,' I said.

'Fuck, don't worry about me, Jon! I'll just pick up a gun and shoot my way out if I have to! Maybe I'll end up a fucking Georgian general!'

'Wouldn't be surprised.'

We threw the gear into the refrigerator and climbed into the truck cab. After a few tries the engine kicked over and we headed out of Sokhumi. Past the hundreds of lost souls along the road looking for an escape from the brutal end. Shevardnadze and his army might fight on but the people were running for their lives. I could feel Abkhazian gunners in the hills looking down on the exodus. Drunk as skunks and laughing it up with their Russian advisers: 'Say, Ivan! This ethnic-cleansing shit really works!'

I listened to the gears clanking and grinding and carrying me away from the shells. I watched late-afternoon light through the trees. One of my favourite joys, warm light and backlit leaves. My head out the window and breathing deep the cool air. My heart still running through the streets of Sokhumi. The fear monster closing in. *No, not now. Please, not now.*

The airport was surrounded by thousands of desperate civilians wandering blank-eyed everywhere and nowhere, pacing and knowing there was no escape. Julian paid off the driver and had Oleg ask for a receipt. The driver was confused. I was confused.

'You want a receipt, Julian . . . now?'

'Oh, Jon, please. Fucking bean-counters!'

As if they handed out awards. Most Accurate Expense Report in War Zone. Applause.

We're all very proud, Julian.

Thank you . . . thank you.

'Oh, fuck it. Let's go.'

We pushed through the mob and found the administration office. A tired Georgian army captain sat with an AK47 on his lap, cigarette in his hand and his fingers tapping the trigger in staccato time. He already knew we were coming. His orders were to get us on the next jet out of Sokhumi. Eduard Shevardnadze might be losing his whole world but he still understood the power of television. A young policeman came into the room and was introduced to us through a cloud of cigarette smoke.

'This police officer will help you leave.'

We shook hands. I forgot his name instantly. The policeman stood solemn and calm listening to orders until the captain waved him away. The captain wished us well and lit another cigarette. I wished him luck. He saluted and drew a long drag, slumped back into the chair and let a blue cloud flow from his lungs. Like watching mad visions in the smoke.

'Save your words. You still may die in Sokhumi.'

More mad visions in the smoke.

Out the door.

'Uh, well . . .'

'Fuck me.'

An Orbi Tupolev 154 on the runway. Jet engines whining over thousands of refugees. Same scene as twenty-four hours ago. Same faces, same begging hands, same shadows in dark corners. The hot tarmac soaking up the same pathetic tears. The young policeman escorted us through the mob towards the plane. Suspicious eyes following with angry thoughts.

'Where are they going?'

'Look! The strangers are leaving!'

The hopeless voices chased after us.

Georgian troops held a line round the jet as the mob pushed forward. Hatches sealed, engines cranking to a higher pitch. Shit! The pilot was pulling out . . . like now! Women hurled themselves under the forward landing gear. Live rounds and rifle butts forced them back. The policeman turned and told us to wait. He pushed through the mob to the line of soldiers. He pointed to us and then to the plane. Voices around us squeezed closer. Hot air like a vice.

'Help us.'

'Do not leave us here.'

'Look at my child. He is dying!'

This was not going to be easy. A squad of Georgian soldiers reached through the voices and pulled us ahead. Dark eyes in the mob strained with anger, voices spitting curses.

'Shame!'

'Listen!' yelled the policeman. 'They are journalists, they must leave to tell the world what is happening here!'

'Cowards!'

'Let us go! We will tell the world!'

A rolling gangway ten yards from the jet. Soldiers fired close over heads and cleared a path to the steps, the young policeman pointing ahead as if showing us our seats in the cinema. The mob pushed back as soldiers wheeled the gangway to the jet. I framed the faces below the lens. Urgency and panic, hands reaching and babies held into the air screaming and crying, insanity dripping from eyes. The gangway slammed into the fuselage. A soldier hammered the hatch with his rifle. Julian banged me on the shoulder and pointed towards the cockpit.

'Jon! The pilot!'

Pan up. The pilot hanging out of the small window, his hands waving us away.

'*Nyet! Nyet!*'

Hands waving and pleading.

'They are journalists! You must take them! Orders!'

The pilot pointing down to the angry mob.

'Look down there! If I open the doors we'll be trampled! We will all die!'

Pan down. Thousands of images in black and white filling the frame with hate. A woman with a child in her arms spits and screams. 'Why should they go? They are men!'

'Cowards!'

And something hard zipping by my skull. A rock. A bloody riot bubbling at our feet. I switched off the camera and laid it at my feet.

'Uh, well . . . a wise decision,' said Oleg.

The soldiers still pleaded to get us on the jet, the pilot waved 'fuck off' some more and sealed his window. The gangway slid back from the plane. My heart had finally caught up with me from the city and it was sinking in my chest . . . and the fear monster was laughing in my guts again.

'Know somethin', comrade? I think we're in deep shit,' I said.

And Oleg standing there. Nothing to say, not even an old Russian proverb. The young policeman's hand touched my shoulder. 'Please, you wait.'

'Yeah, sure.'

He edged down the stairs and forced his way through the mob and the slapping hands and the venom curses.

'Traitor!'

'Coward!'

And we stood on the gangway surrounded by soldiers and AK47 assault rifles protecting us from an angry mob of old men and widows and mothers. Dizzy panic running like a wild river through every soul on the tarmac. My brain doing more sums. It was only a matter of time before the rebels hit the airport. My bodyweight was gold. Two women, maybe four children, could easily take my place. I added it up with the lofty ideas racing through my head about the valour of journalism. But now my camera was on the ground. Nothing to hide behind now. I was just another refugee. And I was afraid, very fucking afraid. I wanted out. Now, dammit!

Oleg nudged my side and his eyes peered over the rims of his glasses towards the jet. Silhouette hands reaching for the plane. A girl perched on shoulders fumbles and claws at the rear-door latch. She finds it, pulls hard, the stairs fall open like the gates of heaven and the souls rush in till the jet can take no more. Soldiers run over and fire live rounds. Each volley closer to the heads of refugees. The mob scatters and the gates of heaven slam shut once more.

'There's our man,' said Julian.

The young policeman at the foot of the gangway calling us down.

'Uh, well . . . that is it.'

'Swell.'

We all sighed and made our way down into the mob. It parted easily, we were no longer a threat. The policeman cut a path towards the terminal. We would be escorted back to the captain's office and offered apologies in place of coffee. We would wait while he smoked Russian cigarettes and listen as he filled the room with smoke and told us of his mad visions of death. Real swell. The young policeman stopped and put his hands on the hood of a big old Kamaz truck. 'Please, get on.'

'Oleg?'

A quick babbling of Russian.

'Uh, well . . . he means get on the front of the truck!'

'What the fuck for?'

'Uh, well . . . do it!'

Refugees gathered around. I saw panic in the young policeman's eyes for the first time.

'Please! We must hurry!'

Four men and camera kit jumped on to the truck as it jolted into the mob heading for the starboard side of the jet.

'Anyone know what's going on?'

'No fuckin' idea!'

The mob swelling with suspicion, the truck moving faster. I felt myself slipping down and held the camera close to my chest. Oleg's hands, like a power tool, grabbing the back of my flak-jacket and holding me steady. Frantic voices chasing after us. Twenty yards, ten yards.

'Uh, well . . . hold on, Jon, we only have one chance at this!'

'At fuckin' what exactly?'

The starboard hatch flew open and hands waved us up. I tossed up the camera and the hands grabbed the shoulders of my flak-jacket and lifted me up on to the deck. I grabbed the camera, switched it on and spun round. Oleg and Julian and the policeman and deadly mob screams . . . all rushing through the lens. Then the tiny hands of a boy and bigger hands hauling him in, then another boy, then a woman in black. Then the faces below crying to be saved, begging, screaming, and the hatch slams shut.

Silence.

The crew pushed us back into a black storage space behind the cockpit. Sweat and stench and heat mixing with the hum of jet engines inside the blessed hull. The flight crew flipping switches and talking to air-traffic control. I let a heavy breath gush into the dark. All was right with the world.

Oleg found a bottle of water in the kit and passed it around. Long deep gulps. Thirsty mouths watched. A woman asked for a drink. Her child was sick in the heat. I shook the last of the water and watched it splash around. 'Here.'

The poor kid sucked it down in seconds.

The camera was on its last battery. Half dead. But I needed to work. Up out of the storage compartment and into a mass of sweating bodies. A gang of soldiers admired my flak-jacket. I pulled one of the ceramic plates from the vest. They tapped it and let the weight bounce in their hands. I explained which bullets at what range would be stopped by the plate, like I was talking about gas mileage in a used car.

They nodded and smiled and I wondered what the hell able-bodied soldiers were doing on a jet *out* of the city. I pushed through them and wound into the main cabin. Seats gone, not an inch to spare. Couple of hundred people crammed together like cattle on the way to the slaughterhouse. Only the crush of stinking flesh kept everyone standing. And under their feet, the wounded and the dying and the dead. No one spoke, no one cried. Silent seconds passing in quiet panic.

Clunk. Swoosh.

Fresh air and terror rushing through the hatch. Soldiers screaming from outside the jet. One more wounded body crammed into the cattle car. Cries of refugees seeing their last hope and rushing up the gangway forcing a mass of frightened bodies into the open hatch. Screams and panic.

I fell back with the camera. Soldiers on the jet rammed their weight against the door and heaved once, twice, and again but the panicked refugees slammed back. I braced against bodies and tried to keep the camera steady and focused. The crush pushed and gouged and threw me off my feet and back on to Julian and Oleg. Claustrophobic horror rushed through the jet like a plague.

'What the fuck is going on?' yelled Julian.

'How the hell should I know?'

I wanted to hit something, might as well be him.

Julian cursed and forced himself into the panic, his voice barking amid the screams. I pulled myself up and shoved the lens above the heads. Soldiers pushed hard and harder against the cries of women and children. Julian wobbled back and forth as if battered by some terrible dream. I crawled back to Oleg's side. 'It's getting spooky, comrade.'

'Uh, well . . . just what is this "spooky" word?'

Julian shoved his frame back through the crush and into the storage compartment. He sank down in the dark and mumbled sounds without words. Fear circled in the sweat and the stench, quicksand fear sucking all of us down and down and down. Rifles blasted through the screams then came the pressurized slam of the hatch. Clunk! The jet was sealed and a quiet hum swept through it once more. Screams fading against steel and glass. And the sweat and the stench and the dripping heat seeping through my pores.

'. . . you still may die in Sokhumi . . .'

A fat Georgian civilian jammed in next to Julian, flipping his cigarette lighter on and off, on and off. Faces flashing with firelight then dark, flashing again, and annoying click-click sounds over and over again.

'Would you stop that?' yelled Julian.

'For Christsake, Julian!'

'This stupid man here—'

'We all stand a chance of gettin' killed here! That stupid man is just as scared as the rest of us!'

'Boys! Boys!'

Oleg, like a teacher separating kids in a schoolyard scuffle. And he shot me a look that nailed my mouth shut. Could he see the fear monster inside me? Did he know? Fear without the buzz is just fear. I came here to play, not die in some sweaty jet.

'You know, I always thought I'd rather buy it on the job than get hit by a bus.'

Julian chuckled. 'That, Jon, is one of the more ridiculous things I've ever heard.'

And we laughed. Not much, just a bit.

The pilot radioed the tower. Engines revved up a few more notches and we were moving. Across the dark, the woman and her two boys who'd climbed on with us. They sat under a small round window and gold light fell across the brown faces and dark eyes. I framed the shot and rolled. Silhouettes in the lens. The woman touches her boys and signs herself with the Orthodox cross.

The jet rumbled to the end of the taxi ramp. Only seconds now, only seconds. Pump a shitload of fuel into the engines and roar down the runway and we're outa here. Forty-five minutes to T'bilisi and that's a fucking wrap.

'Oleg?'

'Yes, Jonka?'

'Know the first thing I'm gonna do in T'bilisi?'

'No.'

'Kill an ice-cold beer.'

'Yes . . . beer.'

'Then you know the second thing I'm gonna do?'

We were dreaming away.

'No.'

'Kill another one.'

'Oh, yes . . . beer . . . cold.'

Julian was in Best British Apology Mode to the fat man with the lighter and was taking a keen gentlemanly interest in just how many times Pudgy could flick it on and off in the space of twenty seconds. We were snug as fleas on a dog. Everything moving nicely except the jet. Radio traffic in the cockpit. Nervous chatter. Oleg listening to every word.

'There is a plane coming in to land. They want us to wait.'

'OK, then.'

More nervous chatter. Our pilot wanted to get the fuck off the runway but the incoming jet had its wheels down for final approach . . . low on fuel . . . must land. Then silence. Long silence. The fear monster in my guts shaking and chewing at the bars of his cage.

'Holy fuck!'

'Jonka?'

'Oh, holy fuck!'

I knew! I fucking knew! Voices screaming over the radio, transmissions distorting with panic. Oleg's face gone white.

'It's disappeared!'

More distorted voices screaming through the airwaves.

'Yes! The jet! The jet! They shot it down!'

I grabbed the camera and forced my way into the cockpit. The pilot pointing out to the Black Sea towards a column of smoke and fire. An Orbi jet packed with soldiers and journalists. Blown out of the sky, seconds from safety. The Abkhazians now surrounded the airport. Their anti-aircraft guns in place and ready. Waiting patiently to kill anything that moved. Small boats chugged out across the water to the smoke. Abkhazians looking for survivors to finish off. There were none.

Oleg fell back to the floor, shaking like ice was running through his blood, rubbing his hands across his face and curling into a small ball for warmth. I moved close to him.

'Oleg, what is it?'

'Jonka. We were to go first.'

Terror in his eyes.

Julian sat quietly in the dark.

Shit! Pictures!

I flipped on the camera and focused through the cockpit windows. Smoke and boats floating above black waves. Couldn't get it. I shut down the camera to save whatever battery I had left. The radio sparked with voices from the tower. The air-traffic controllers could see the Abkhazians at the end of the runway. The only way out was through the sights of rebel guns and rockets.

The pilot smashed his hand on the controls and cursed. He took a deep breath. Then he taxied back down the runway towards the terminal.

'Only a handful of refugees on the tarmac.'

'Shootdown must have chased them away.'

'Uh, well . . . no shit.'

The jet engines whined down and fell silent. The pilot unhooked his seatbelt and climbed out of the cockpit. He opened the starboard hatch, climbed down and ran over to the tower. The gang of soldiers on board opened the port side and the gangway rolled up to the door. A stampede of refugees poured off the plane. Orbi Airlines wasn't the way to safety any more. It was a fucking death-trap. A desperate need to run and hide, chasing the refugees out of the jet and down the steps.

Back in the main cabin. Twenty-five wounded, one nurse, seven civilians, five soldiers, an ITN crew, one young Georgian policeman . . . twenty bloody bodies stacked in the back. Fresh air swirled around the jet and carried dead-body smells to each of the living. Death-trap, hell. This was a flying coffin.

Julian checked his watch. Nearly six p.m. News. He dug around through the backpack stuffed with tapes and batteries looking for his short-wave radio. BBC World Service. Lifeline to reality.

Oleg was talking to the mother of the two boys. The boys leaned into the cockpit, wide-eyed and playful. Her husband went to the front weeks ago. Messages came back every once in a while, then they stopped. Her husband's words before he left: 'If anything happens to me get my sons out of Sokhumi.' The woman's voice full of pain and tears falling down her face.

Oleg listened and looked at me. 'She wants to know if it is safe to stay on the plane.'

'No idea. Co-pilot's still here, but who knows?'

'She is terribly frightened.'

'Yeah. Tell her to stay and we'll help her.'

She smiled and tears came again. The youngest boy came near and pressed his little body into the folds of her black skirt. Tears on his face. He did not want to go without his father . . . please, please. The woman stroked his hair with the tenderest touch.

'My God, what will happen to us?'

'This is the BBC World Service . . .'

We gathered around the small radio. A bit strange hearing what was going on in Sokhumi from some guy in a London studio a thousand miles away. Sokhumi was the lead story. The presenter reading the news in perfectly proper BBC-speak. Nice civilized way to hear that the world was going to hell in a hand basket.

'. . . Abkhazian rebels have fought their way into Sokhumi . . .'

No news about the jet blown to the bottom of the Black Sea. Just the usual time-will-tell crap.

'. . . and there are reports of shelling at the airport . . .'

Julian let go with one of his chuckles. Ruptured eardrums all round.

'I wonder where the BBC gets its information.'

And me and Oleg looking at each other, then out the hatch towards the green trees and fading light. Seemed quiet enough. We looked at each other again and shrugged our shoulders.

'Hang on a second.'

'What is it, Jonka?'

'Where the hell . . .'

'. . . is everyone?'

Boom. Boom. Boom. Three launches . . . Katyusha rockets . . . then roaring whistles and fire from above.

'Fuck me!'

And diving back into the jet as the rockets blasted on to the runway.

Somebody at the Beeb had a crystal ball. Julian jumped up and stuck his head out the door. BBC-speak babbling through explosions: '. . . attempts to resolve the crisis . . .'

'They've hit the runway!'

'No shit!'

I crawled under him and switched on the camera. The battery warning light flashing in my eyes . . . shit! Three or four minutes of power. Smoke and fire at the edge of the runway. Shrapnel skidding along the tarmac. I grabbed a few quick shots and shut down the camera.

Silence.

'Hmmm,' hummed Julian.

'Like I said, no shit.'

Julian slid back in the dark with Oleg. Weariness coming down hard. I slumped into the jump-seat and waited with every soul on the jet. The woman and her boys staring at me. And me hoping she couldn't see the fear pumping faster and faster. The fear monster tearing at the cage and howling in my guts. The airfield was the target and our blood was the prize.

I bit my lip trying to draw blood. Penance for my thoughts. I'd told the woman and her sons to stay. I'd taken what was left of a Georgian family and turned it into target practice. I couldn't even save a dying puppy, for Godsake. What the hell did I think I was doing? I couldn't look at them any more or maybe I couldn't have them look at me. I pulled the camera on to my leg and leaned out the hatch. My hand found the power switch and my eyes looked down the lens.

Another sunset in Sokhumi. Orange fire falling into the sea. Black waves dancing over bodies and souls blasted from the sky. Red blood streaks splashing across alabaster clouds. I thought of all the sunsets I'd seen around the world. A soft breeze. I took a deep breath. I could smell the sea. And I panned across the horizon and the smoke and the light . . . waiting.

'Jon,' said Julian softly, 'aren't you a little exposed out there?'

I didn't answer. I didn't want to tell him it didn't matter. One small fire-hot shard from a shell cutting into a jet wing full of fuel. Hell, no, it didn't matter one bit. A man walking towards the plane, just a shadow on the tarmac. Quiet and calm. Roll. My eyes hid in the world of black and white images. My ears heard sounds from the real world around me. Faraway booms like whispers in my soul.

'Here we go, motherfucker . . . incoming.'

My heart stopped. My breath stopped. Only the camera lived. The fear monster out of his cage tearing and shredding my guts. And the sky opening with rage and fury and howls as seven monster shells exploded along the runway. Closer and closer. And one deafening roar screaming overhead . . . KACRASH!

'Missed! Fuck me! Missed!'

I whipped the camera from side to side grabbing anything and everything. The terminal in flames, a jet ten metres away peppered with shrapnel, flashes of fire and smoke and waves of heat and explosions roaring like slobbering monsters and drooling with chunks of jagged death. We will kill you! We will kill you! WE WILL KILL YOU!

Then . . . the perfect quiet of another sunset in Sokhumi.

'Everyone off the fuckin' plane.'

'Now? You mean now?' asked Julian.

'What about the bags?' asked Oleg.

'Leave 'em. Trust me on this. We have to go now! They got our range and they ain't gonna miss next time!'

Oleg and Julian grabbed their helmets and followed the co-pilot out of the jet. I dug through the kit for another battery hoping I'd have enough power till – till – till when? The woman and the boys watching me. I pointed to myself and them, too fucking scared to remember the Russian words.

'Look! Just stay with me! Got it? Stay with me!'

She nodded and grabbed the hands of her terrified children and we headed for the door. In the main cabin the wounded soldiers and the nurse. She would not leave. She couldn't leave them behind. Worn and suffering faces. Twenty-five men and a woman left to die. Outside, a dark-dusk blanket falling over the sky. I ground my teeth, rocked on my heels and slammed my fist into the bulkhead. Shame ran through me. 'Fuck!'

And down the stairs and into the night with the terrified woman and her two boys behind me. I heard their steps. I could hear them breathing. Across the tarmac Julian and Oleg running towards the control tower and me crouching and turning to the family and pointing to the control-tower bunker.

'Come on this way!'

Two shells smashed down on to the runway. I fell and rolled into a ball. Vibrations rumbling through the concrete. On my knees looking through the dark. The woman running away towards the burning terminal, dragging her screaming sons behind her.

'No! Goddammit no!'

Whoosh . . . KACRASH! KACRASH!

Fire and light and then the dark once more.

I scraped myself off the ground and focused through the dark. Gone. They were gone. I ran a few steps towards the terminal and stopped in terror, remembering the pillow on my face and the dark and the heat and no air and begging the fear monster to stop – 'I won't do it again! I won't do it again!' And shaking myself in the dark and remembering it was a long time ago and not now, but feeling the fear monster crawling up my gullet and grabbing my throat. 'Shit!' And I raced away like the little boy, still remembering and still afraid. Visions of body parts spread across the tarmac.

'Goddammit! Goddammit!'

I caught up with Julian and Oleg and the flight crew behind a stone wall. Nearby, the soldiers and a few civilians from our tour group. The young policeman keeping everyone together and quiet. The fading dimness turned black and the shelling died away. Heavily armed troops crawled out of the trees and walked by without shooting us.

'Uh, well . . . Georgians, I suppose.'

'That woman on the plane, the one with the boys. They went the other way.'

My voice, like telling a terrible secret.

'Into the shelling?'

'Yeah. What the fuck was she doing?'

'It is not your fault, Jonka.'

'You sure 'bout that, comrade?'

Julian wandered over and sat down. 'Quite a mess. And not too many options, it appears.'

'Guess we'll have to hunker down. Over there, maybe. Small concrete building in the trees. Hard target to hit unless you're lucky.'

'So far, the Abkhazians seem to have all the luck in the world.'

Julian wasn't really talking, I wasn't really answering. Just the comfort of shared voices.

'You know, Jon,' said Julian, 'we ran off that plane straight into a minefield. Soldier started yelling, "*Miny! Miny!*" Can you fucking believe it?'

'S'pose that means things'll only get better.'

'Uh, well . . . I do love that American optimism while sitting in a pile of shit.'

The pilot scurried to the tower and I tried to work more sums through my tired brain. Stay the night at the airport and hope to hell we don't get blown to hell, not good. Make our way back to the city in the morning if we can get through the confrontation lines in one piece, not good either. Added up to a big zero. Nothing to do but stay down and stay alive.

The pilot was back, calling his crew and Oleg. They huddled away from the rest of us. The pilot speaking, his hands moving quickly. Oleg listening, nodding in slow, thoughtful moves. The pilot and co-pilot left him standing alone and staring at the ground. I crept up on his thoughts. 'Oleg?'

'Uh, well . . . he says that he will go . . . the rebels will not stop till they get his plane. Two of the wounded on board have died already. So . . . well . . . he believes he must go. And he says the captain will try to take off. Uh, well, he thinks . . .'

'Oleg . . .'

He looked over the rims of his glasses and into my eyes.

'. . . what you're sayin' is, if we go with him there's a very good chance we may get blown out of the sky.'

He pushed his glasses up his nose. He smiled like an old friend. 'Uh, well . . . yes.'

We sat with Julian, and Oleg explained the plan. 'The pilot will make a break for it. No lights on the jet and no lights on the runway. Blackout. He will throw the jet down the wrong end of the runway into the mountains.'

'That's it? That's the plan?'

'Uh, well . . . no. He hopes he can pull up high enough to miss the mountains and fast enough to miss the guns of the rebels.'

'I thought the guns were by the sea.'

'They are everywhere now. But the pilot thinks going into the mountains is not what the rebels will expect.'

'Why's that?'

'Uh, well . . . no one has ever taken off that way before. Only out over the sea.'

'Holy shit.'

'*Da*. He hopes it will work.'

I watched Julian listening. He was looking like a rundown mule, just like me. This was a fine mess. We'd come to Sokhumi to do a story on Shevardnadze and now look at us. Few days ago, back in Moscow, we were debating whether the story was worth the effort. Our Cold War relic wire machine had dinged a fact of some sort. I ripped and read quickly to Julian: 'Shevardnadze dies in arms of BBC correspondent.'

Julian looked up from his desk. 'I beg your pardon?'

'Just kidding.'

Now we were dodging shells and running for our lives and asking each other what we thought for the zillionth time.

'So what will we do?'

'We've got no water, no food, no power for the camera. Can't think of anythin' worse than being stuck here and not bein' able to shoot a frame.'

'I think so too,' said Julian.

Oleg looked to the pilot. They nodded to each other.

'Jesus wept. What a long fucking day,' said Julian.

'Fuckin' hell.'

'Uh, well . . . I agree.'

Pretending everything was going to be swell. Just swell.

Automatic rifles cracked in the night. Sniper fire round the airport. Nothing heavy, just enough to grind down our nerves. Hopefully the Abkhaz gunners were settling down to brandy and drunken conversation. The pilot looked at the dark sky and then the small luminous dials of his watch. He waved and signalled. Time to go. And the tiny band of refugees, Georgian soldiers and one ITN crew ran on to the runway.

The jet sat like a giant shadow dark and still against a half-moon sky. Fresh air off the sea blowing cool across the grass. Under the round belly to the gangway. Two soldiers stood at the bottom of the steps. They wouldn't be leaving. Someone had to stay behind and roll back the gangway.

No greater love, I thought.

'Hurry! Please hurry! Do not wait! Go!'

Into the flying coffin. Jet turbines kicked to life. The pilot wasn't wasting any time. The rebels would hear the engines and arm their guns. The co-pilot sealed the hatch as men with Kalashnikovs bolted from the grass. Georgian soldiers racing up the gangway and smashing their faces into the window, pounding on the hatch with rifles. Deserters.

'Let us in! Let us in!'

The pilot ripped open his window and leaned out the cockpit. 'Get away!'

'Open the door! You will take us!'

'Men are dying on this jet! Get away!'

Rifles blasting on the gangway.

'No! Take us!'

The co-pilot hit the door again and again.

'We only have seconds! Think of your brothers and pull away the stairs!'

Rifle butts slammed the fuselage with savage fury. The pilot begging, the deserters threatening.

'We will shoot out the wheels if you move! We will shoot you down ourselves!'

I sank into the jump-seat behind the cockpit. I was suddenly very tired. Julian and Oleg were tucked into the storage space. The entire jet in nightmare dark but for small red and green lamps on the control panel spilling light through the cockpit door. Oleg's glasses reflecting tiny sparkles of festive colour.

'Only ninety more shopping days till Christmas. Know that?'

'What are you saying, Jonka?'

'Nothin'.'

Goofy thoughts while trying to keep myself from choking on fear. The co-pilot jumped over me and argued with the pilot. There was no choice.

'Open the door!'

Clunk. Swoosh.

Six silent soldiers. They would meet no one's eyes. They stepped over the wounded and cowered with the dead. I could feel their panicked hearts beating. They'd started the day as warriors and now they were running from their fear, just like me. The jet lunged forward and tore down the tarmac as if the steel hulk itself knew, through every rivet and bolt, that this was its only chance of escape. The pilot turned back and waved through the door. Grey hair and big hands. He yelled Russian words to my tired ears. Then he looked to his co-pilot and flight engineer . . . ready. Like tasting death and swallowing hard.

'Jonka!' Oleg shouting through the noise and the dark. 'The pilot says if we make it through the first thirty seconds we will be safe!'

'Swell!'

The jet spun on its wheels and the engines growled. Power surged and strained at the brakes. The jet fought and reared like an unbroken stallion tearing at the bit. The engines whined to an earsplitting screech, pulling and tearing and higher and higher and ... now! Wheels spun on the asphalt and the jet shot ahead and slammed me back into the bulkhead.

You may still die in Sokhumi.

Faster. Faster. The jet shook and rattled. Faster!

The pilot's big hands grabbed hold of the reins of the beast waiting for speed. Then his voice calling to God as he pulled the controls to his heart. The nose lifted from the ground and forty tonnes of steel screamed into the night. Take off! Thirty seconds! Twenty-nine, twenty-eight, twenty-seven! The jet banked right and steep. Outside the window, red flashes split the night with rage. Abkhazian guns lashing fire at the invisible roar. Twenty, nineteen, eighteen! I held the camera to my chest and closed my eyes. Ten, nine, eight! It happens so fast. One moment you live, one moment you die. Like the next breath. And now that breath was chasing after me. Sleepy deadness wrapping round my neck. Reaching and grabbing and dragging me down to the bottom of the Black Sea. Four, three, two!

'Come and get me, motherfucker.'

And the touching of a hand on my arm.

'OK ...'

And looking up into the face of one of the pilots.

'... we are safe. We made it.'

'Yes! Yes! Yes!'

Like hitting the needle and letting go the knot round my arm and high-grade junk pumping into my veins and all the tension and all the fear washing away on a rush of bliss and joy and ecstasy.

'Fuck me! I love days like this!'

The pack of refugees let go a sigh. The Tupolev 154 banked left and sailed with the stars towards T'bilisi. I flopped down with Oleg and Julian. We laughed and talked. I can't remember the words, just the sounds. Twenty minutes into the flight the jet fell silent. My mind flew back across the night. Faces and voices. I could see them. I could hear them. I could feel them.

'Uh, well ... Jonka. Anything wrong?'

'Dunno. Just nerves.'

'Maybe some shots in the back?' offered Julian.

'Yeah.'

I grabbed the camera and walked into the main cabin. Find a closing shot. Something to end the last twenty-four hours. Find the picture and maybe the faces and the voices would go away.

The jet flew straight and smooth. My eyes panned the deck. Switch on and focus. The policeman who saved our lives, his hands now holding the head of a wounded soldier and giving him cool water and soft words. In the rear, the deserters crushed with shame staring at the shrouded bodies of their dead comrades. Blood dried black on white cloth. The lens absorbing the shapes and the blood and the silence.

Over there. A soldier on a cot. Ghost-white skin, eyes fixed. He was alive only hours before, his weak pulse beating against my fingers. His breathing laboured and shallow. Reddish hair and brown eyes. I'd wiped the sweat from his brow. He said he wanted to be on TV. I said he would be with his family soon and he smiled. But the long afternoon trapped in a stinking hellhole jet had broken his will. I knelt with the camera on my shoulder. I pulled a bloodstained sheet over his face. I made the sign of the cross over my unbelieving heart. Maybe he'd believed in something. Maybe he'd murmured one last prayer.

Help us! Help us!

Something calling and me turning to see a young woman never there before. Long black hair like a veil and a sleeping baby in her arms. She rocked in peaceful rhythms back and forth. All around her, the wounded and the blood and the smell of death. She watched me with quiet eyes.

I stood and circled about her looking for the picture. Her quiet eyes following me. Never blinking, never turning. I went down on the deck easy and slow and waited for her to look away.

Now.

Zoom across the jet.

Focus the frame.

Roll.

A bloodied shroud of a dead Georgian soldier. Reddish hair peeking from under the cloth. Counting the seconds. Fingers on the zoom control and pulling slowly. The picture opens from the bloodied shroud . . . the black hair veil of the young woman comes into frame . . . then her arms and hands . . . then the sleeping child . . . the bodies and death around them. There, hold the shot. Don't breathe, don't move.

The woman's quiet eyes staring out beyond the hull and beyond the stars as if in a trance. She looks down to the child and touches the face and tucks a bit of ragged blanket under the baby's chin. She watches the baby sleep. And all the time, rocking back and forth and back and forth.

My fingers on the button . . . that's it . . . closing shot . . . finished.

Till the woman's eyes looked up into the lens and into my soul. Eyes no longer quiet. Dark tunnels to terrible visions of broken lives condemned to die while I lived.

'Look at us!'

'Help us!'

Deeper into her eyes.

Jets blown to bits, crashing and burning. Arms and legs floating in the Black Sea. In T'bilisi, me pleading with a skinny, blonde-haired freelance writer named Alexandra Tuttle not to take another flight into Sokhumi.

'They are shooting planes out of the sky, for fucksake!'

And she craving a scoop for the *Wall Street Journal*. And liking the taste of war and the way it burned in her blood. 'I really want to do it!'

And me looking her over. Thin black dress, city-life shoes. Nothing but a laptop computer in her hands.

'Fuckin' hell. Here, take my flak-jacket and helmet.'

Watching her face in the window of a jet rolling down the runway and drifting away.

Deeper . . .

Sokhumi falls into flames. Eduard Shevardnadze wanders the streets of his burning city, hoping for a bullet. The Abkhazians march in. Bodies and blood. Smoke and fire.

'Please!'

'Help us!'

And Eddie Parker snapping stills of charred bodies in the smouldering wreckage of another jet blasted from the sky. A thin black dress wrapped round a dead shape, twisted and torn and burned beyond recognition. A patch of still blonde hair was all that was left.

That's odd, Eddie would think. I wonder who she was.

And all the while the pitiful tears.

'Look at us!'

'Save us!'

'*In the name of God! Don't leave us here.*'

And the visions faded and the young woman's eyes were quiet once more. And she turned away, saving her mercy for the sleeping child in her arms.

And voices screamed through my mind and echoed and cried. I couldn't listen. I didn't want to remember. Too many screams, too many screams. Hide in the lens. Hide in the picture.

Madonna and Child on the last flight out of Sokhumi.

The camera shaking in my hands. The battery warning light flashing.

'Please don't stop. Please . . .'

The camera died. And the picture flickered to black.

3

BACK IN THE USSR

Boris Nikolaevich Yeltsin did the worst possible thing he could have done to a Moscow-based journalist out of town on a story. He made news. Big news. The day we escaped from Sokhumi, Yeltsin dissolved the Russian parliament, fired Vice-President Alexander Rutskoi and announced to the world, 'I've had enough of this crap!'

A few thousand Commie True Believers dug out their old Soviet flags and rushed to save the White House from the 'Evil Jackal Yeltsin'. They spent the night shouting and chanting for foreign TV cameras.

'*Yeltsin, vrag naroda!*' Yeltsin, enemy of the people!

The Russian army grumbled.

Western leaders shit their pants.

A mad dash back to Moscow, up the elevator of Marksiskaya Dom 1 to whatever floor it was, smack into chaos. ITN had sent out a cast of thousands while we were gone. Defence Reporter Geoffrey Archer was doing *News at Ten*, James Mates was sent in as diplomatic correspondent; Angela Frier and Ian Glover James held the fort as producers. Our own bureau producer, Bridget Else, was off dodging bullets in Yugoslavia on her First Big War Trip. Now she was listening to the news from Moscow over a short-wave radio, staring at the four walls of a house in Central Bosnia and wondering, What the hell am I doing HERE?

There was no time for the polite hellos or 'How was the weather at the Black Sea?' Everyone was too busy crashing together packages on the Biggest Story of the Year: 'Yeltsin Goes Nuts'. Me and Julian were assigned five minutes on our holiday in Sokhumi.

'This is bullshit. We're gonna get dropped.'

'Don't be so glum. We'll make it, Jon,' said Julian.

'Yeah, yeah.'

News at Ten was going out in two hours. Julian had written most of the words on the flight from T'bilisi. He ran it by me once so I had an idea of where he wanted to go. I replayed shots through the camera and logged time codes to buy some time. We ran through the bureau, hijacked the edit machines and recorded Julian's words up to the first 'Bang!' I threw him out of the room and painted the pictures together with sounds.

Weird. Images of war racing across the screen at twenty frames per second but somehow it was like I was never there. And that was good. The story came together like a roller-coaster ride and ran second out the gate after Yeltsin's Moscow meltdown.

'A poetic feel,' critiqued Julian.

'Almost killed for story number two. What kind of fuckin' job is this?'

'Uh, well . . . the only job you have,' offered Oleg.

One a.m. Time for beer.

Me and James Mates and Julian landed in a sleazy casino under one of Stalin's skyscrapers. Julian and myself still a bit shell-shocked. James buying rounds of beers and listening.

The son of a well-known British MP, James had inherited his father's sharp mind, bushy eyebrows and strong desire to bang away on pianos. He was the Moscow bureau chief before Julian and often referred to it as 'The Mates Dynasty'. During his reign we argued and yelled our way into a solid friendship. I was grateful to see him now.

'Another round?' asked James.

'No shit.'

Gulp, gulp, gulp.

'So, James, what *is* going on in Moscow?' asked Julian.

'How the hell should I know? I got here just before your good selves. Next thing I know I'm standing in front of a camera with Trevor McDonald's voice in my ear, inviting me to enlighten fifteen million viewers on the significance of today's events.'

'So what did you tell them?'

'Bugger all, I suspect. More beers?'

'Yup.'

We talked for a long time. Drinking till the numbness came. Then we went our separate ways. I found my Volvo and pulled into the dark Moscow streets. Rain and lamplight reflecting on asphalt. My eyes panning round for the dreaded GAI, Moscow's traffic police. Few cars were on the road at three a.m. and my K-001 licence plate made for easy hunting. Russian coppers would nudge each other awake in their patrol cars.

'Observe, comrade, *Britanskii korrespondyent*. On the streets at a most unrespectable hour.'

'*Da*. We must seize him and protect the purity of Russia.'

The GAI had a sixth sense about knowing if a foreigner was pissed behind the wheel. It was a serious offence to have any booze in your blood while driving. Not even a drop. A stern lecture would be followed by a threat to drag you down to the local police station for a blood test, the officer's colourful descriptions of AIDS-infected needles adding to the moment. This opened the conversation to the subject of a 'proper fine'. Didn't matter how smashed you were, thirty or forty dollars was usually enough to protect the purity of Russia. Then you'd be sent on your merry drunken way.

Moscow was that kind of place. A little strange, always fascinating, sometimes funny. Weaving through the streets in outrageous out-of-the-way loops, because left turns are illegal in the city, I wondered if Moscow was about to lose its sense of humour.

Boris Yeltsin's theory of democracy was a joke. In his battles with the leftover Soviet Parliament, Yeltsin gave up any illusion of democratic rule. Boris Nikolaevich ruled by decree . . . fuck Parliament. Yeltsin's aides would drop some piece of paper on his desk and hope Comrade President was sober enough to scribble his name across it. It made for an impressive body of work: 1399 decrees covering everything from wage/price controls to the temperature of meat sold on the streets.

Parliamentary deputies growled like Russian bears. For them, Yeltsin's reforms were leaving millions of Russians on the trash heap. Hospitals, schools, pride, pensions, sense of nationhood. Their entire way of life junked. In Yeltsin's Russia, teachers parked cars for a living if they were lucky. Old women couldn't buy bread. Miners in Siberia and factory workers all over Russia hadn't been paid in months. Boris's way of balancing the books was defined in two words: 'Fuck 'em.'

Didn't take long for most Russians to form their own opinion of the new world order. Democracy was bullshit! Look at it! Mother Russia out on the street like a hard-currency whore and Boris Yeltsin the pimp! My God, Mother Russia!

Parliament and the Supreme Congress growled again and again by voting down Yeltsin's plans for privatization and dismemberment of the State. Parliament issued credits worth billions of roubles to worn-out factories and towns so people could eat. And all the while the deputies demanded Yeltsin fire his reformist ministers. Yeltsin went through the motions of negotiations till he thought he could dump Parliament and the Commies like dead fish. Only one problem: the Constitution.

The Soviet-era document might be a relic but it was still the law of the land. Even Uncle Boris swore an oath to protect it when he became President. It was wildly bent in favour of the Communists and no matter how hard he tried, Boris couldn't find the votes to change it. Fact was, Uncle Boris had barely enough votes to avoid impeachment. He was hanging on to his political life by a thread. The Great Democrat didn't help himself by getting stone drunk before one parliamentary session and choosing that particular moment to take to the podium and tell the deputies they were all a bunch of wankers. Palace body-guards carried him out of the Kremlin. He was so drunk he could barely walk. One of Yeltsin's more Noble Moments, broadcast live across the country's eleven time zones.

But that didn't bother the reformers. So Yeltsin was a drunk, Bolshoi deal. He was a 'Reformist drunk'! For the reformers, Boris was all that stood between a fluffy economic future and all those nasty Bolsheviks pounding on the Kremlin gates with little bronze busts of Vladimir Ilyich Lenin.

'Look!' the reformers would shout. 'The sky is falling!'

A fear Yeltsin exploited throughout the world. He held himself up as the Only Hope. It was Boris or the Commies. A complete insult to the Russian people, but it worked.

Western leaders, terrified that they might miss out on the biggest garage sale since God created wholesale, were quick to agree. A flood of political luminaries rallied to Yeltsin's side: Bush, Clinton, Kohl,

Mitterrand, Major, Thatcher. Pilgrims of the Photo-Op, flying into Moscow for a few happy snaps with Uncle Boris. A joint press conference would follow, and Whichever Western Leader of the Week would spell out his own unique view for the cameras.

'The sky is falling!'

It was always the same.

Yeltsin sat nearby like a fat and happy cat. A smile on his face. Canary feathers on his lips.

Pass the vodka. Burp.

Billions of dollars and marks and pounds and francs and whatever else were promised to 'help the Russian people in their brave struggle'. And Yeltsin never missed a chance to remind the West that he and he alone knew what was best for the Russian people.

Equinox, 21 September 1993. Yeltsin decided he had the fear of the West in his pocket. He went on national television. He took a sip of *chai* from a dainty Russian teacup. He held a pen for all the world to see. Then he signed Presidential Decree 1400: No more Parliament, no more Rutskoi, no more Constitution, just Boris Nikolaevich Yeltsin.

Urah.

CNN banged the drums before and after every commercial break and 'Crisis in Russia!' was born.

As the ink dried on Decree 1400, I was running for my life in Sokhumi. Twenty-four hours later, driving through Moscow's wet streets, 'Crisis in Russia' felt like a power struggle between morons. I turned on to Ulitsa Zholtovskovo and parked behind a broken-down bus next to my broken-down apartment house. Home, sweet home. I locked the car, hoping no one'd steal it before morning like my last car. Wind swirled in the trees and I watched autumn leaves tumble down the road and up around my legs. And through the wind and the leaves and the dark I saw it. Dried Georgian blood on my boots.

Then it hit me. The morons have guns.

Next day. No blood on the streets. The bean-counters in London got nervous and recalled the cast of thousands from the Moscow bureau. Ian Glover James would stay on to run the show, which suited him just fine. Rewind to 1985. Ian was ITN's first reporter into Moscow. Working under tough Soviet control and tougher living conditions. Long, difficult hours right up to the moment the Russians accused him of being a spy and tossed him out. These days, all was forgiven and Ian was happily tasting every bit of the new Russia. He never slept. He didn't want to miss a thing just in case the Russians threw him out again.

A dashing and talented cameraman from Northern Ireland was asked to stay on as well. He was not happy. Eugene Campbell had just left Russia on the back of a two-year stretch for ITN's *Channel Four News*. Eugene couldn't wait to leave. He hated the country, all the food, most of the people, including me. Eugene let it be known that I wasn't his favourite choice as a cameraman or editor. Russia's weird karma found him smack back in the middle of Moscow with me shaking his hand weeks after he'd left.

'Hi, Eugene! How you doin'?'

'Oh . . . all right . . . you know.'

We worked in separate teams. Go out and find some shots and bring them back to base. Julian and tape editor Brian McVeigh would sort through the pictures and cut three packages a day. Every once in a while me and Eugene made separate trips to the edit suite to see how many of our own shots made the package. Cameramen can be very strange about their pictures.

But as me and Oleg cruised the streets it didn't seem there were enough pictures to go round. Down along the river under the Kremlin walls, the secret archway built for the Tsars to escape from angry peasants and jealous tsarinas was still sealed and shut. Tourists still strolled through Alexander's Garden, taking in the autumn sun. And over by the Lenin Library, kiosks were still stuffed with Coca-Cola and Snickers and other symbols of economic reform. Everyone open for businesski. Down Novyi Arbat towards the White House, old women still selling what was left of their homes. Battered pots and teasets, Russian china and old clothes. Oleg spotted a truckload of Interior Militia behind the Mayor's Office. Their mission: sit in the truck and wait. They did it well. Half the men were snoring while the others were bored senseless.

'Best fuckin' picture so far.'

'*Da*. The protectors of Russian democracy hard at work.'

'C'mon. Let's have some laughs.'

I pulled up on the pavement and blocked the truck from the street. No one seemed to care – after all, this was just the same old shit. Every weekend there was some kind of anti-Yeltsin demo in Moscow. Red flags waving and Commies shouting and militiamen watching. When they all got tired, they all went home.

I grabbed the camera and locked the car. Quick hop up the steps for a shot of the militiamen then a short-cut across the road to the White House. A line of even more bored police at the top of the stairs.

'*Nyet*,' announced a pimply-faced cop.

Oleg did his usual number. Wave press documents, point to the camera, roll over and play fetch.

'*Nyet*.'

'What does he mean?'

'Jonka. I cannot believe you have been in this country for a year. *Nyet* means "no".'

'I know that. What does he mean by "*nyet*"?'

'Oh. Uh, well . . . he says this walkway is closed for the security of Russia and that we must go to the corner and up Konyushkovskaya Street to the White House.'

'Lemme get this straight. We pull up behind a truck of militia and block them in and that's OK.'

'*Da*.'

'But we gotta walk twenty yards that way to get to the White House?'

'Uh, well, *da*. Democracy must be stupid if it is to have any chance of survival in Russia.'

The cop picked a zit. We left.

Down the steps to the wide square at Kalininskii Bridge. The White House dominating the sky like a giant geometry puzzle. A tall oval sitting on a wide rectangle. All marble and white and sparkling in the sun. The gold crest of the Soviet Union still gleaming above the main doors and shining down stairs after stairs after stairs to the embankment road and the Moscow river.

Across the bridge and the river. Spiky monster towers of the Hotel Ukraine and a wide avenue straight out of Moscow.

'The tanks will come from there,' mused Oleg. 'Just like the August coup.'

'Don't know 'bout you, comrade, but my nerves are still in cover-your-ass mode.'

There was a big old apartment building across the road. Huge windows and balconies. A pedestrian tunnel stretching under Novyi Arbat. Easy run back and forth. Concrete barriers and parking ramps offering protected views of the White House.

'Get along the ground and scoot over there, maybe, if the shit starts to fly.'

' "Cover-your-ass mode" . . . "if the shit starts to fly" . . . What are you talking about, Jonka? Do schools in America actually teach such things?'

'I'm sayin' we may need to hide.'

'Ah. *Konyechno*.'

Seemed silly. Only a few hundred Russian cops guarding the place. Muscovites who didn't give a damn were allowed to pass through the White House grounds on the way to Babushka's house. Comrades who did care were free to join the fun and shout a few *Yeltsin vrag naroda*s and move on. CNN might be banging the drums non-stop, but 'Crisis in Russia' was shaping up as a minor inconvenience. Just that morning Boris Nikolaevich and Moscow's Munchkin Mayor Yuri Lushkov had taken a stroll through Pushkin Square, giggling and smiling for the cameras.

'We shall settle this without violence,' promises Yeltsin. 'There will be no blood.'

Yuk, yuk, yuk.

Mayor Munchkin's bald head bobbing up and down like a happy baby's. His happy baby hands controlling vast amounts of real estate in Moscow. Rents like toys, flying through the roof. Reform was profitable. Blood was messy.

Oh, yuk, yuk, yuk.

Up in the driveway of the Hotel Mir, plainclothes thugs in leather jackets and shades sitting in black Volgas, smoking Cosmos cigarettes and watching the action across Konyushkovskaya Street. An endless drone of 'Yeltsin traitor!' and 'Yeltsin pig!' keeping them awake while their shaded eyes scanned the White House balcony and the entire plaza below. There was one path out of the plaza through the far trees. Nothing and no one was going in or out of the plaza without being seen from the Hotel Mir. We asked for rooms. A man in an ill-fitting suit told us to go away.

'No foreigners. Besides . . . all rooms taken.'

His eyes jerked round the lobby. Wall-to-wall plainclothes thugs in leather jackets and shades smoking Cosmos cigarettes.

'KGB?' I whispered.

'Uh, well . . . in the new Russia, they are the FSB.'

'The difference being . . .'

'. . . the alphabet.'

We wandered over towards the red flags. Bits of wire and steel piled across cardboard crates. Barricades of the Revolution. Fevered eyes watching us. Beyond the eyes and under the balcony, a crowd cheering yet one more impassioned plea to end the suffering of the Soviet Peoples at the hands of the Evil Jackal Yeltsin.

'They do like a good speech, don't they?'

'*Da*. Preferably long.'

Hard-faced and pissed-off revolutionaries at the barricades saw us coming and charged into us.

'Lying western pigs!'

Normalno. These guys thought the media was pro-Yeltsin. Sure looked that way on Russian TV screens. Yeltsin cronies controlled the airwaves of Ostankino Television. Boris was always presented in reverential tones while opposition figures were seen as dangerous loonies. Yeltsin thanked his pals by letting them stuff their pockets with western advertisement dollars.

The Commies didn't help themselves much. Any 'Bring back Stalin' rally featured some old survivor of the socialist struggle pushing his finger into my chest.

'*Kakoye televideniye?*'

'*Kompaniya Britanskaya* ITN.'

One of the Russian channels ran our news programme. Oddly enough, a lot of Russians knew who we were.

'*Skolko lyudey vy vidite zdes sevodnya?*'

Oleg looking at me and pushing his glasses up his nose not bothering to translate. 'Uh, well . . . the same old question.'

And me looking round in serious fashion as stern Commie faces watched me count the same three hundred heads over and over again.

'Oh . . . s'pose you got five or six thousand head of people.'

'Humph!' And groans of disbelief.

'Lying western pigs!'

'There are at least two hundred thousand people here!'

I stepped over the wire and steel. The hard-faced and pissed-off revolutionaries pushed me back.

'*Nyet! Nyet!*'

'You need a serious PR makeover, dickhead.'

I stepped ahead again, the camera rolling. Spitting Bolshoi faces closing in through the lens. Fists and slugs and kicks and me pushing back again. Down in the corner of the frame, a man's hand and something heavy hanging at his side. A brick wrapped in burlap swinging up and down towards my head. Oleg's hands pulling me back fast and the brick smashing the tip of the lens.

Whack.

I shoved the camera into Oleg and went for Comrade Bozo's throat. 'You son-of-a-bitch!'

Sticks and stones and fists.

A militiaman jumped in, hauled me out and yelled in my face. Oleg shoved the camera into me, grabbed my coat and pointed down the street. 'Uh, well . . . we shall go there.'

'But—'

His iron grip dragging me down the street like a naughty child. 'Sometimes I think I should keep you locked up!'

'Ah, hell. Just havin' some fun!'

I fiddled with the lens. The focus ring was a little bent and stiff. Worked well enough, though. Damn, little to the left and the bean-counters at ITN would have to cough up a new lens.

'Maybe we should go back.'

'Don't make me spank you.'

'Yeah, yeah.'

'Jonka, do you ever think that some people are not happy to have you stick your thing in their face?'

''Scuse me, comrade?'

'Uh, well . . . I mean your lens.'

'Yeah, yeah.'

Oleg was right. He was always right. A few hours into the revolution and already a feeling of bitter defeat running through the hardliners. Parliament called for national strikes to oust Yeltsin. Nothing. Then a plea for the Red Army to join the not-so-teeming masses at the White House. Zip. The deputies branded Yeltsin a criminal and voted for his impeachment. Alexander Rutskoi was even sworn in as the new president of the Russian Federation. Still nothing. Some revolution. Boris sat in the Kremlin guzzling vodka and painkillers with that dumb-ass 'What? Me worry?' grin on his face.

Old boy didn't have to worry. It'd all blow over in a few days. Always did . . . burp. The Western Leaders' Chapter of the Boris Yeltsin Fan Club breathed a sigh of relief. All this unpleasantness just a rude fart on the road to Democracy and Huge Profits.

'So, it ain't gonna be like May Day, huh?' I asked.

Rewind: May Day. Five months earlier. A Moscow street near Yuri Gagarin's statue. Me and Bridget Else, the ITN Moscow producer, had found ourselves in the middle of a bloody riot. A young soldier crushed between two trucks. Blood pouring from his mouth. Thick and black. I zoomed in on his face and watched his life drain on to the asphalt. Above his unseeing eyes through the smoke and fire, a banner stretched across the road. 'Happy Holiday, Dear Russians!'

'Oleg?'

Not wanting to answer. Not wanting to think, not yet.

'Let's go find someone who may appreciate your wobbly lens,' he said.

A footbridge from the nineteenth century connected Konyushkovskaya Street to the White House grounds. Young believers and timber and wire at the crest of the bridge. Young, hell. Front-line kids.

'Why ain't these kids in school?'

'They have enrolled in the School of Revolution, Jonka. Perhaps they will learn such clever concepts as covering one's ass from flying shit.'

And they all liked the idea of TV. They smiled and helped us across the barricades and into Revolution Class.

Men and women. All ages and all walks of life, tearing at the cobblestones. Neat rows of jagged rocks arranged like a caveman's arsenal. Ancient missiles ready for war. Eyes turning to me for a second, curious and innocent. I lowered the camera and looked into their eyes. They looked at each other for a moment then went back to work. The lens zooming into the digging hands. Young hands and old hands.

'Welcome to the USSR, Jonka,' said Oleg.

'You!'

A miner standing next to me. A red hammer and sickle painted on his yellow miner's hat. His coat smelling of deep and dark earth.

'You! Understand this! We must defend our parliament!' he said.

And he went down on his knees and dug his black fingers into the stones.

Oleg poked me in the ribs. Over there. A huge statue commemorating the 1905 revolution. The form of a woman with a flag held high over her head. She calls behind her. A man in a worker's smock crouched nearby . . . a rifle in one hand . . . a fallen comrade in the other. Dreamers in bronze. A man of flesh and blood scampers up the statue and unfurls the flag of the Soviet Union. Red on bronze. Like remembering. Like blood.

I walked over and framed the statue against the White House. The flag of Yeltsin's Russia still waving atop the marble tower. Like sitting atop a faraway mountain.

This was sacred ground for the anti-Yeltsin crowd. Twelve years before October 1917, Moscow workers had rebelled against the stupidities of Tsar Nicholas II. And for a moment it had seemed the workers just might pull it off. But the Tsar's troops stormed through the streets, crushing the dreamers under the hoofs of well-groomed horses. The statue marked the Last Stand of the Last Battle of 1905.

'*Urah!*'

The impassioned words from the balcony finally finished and the loudspeakers exploded with solemn music. The Soviet National Anthem. Hats and hands to hearts. Red flags above faces. Teary eyes. Mouths shaping the scared words as if praying for strength. The lost tribe of the Soviets holding on to tattered shreds of Commie dreams. Between the pictures a flash frame raced through my eyes.

'Oleg. How many people stormed the Winter Palace in 1917?'

'A few hundred at most. However, in the Eisenstein film it was depicted as tens of thousands but that, well, of course, was part of the propaganda and myth that Communism was the greatest thing since sliced caviar and, of course, Lenin wrote a treatise on the press and the importance of controlling the telegraph . . .'

And me looking round at the thousands of dreamers thinking Boris Nikolaevich might have something to worry about after all.

Inside the White House the Polite Parliamentary Police were asking for news from the outside. The phone lines had been cut . . . Is it true what they say of marches? Has Yeltsin fled the country? Are police shooting people in the streets? Rumours were the only lines of communication now.

'Things are calm,' says Oleg.

'*Spasibo.*'

Up the stairs to the main foyer. Giant chandeliers sparkling with light and huge windows open to the balcony, framing the dreamers below like a portrait. And everywhere about the foyer, the true victims of 'Crisis in Russia', the ladies and gentlemen of the international press. Coke cans, pizza boxes, cups of tea, sleeping cameramen, panicked producers on mobile phones, everyone wondering how long this torture would last. Twenty-four-hour News was a hungry beast to feed. Roll the promo, cue the drums . . . 'CNN. The World's Most Important Network!' . . . cue coiffed announcer in tailored suit designed to accent the weight of the world on his shoulders.

'So tell our viewers, what's the situation now?'

Reporter looking for yet another way to say, 'Same old shit.'

'The stand-off continues.'

Oops! Roll another promo! Bang the drums! Get out that Thigh Master advert. 'We'll be back with more "Crisis in Russia". Stay tuned.'

Parliamentary deputies still registered with clerks outside the doors of the chamber. That way they could still collect their attendance fees.

'Uh, well . . . it might be revolution, but a man must still get paid,' observed Oleg.

'Seems so.'

Inside the chamber debates and law-making rolled on. Didn't matter that no one else in the world gave a damn. This was the seat of the New Russian Government. Ruslan Khazbulatov sat on the dais as head of the Congress trying to keep the show on the road. It wasn't easy. His voice mumbling with stuffy nasal sounds. Hard to understand. Annoying if taken in large doses.

Yeltsin had a secret weapon in Khazbulatov's dark hair, dark eyes and olive skin. Raised in the provinces of Chechnya, Khazbulatov did not look Russian. And with the well-chosen word Yeltsin could easily deal the race card by suggesting to fellow ethnic Russians that Khazbulatov was not one of their own kind. A play on the common

Russian prejudice that all Chechens were filthy criminals. Less than human.

A man who looked totally Russian walked out of the chamber. Iona Andronov, conservative deputy from the Siberian *oblast*. Cameras swooped down quick. Andronov was always good for an English soundbite.

'What is the matter with the West? How can you support this drunkard as our president? If you love him so much, give him asylum. We will give you a plane to take him. He's yours, please.'

And all the reporters pretending they were auditioning for *60 Minutes*.

'But of course he was a freely elected president, *wasn't he*?'

'Well, so was I! In my region I stood against seven candidates!'

'But, of course, the parliament was elected under the old Soviet system, *wasn't it*?'

'What is the matter with you? So was Yeltsin!'

'But isn't this parliament *illegal*?'

Andronov rolling his eyes.

'Oh, shut up, you idiot!'

Andronov pushing through the cameras . . .

'We were elected to serve and we shall stay and try to make peace with that drunkard.'

. . . and not believing he must defend his constitutional right to exist to a pack of reporters from the wonderlands of democracy.

'How would you feel if your president threw out your parliament?'

Nobody answering and the lens following him down the hall into the dim light, till I saw them. Two men in battle fatigues walking round a corner. A tiny bead of lamplight reflecting off the dark metal tubes across their backs. Guns. Machine-guns.

'You see that?'

'Uh, well.'

'I mean, you did see that?'

'Uh, well.'

'Me too.'

We ran down the hall into the dimness and rounded the corner and slammed into the mysterious warriors waiting in ambush.

'What do you want?' one sneered.

'Do not follow us!' said the other.

We obeyed like well-trained monkeys and ran away.

'Nice guys. Who the fuck are they?'

'The White House is stuffed with weapons, Jonka. Hundreds of automatic rifles and thousands of rounds as an arsenal for Yeltsin's defence in the August '91 coup.'

'You're shittin' me.'

'No. The police in this building are separate from the national police. They take their orders from Parliament, not Yeltsin.'

'And Boris let them keep the weapons?'

'It is not like he could remember too much. There were many happy celebrations and lots of vodka.'

Quick sums.

'So the same guns used to defend Yeltsin two years ago are now being used to protect . . .'

'Uh, well . . . Rutskoi.'

'The guy tryin' to take down Boris.'

'*Da.*'

I kept adding it up like a tricky maths problem. 'Doesn't make any fuckin' sense.'

'Is this not a wonderful country, Jonka?'

'Let's go find him.'

'*Nyet problemy*. Of course, we could go this way but then those fellows might shoot us. But if I remember there is another way by the rear stairs . . .'

And we were off through a maze of stairs and hallways and back rooms. The White House was built in typical Soviet fashion. Like some mad Russian experiment to drive mice nuts. Oleg ran the maze like the head mouse.

'. . . of course, we must go back this way and circle through the . . .'

Down elevators and into more halls. Up elevators and through doors. Corners this way and corners that way and through a set of doors and face to face with Thomas Roth and Rory Peck.

'. . . and *urah*. Success.'

'No shit. Hello, Rory, Thomas.'

Thomas with his usual smiling face and Rory with his usual brown fedora. They'd been waiting for two hours. Thomas wanted a one-on-one interview with Rutskoi.

'OK, I'll stay out of the shot but I'm crashin' the interview.'

'No access Germany?' he asked.

'No access UK?' I asked.

'Done.'

We stood in a lobby outside two opaque glass doors. Beyond the glass, the offices of Alexander Rutskoi, newly elected president of a Russian government no one in the world cared to recognize. Two heavily armed guards stood between our cameras and Rutskoi. Rory took a casual drag from his cigarette. We stood around some more.

'I saw your stuff from Sokhumi,' said Rory. 'Well done . . .'

And he finally let go of the smoke.

'. . . When this all settles down you must come out to the dacha for dinner.'

Have you heard about Rory?

'Thanks, mate. Look forward to it.'

The doors popped open and out stepped Andrei Fyodorov, Rutskoi's most trusted aide. We begged, he listened. Fyodorov liked Oleg and ITN. He thought we were always fair to his boss. He nodded and slipped behind the glass. We waited another hour.

'How long you think this'll run?'

'Uh, well . . .'

'A week.'

'Less. Maybe.'

'All depends on the army.'

'They won't get involved. Too fucking messy.'

'Could use some coffee.'

'Yeah, I'm starvin'.'

'When's your feed?'

'How's Juliet?'

'Soon.'

'She's very well, thank you.'

A gaggle of Russian snappers bounding up the stairs. Still cameras loaded and ready.

'Uh, well . . . a good sign.'

'Word's gone out.'

'The Man will speak.'

'Soon, please, soon.'

And Andrei Fyodorov standing at the doors waving us in. Thomas and Rory first, then me and Oleg and the snappers behind. All of us knocking over tables and lamps and priceless Russian blue vases.

'Careful!'

'Oops!'

' 'Scuse me.'

And into a long room lined with shades of daylight. A huge flag of the Russian Federation twirled and dangling from the far wall and Alexander Vladimirovich Rutskoi standing at the end of a table. He was lighting a cigarette. Yellow flame flashing across his silver hair as he looked up into the approaching lenses like a movie star.

'Yeltsin's Moustachioed Rival' was the usual description.

A fighter pilot in Afghanistan. Proud to serve his country flying countless combat missions through the treacherous mountains round Kabul. Shot down and taken PoW. Alexander Vladimirovich was having none of it. He got hold of a side arm and blasted his way out of jail. Soon as he got back to his comrades he climbed into another jet. More missions, more near-death. Till once more the Mujahideen unlocked their courtesy-of-the-USA stinger missiles and blasted him out of the sky once more. He came down in a small Afghan village. An old woman saw him bail out and land. All he had to do was kill her and shut her up for good, but he couldn't do it. He ran as hard as he could. The old woman told the Mujahideen and they tracked him down and threw him into another PoW camp. Rutskoi stayed there, trying to comfort and rally his fellow Russians lost in a fucked-up war.

War hero was the other description.

Rutskoi stood at Yeltsin's side during the August coup in '91. He led the flight to Sochi to rescue Mikhail Gorbachev from house arrest. He was the freely elected vice-president of Russia under Yeltsin. Rutskoi didn't take shit from anyone. That was his problem.

Alexander Vladimirovich lost heart at the decline of his beloved Russia, the Russia good men died for. Rutskoi could only see the suffering in this New Improved Russia. Like letting an axe murderer run amok through the land. He railed against Boris and his gang of money-licking 'reformers'. Yeltsin watched Rutskoi jealously and decided there was only one answer, get rid of him. Yeltsin suspended Rutskoi on phoney corruption charges. *Nyet* due process, *nyet* legal redress, *nyet* proof.

And the Western Leaders' Chapter of the Boris Yeltsin Fan Club sat with fingers up each other's bottoms, looking the other way.

'Internal matter, you understand.'

Cough, cough.

'Please sit down,' said Rutskoi.

Rutskoi drew smoke, let it go and sighed. He took the chair at the head of the table. His hands moving with grace. His deep voice filling the room with words. 'Democracy'. 'Constitution'. 'Legality'.

'Parliament is a legal arm of the Russian government. How can the world allow Yeltsin to say it simply does not exist?'

His warrior hands pounding the table, outraged that the West could just fall to its knees before the myth of Boris Yeltsin.

'Is he some kind of saint? Is he a god? Has the West no idea of the horror about to be released in Russia?'

Rutskoi's hands holding a document. More of his own words, handwritten on a scrap of paper. A call for mutual elections of both the presidency and the parliament to be held at the same time. All political factions allowed and invited to stand. His steel-blue eyes looking down the lens once more.

'There is no other way to avoid bloodshed.'

I checked my watch. Still a bit of time before deadline. Another trip through the maze and out on to the balcony for one last top shot. The White House casting a long shadow over the dreamers on the plaza. Late-afternoon sun sinking into the Russian steppe and the wind blowing in with a chill. The cold soul of Russian winter just weeks away. Campfires glowing under the trees. Speeches and newspapers circulating amid the masses. Flags fluttering with every colour out of the crayon box. Nationalists, Monarchists, Fascists.

'So what the fuck is happenin', Oleg?'

Oleg took a breath and thought and breathed again. 'Uh, well . . . Rutskoi is trapped. And so is Yeltsin. Yeltsin has no choice but to squeeze and squeeze till he gets what he wants.'

Me thinking about the flags and Oleg thinking about something else.

'Yeah, and what's that?'

'Blood.'

My ears zoomed into the word. 'You are jokin'.'

Oleg didn't smile. His eyes focusing on the dreamers below. 'Look at them. Mothers and fathers and children. Rutskoi stated a fact. What Yeltsin has done is illegal. And to get away with it, our glorious president must convince the world that these people are evil. Animals, not worthy of life. So he will provoke them till they bite. Then he will hold up his bloodied hand to the world and then he will strike.'

Oleg leaned into the balcony. His fifty-one-year-old hands tapping the marble in time with his thoughts. 'Jonka, can you imagine what has happened to my country?'

Down on the plaza, a band of dreamers gathered around a lanky stretch of man wrapped in a long black coat. He held an accordion in his hands. Never knew his name but he was a regular at any anti-Yeltsin demo in Moscow. Like a DJ at a Commie rave. The brown cap on his revolutionary head always tilted to the left as his fingers danced over the ivory keys. He led the dreamers with Songs of the Great Patriotic War against Hitler. Voices floating up the marble stones and echoing round the plaza. 'Arise the Great Country!'

Hearts stirring to life. Hope and glory one more time.

'Oleg, why is it the Commies have all the best music?'

'Uh, well.' He laughed.

We wandered down on to the plaza for close-up shots. Two babushkas hiding from the wind. A shelter of blue plastic sheeting. Wool coats and itchy scarves. Oddly coloured knitted hats and thick boots. Icons of Soviet fashion. A small fire at their feet and a small kettle on the boil.

'*Kakoye televideniye?*' asked the one with most of her teeth.

'*Britanskoye televideniye.*'

'BBC *ili* ITN?' asked the other with no teeth.

'ITN,' said Oleg.

'*Khorosho!*'

They both nodded. The one with teeth leaned close. A twiglike finger on a wrinkled hand pointing to the lens. 'ITN *govorit pravdu*,' she said.

'Uh, well . . . good news,' said Oleg. 'It seems more revolutionary grandmothers prefer ITN to any other British news.'

We were offered tea while I was given a lecture on the stupidity of being outside without a hat. The babushkas giggled and wiggled like Jell-O.

'*Urah!*'

An encore performance at the White House. The thousands of dreamers moved into the arc-lights of camera lamps washing down from the balcony. Ruslan Khazbulatov at the microphone, warming the crowd before the long cold night. Fists and flags and patriotic rage rising as one into the sky.

'Long live the Soviet Union!'

'*Urah! Urah! Urah!*'

Oleg pulling my arm and the lens dropping into shadows along the walls. Dim light and the shadowy forms of men moving quickly and quietly and then disappearing into the White House. Automatic rifles in their hands.

Me and Oleg spent the next few days in the White House cafeteria with the rest of the media circus, munching stale bread and sipping sweet tea, watching the balcony and plaza below. CNN's 'Crisis in Russia' was creeping along like a drowsy snail.

The TV agencies did all the head shots of balcony speeches and meetings in the chamber. That left me free to wander the halls and the grounds looking for bits of colour but even those pictures were all looking the same. So we had more tea and took a nap. Somewhere, when I was dreaming about someplace wonderful, Rutskoi and Khazbulatov came pounding down the stairs after yet another speech on the balcony. Fifty tea-glasses hit tabletops like the single stroke of a drum. Cameras and reporters and producers raced to head 'em off at the pass.

'Don't you think Yeltsin *is winning*?'

Rutskoi stops and glares. 'Look...' His hands moving over an imaginary table. '... this is a chess match.'

'Yes, *so*?'

'Simple. A few more moves and checkmate.'

And Rutskoi's bodyguards pushing aside the cameras. Reporters searching their notes with *that's-it?* expressions. Oleg rolling his eyes.

'Hmmm. How was that for you?'

'Think the guy's losin' his fuckin' mind.'

'A most astute political observation, Jonka.'

Another cup of tea from the samovar then time for a walk round the plaza. Woodsmoke mist swirled through autumn trees and the warm sun cut through the shadows and shivers of early morning. Light through thick clouds hanging over an ashen steel kettle. A woman amid the steam with a zigzag-shaped log in her hands. She shoves the log into goo and she stirs and stirs till it's just right. Then she dishes up bowls to the cold and hungry faces.

Out across the thinning barricades, more and more militiamen.

'Where do all those guys come from?'

'Some factory is stamping them out like cookies,' said Oleg.

Heavy grey coats. Black boots. Doughboy steel helmets atop an endless line of boys. The Red Star of the Soviet Union still engraved on the brass buttons of their uniforms. Oleg laughing and shaking like Chuckles the Clown and turning red with stupidity.

'Tasty Militiaman Cookies.'

Laughing harder.

'Mmmm, good.'

'We gotta find some fuckin' pictures before we both go nuts.'

We strolled through the park, coming across small fires and half-asleep dreamers ready to '*Yeltsin vrag naroda!*' one more time. Quick headcount, maybe seven hundred true believers in total. Lot less than yesterday and that was a whole lot less than the day before. The angry thousands had gone home. 'Crisis in Russia' was close to a wrap. One guy was running in circles round me to get his blood going.

'Allo! Glad to see you!' he shouted in Russian. 'Yeltsin will never attack as long as you're here!'

And him slapping me on the back with fraternal brotherhood and me slapping his back and smiling and speaking in English . . .

'Don't count on it!'

. . . and him laughing and slapping my back some more thinking I'd just said, 'No shit, comrade! Forward together!'

'Uh, well . . . forward this way, Jonka.'

Over near the side entrance of the White House through a cluster of dreamers and giddy applause as a column of men in battle fatigues marched into the sunlight. A tall Cossack officer in a peaked sheepskin hat, goose-stepping out front of the troops and shouting commands, his shiny black boots slapping the pavement and his hand wrapped tightly round a cavalry sword. A spark of light gleaming on polished steel.

I moved in close and stuck the lens through the crowd.

Strapped across the back of each man . . . AK54 rifles. Light and vicious. Compact-size death. The Cossack screams and the column halts. Another scream and the men spin on heels and snap to attention.

Close-ups. Young men and old men. Mismatched uniforms and uniforms just out of mothballs. A few bellies bursting at the buttons but all the faces proud. Like the proud faces of the true believers, because now they had more than sticks and stones: now they had a fuckin' army.

Pan right. The lens frames the tall Cossack. His eyes flash. A mad leap towards the camera and a hand reaching and grabbing. 'If you do that again I will kill you!'

'Swell.'

Oleg stepped in to offer a polite explanation. 'Pardon me, but you must excuse my American colleague. He does not understand that—'

'And I will kill you too!'

And the soldiers glaring.

'Me first, sir!'

The crowd spat and we backed away and crouched down. A colonel strolled through the dreamers and down along the line of volunteers. He called the Cossack officer over for a chat. A quick spin and a few goose steps later, the sheepskin hat was awaiting orders. I handed the microphone to Oleg.

'Let's interview the colonel.'

'Uh, well . . . have you been taking drugs again?'

'Oh, you don't think that guy would really kill us?'

Oleg looked at the sheepskin hat still listening to orders and then back to me. 'But he is a Cossack.'

'Yeah, yeah. Still has to take off his sheepskin hat to piss, don't he?'

'Does that mean anything in particular?'

'No. Don't think so.'

'You are taking drugs again!'

'No. Just sounded funny in my head.'

'Uh, well . . . you go first.'

'Me? You're the Russian speaker!'

'And you have that big camera!'

'Now who's on drugs?'

'Maybe I should try some!'

'Later. I got some great Uzbek grass.'

'Aha! I knew it! You are taking drugs!'

The faces of the crowd, the volunteers and one bloodthirsty Cossack watching us in silence.

'Now would be a good time, Oleg.'

We stepped to the colonel and introduced ourselves. He bowed. '*Pozhaluista*,' he said.

The Cossack stood ready to take off our heads if needed, and I waited while Oleg did his magic. I would wait and wait, listening, not knowing the words but hearing the sounds, feeling the sounds, till Oleg winked and it was time to roll.

'I was a career officer in the Red Army, proud of my country, proud of the army, proud of Russia. Since Yeltsin came to power, look! The army has been decimated. Men in uniform are going without pay! Without food! The Red Army! The Red Army that saved Russia!'

'But are you ready to fight?'

Sadness in his eyes. 'Yes. If we must.'

'Are you ready to die?'

Hopelessness in his voice. '*Da*. We will lose lives. Many of us will die. But those lives will have fought for a country taken away from us. Those lives will have fought for the chance to take it back!'

Yeltsin was not happy. Pictures of armed volunteers marching in and out of the White House broadcast around the world? Serious men with guns telling the world they were ready to defend their parliament and die for what they believed in? This was not in the script.

Script says: Boris rips up the Constitution and everyone goes home. What were they talking about 'defend Parliament'? Didn't they read Presidential Decree 1400? There is no parliament. Only Boris, Boris, Boris!

Yeltsin mused: *Bolshoi* problem. Doesn't look good. Sissy Western leaders getting nervous. Time for another Presidential Decree.

'The White House has been taken over by dangerous armed lunatics! I order the White House to disarm and stockpile their weapons within twenty-four hours!'

Twenty-four hours later the angry thousands were back at the White House. Miners, teachers, ruffians, boozers, unemployed factory workers, unpaid scientists, all shapes and sizes, lining up and marching into the White House maze, the dreamers cheering them on like heroes. Yeltsin's latest order had come down like a drunkard's threat.

'Why couldn't he just keep his mouth shut?'

'Jonka. You must understand that to ingest vodka, Yeltsin must first spew senseless words to allow room for the greatest amount of consumption.'

We wound our way up to Rutskoi's office. Nobody'd seen him since Yeltsin's order. The hallway to his office wing was blocked and guarded by a nineteen-year-old kid. Quick pan down his back and belt, no weapons. Quick glance through the half-opened door, some men in suits but most in fatigues, all of them armed to the fuckin' teeth. A volunteer pulled open the door.

'No pictures!'

'OK, then.'

We had a decent relationship with Rutskoi's guards and I didn't want to blow it. I put the camera on the floor, but pictures of rebel guns was today's story and I wanted it. Steps from behind us. A squad of volunteers coming up the hall, their hands on slings and rifle barrels popping up over their caps.

'Comrade, in five seconds sit on the window-ledge.'

'Uh, well . . . ledge.'

Down behind Oleg. Reach for the power switch, spin the focus ring, hit the roll button and look, Mom, no hands. Armed men and hard steps through the frame. Fierce eyes glancing towards the camera and me with my hands scratching my head and looking stupid.

'Some day, Jonka . . .'

And the door pulls open and another squad marches down the hall. Better picture. Black barrels and rifle stocks and banana clips. AK47 silhouettes. One good shot in the can.

'. . . you will get me into big trouble.'

Back through the maze of more volunteers and more rifles, bullets spilling out on to desktops. Last week's parliamentary secretaries with big hair and bad dresses, this week's ordnance-supply officers, busily arranging bullets in neat little rows like paperclips. Big ones here, little ones there.

Nervous tension snapping through the maze, out on to the balcony and down on to the dreamers like a whip. Hundreds more crowding the plaza. Rumours racing. 'Special army commando units are taking positions in the high buildings around the White House!' 'Tank divisions have been mobilized!' 'OMON riot troops are pouring into Moscow!' Men and women huddled round a small radio as the voice of Yeltsin's interior minister blubbered more threats over the airwaves. 'The time for decisive action has not arrived . . . *yet*.'

And everywhere, stones and bricks and rocks strategically placed in piles along the barricades. Steel bars and lead pipes and wood clubs. The footbridge to Konyushkovskaya Street now a fortress of boxes and wire and metal junk. More volunteers marching into the White House. Picks digging trenches along the roads. Heavy logs dropping into place round the perimeter. The barricades rising higher and higher. The Commies were looking for a fight.

The Western Leaders' Chapter of the Boris Yeltsin Fan Club got twitchy. Fingers were diplomatically removed from each other's bottoms and Casper Milquetoast statements were issued to the world. Polite, calm. All about support for 'the embattled Russian President' and 'the need for negotiations'. Meanwhile hotlines into the Kremlin were burning with diplomatic panic. 'Boris! What the fuck is going on?'

Pass the vodka. Burp.

Night fell over Moscow. The White House plaza like a village square, full of accordion music and campfires. Boys and girls holding hands, men smoking near radios once more and listening, 'Negotiations still continue', 'The President reaffirms his promise not to use force'. And then lighting more cigarettes and talking and debating. A megaphone moves through the village calling and shouting political slogans like a street hawker. A woman arranges flowers in a tin can, keeping her eyes on the kettle of stew simmering nearby. A little boy wearing a miner's hat sitting under a red Soviet flag glowing with firelight. Faces through the flames. Handshakes and tea and rubbing arms against the cold, fire sparks crackling and exploding and rising like fireflies.

And the White House bathed in spotlight and looking like a university art project. Windows like a giant stack of television sets, each one tuned to a different channel. Deputies talking on floor eleven, a man reading papers on fifteen, a maid dusting window blinds two floors below. Up on the tenth floor a man undoes his tie and settles down for another night on the couch.

'Think anyone's gettin' laid in there?'

'Uh, well.'

We strolled through the village to the fires along the west barricades. Across the front-line and through the smoke. The grey coats and steel helmets of the militia still watching and waiting. I knelt on the ground for the last shot of the day. Zooming through the wire, wavy shapes come into focus with tired soldier-boy faces. All of them stomping their boots on the ground to chase away the cold.

'Christ. Fuckin' thousands of 'em out there.'

And then black.

Thousands of voices at once: 'Whoooa!'

I spun round on my knees.

The White House was gone.

Boris had pulled the plug. The massive building was lost in the dark. Panic in the village square, women pulling children to their arms, men and boys grabbing sticks and stones ... and waiting. Silence. Any moment now, the first shots of Boris Yeltsin's drunken rage were gonna fly. But back across the barricades and firesmoke the grey coats and steel helmets of the militia stood motionless like shadows against the street lamps. Then thousands of voices calling in the dark: 'Rutskoi! Rutskoi! Rutskoi!'

Up on the balcony, Alexander Vladimirovich Rutskoi with a single camera lamp behind him. His silver hair backlit and shimmering in the dark. His arms reaching for the frightened ones below, like a comforting father.

'Comrades! Comrades!' he called.

We ran with the masses, thousands of fearful bodies crushing together. Rutskoi hitting the microphone ... dead. He calls for a megaphone from the crowd and one is raised up to him. Everything told me the guy was about to give the speech of his life and I should stay put and get what I could.

'Fuck it! Let's go!'

We ran to the entrance. The parliamentary police slammed the doors in our face. Oleg banged on the glass. The police waved AK47s in our eyes. Women and men surrounded us and cried to be saved. Rutskoi's powerful voice cutting through the fear. 'Comrades! Listen to me!'

'Shit!'

Oleg banged harder and the police screamed. Deputies shoved us aside and the doors opened just a crack. Oleg threw himself into the guards. A frightened mob smashing us forward like a trash compactor.

'*Pozhaluista!*' Oleg yelled.

The police threw him into the stone wall.

'*Nyet!*'

The camera rolling and Oleg waving his credentials in the cops' faces. Rutskoi's voice echoing through the screams . . .

'Comrades! Comrades! Listen to me!'

. . . and the police lifting Oleg off the ground and slamming him back into the wall. Me pushing hard against the door. A rifle butt crashing into my guts.

'Fuck me!'

'*Pozhaluista!*'

'Comrades! What does Yeltsin think? Listen to me, comrades!'

'*Nyet!*'

'Goddammit!'

'We are not children! We are not afraid of the dark!'

'*Urah!*'

Trying to grab my breath and holding on to Oleg's jacket for the ride. The police threw us into the wall over and over again. Oleg never shut up. His mouth racing with begging words in six different languages till he'd had enough of this shit and plastered his press card hard on to the nose of one very pissed-off cop.

'*Pozhaluista!*'

Rifle barrels pointing at our heads.

'Bastards! Next time we shoot!'

And once more into the wall . . . Wham!

We sank down in slow motion like busted cartoons.

'Uh, well . . . that was fun.'

'Oh, yeah.'

The panicked mob rushed the doors again and the police turned to smash somebody else's face. Bodies pushed and pulled, and we crawled between their legs.

'Any second I know a bullet's gonna fly up my ass!'

'Uh, well . . . crawl faster!'

Down three or four steps and safe.

We ran through pitch-black hallways chasing Rutskoi's voice echoing and vibrating through the dark and the true believers' cheers washing away the sins of their fear. Tripping up stairs and round a corner and into a line of assault rifles. Doors to the balcony stuffed with darting eyes and nervous trigger fingers. And through the protecting ring of AK54s, Alexander Rutskoi was indeed giving the speech of his life, surrounded by every camera in the world but mine.

'Rutskoi! Rutskoi! Rutskoi!'

There was no way we were getting close to him.

'Ah, allo, ITN.'

Andrei Fyodorov's chubby hand reaching through the weapons.

'Evenin', Andrei.'

'Yes. Exciting evening, don't you think?'

Rutskoi shouting to the crowd and raising his hands and reaching for the stars, and the true believers roaring like Jesus himself'd come down from the heavens to save them.

'Guess we missed it,' I said.

Bodyguards tossed aside the cameras and reporters. Assault rifles tucked in close and surrounded Alexander Vladimirovich, shielding him from the crush and hustling him off the balcony quick.

'No questions!'

'Get back! Back!'

A small army rolling our way at high speed.

'Stay where you are,' said Andrei.

''Scuse me?'

Ooof!

Machine-guns bulldozed us into the White House with Rutskoi in tow. I looked over the heads of the bodyguards. The entire press pack trapped out on the balcony. I waved. Down a stairwell and into total blackness. Zippo lighters flicking in the dark. Two guards held us in a corner as the rebel band squeezed through a narrow door. They stood for a moment trying to find their way in the dark.

'Uh, well . . . I don't think they will let us . . .'

'Yes, they will!'

And I kicked on the camera lamp and flooded the blackness with light. The guards waved us through. Swell, ITN was blazing the way for the leader of a revolution. I ran along the walls and locked Rutskoi in the lens. Hurried steps. The general under siege. He orders, he commands, he leads. Fingers pointing and his fist slamming the air with determination and resolve. And me falling back and letting the small army pass through the frame and dropping the camera low and stuffing a double-clipped AK54 into the lens wanting the picture to look as big as Texas. Wanting the picture to say, 'Fuck you, Boris.' And wanting the shot to run as fast as the hurried steps up some stairs and down more halls to the outer rooms of Rutskoi's office till the guard turns and waves the killing thing in my face. Message received, loud and clear. I switched off the lamp and Rutskoi vanished into the dark. I backed away and tried to hide in a dark corner. Oleg came close.

'Jonka, what are you doing?'

'We need an interview.'

'Uh, well . . . now?'

'Everyone's got him outside. We got the only pictures inside this fuckin' place. If we can get him to talk we've got somethin' big!'

He took a breath and stepped out of the dark towards the bodyguards. Hands slapped rifles ready. Oleg mumbled in a quiet voice and pointed back towards me. I stepped out of the shadow. Candles glimmered through the bevelled glass of Rutskoi's office and a warm light fell across our faces.

'Tell him, "We helped you, now you help us." '

Oleg said the words. The guard nodded and went through the doors and was soon back with Andrei Fyodorov.

'No, no. He is very tired. He doesn't want to talk now. Perhaps a press conference tomorrow.' He held out his hand to say goodnight.

'Look, Andrei, things are tense just now. The entire fuckin' world . . .'

'Uh, well . . . Jonka.'

'. . . yeah, yeah, 'scuse me. The entire world is wonderin' what the hell's goin' on in this building.'

Andrei's eyebrows looking curious.

I looked at my watch. *News at Ten* was on the air in seventy-five minutes. 'Andrei, you know CNN uses every bit of our stuff. Russian TV broadcasts our news from here to Vladivostok. And right now Boris Yeltsin is tryin' to cut your fuckin' balls off –'

'Jonka!'

'– but I promise you that minutes after Alexander Vladimirovich Rutskoi Presidyent speaks to this fuckin' camera his voice is goin' to be heard around the entire fuckin' world!'

Fyodorov smiled. 'Let me see.'

He slipped behind the doors.

'Uh, well . . . a most interesting presentation, Jonka.'

'Think so? I think it went OK.'

I wandered around looking for images to capture the moment. Volunteers stomping through the dark. Ammo clips snapping into steel chambers. Candlelight swelling up the stairs and the stairwell glowing like a mineshaft deep in the earth. Voices calling, 'All clear!' from far below. The doors drew open slowly and Andrei Fyodorov signalled us in.

'Just a few minutes. He must sleep.'

Candles lining the entrance, like a chapel. Assault rifles against the walls. Rutskoi sitting in a pool of yellow light at the end of the table. A small candle burning next to him. His jacket thrown over the chair. A cigarette with an impossibly long ash smouldering in his hands and a graceful move inviting us to sit next to him. His voice deep and calm. The candlelight smoothing the strain of the last days from his face.

'Alexander Vladimirovich . . .' Oleg whispered '. . . is this checkmate?'

Rutskoi held up a hand, silence. He wasn't interested in questions. He sat thinking quietly for a moment. A deep pull on his cigarette, a smoke-filled sigh. His steel-blue eyes falling on the candle flame before him.

'You know. I have always been a man of fixed principles. And I always knew it would end this way.'

And his hand reaching and holding the fire high into the dark room.

'With a candle like this, burning as a memorial to democracy in Russia.'

And hearing it ring in my head. Soundbite . . . yes! The man can talk all night but he ain't gonna top that. Thank you very much. Time to go.

I slid back for a few wide shots. Oleg made our goodbyes to Andrei Fyodorov and we bolted through the door and passed the bodyguards till another stupid idea raced through my head.

'Oleg. We get this tape out then we come right back. We tell Andrei we want to sleep on the floor.'

'Uh, well . . . floor. Why?'

'Christ knows what's gonna happen tonight.'

'I was afraid you would think something like this.'

And he ran back into the candlelight.

*

Crashing thuds shook me awake. Not that I was really sleeping, more like freezing with my eyes closed. The heat went off with the lights. Chills and cold prowled the empty halls.

I crawled to a window and wiped fog from the glass. Way down below, a buzz of activity through the night. Kamaz trucks packed with huge concrete blocks and timber pulling up near the White House. Volunteers tossing massive chunks of debris on to the driveways and pavements. Dreamers tying ropes round stones and dragging them into place like the Hebrew slaves at the Pyramids.

From another window, Greycoats of the militia still stomping in place keeping warm and watching the rebels build their defences. A line of army trucks rolling across Kalininskii Bridge, stopping and waiting, then pulling away down a dark street.

Out over the plaza, hundreds of dreamers huddled near the barricade fires, watching and waiting with the rest of the world. The accordion man in the tilted cap sat amid the crowd, playing his music and singing about somewhere over the Soviet rainbow.

Drops of soft rain trickled down the window. I stepped back and did a few sums. Ten feet across, twenty feet floor to ceiling, floor after floor of the same fuckin' thing.

'Christ. Goddam place is a monument to glass.'

My voice echoing through the dark. Quick spin round the halls. Sofas, chairs, bookcases, anything and everything turned over and stacked high against the windows. Like, so what? Bodyguards sat outside Rutskoi's office and smoked and fiddled with their assault rifles. They waved and smiled as I wandered through the room, offering me cigarettes and being very sorry there was no tea.

A lone guard sat in a faraway corner, cleaning his AK47 by candlelight. Bullets and oily rags and banana clips like a still-life painting. Oleg was rolled up on a small carpet nearby. His wool cap pulled down, his arms wrapped round his chest, one eye open as I flopped down next to him.

'Normalno?'

''Cept for some guys throwing down concrete and shit.'

'Tank barricades.'

'Swell.'

I laid my head on the camera and counted the concrete thuds like sheep.

'Were you ever a Communist, Oleg?'

'Uh, well . . . my grandfather was a bee-keeper.'

A long quiet and more thuds.

'Is there more to that thought or was that it?'

'I was just thinking about him.'

'Were you close?'

'No. He is only a photograph. Comrade Stalin had him arrested and sent to a Siberian gulag where they put a bullet through his head.'

'What the hell for?'

'For the high crime of being a good bee-keeper, I suppose.'

'Fuck me.'

'A few years later my father was killed in the Great Patriotic War trying to save Comrade Stalin's ass from Herr Hitler.'

Oleg turned and propped his head on his arm and sighed.

'They both died before I was born. I never knew them, they never knew me. They have only been photographs in my life.'

'Nothin' more than pictures.'

'Yes, Jonka, nothing more than pictures.'

And now the third generation of Yuriev men in the line of fire. I saw his wife and kids then images of another family on a dark runway in Sokhumi ripped to shreds following me, believing me. What the fuck was I doing?

'Oleg, maybe we should be goin'.'

'Do you know about his fingers?'

'What?'

'Yeltsin. He has two fingers missing from his left hand. When I was a little boy I would always find bullets from the war. And I would build fires and hide behind trees and throw these things into the fire and cover my ears and hear them explode.'

And Oleg remembering . . .

'My mother would come out and beat me. Oh, she could scream. But it was something Russian boys did after the war and we knew enough to hide when playing these games.'

. . . and giggling.

'Earth to Oleg. Earth to Oleg.'

'Uh, well . . . yes. When Yeltsin was a boy he found a grenade and set it on a rock and found a hammer and he started to hit it!'

'Silly things that children do.'

'Children? He was fourteen years old!'

Oleg laughing, then not laughing.

'Imagine, Jonka. There is a man out there, with one of the most powerful armies in the world ready to attack this building, who at fourteen years of age did not know you do not hit a grenade with a hammer.'

'No shit?'

'And when his mother asked him why he did it he said, "I wanted to see if it would blow up." '

'No shit?'

Suddenly the White House felt like a very large grenade. 'Nuff vodka, big old hammer, and boom.

Thud, thud, thud.

And Oleg drifting off to sleep and me wrapped up in my leather jacket trying to get warm, thinking how I was always afraid of the dark as a boy and how that fear never left.

The guard set his rifle on the floor. He opened a closet, dug through a pile of stuff and pulled out two heavy wool militia coats. He laid one over me, the other across Oleg, and he walked back to his chair and sat with his weapon in silence.

'*Spasibo*,' I said.

He lit a cigarette and locked a bullet into the chamber of his rifle. '*Nyet problemy*.'

I closed my eyes and saw an old man kneeling in the snow, hands tied behind his back, a dirty rag tied over his eyes. Bees buzzing round him till someone put a bullet in his head.

Scratch, scratch, scratch.

I opened my eyes to a threadbare broom inches from my nose and little puffs of dust in my face. I rolled on to my back and saw an old woman leaning over me, snapping with Russian indignation.

'*Dobryi dyen*, Jonka,' yawned Oleg. 'And by the way, Babushka says she has been sweeping this carpet since before you were born and who do you think you are, sleeping on the floor and upsetting her routine of cleaning duties?'

The babushka chopped at the dirt and the dust and shovelled it around my face and down the stairs.

'Where's she goin' now?'

'I would think she has been sweeping that same pile of dirt since before you were born as well. She just keeps moving it around the building year after year.'

Oleg looked at the wool coat over his legs. I pointed to the sleeping cop, rifle still on his lap, the nearby candle melted to a blob of wax. Hazy light poured through the windows. The entire floor was crammed with sleeping bodyguards, assault rifles, and empty packs of Marlboro cigarettes.

'Guess Boris couldn't find a hammer.'

'Uh, well.'

We left the coats on a chair and wandered through the White House maze, hoping for a cup of tea.

'Hear that?'

'*Da*, voices.'

'Yup. Comin' through microphones.'

We looked up to the ceiling.

'And the lights are open again.'

'Let's have a look-see.'

We opened the doors of a crowded conference room. No one stopped us so we walked right on in. Ruslan Khazbulatov was sitting under a huge seal of the Soviet Union and all down the table, the entire think-tank of the rebel parliament. Sergei Burbrin and Iona Andronov and all the Commie high holies. Lesser gods stood against the walls. They were not happy campers.

Khazbulatov looking like everyone else felt. Black unwashed hair sticking out at right angles to his head, his clothes rumpled as if he'd slept in them. In fact he had. In fact we all had. It was a room full of people with rumpled clothes and hair at right angles from heads. All but General Vlyachslav Achalov. A fat Russian bear in crisp Soviet uniform. The general roared and yelled. The deputies yelled back. Khazbulatov pounded the table with his fist.

I framed it up and hit the roll button. A roomful of red eyes and bad hair stared into the lens then went back at it again. Yelling and fists and the strain of holding out day after day filling the lens. Some deputies screaming for negotiations, other deputies screaming to kick ass. General Achalov screaming to kick the fucking press out of the White House. His fat claw pointing to my camera lens.

'They are foreigners! They are giving secrets to Yeltsin!'

Achalov was defence minister for the rebel parliament. He was tough and unafraid of spilling blood for Mother Russia. When the Soviet Union cracked down in T'bilisi, Vilnius and Baku, General Achalov spilled lots of it.

Zoom into the old soldier's face. Clean-shaven, slicked-back hair, eyes of a well-disciplined killer. Irony framed in glass. This was the same man who had planned the assault on Yeltsin's White House bunker in August 1991. Now the fat soldier roared again, like wanting just one more chance to take out Boris.

Ruslan Khazbulatov had had enough and waved his arms and stormed out of the room, as if running from a pack of flies. Deputies broke into groups and yelled some more. We edged close to General Achalov.

'Excuse us, Comrade General, may we ask about your defences?'

'Fuck off!'

'Yes, sir.'

Sunday. Red Square. Mstislav Rostropovich, Soviet *refusenik*, cellist, Russian *émigré*, and now conductor of the National Symphony Orchestra in Washington, DC, performs with his *Amerikanski* orchestra under the domes of St Basil's Cathedral.

And Boris Nikolaevich Yeltsin stands with thousands of Russians listening to Tchaikovsky's '1812 Overture'. The sun bright, the wind cold. Rostropovich in the lens. A man gloriously possessed with music, like Merlin with some magic wand, conjuring sounds and casting them like a spell over the Kremlin walls. A small cannon sits at the edge of the stage. Merlin spins his magic into a powerful climax and the cannon fires.

Kaboom!

Then again and again.

Whip pan and focus.

Boris Yeltsin smiles.

RRRINNNGGG!

'Oh, please. Gimme a break.'

RRRRRRINNNNNNNGGGG!

'Shit.'

Sleepy hands slap the table.

'Hello.'

'Jon. Ian Glover James.'

Ian sounding tense. Then Ian always sounded tense. My eyes stay closed. 'What's up, Ian?'

'Yeltsin has sealed off the White House.'

Instant awakeness. Into yesterday's socks and jeans and find my boots. Grab the camera kit and zing out the door. Three minutes down the ring road and a quick right at Novyi Arbat. A line of water-tank trucks pressed nose to tail across the road. Soldiers with bales of razor wire. Cutting, pulling, stretching. Dump the car on the pavement and grab the camera. Run into the road and round the trucks. Militiamen close ranks and shove a wall of riot shields in my face. Like hitting a big tin can.

'*Nyet!*'

Wham.

'Not again!'

I ran round the entire building. Grey coats and steel helmets and riot shields every step of the way. I rolled off a few shots of the White House and the Mayor's office and the endless line of silver shields. I needed something bigger and higher.

'It seems the Militiaman Cookie Factory has been working over-time.'

As if by magic, Oleg standing behind me.

'Where the hell did you come from?'

'I was born in the northern Ukraine. Why do you ask?'

Over his shoulder the tall apartment building with the big windows. Big windows looking straight down on to the White House.

'Let's go see the neighbours!'

I took off with Oleg nipping at my heels.

'Then, of course, I was educated at the Moscow University.'

Up to the doors ready to rip them open 'cause none of the security locks in Russia worked anyway.

'Then I was sent to Africa but, of course, I much preferred my time in Cuba.'

Pull hard.

'Shit! Locked!'

The lock clicked and a crooked old woman pushed at the door. There was a small dog stuffed in her coat. I was gracious enough to yank the door wide. The woman flew out on to the step with her hand still glued to the brass handle and the dog looking airsick. The woman's squeaky voice worried and nervous, the dog growling. I smiled and bowed and shoved her over and in we went. We jumped into the lift and headed for the roof.

'What was the old gal saying anyway?'

'She was complaining about the price of cabbage. She doesn't know how she will buy food. Her dog is crazy from all the noise. And her bones ache in the rain.'

'It's raining?'

'Uh, well . . . yes.'

'Huh.'

The lift clunked to a stop. Up a few stairs to the metal roof door. Pull hard. Locked again.

'Since when did this country decide to fix every fuckin' thing?'

A cough from below. An apartment door opening just a peek. Elderly eyes looking us over. Oleg walked down, mumbled Russian for a few minutes and came back up the stairs. 'I have spoken with the man and he will let us – of course it is his wife hiding behind the door giving the orders – but he will let us into the flat. But they want money.'

'How much?'

'A hundred dollars.'

I dug a wad of cash out of my pocket.

'Make it two. But we get to come back and no other TV company, 'specially the BBC, gets into the flat.'

'Jonka, you want me to negotiate exclusive television rights into some poor Russians' flat?'

'Yup.'

Oleg mumbling down the stairs.

'So that is how market economy works, then. Nobody makes any-thing. You just pass money around for stupid things like exclusive rights to do this and that. It's like the Russian proverb. This hungry fox meets a very stupid bear near a stream. But I cannot remember the rest just now.'

We stepped inside and said hello to the residents. He was a nice old chap with hunched shoulders and a Russian newspaper in his hands and she was a squatty little thing in a frumpy dress and apron the same colour as the wallpaper. Some sort of green not found in nature. Madam snatched the money out of my fingers and replaced it with a pair of fuzzy blue house slippers.

'*Snimite botinki! Nye sorite v moyom dome!*'

'Uh, well . . . Babushka demands we remove our boots and not dirty her house like capitalist dogs.'

' 'Scuse me?'

'Oh, I added the part about capitalist dogs. I was carried away.'

We pulled off our boots, put on our slippers and raced into the flat.

Yank back the heavy drapes and open the tall wood frames of heavy glass. Rain and diesel and pictures rushed into the room. The White House in grey wet light. Water trucks roped round the building like a hangman's noose. And inside the rope line thousands of Interior Ministry troops. Tight formations of well-trained men marching through the rain and splashing through puddles, boots pounding like soggy drums. Riot shields and truncheons and rifles. APCs up and down Konyushkovskaya Street. Heavy Draganoff machine-guns in the faces of the true believers.

A radio echoing down the hall from the kitchen. A Russian voice broadcasting in double time. Like he was in a hurry to get out of town before the shit starts. '*SevodnyaPresidentYeltsingovorit . . .*'

'Uh, well . . . Yeltsin has announced the White House has been taken over by illegal armed formations that have made the situation dangerous and unpredictable. And . . . well, demonstrators are free to leave but no one will be allowed through military lines into the White House.'

Down behind the barricades, a handful of dreamers with their rocks and steel bars and clubs. And up in the windows of the White House, stunned faces. Yeltsin's noose squeezing eyeballs from their heads. Pan down and along the barricades. Quick sums in the lens. Only a few hundred men, tops.

'Christ. It's brilliant. It's a fuckin' siege, Oleg. Boris'll starve 'em out.'

Oleg giggled and shook his head. 'No lights, no heat, no food, no water. So what, Jonka? This is Russia. These people would only go home to the same thing.'

Across Kalininskii Bridge. More trucks and more troops and more guns. I leaned out the window. Way down on the steps of the apartment building, the old crooked woman with the achy bones and the small dog stuffed into her coat, right where we left her, motionless, like a pillar of salt melting in the rain.

And the rain fell cold in the night. We cruised the wet streets after a long day of riot shields and '*Nyet!*', turning on to Novyi Arbat when shapes and shadows raced through headlamps. Angry men, enraged men. Stones and bottles and metal bar smashing into the windshield.

'Shit!'

Hit the brakes and jump out of the car and into a riot. Curses and shouts, rocks and bricks whipping by our heads. Every possible bit of roadside junk sailing through dark and crashing on to asphalt.

Switch on the camera, hit the roll button, and . . . nothing.

'Fuck me!'

'What is it, Jon?'

'Dunno! Camera!'

'Uh, well . . . great.'

Open the camera and yank out the tape. Safety button locked. Pull and it snaps in my hands.

'Holy fuck!'

Spare tape in the car. No time. Spinning blue cop lights. Rip off a piece of gaffer tape and slap it on the cassette.

'I can't believe this shit! First hint of trouble . . .'

Cram the cassette back into the camera and slam it shut. Bad guys running back into the shadows.

'. . . and I can't get a goddam inch of it on tape!'

Flip the camera on to my shoulder and roll. Moscow cops leap from cars ready to beat the shit out of anything that moves. We make like a couple of nobodies. The coppers kick and shove me and Oleg and the rest of the junk off the street. 'This is your fault!' a cop screams. 'You instigate them with your cameras!'

Few quick shots and get the hell out of there.

Back at the bureau. Oleg eating three-day-old pizza and me drinking beer and us watching Julian's package hit the satellite with the pictures from Novyi Arbat. Serious Julian voice. Ominous Julian tones.

'And tonight the first signs of sporadic violence in Moscow.'

And Oleg leaning over the table, spectacles sliding down his nose.

'Actually, ladies and gentlemen, our wonderful hotshot cameraman screwed up . . . and, well . . . these are the first pictures of the first clean-up after the first signs of sporadic violence . . .'

'Yeah, yeah.'

A thousand umbrellas in the rain. The banished dreamers caught outside Yeltsin's noose. They march down the tiny road off Krasnaya Presnaya near Dom Kino Cinema. Soviet mantras calling through the wet and grey and cold. Me and Oleg were inside the Cinema Café drinking bad coffee and drying out, waiting for something BIG to happen. We got a weird parade instead. Red flags popping out from under black umbrellas. Furious waves.

'Fuck me. Looks like the First Soviet Congress of Communist Turtles.'

'Does your corrupt western mind always see such things?'

'You mean you don't?'

Water trucks and grey coats and steel helmets and riot shields formed a front-line across the road. The militia sporting something new with their ensemble: bullet-proof vests. The dreamers bumped into the Greycoats two hundred yards from the White House. Gentle pushes back and forth.

'Uh, well . . . they seem to want to get back into the Promised Land.'

'No fuckin' way.'

'It cannot go on like this for ever, Jonka.'

'Why the fuck not?'

Oleg tapping his fingers, waiting for me to grow up.

'Yeah, yeah. Let's go.'

Three or four men scampered up on to a truck alongside the road with megaphone and banners and angry words.

'Bring Yeltsin's band of criminals to trial!'

'*Urah!*'

I scampered up behind the leaders. The megaphone screeched and the crowd cheered again. Guess they thought I was going to make a speech because they just stared at me, waiting. So I bowed.

'*Urah!*' they cried.

Black turtle umbrellas squeezed together in the cold. Red flags soaking wet, dripping and drooping.

'*Yeltsin vrag naroda!*'

'*Urah! Urah!*'

Zoom over the water trucks. Trucks and buses packed with troops of a different colour. Black berets. Black riot vests.

'Who's those guys, Oleg?'

'Otryad Militsii Osobovo Naznacheniya.'

''Scuse me?'

'Let us say Seriously Mean Bastards. OMON, for short.'

'Got it.'

An OMON commander pacing nearby with a radio in hand like a football coach on the sidelines waiting for just the right moment to send in his boys. Voices screeched through the rain and the banished dreamers pushed harder against the riot shields and greycoats pushed harder back again. Little more each time.

'Long live the Soviet Union!'

'*Urah!*'

Amid the black turtle umbrellas, one guy wrapped from head to toe in a white plastic sheet. Cut-outs for his eyes and arms and a red banner stretched wide in his hands. Like Lenin's ghost looking for the way home.

'How does it look from up there, Jonka?'

'Didn't think it could get any weirder, but then it did.'

'It is all the drugs you smoke. What do you expect?'

'Yeah, yeah.'

The long days slipping into stoned goofiness.

Inside the White House, parliamentary deputies sat by candlelight singing patriotic songs and passing laws Yeltsin ignored. Down the road in the Kremlin, Boris Nikolaevich poured himself a round, then another, and issued more ultimatums the deputies ignored. Out in the streets it was just cold and wet. Day after goddam day.

I passed the camera down to Oleg and slid off the truck to a round of applause from the flag-waving First Soviet Congress of Communist Turtles. The lens pushed through the crowd and settled next to the riot shields smack between the face-off. Like watching nasty neighbours argue over a picket fence. Soviet fists inches from militia noses. Spitting faces and pointing hands. Militiamen biting their lips and chewing their teeth and listening to the same crap over and over again.

'And another thing, you Fascist pig!'

'How can you defend this illegal act?'

'Are you not Russians?'

Bitter words pouring into the cold in little puff-clouds of rage. And the soldiers, rain-soaked and tired, feeling their own rage and biting their lips.

'Where is your pride?'

That one hurt. Cringing and shame in the lens. Militiamen knowing this was not decent work for men in uniform, but orders were orders. Close-ups. Greycoats biting their lips harder, patience slipping.

'You are selling out your country!'

'How can you accept blood money?'

Like a cold slap.

Just the day before Yeltsin issued another of his whiz-bang decrees. Not only would the militia get all their back pay but how about a big fat bonus to boot? Not a bribe to keep the troops in line, you understand. Just a little Presidential Something to say 'spasibo' for all those cold days in the rain.

'How could you sell your soul to a drunkard?'

'Traitors!'

Soldiers' faces scowling into the lens.

Hate cutting through glass.

Seeing their shame.

Patience slipping fast.

A gang of babushkas came out from under their umbrellas and surrounded us. Voices shouting all at once and Oleg doing simultaneous translations in fluent Oleguese.

' "Which television company are you?"; "Now you can clearly see Yeltsin's crimes!"; "Do not tell lies!"; "My son is in the White House!"; "Rutskoi is President!"; "Why is this cameraman outside without a hat?" '

'Izvinite.'

I turned to a young Russian. He had a hat. It was wet and drooping down round his face. Thick glasses. His skin-thin coat soaked with rain.

'Where are you from, please?' he asked. A slow and trembling voice. Glasses clouded with raindrops and steam.

'America.'

'I would like speak you.'

'Sure.'

'I not Communist. Never Communist. I study history in university.

Now I stand here. I not wish to be ruled by any men. Russia ruled by tsar, then Communist Party, now Yeltsin. I want rule with law like in America. Do you understand? I am sorry. My English very poor.'

'No, please. *Ponimayu*. I understand.'

He held out his bare wet hand in the rain; he was shivering. I pulled off my forty-dollar fur-lined glove and took his hand. Freezing cold skin.

'Thank you very big,' he said.

And he turned and walked back to the riot shields and stared straight into the eyes of Yeltsin's bulletproof militia. Trembling courage in the cold rain.

And me slipping into my glove and feeling warm and ashamed, but still waiting for something big to happen. Anything.

Thunk! Thunk! Thunk!

Truncheons banging on shields like war drums.

'Jonka, I think—'

'Yeah . . . trouble. Finally.'

Flip on the camera. Roll.

Truncheons smashing down on heads. A line of grey coats and steel helmets and riot shields plough through the crowd. Terrified faces run through the frame. Truncheons smashing harder still. An old woman falls to her knees and makes the sign of the cross. The Greycoats march over her, digging in their boots for traction. Closer and closer and bigger and bigger in the lens.

'Swell.'

Shields crashed into the camera and I fell back. Oleg had me by the collar and pulled me up before I hit the ground.

'Stay on your feet, Jonka!'

A truncheon smashed into my shoulder and I went down again.

'Goddammit! I'm tryin'!'

Oleg pulled me back and I kept rolling in the faces of the militia. Mean eyes squinting meaner and voices screaming into the lens.

'Enough of your fucking cameras!'

A Russian stills-shooter grabbed by the militia and dragged behind the shields. Truncheons smashing hard across his back. I was pushed into the riot shields trying for the shot. Oleg hauled me out like an errant child. 'Jon! They will arrest you! They will hurt you!'

'Fuckers! Fuckers!'

We fell into a pile of photographers.

'Listen, we stay together!'

'*Da.*'

'Anyone gets taken down, the rest of us shoot it, OK?'

'*Konyechno!*'

The steel plough rolled ahead and beat the crowd off the street and through the park behind Barrikadnaya metro station. Into the thick mud of days and days of rain. A woman struggles with a pram, trying to escape. The baby screaming blue in the face and the woman screaming for help. Riot shields push her down and the steel plough swallows them whole.

An old war veteran tumbles into the slop. Medals cross the breast of his old army coat. A hero of the Soviet Union. Militia boots grind his face into the mud then kick him aside like rubbish.

Thrum! Thrum! Thrum!

'Ooooommmmmmm.'

Pan left. Three Buddhist monks. Saffron robes and sandals, banging away on little drums and chanting for inner harmony and enlightenment.

'OK, then, who the fuck are these guys?'

'I have absolutely no idea, Jonka.'

The Greycoats went for one last thrill and shoved the crowd into the heavy traffic of Krasnaya Presnaya. Cars, trucks and buses skidded and screeched to a stop. The militia fell back and formed a new front-line along the pavement.

'Fascists! Fascists! Fascists!' the Commies screamed.

Pan round to the voices. Pull wide and roll.

Junk and fire crashing into the road. Metal doors, pipes, broken radiators, wood slats, a water-heater, a wooden table. A giant billboard for some Russian trading house. Flames burning through its message of 'Strength through Success!' A dumpster turning over and spilling trash on to the fire. A Soviet flag lashed to the wheels. More junk and more smoke. More fists and cries.

'Fascists! Fascists! Fascists!'

Passengers fleeing buses. Tyres slashed. Instant barricades.

Interior Ministry trucks raced up from Konyushkovskaya and slammed to a halt. Hundreds more militia piled into the street. Hundreds more clubs and boots and riot shields charging hard and cracking heads. The beaten-down protestors crawled up the slick cobblestones towards Krasno Presnenskaya metro and slipped away. A long trail of smoke and junk and crumpled black umbrellas scattered in their muddy steps. The Greycoats lit fags and drew long pulls of smoke. Shields dragging across cobblestones. And me and Oleg sitting in the middle of the trash heap. Breathin' hard as worn-out dogs.

'Uh, well.'

'That's all you gotta say?'

Cold rain turned to colder fog. APCs appeared from outa nowhere and took up positions in the newly conquered land. Heavy machine-guns swivelled on turrets as Yeltsin's soldiers locked their sights on the White House.

'Uh, well.'

'No shit, comrade.'

Back at the bureau again. Oleg eating more leftover pizza and me feeling sore and tired because there was no more beer and the bruises on my back and legs hurt like hell and all my dope was stashed in that little Yeltsin Matrushka doll back home. Sounds of tape spinning on heads from the edit suite. Julian cranking out stories like a sausage factory.

'Oh, Jon,' calls Julian, 'that screaming woman! Great stuff!'

'Yeah, yeah.'

CNN on the tube. Blah, blah, blah, blah.

And me thinking I might mix a bit of hash into the grass for some extra mondo bongo later on. Across the room, Ian Glover James sat with three phones hanging from his ears.

'Jon, the opposition has called for a demonstration at Krasno Presnenskaya metro station.'

'They just fuckin' left.'

'They're back. I think it might be a good idea if you and Oleg went down . . .'

We were already running out the door and heading down in the lift. Me slapping a fresh battery into the camera and Oleg holding a small aluminium step-ladder.

'Good thinkin', Oleg. May have to get above the crowds.'

'Uh, well . . . actually I think it's time we had our own shield.'

'Yeah. That too.'

*

Like a scene from a low-budget horror flick.

Spiky towers looming in the night. Wind in the trees, cold rain. Weird orange light squiggling on icy wet cobblestones. And thousands of angry Muscovites marching up the road, screaming for the head of Yeltsinstein's monster.

Action!

Greycoats swarmed in like armour-plated killer bees. They cut the demonstrators in half and hit hard. Something in the dark making it feel extra mean as riot shields herded the crowds into tiny head-bashing pens.

Whack, whack, whack.

A small band of protestors in the middle of the street, their leader calling for them to draw close . . .

'Sit down! Do not fight back! Do not fight back!'

. . . and forty troops surround the sit-in and smash heads like hammers on meat. I drop to my knees and frame the bloodied hands and twisted faces, the killer-bee soldiers spitting in the lens.

'Look out!' yelled Oleg.

Shields hit us from behind. Truncheons swinging down and Oleg's ladder going up . . . crash, crash, crash! We crawled away and watched the protestors melt into the cobblestones, their bodies splayed out like roadkill. Orders of the day from the Uncle Boris: swing hard and swing often, earn that fuckin' pay rise! Half the demonstrators escaped over the hill, half were still trapped at the doors of the metro station.

'Oleg! Let's get to that mob!'

Oleg used the ladder like a can-opener and prised a path through the chaos. We popped out in front of the demonstrators and into a line of oncoming shields and clubs.

'You and your fucking cameras!' screamed the Greycoats.

'Shit, not again!'

Wham! Crash!

On the ground. Soviet army-issue boots kicking into our sides.

Demonstrators pulling us to our feet and spinning us round like tops and tossing us right back into the shields and clubs.

'You and your fucking cameras!'

Wham! Crash!

And down again hiding under the ladder.

'What the fuck is goin' on?'

'Uh, well ... the rebels probably think it is good the world sees foreign journalists getting the shit kicked out of them!'

'Oh, swell!'

Black boots kicked us down the slick cobblestones as another line of pissed-off Greycoats charged. I got to my feet and shoved the lens into their face-guards. 'OK, you fuckin' bastards! C'mon!'

Oleg's warning lights went off and he executed the classic 'Oleg Rescues Jon From His Big Mouth' manoeuvre, grab hold and pull hard. We fell into a concrete wall with nowhere to run. Truncheons and shields marching closer still.

'Great fuckin' rescue, Oleg!'

'This way, Jonka!'

He pushed me sideways like he was sending me to bed with no supper. We crawled behind a tree and hid with two Russian snappers. The Greycoat squad commander shouted new orders and the shields and clubs turned back into the demonstrators for more backhand and overhead smash drills. One of the snappers held up his camera, smashed to pieces.

'Jonka, they are attacking cameras. Two photographers have been badly beaten.'

'OK. I'll keep quiet.'

'Good boy. When this is over I will give you a candy.'

'Yeah, yeah. But I want pictures of those fuckin' clubs.'

'I was afraid you would say that.'

Slide down the cobblestones to the end of the shields, a quick dash behind the Greycoats, then back up the slippery hill and into the crush of screams at the metro-station gates. Fluorescent light pouring through the doors and on to the police helmets and silver shields all shimmering with otherworldly light. Truncheons smashing down over and over again.

I pushed into the backs of Greycoats and focused through the clubs. Fiery eyes of rebel rage. Sweating and bloody faces, faces that would not surrender. Never, never! And the clubs whipping through the frame again and again, pounding harder and harder like trying to kill the screams.

'Traitors! Traitors!'

'Bastards!'

'Long live the Soviet Union!'

Oleg's hands grabbing my coat. 'Time to go, Jon!'

'Not yet!'

'Uh, well . . . now!'

And Oleg twisting me round with my face still locked to the viewfinder. Spinning images of black and white in my eyes till focus. A massive wall of riot shields and savage-eyed troops charging into the lens . . .

'Oh, fuck!'

. . . wham!

Protestors and Greycoats and me smashing into kiosks and glass. Shields cutting and stabbing like knives. Truncheons dancing on skulls. And me on the ground under the bodies trying to hold on to the camera. Voices crying and screaming and raining down in the breathless dark. Then all the voices lost in a waterfall of dull, sickening thuds.

'Fuck me . . . this hurts.'

Stoned to the gills. Land of dope coming on smooth with Buffalo Springfield booming through the stereo. Neil Young picking those same two high notes over and over again like submarine pings from the far beyond. And Stephen Stills jamming riffs on his acoustic guitar and wailing away with that blues-gravelled voice of his from 1966.

'Something's happenin' here . . . what it is ain't exactly clear . . .'

And the TV flickering firelike in the dark. Not a word on Russki Newski about riots at Krasno Presnenskaya. Like it never happened. Just pictures of this fat Russian guy with white hair trying to stand up straight and not fall over while walking into a *Wizard of Oz* kinda room with chandeliers and cameras flashing. Seems the fat guy wanted to say, 'Howdy,' to this other Russian guy in a big eggshell hat all covered in gold and jewels and a big gold cross on top. The two Russian guys shook hands.

Another hit of Uzbek grass and stoned wisdom takes hold. Seems the fat guy is Boris Nikolaevich Yeltsin, President of the Russian Federation, and the guy in the big eggshell hat is Alexei I, Patriarch of the Russian Orthodox Church. Uncle Boris was looking for a photo-op with the next best thing to God.

'There will be no blood sacrifice on the streets of Moscow,' promises Uncle Boris.

'Let us pray for peace,' intones His Holiness.

They bow their heads for the cameras.

'. . . *there's a man with a gun over there . . . tellin' me I've got to beware . . .*'

4

THREE DAYS IN OCTOBER

Saturday. Clear, cold skies

Old Arbat Street was having a birthday. Five hundred years old today. *Urah*. Muscovites wrapped their kids in the usual fifteen layers of clothes, no matter what time of year it was, and went for a stroll amid the balloons and jugglers and clowns. Yesterday it was a riot, today it's a carnival.

'And you're tellin' me none of this seems weird to you?'

'Uh, well . . . why?'

'I mean, look. Down the road the White House is surrounded by a fuckin' army and we're here watchin' a few hundred families wander round a birthday party for some old cobblestones.'

'Democracy must be fun, Jonka.'

Nearby, construction workers were putting the final touches to a huge stage at the end of Old Arbat Street. Unused steel frames and bars and bolts tossed in a big pile behind a row of scraggly bushes.

Clank. Dink. Boink.

'What's the stage for?'

'Uh, well . . . there is a concert this evening. Some terrible Russian pop band. You would think it could be classical music, Prokofiev or Borodin, but no, modern Russia has no room for such beauty.'

My eyes ran up the walls of the Foreign Ministry Building next to the stage. Thirty floors above the trees with pointy towers and gargoyles scraping the sky.

'Looks like the *Daily Planet*.'

'Shtoa?'

'*Daily Planet*. You know, Superman?'

'Superman.'

'Yup. Faster than a speeding bullet. More powerful than a loco-motive. Worked as a newspaper reporter for the *Daily Planet* in this huge skyscraper in Metropolis.'

'*Da*, I remember. Bullets bounced off his chest and he wore a cape. He liked to fly and make the world safe for capitalism.'

I pointed up to the windows high above. 'Sorta looks like Superman might fly outa there any second.'

Oleg looked up and then down. 'Uh, well . . . your western brain is obviously corrupted by too many comic books.'

Clank. Dink. Boink.

The pile of steel bits growing bigger.

'Then again perhaps you were hit on the head once too often last night.'

'Yeah, yeah . . . maybe.'

Music cut through the morning chill. Five comrades in cowboy hats and silly grins grabbed their guitars and fiddles and one lone banjo and started pickin' a double-time rendition of 'The Orange Blossom Special'. Russian families gathered round for some down-home, toe-tappin', Amerikanski Bluegrass. Yee-hah! Oleg's ears cringed, like hearing fingernails on slate.

'My God, what is it?'

'Good old American fiddle music, Oleg.'

'Why could we not have been conquered by the Germans? At least we'd be listening to Beethoven now. My poor stupid country. It is hard to imagine Comrade Stalin walking this same street on his way to the Kremlin.'

'Stalin walked to work?'

I looked round the narrow street. Old Russian buildings with spank-ing new façades . . . Haägen Dazs ice cream, Benetton, and McDonald's golden arches at the end of the street. A long queue of Russians ready to feast on Bolshoi Macs and fries at ten a.m.

'Stalin'd probably be first in that queue, I s'pose.'

'Of course, Jonka. Everyone else would be shot.'

Clank. Dink. Boink.

Then a handful of men and women marched through the crumbling arches of Smolenskaya metro station. No kids in tow, no party hats, no balloons. Just red flags and angry faces. The same faces from yesterday. A little black and blue from yesterday's riots, but the same faces with that same banished-dreamer look in their eyes. Then a few trucks of Yeltsin's militia pulling up along the ring road near the back of the stage. Greycoats fell out of the trucks like chunks of canned tuna. Me and Oleg wandered over for a snoop.

'This demonstration is illegal!' yelled an officer.

'But will you stop it?' asked Oleg.

He turned and spat. 'This demonstration is illegal!'

The red flags and angry faces snaked down the steps to the pedestrian tunnel running under the ring road then up more steps into a small park of dreary trees. Like a forgotten island in the middle of eight lanes of traffic. Usually the park was packed with gypsies jumping in front of cars, begging for roubles. Today it was seven hundred grumpy Commies, begging for socialist salvation. I grabbed the camera and threw it on my shoulder. Oleg grabbed the ladder, tucked it under his arm, and we fell in behind the march.

'Weirder and weirder, Oleg.'

'Jonka, it is like the Russian proverb. A village girl warns her little brother not to drink from this pond in the forest or he will turn into a lamb. But, of course, the boy does not listen and he drinks from the pond—'

'Not much of a turnout!'

Julian Manyon bellowing behind us.

'Hey, Julian.'

'How are you? Jon, Oleg?'

'Nothin' a few days off wouldn't cure.'

'Tell me about it. The days seem endless.'

The Commies convened into different groups, each with their own ear-blasting megaphone, each screaming their own version of 'Fuck Boris!' into the cold wind . . . cold and bitter as the mood. Babushkas tucked scarves into coats and men pulled hats low on heads. Red banners fluttered with battle cries to stir the heart.

'Today the White House! Tomorrow Yeltsin dictatorship!'

'Workers from Some Iddy-biddy Town in Siberia Pledge Support!'

And posters floated from meeting to meeting.

'The White House is Yeltsin's Concentration Camp!'

'Arrest Yeltsin's Gang!'

Greycoats moved across the ring road and surrounded the Commies on the island of crummy trees. Truncheons tapping shields in nervous time.

'Think anything will happen?' asked Julian.

'So far it's horse shit.'

Julian's eyes rolled with exhaustion. He didn't notice the megaphone popping up behind his head.

SCREEEECH . . . *'YELTSIN VRAG NARODA!'*

And Julian three feet into the air and down into Oleg's arms. 'Jesus wept!'

'DEATH TO TRAITORS!'

We stumbled away, ears ringing.

'Noisy. But that's about it.'

'Got that.'

'Uh, well.'

The mob stomped around the park trying to keep warm and get things moving but the rally seemed to be running out of fuel.

'Looks like a fairly lost tribe,' I said.

'I don't think this will make news.'

'Nope.'

Oleg's eyes watching. 'Uh, well.'

'I suppose I'll head back to the office and check the wires,' said Julian.

'Sounds good.'

Oleg's eyes following something, someone. 'Uh, well.'

And me finally hearing that tone in his voice and tuning my brain to Olegvision. Over there, a small pack of quiet men moving through the banners and megaphones . . . selecting, choosing, gathering . . . and one man with squirrelly brown hair and squinty eyes in the middle of the pack. Victor Ampilov. One of the last fire-breathing prophets of the Soviet god.

'Seems all the other cameras are leaving,' said Julian.

'Think we'll stay a bit.'

I switched on the camera and Oleg grabbed the ladder, and we moved towards the pack of quiet men.

'Right, then! Let me know if anything happens!'

'Yup.'

Ampilov glared through the trees towards Yeltsin's militia. He didn't like it, not one bit. His teeth snarling and gnashing like a barnyard dog. He ripped a megaphone from someone's face and climbed on to a park bench.

SCREEECH . . . 'COMRADES!'

Thunder and lightning and voices shamed into silence as the lost tribe turned to the Commie Moses come down from the mountaintop.

'Comrades! We are in danger here! The soldiers have us surrounded! Everyone! Quickly! Across to the Arbat! We will be safer there!'

Murmurs of fear. And Moses pointing down to the lens of my camera. 'Comrades! If they beat us the world will see and condemn them!'

I looked at Oleg. Big grin on his face. 'Another endorsement of your fine camerawork, Comrade Cameraman.'

'Swell.'

Ampilov rushed the mob down the steps and back through the tunnel right under the black boots of the Greycoats then up the other side of the street till the multitude was assembled beneath the Great Seal of the Soviet Union, stone-carved and massive above the doors of the Foreign Ministry building. Boris Yeltsin's militia was left surrounding the park of crummy trees and nothing more.

Ampilov jumped on a wall and opened up with high-powered rounds of rapid-fire Russian. The camera up behind him, frame his face and his megaphone, his angry fist . . . pull wide and focus down on the Commie dreamers. Hunger and answered prayers rising into the lens.

'Comrades! I want to tell you! Yeltsin is a criminal!'

'*Urah!*'

'He will be held accountable!'

'*Urah!*'

Close-ups. Faces of hope.

'Yeltsin will go to jail with the rest of his gang! Rutskoi *Presidyent*!'

'*Urah!*'

Pan left. A Second World War veteran on crutches. One decent leg and one wooden peg. Ragged clothes and a worn-out shoe. His fist pounding the cold air and his quivering lips shaping the sounds . . .

'Rutskoi *Presidyent*! Rutskoi *Presidyent*!'

Wide shot. More fists and cheers and banners. The Greycoats rushing across the street and boxing in the mob with steel shields. Then two more trucks slamming to a stop on the ring road. Heavy grilles on windows.

'Rutskoi *Presidyent*! Rutskoi *Presidyent*.'

'*Smotrite!* OMON!'

The cheering voices fell silent. Eyes watched men the size of tanks leap from the trucks. Thick arms and huge chests. Grey combat uniforms with black berets. Pistols strapped to belts and truncheons slamming into fists ready to swing. The mob wilted at the edges. Ampilov curdled with rage.

'Stop! Are you Russians or are you scum?'

Seven hundred Commies froze in their tracks. Me too, with a sideways glance towards Oleg.

'Actually, now that he fuckin' mentions it . . .'

'Uh, well . . . I was thinking the same thing.'

'Comrades! Defend yourselves!'

Down off the wall and a quick huddle with Oleg.

'Rule number one. Always have an escape route.'

'And rule number two?'

'Get on the side with the guns.'

SCREEECH . . . 'You men! Surround the meeting! Join hands! Protect the women!'

The Soviets found heart and snapped together like a rubber band. Men faced off with the militia and pushed into the shields and shouted curses at the OMON troops. Ampilov's voice roaring in the megaphone. 'Stand firm! You are Russians! Stand firm!'

Quick run to the ring road and round to the guns. Ampilov's voice chasing after us. 'Look at these soldiers! Barbarians! This will be their shame! Soldiers clubbing defenceless women! Shame on them! Stand your ground! Shame on them! Shame!'

Focus tight and roll. A soldier's hands and a well-polished Tokarov pistol, like some killer priest with a deadly sacrament, his fingers caressing an ammo clip of live rounds. The picture saying, 'Fuck that rubber-bullet shit. Lock and load. Amen.' Wide shot. OMON fixing berets and preening and flexing muscles like some macho circle jerk.

'On to the Arbat! March to the Kremlin!' Ampilov screamed.

'Jonka! They are moving!'

'Shit.'

Dash back round the stage. Ampilov's mob forms into marching order and moves up Old Arbat Street. Red flags in the cold wind. Marching forward, round a corner, then smack into the clowns and balloons and families listening to the bluegrass band, still grinnin' and pickin' ten yards up the mall.

'Stop! There are children!' yelled Ampilov. 'We must go back!'

But the OMON jammed their trucks up behind the stage cutting off any retreat. Black beret troops crept round to seal the trap and the Soviets had their backs to the walls of the Foreign Ministry with nowhere to go. The OMON crouched like beasts, wicked clubs slapping hands, nasty smirks.

'How the hell did we end up in the fuckin' middle again?'

Me watching the OMON edge closer and Oleg watching the mob step back once more and once more . . .

'Uh, well.'

'What now?'

'Look where these stupid boys are pushing them.'

. . . right on to the scrap heap of steel bars and heavy bolts and jagged pipes.

'Oh, swell.'

'Comrades! Defend yourselves!'

'Attack!'

And a blur of combat grey charged. Men and women scattered. Vicious thuds crashed on heads. Faces stretching like horror masks in the lens. Buzzes and screams and fear spinning out of control like a carousel tumbling over a cliff and Oleg grabbing my collar and holding the ladder over our heads and down our blind side and drifting into the shot.

'Keep that goddam ladder out of the shot, Oleg!'

'You just take the pictures and be quiet!'

Pools of blood on the old stones of Arbat street. Men fall to their knees taking the full brunt of OMON fury. A man crawls out from under OMON boots, his head pulsing with thick blood. Spit-shine boots slam into his ribs till blood spits from his mouth. And it was pouring into the lens. All of it.

Over against the Foreign Ministry. Ten Soviet dreamers pressed against the wall. A man falling to the ground. A deep gash in his skull. A babushka stumbling through the truncheons. Her arms and hands begging and praying. 'Please, my sons! Please stop! For God's sake!'

A man dragged from the blood and laid on a patch of concrete. Hands pounding on his chest. A woman blows air into his mouth. A screaming voice. 'His heart! His heart!'

And the OMON smashed their way deeper into the broken dreamers. Few more whacks and it'd be over.

I dropped to my knees. More pictures and more non-stop rolling. Pan left, pan right. Then one man's hand framed in the lens. Reaching into the scrap heap and finding a club of steel and raising the thing into the air slowmotionlike. And my eyes drilling into the picture, knowing that everything was about to change. The steel went higher till it smashed down hard. An OMON soldier wobbled dazed and confused in his slightly off-kilter beret. An unbelieving 'Huh?' plastered on his bloodied face.

Then another steel pipe swinging and another. Then steel bolts flying at the heads of the OMON. Then days of rage breaking loose and charging back at Yeltsin's troops. An old woman winding her handbag like a propeller and letting it smash on to OMON heads. Yeltsin's boys fell back round the stage towards their trucks with seven hundred rebels and one ITN camera close on their boot heels. Twenty feet apart and OMON troops spin round. Hands up from belts and a glint of sun on metal. Guns.

'Fuck me! Get down!'

Six rounds ripped over our heads. The rebels ran back, and me and Oleg were left staring down the barrels of ten Tokarov pistols. Crash zoom. Focus on OMON faces. Wide eyes, shaking hands, fear.

A steel bar crashed near OMON boots. Pistols snapped ready but didn't fire. Quick sums. Six barrels on the mob, four at our heads, everyone scared shitless. Equals not good.

OMON reinforcements spread out in the street. Commanders ran up and down the line shoving Kalashnikovs into the hands of the troops. Like not only 'Fuck the rubber bullets' but 'Fuck the pistols'. Like the first shots were a warning. Like the next shots would kill.

Banana clips slapping into rifles and bullets snapping into chambers. Rebels waving their fists and clubs from a distance, holding their rage in check. And behind them, a steady stream of army trucks and hundreds of militiamen taking positions across the ring road. And me and Oleg still on the ground and wondering what the hell was gonna happen next.

'Jonka, you realize we have broken both your rules.'

'Yup.'

'Do you have any more clever rules of survival?'

'Nope.'

'How inconvenient.'

Rifles ready. Silence.

'By the way, Oleg, what happened to that kid?'

'What kid?'

'The one who drank from the pond.'

'What pond?'

'You were tellin' me some Russian proverb about a kid who drank from a pond.'

'Just now this seems important for you?'

'Yup.'

'He turned into a lamb, of course.'

'Swell. Then let's get the fuck out of here.'

Slowly. My press pass up from the ground, letting the soldiers have a nice long look. My hands shaking as much as those of the boys with the guns. Me and Oleg crawled off with gun barrels following us the whole way back to the rebels.

I looked round. The busiest road in Moscow shut down by a handful of Commie dreamers. Dreamers now trapped between deadly Kalashnikovs and thousands of Greycoats. Rebel eyes whipping back and forth like a tribe of Davids waiting for an army of Goliaths.

Then hands let the steel clubs and bolts and bars fall to the road.

Clangclangclang! Clang!

'Now what?'

'Uh, well.'

Clang! Clank! Bang!

The rebels ripping at the giant stage. Steel supports and floorings and crossbars. And across the road an abandoned construction site. Lumber and concrete blocks and tons of junk. All of it flying and sailing on to the Ring Road. Bits of steel and wood sewn together and stacked higher and higher. In a matter of seconds, eight lanes of traffic covered and blocked.

'It's a wall! They're buildin' a fuckin' wall!'

'Democracy must be inventive, Jonka.'

Clang! Crash!

An entire corner of the stage collapsed. Rebels rushed in and grabbed for treasure. Hands ripping and tearing, slamming into more supports, trying to knock the entire stage down. A steel plate the size of a car, up on end and dragged to the wall. Rebel faces in the lens.

'Let the bastards shoot!'

'Long live the Soviet Union!'

'*Yeltsin vrag naroda!*'

A long metal shaft, a wooden table, a park bench, bedsprings, trash bins, steel doors and more logs. Higher and higher. Soon the wall was ten feet high all across the roadway. And then another wall a hundred metres down toward the Greycoats. And men and women and kids coming out of the woodwork like carpenter ants, everybody carrying something to the wall and lining up along the barricades to stand their ground. Proud, determined faces.

Down amid the twisted steel. An old woman's wrinkled hands and an icon of the Madonna and Child. Boys smash concrete blocks into fist-size stones and stuff rags into small bottles of petrol. Smoke-curls from woodpiles as fires flicker to life. A woman walks along the wall, her hair in a bun and a shopping bag dangling from her arm in a very neat fashion. She stops and opens her bag and sets one well-chosen chunk of wood in the smoke, as if setting a cake in an oven, then closes her bag and walks away. And everywhere else, men filing bits of metal into deadly shapes. Spears and knives and swords. This time the rebels would not run away.

Dark clouds rose with the flames. We wandered out into the road and caught our breath.

'Jon, Oleg. Hi!'

'Hey, Julian. Welcome to Fort Moscow.'

'Fucking incredible! I've only been gone thirty minutes!'

'That kinda day, Julian.'

Whistles and boos as thirty OMON troops marched towards the barricades. Truncheons and shields and helmets ready for battle.

'Aren't we sort of in the middle out here?'

'Like I said, Julian, that kinda day.'

'Meaning what?'

Then hundreds of rocks tore by our heads and we dropped to the asphalt. I zoomed up from the ground towards the OMON. Two metres from the barricade they fell behind their shields as a skyful of stones crashed down. A second OMON line ran up and raised shields to the next incoming wave of rocks and stones and bottles.

'We could really use some helmets,' said Julian.

'I could use a joint.'

And me up with the camera and sticking the lens through the barri-cades. Rebels scurry for the perfect rock. Women shake their fists and scream. Bottles and bits of steel ready for blast-off. Spin round and focus on OMON once more. Another skyful of jagged rain crashing hard on polished shields, again and again, till the shields crawl away like a fat armadillo on a Texas highway. Cheers and shouts from the barricades.

'Might I do a stand-up?'

'Sure. Over on the sidewalk.'

Oleg tossed Julian the microphone and I jumped on a lamp-post to cram the scene into the shot. Fires crackled and burned. Greycoats now three deep along the far barricades. The rebels occupied a patch of Moscow the size of a football pitch, all of it surrounded. And still, they smashed stones and gathered their bits of steel and set more woodpiles alight. Flames and thick black smoke and Julian Manyon looking like he was reporting from the depths of hell.

'Today was supposed to be a celebration of Moscow's history. Instead it's been one of the most violent of recent times. And now it's difficult to see how Boris Yeltsin can quench the hatred that divides the two sides in Russia.'

'Good.'

'Think so?'

'Yup. Real good.'

Through the smoke, hundreds of Greycoats drew up behind the OMON line, fading in and out of the smoke like ghosts. Then an APC mounted with water-cannon rolled towards the rebels. Shields and clubs and guns formed up once more, ready to counter-attack. Rebel voices screaming in fury and hate.

'Come on, you son-of-a-whore!'

'Cowards! Bastards!'

The APC rumbled forward and washed rebels from what was left of the stage. A fusillade of steel and stones sailed over the barricades and down on to the water-cannon. The APC roared and spewed smoke and lunged ahead. The water-cannon swivelled down and fired a rush of high-pressured water into the barricades. Rocks and steel flying through the stream. OMON pounded their shields ready to charge. The APC circled round for one more blast, just enough to break open the walls of Fort Moscow.

The APC roared and lunged. Rebels hunkered down and the hammer spray blasted into the barricades and then . . . it fizzled into drips as if someone was standing on a garden hose.

'What the hell?'

'Jonka! It's like an old man's dick!' yelled Oleg.

And the rebels pounding the APC with rocks and bottles and steel.

And the mighty steel machine slunk away with its tail between its legs and the OMON chasing behind in their sagging black berets.

'Ain't really a good day for machismo.'

And Julian sputtering and shaking the ground with laughter.

'I can't believe it! Unfuckingbelievable.'

Clang! Clang! Clang! Clang!

A lone rebel atop the barricades slamming steel against steel.

'What are you doing? Soldiers of Russia! Where is your pride!'

And the rhythm caught like fever and spread fast.

Clang! Clang! Clang!

The sound swelling like cathedral bells and bouncing off the stone walls along the ring road and falling fast and slapping the faces of Boris Yeltsin's militia.

Clang! Clang! Clang!

'Comrades! Comrades! We are fighting for the heart of Russia! Stand firm! Stand firm and we shall win!'

'*Urah!*'

'All power to the Soviets!'

'Long live the Soviet Union!'

Clang! Clang! Clang! Clang!

'Listen, Jon, I must grab the tape and edit.'

'*Nyet problemy.*'

Swap tapes and say goodbye.

'Hate to leave.'

'Yeah, well, you're the lips. That's why you get the big bucks.'

'Yes . . . yes. Of course. I think.'

And Julian walked off through the wreckage of Fort Moscow with that odd walk of his, like he was about to fall over any second.

'Uh, well . . . may I ask what do lips have to do with someone's salary?'

'Depends on your profession. Reporters and hookers fall into the same category, comrade.'

'Ah. Some of your corrupt western humour.'

'Nope, not really.'

Smoke and haze choked the air out of the sky. Wood and tyres, garbage and cardboard, anything that would burn was set afire. I walked around breathing in acrid smells and the pictures. Banners through flames, thousands of Greycoats waiting through the smoke haze, razor-edged spikes sticking out of the barricades like pissed-off porcupines.

A boy wanders into the frame, a cloth-wrapped stick and a jar of petrol in his hands. He pours fuel on to the cloth and jams the stick into the flames. It flashes alight and he walks along the walls of Fort Moscow setting more and more fires to the barricades till he's satisfied and he shoves the torch into the flames and watches it burn. He turns and stares into the lens. Just a kid. Enemy of the State at twelve years old.

'Uh, well . . . you can see the White House.'

'Huh?'

'Over there, above the trees.'

The White House clock tower still dark and cold and trapped behind Yeltsin's militia. I balanced the camera on a mound of rock and steel and zoomed in slow. Images of the Promised Land shimmering through a flaming haze.

'That's the picture of the day, Oleg. Everything else was good but that was the best. All yours, pal.'

'Uh, well . . . I will see if I can find out what is going on now.'

'Hullo, lads.'

'Hey, Eugene. How are you?'

'Oh, you know.'

And out of the smoke a brown fedora and the certain style of a country gentleman. Camera in one hand and cigarette butt in the other.

'Rory. Where the fuck you been?'

'Out at the dacha when it started.'

The rebels settled into quiet revolution. Fires turned gold in the fading blue light and the smoke drifted by, harsh and choking. Rory pulled another fag out of his well-worn field jacket and lit up anyway.

'Seems to be a stand-off.'

'Yeah. Maybe.'

We talked awhile and waited.

'Yeltsin was at the White House today.'

'Yeah? I've been down here since dawn. What's up?'

'He went to pat his troops on the shoulder and say, "Well done." '

A long drag of smoke in a world of smoke.

'Something else. Yeltsin says the rebels are holding hostages in the White House.'

'No shit?'

'Indeed. Sounds rather ominous.'

'. . . *one shot to the head* . . .'

Down near the far barricade. A truck with its tyres slashed and the body picked clean of engine parts and headlamps. A rebel silhouette climbing on to the top of the truck. A long pole passed up behind him and the flag of the Soviet Union unfurled in the smoke. The setting sun flowing through the red cloth, like blood.

'Fuck me. Look at that.'

'Best flag in the world for a camera, isn't it?' said Rory.

'Yup.'

After a time Rory sauntered away and perched himself in a window above the flames. He looked bored up there. Rory liked guns and lots of bangs. I couldn't take my eyes off him. Firelight glowing all round him. Perfect balance of light and colour and Rory Peck looking somewhere far away.

'Wish I had a still camera, Rory. Make a nice shot.'

He tipped his fedora and nodded, then lit another cigarette. 'Next time, Jon.'

Oleg made his way back through the smoke. 'I have been talking and they have agreed. Well, actually the police and the rebel leaders who come from Ekaterinberg, and they say it is very interesting about the budget for coal-mining operations and—'

'Earth to Oleg. Earth to Oleg.'

'*Da*. Let me see if I can remember . . . ah, yes. They have agreed that everyone will leave at nine o'clock tonight.'

'They're negotiatin' a riot?'

'It seems so.'

'Great way to run a revolution, eh?'

And me kicking stones into flames.

'Jon. You and Oleg take off. You had most of this today. I'll stick around.'

'Yeah. Fuck it. You hungry, Oleg?'

'Uh, well . . . does a bear pee in the woods?'

'Close, Oleg. Close.'

And walking down through the fires of revolution and packs of teenagers smoking dope and singing Visotsky songs about drunken heroes and broken hearts. And around the rebels drinking tea and vodka and watching the flames and ashes and embers stir like a bubbling cauldron and thinking and wondering what would happen next.

'*Smotrite! Smotrite! Belyi Dom!*'

The rebels rose from the ground and flames flashed in their eyes with a new light. Out there above the trees. The clock tower of the White House flooded with brightness and the marble walls glowing white. The once dark windows full with lamplight.

'*Urah! Urah!*'

'Fuckin' hell.'

'A small victory for the rebels, Jonka.'

'Yeltsin caves in again. Bastard'll be drunk as a skunk tonight.'

'Long live the Soviet Union!'

'*Urah!*'

And me and Oleg shaking our heads and wandering through the cheers and smoke and off the Ring Road and through the crooked alleys of coffee-houses and gypsies selling lace, bums selling lottery tickets, old women selling two-day-old sausages.

Up the stairs of the Irish House. One of Moscow's favourite haunts for International Bright Young Things. Expat business types with loads of cash, young and beautiful hookers who swallow green, Russian *mafioski* frowning over their first taste of Guinness. *Saturday Night Fever* in Moscow. A twenty-five-inch Sony blasting the bar with MTV.

Rock and booze and giggles and sex. Spinning images from Planet Whogivesafuck. We found a table in a corner. I put the camera on the floor and smelt my clothes. Smoke and sweat. Not pretty.

Two plates of lasagne and bolshoi beers.

We sat and ate, happy as pigs in slop.

Up at the bar, a gorgeous Russian babe in black almost nothing lifting a cigar from the mouth of some goofy expat. She slides it between her red lips and slowly demonstrates what she'll do with his other Havana if the price is right.

'Ah, yes . . . I see. Lips. A most entertaining place, Jonka.'

'If you like stupid idiots. They got no idea, these people. No fuckin' idea.'

Oleg sat quietly next to my mood. Downtime was thinking time, then again fuck it. I ordered more beers and sucked them down, counting the minutes till I could crawl away and get stoned and not think some more.

'Jonka, what is it?'

'Whatchameanwhatisit, comrade?'

'Sometimes it's like a demon switches out the light inside your head and everything goes black.'

My eyes panned up from the glass. The Saturday Night Expat Slurp and Leer Fest roaring into high gear. The Russian babe had the cigar down her throat. Expats' eyes wide as kids' at a circus.

'I hate these fuckin' expats. I hate them all.'

More beer.

'Why? Because they are normal and you are crazy? They have girlfriends and jobs and a normal life. Jonka, you are so much like Russia. Uh, well . . . of course, not this Russia. But the Russia down the street.'

'Fucked up and going up in flames, you mean?'

'Uh, well . . . yes. I watch you every day, Jonka. The risks you take. The chances. As if you are trying to drown yourself.'

'You're there every step of the way, comrade.'

'Uh, well. That is another subject for another day.'

And drinking more beer and loving the fucked-up and going down in flames. Third marriage crashing bad. Losing my balance. Wanting only drugs and booze and war in my blood. Hands shaking and wanting to grab the gorgeous Russian babe in the black almost nothing and take her home and fuck her senseless and fill her with all the rage and fury of . . .

'. . . of my fuckin' life.'

And Oleg still sitting and listening to my thoughts.

'Weird, ain't it? This morning boys held us in the sights of their guns. And now look around.'

Oleg with that half-pissed look on his face. Sort of looking round the bar through cock-eyed glasses hanging off the tip of his nose.

'*Da*?'

'We are now in a bar where the biggest concern in life is getting laid.'

'Uh, well . . . yes.'

And clearing his throat and coughing.

'But let us hope foreign water-cannons work better than Yeltsin's.'

And Oleg breaking into a bad case of the blush and giggles. All I could do was laugh.

'You're a life-saver, Oleg.'

'As long as I can keep you from killing yourself, Jonka.'

He spotted some Russian stills-shooters across the bar and wandered over for a chat. They stood and shook his hand. Seemed like everybody in this town respected Oleg Nikolaevich Yuriev.

I lifted my camera off the floor and dusted off the Ring Road Riot.

'Hey! You with the camera!'

An American voice cutting through the slurpfest.

'Yeah . . . you. You hangin' out with those Commie jerks down the street?'

A table crammed with cut-outs from a Ralph Lauren advert. Early thirties, clean-shaven and moussed, styled hair, casual taste-for-adventure clothing. Nice white teeth.

'S'pose I am.'

'Well, how's it goin'?'

' 'Scuse me?'

'Ya know, man. How's it goin'?'

'Swell. Just swell.'

'Yeah, well, just make sure you tell the truth. You reporters are always makin' it look so bad over here, ya know? Bad for business. There's big bucks and lots of pussy up for grabs here, man.'

'You don't say.'

'Yeah. I mean, what's gonna happen that's so bad?'

All round the table. Smiling with those perfectly formed American teeth. My countrymen. I wanted to smash the heavy battery end of my camera into their gleaming bicuspids.

'People are gonna die.'

Unflinching smiles.

'Bummer.'

Party on.

Sunday morning. *Déjà vu* all over again

Fort Moscow lay in a heap at the side of the Ring Road. Ladas and Volgas coughed and burped along, slowing just a bit round the four buses parked at the top of Old Arbat Street. Just enough to see sleeping and unshaven soldiers' faces scrunched up against frosty glass. Yeltsin's Greycoats. They'd been there all night. A tiny band of Soviet pensioners, small bouquets of flowers in their hands, walked down the pavement.

'Some old Commies and some snoozin' militia. Seems to be it.'

'Uh, well.'

'Remind me, Oleg. Why the hell are we here?'

'It was your idea.'

'When?'

'Last night. You were drunk.'

'I don't remember you being much better.'

Cold wind snapped up from the river. I closed my leather jacket over today's fashion statement. A bulletproof vest.

'This my idea too?'

'*Nyet*. Mine.'

'Why?'

'Because, Jonka, today is going to be a very bad day.'

'Oh. Right.'

Tapping the armour and reading 'Steele/Blood type: O-Negative' across the breastplate.

'And who said it was gonna be a bad day?'

'Jonka!'

'Last question. I promise.'

'Uh, well. You did.'

Some sort of Commie rally was planned over at Oktyabrskaya

Ploshad under Lenin's statue but that wasn't till noon. So far all was quiet on the Eastern Front.

'Fuck me. I'm confused.'

Oleg nodded towards the Arbat. The old Commies gathered under the walls of the Foreign Ministry building near the spot where the old boy's heart gave out during yesterday's riots. Oleg tossed the camera into my lap.

'Just now you will work, Jonka. You will feel better.'

'Yeah, yeah.'

A small circle of white rocks arranged like a grave. Small candles shivering in the wind. Hands of comrades arranging flowers round the tiny flames. A chunk of cardboard for a headstone and a handwritten scrawl: 'Vot OMON Ubil Cheloveka.'

'What's it say?'

' "Here OMON killed a man." '

'Not a bad shot to start.'

An old woman with a small tricolour cloth and a candle in her hands. She sets fire to the flag of Yeltsin's Russia. And it burns and curls and falls on to the flowers.

'*Da*, except he is alive.'

Hit the roll button. Cut.

'OK. Now I really am confused.'

'The man is in the hospital, but he is very much alive.'

I looked back at the solemn ceremony. Grief and tears.

'Are you sure? How can these people stand here and cry if the guy ain't dead? I mean, there's fuckin' flowers and everything!'

'Yeltsin has his lies. And the Communists have theirs.'

'Yeah, but look at 'em. It's like they believe it.'

And Oleg rolling his eyes like a professor who can't get his dim-witted student to figure basic maths.

'Jonka. So does Yeltsin.'

'You guys got one weird country.'

The clank of metal and the shuffle of heavy boots. Greycoats off the buses and surrounding the make-believe funeral service. Fifty more militia marching down the Arbat, AK54s hanging from their shoulders.

'And it's gettin' weirder and weirder by the minute.'

Thunk! Thunk! Thunk!

Black militia boots marched in and kicked through the grave and the rocks and the flowers and the candles and ground them into the concrete. A Greycoat rips the cardboard headstone to shreds. Shields close in and shove the old Commies off the Arbat as easy as shooing flies off a Sunday picnic. Bit of a shrug, that's all . . . then light up that first fag of the day. Sucking in the warm smoke and shaking off the chills.

'Jon, Oleg. Good morning.'

'Hey, Julian.'

'So the grannies are back.'

'Yeah, but Yeltsin's boys don't seem in the mood for any shit today.'

'Mmm.'

'What's happenin' at the White House?'

'Usual nonsense. Negotiations, more negotiations.'

'And Yeltsin?'

'Still out at his dacha,' said Oleg.

'He didn't come back after the riot?'

'*Nyet.*'

'So who's runnin' this show anyway?'

And Julian's eyes rolling.

'God knows.'

'Fuck me. This *is* gonna be a bad day.'

Sounds of a small rumble yards away. Demonstrators at the edge of the Arbat getting the shit kicked out of them. Rebel Deputy Vitaly Urazchev and thirty more rebels soaking up clubs and shields like punching bags. Rebel faces in the lens, way beyond anger and way beyond hate, wanting to kill.

'Uh, well . . . Jon.'

And Oleg throwing me out into the street.

More rebels holding hands all across the ring road. Cars and trucks hitting the brakes. A fourteen-wheeler turning fast and almost jack-knifing on its side. Rebel knives went to work on screeching tyres . . . instant parking lot.

'You gotta be kiddin' me.'

Another crowd tossing big chunks of Fort Moscow back on to the Ring Road. Bangs and crashes and Julian laughing like he's watching a Monty Python sketch.

'Bit of *déjà vu*, wouldn't you say?'

'Over and over again.'

... the same rocks and the same bits of steel and the same bits of charred lumber as yesterday. Same desperate hands in the frame, searching for weapons, looking for vengeance. Then hundreds of Greycoats charged on to the Ring Road.

'Jonka! Rocks!'

'Get down!'

Stones tore over our heads and hit well-dented police shields like bulls' eyes. The Greycoats kept coming and we dashed to the side of the column and marched along till the shields slammed into the rebels and stomped them underfoot. The rebels fell back. Their killer faces spitting in the eyes of the militia. And me falling back with them till I tripped over something big, and looking down and seeing an old man crawling through the militia's boots, blood oozing from the side of his head. I rolled over and stuck the lens in his face. Merciless black boots and gushing blood and an old man's terror screaming into the camera. 'Please! Please! I was only going to the metro! Please! I have nothing to do with this!'

And a final kick into the old man's guts.

Rebels dash in and drag the bleeding man off the road and lay him behind a fence. The lens follows a trail of blood dripping in the dirt.

'Look at what the bastards have done!'

'See their crimes!'

Pull wide and watch the old man suffer for twenty seconds, waiting for just the right look in his face, then cut. I grabbed a field bandage from my body armour. 'Here! Take this!'

'No! Take his picture!'

'Yeltsin is a criminal!'

'For Christ's sake I got the picture!'

And me ripping open the bandage and cramming it into the rebel's fist.

'Get him to a hospital before he bleeds to death, you fuckin' moron!'

'*Yeltsin vrag naroda!*'

'Fuck off!'

Hundreds of Greycoats raced in and locked down the Ring Road. The outnumbered rebels fled down alleyways. Ambulances picked up the wounded. Fort Moscow lay in a dusty heap once more.

'You see the faces on those guys?'

'Seems you were right, Jonka. A very bad day.'

And Oleg just shaking his head.

'Just about noon. We'd better get to Oktyabrskaya.'

'I was afraid you would say that.'

Vladimir Ilyich Lenin stretched thirty metres into the blue sky above Oktyabrskaya Ploshad, a giant in bronze. His dead Commie eyes looking out over his lost Commie kingdom. On any what-used-to-be-a-Commie holiday, red flags would flutter under Comrade Lenin's monster feet and voices would '*Urah!*' for the return of Soviet glory. But not today. A thousand Greycoats stood shoulder to shoulder and shield to shield, truncheons ready. The metro stations sealed and traffic shut down. No way for the Commie bastards, not today.

Eugene and Julian on the roadside shooting a stand-up.

'So far the violence has not been as bad as yesterday. A rally is planned for later and the army is prepared for trouble.'

And me and Oleg looking round the square, taking in the emptiness of it all. Couple of old ladies sticking V signs into the faces of Yeltsin's militia here and a little pushing and shoving from a tiny tribe of true believers over there. Looked to be more cameras than Commies.

'Well, I'm off to the bureau to edit. I've got a stand-up to cover any trouble.'

'OK. Later.'

A few comments on the weather, our eyeballs panning round every few seconds.

'Be a wee bit difficult to hold a rally here,' said Eugene.

'Does seem to be calm,' said Oleg.

'Yup.'

And me thinking about a long time ago, standing on the Gulf of Mexico waiting for a hurricane to blow in and how the air got so heavy you could see it hanging motionless and thick before your eyes. That kind of calm.

'Calm.'

And wandering round playing bumper cars with the other shooters. Same nervous conversations everywhere.

'*Kak dela?*'

'*Normalno.*'

'What do you think'll happen next?'

'*Nye znayu.*'

'No idea.'

'Anything over there?'

'*Nichevo.*'

'Maybe it's over.'

'Maybe.'

And then noticing the heavy lumps under every cameraman's jacket.

'Fuck me.'

'What is it, Jonka?'

'Every shooter here's wearin' body armour.'

'Jon! Oleg!'

Eugene throwing his own bulletproof vest over his head and pointing way up the road into the hard light of an afternoon sun.

'Oh, swell. Just when you thought it was safe to go back in the water.'

'What?'

'Old American proverb. Seems to fit the moment.'

It moved in silence. Wiggly and miragelike. Then faraway flags and fists poking out from the wiggly form. Hundreds of rebels. Then more and more. I steadied the camera on the ground and crashed the zoom to the long end of the lens till the mirage took shape. A solid line of rebels stretching across the road. Quick sums in my head. Like counting bugs through a microscope. Fifty, sixty across. Ten men deep, no twenty, no . . . *hundreds* of lines deep, *thousands.*

'Holy shit, Oleg.'

'What?'

I looked up into his face.

'There's a whole lotta pissed-off Russians headin' this way.'

Red flags on spears and sticks and pipes and rocks and chains and knives. Vitaly Urazchev, his face swollen and dirty from his beating at the Foreign Ministry hours ago, coming closer in the lens and screaming with laughter and waving his pals forward and forward again.

'Down with Yeltsin!'

'*Urah!*'

'March, comrades! March on!'

The Greycoats around the giant statue of Lenin seemed stunned into submission. They just stepped out of the way, like hoping nobody would notice they were ever born. And the mob washed up like a tidal wave at the feet of their Commie god then settled into a kind of stormy sea. A rebel sea waiting for the next big wind.

'Jonka. The Crimea Bridge . . . look!'

Pan left. An entire army of Interior Ministry troops taking positions across the bridge. A line three or four deep behind a wall of shields. Then fifty metres back another line and then another. Then re-inforcements falling into battle formation in the narrow roads behind the rebels.

'It's a trap. It's a fuckin' trap.'

'*Da*. But for whom?'

Eugene pulling tight the velcro straps of his body armour. Seemed like a good idea. Every photographer in the square was doing the same thing.

'Seem to be boxed in a bit. Your call, Eugene, you were here first.'

'Think I might go down to the bridge.'

'OK. We'll stay and follow the crowd.'

I held out my hand. 'Listen, Eugene. Good luck.'

'Yeah. You too, Jon.'

And me and Oleg standing quiet at the edge of the rebel sea, hearing the cheers and the cries and the fury swell into storm force ten.

> 'Arise the Great Country . . .
> And fight to the death!
> Against the dark forces of Fascism . . .
> Against the deadly horde!'

The voices roared and the winds howled and Vitaly Urazchev raised a clenched fist high above the waves. He screamed and called across the storm . . .

'Comrades! The White House belongs to the people!'

'*URAH!*'

. . . and the rebel sea rushed ahead.

Chaos in the streets. Wreckage and destruction every step of the way. Molotov cocktails exploding like incoming shells. Burned-out army trucks trashed and abandoned, buses in flames. Rebels grabbing militia shields and helmets and truncheons, then chasing down the Greycoats and beating them senseless. Greycoats on their knees, hands up in surrender, a thousand blows the reply. Blood spilling out over the Ring Road. No mercy, no pity.

I crammed the lens into the frenzy. A militiaman stumbling through the mob, his face bloody and swollen. A terrible lostness in his eyes. His hands bloody and shaking and reaching towards the lens till rebel fists slammed into the camera.

'*Nyet* video!'

And a hard fist caught my head and I went down. Knives and clubs flashed before my eyes as another fist smashed into my face. Oleg pulled me back to my feet. The militiaman still reaching and begging me for help, then a club smashed down on his head and he was gone.

'Jonka! Keep moving!'

Dash to Novyi Arbat and down to the White House. Rebels charged the barbed wire and trounced it underfoot then scrambled atop the nose-to-tail trucks sealing off the White House. Fists and delirious voices against a brilliant blue sky. Shapes and sounds of triumph framed against the marble tower of the Promised Land.

'Rutskoi *Presidyent*! Rutskoi *Presidyent*!'

We crawled up on to the trucks and watched the rebel waves rush faster and crash against the sides of the vehicles, smashing at the doors and windows . . .

'Rutskoi *Presidyent*! Rutskoi *Presidyent*!'

Hundreds of rebel comrades jumped ahead with cables and ropes and chains. Quick loops and lashes round the tow-holds of the nose-to-tail trucks, then heave and pull till they were hauled aside and the entire rebel sea flowed on to Konyushkovskaya Street, racing on to the grounds of the Promised Land.

Into the final march. Rebels slapping each other on the back, laughing and singing their Commie songs. Babushkas with ragged Commie flags and fat tears in their eyes. Every soul sucking up the rush like candy, every heart spinning with joy.

'Rutskoi *Presidyent*! Rutskoi *Presidyent*!'

GTTTTRRRRUP! GTTRRUP!

Zing! Zing!

We were on the ground between two smashed-up Ladas.

I poked the camera round the bald tyres. Men and women laid out and crawling across asphalt. Three Greycoats marching over a grassy knoll with AK47s on their hips, spraying the air with bullets.

'Get down, Jonka!'

'It's OK. They're just firing way over us.'

The Lada windshield next to my head exploded to bits. Oleg's hands clawed at my body armour and pulled me to the ground. 'You can still get killed, Jonka!'

Bits of glass in my hair.

'S'pose I can.'

More rapid-fire bullets across the road towards the Mayor's Office building. We ran over the grassy knoll and up the car ramp and fell behind a concrete roadblock. Greycoats inside the lobby sprayed bullets out through the glass doors. Bullets ripping wildly through the sky and zinging off concrete and steel. Bodies down eating dirt. I popped the camera over the ledge and looked up into the eyepiece. 'Fuckin' hell!'

'Stay down, Jonka!'

'Fuckin' hell!'

Armed rebels sprang up like a pack of deadly rabbits and blasted hundreds of rounds into the wide glass panels round the doors. Blasting and smashing sounds and cordite smoke and chinks of shattered glass flying everywhere. Another rebel jumped into an army truck and reversed and smashed through the doors. Then it all went quiet.

'I cannot believe this shit! Like *Shoot-out at the OK Corral*. Made a great flick in 1946. Henry Fonda and Victor Mature. Ever see it?'

'Jonka, I am growing increasingly concerned about your apparent inability to distinguish between real life and movies.'

'Comrade, life *is* a movie.'

And then down over the side, sheets of glass shattering and crashing to shreds. Oleg peeked over the concrete slab. His eyes went wide. 'They are running away!'

'Who?'

'The soldiers! They are running away!'

Up over the wall and roll.

Greycoats smashing through office windows with shields and chairs and kicking away the glass with their boots, then tumbling out through the shards and falling on to the ground on top of each other, then more and more. Hundreds more. And Oleg giggling at the whole craziness of his world falling apart. 'It seems Yeltsin's rats are all leaving the ship.'

'Like I said, comrade, this is one weird country.'

Crack! Crack! Crack!

Back near the smashed doors. Rebels blasting rounds over our heads. Smoking barrels pointing and voices screaming and coming closer.

'*Sdavaites! Sdavaites!*'

'What the fuck?'

'He demands our surrender.'

'Who? Us?'

And me and Oleg looking around for anyone else.

'*Da*, it would seem so.'

Crack! Crack! Crack!

'Fuck me . . . OK! OK! We surrender!'

And raising our hands slowly above our heads and coming up over the concrete wall and seeing the rebels looking very confused.

'*Nye vy! A vy!*'

'Uh, well . . . he is saying not us . . . but them.'

Two long columns of Greycoats walking out from under the parking ramp below us. Bowed heads and hands in the air. The last of Boris Yeltsin's militia in mass surrender. I grabbed the camera and panned the scene wide. The defeated ones marching under the feet of the rebels. Disgrace and conquest in the lens. One rebel let off three rounds over the heads of the Greycoats. Zoom in to the shooter's face. A sneering smile through deadly smoke.

'So can we put our fuckin' hands down?'

'*Da*. Just smile.'

And all around young kids and old women picked up abandoned militia shields and formed a line around the White House. I grabbed the camera and hit the roll button. It was all there in one picture, victory. As impossible as it seemed, victory.

Me and Oleg slumped down, exhausted.

'Fuck me. I'm hungry.'

'*Da* . . . food.'

'He's through, ain't he?'

'Who?'

'Yeltsin. He's fuckin' through, ain't he?'

Oleg pulled his glasses off his nose and wiped the smoke and the tear gas from his face. 'Only a miracle can save him now, Jonka.'

*

'Rutskoi *Presidyent*! Rutskoi *Presidyent*!'

Alexander Vladimirovich Rutskoi looked out over the rebel sea. He'd been trapped for weeks in the cold and dark, surrounded by an army of Yeltsin's troops, and now forty thousand voices chanted his name. He listened to the sounds and watched the faces of victory, knowing that now Yeltsin would have to come wobbling up the steps of the White House begging for forgiveness! And the West! Now the West would be forced to admit their precious Boris Yeltsin was no more than a drunken fool. The Second Russian Revolution was at hand! The word must go out across the land! Rutskoi remembered the teachings of Lenin from the First Revolution: 'Seize the telegraph!' And maybe that was then and this was now but the lesson was still the same. So Alexander Rutskoi spread his hands over the masses and uttered the fatal words that would give Yeltsin the miracle he needed.

'Comrades! Seize the National Television Station! Seize Ostankino!'

'What's that?'

'Someone is making a speech at the White House.'

'Shit! Rutskoi!'

Up and across the road to the plaza just as Rutskoi was going back into the White House. The giant mob was left buzzing with frantic energy. Trucks and cars forming into a caravan. And from somewhere Julian's voice barking through the noise.

'You hear that?'

'*Da*, a uniqueness all its own.'

'Sounds like it's from over there.'

We pushed between the buzz and barks and found Julian finishing a stand-up with Eugene.

'Ah. Jon, Oleg.'

'Hey. You get Rutskoi pictures?'

'Yes. And Eugene says he has some very good stuff from the riots.'

'I bet he does.'

And Oleg's elbow hitting the back of my flak-jacket and coughing. 'Ahjonkagh!'

'Do you have anything worthwhile?'

'Maybe one or two shots.'

'Fine. I should like to take Eugene back to the bureau and help with the edit.'

'OK, then. We'll find Rutskoi and stick with him. Oleg?'

'I will go and find him but, well . . . then, of course, if I go this way . . .' And Oleg took off looking for the man.

'These people'll be going to Ostankino in a bit,' Eugene said.

'Yeah. My guts tell me Rutskoi will do the same to make a speech on TV, but I wanna find him first. Do a fly-on-the-wall thing with him.'

'Good idea. Shall I send a driver?' asked Julian.

'We'll need him to get tapes back fast. Have him meet us over at Kalininskii Bridge.'

'All right. Good luck. Cheers.'

A giddy festive air circled round the White House. People all grinning like Tinkerbell had jacked them up with fairy dust. I sat in the middle of the road, listening to the laughter and the songs, wondering when it was I'd stopped believing in fairy tales, then just watching the rebel caravan take shape and then thinking, Maybe never.

Rebels jumped into cars and trucks. Rifles and ammo clips crammed between arms and legs. A red Soviet flag flapping from the aerial of the lead truck then a brown fedora hanging out the passenger side door.

'Hey, Rory.'

'Hello, Jon! Unbelievable, isn't it?' He was bouncing this way and that way with his camera in the window, hunting for the best point of balance. 'Coming along?' he asked.

'Oleg's just checkin' up on Rutskoi and I'm waitin' for our driver.'

'Right. I'll save you a spot.'

'You do that and I'll bring you a cold beer.'

'Done. Fucking unbelievable, isn't it?'

'Just don't fall outa that truck on the way, Rory.'

'And miss all the fun? I don't think so.'

His eyes wide as daylight moons.

Cheers and yells and last calls for party time. Engines turned over and the rebel convoy sped down Novyi Arbat towards the Ring Road. Daylight started slipping away. Five minutes. Ten minutes. No car. Oleg came running across the street. 'Rutskoi will not speak now but he will go to Ostankino later and we are welcome to accompany him and . . . Where is everyone?'

'Exactly. Where the hell's the driver? We've gotta get to Ostankino.'

'Just now I do not know.'

'Well, fuckin' find out! The convoy's gone, Oleg!'

'Uh, well . . . convoy.'

Oleg ran over Kalininskii Bridge to find a telephone that worked.

'Hurry!'

Fifteen minutes, twenty. A Red Army helicopter cruised overhead and circled the White House. Heavy onboard machine-guns tracking the doors and windows. A quick pass round the clock tower then banking off and away. Below, Muscovites took their evening stroll along the river to see if the rumours were true. A parade of gawking faces along the bridge. And Oleg running out of the crowd.

'Julian wants you to forget Ostankino and go to Reuters for a live shot.'

'What?'

'Uh, well . . . this is what he says.'

'Fucksake! He doesn't need me for that! Where the fuck is the car?'

'Well, I do not know! The driver says he cannot find us!'

'I am standin' in the middle of the fuckin' road! I wanna get to Ostankino! Live shot, my ass!'

'But Julian—'

'Fuck Julian! I want the goddam driver now!'

'Well, I do not know where he is!'

'Goddammit! He's just too fuckin' afraid!'

'Jonka, calm down! He is not afraid! He could not find us!'

'Fuck it! I just shudda gone with the convoy! Fuck this shit! Stupid fuckin' people!'

Oleg turned away and stared at the river. Big orange clouds reflecting in his glasses. A deep sigh and his body slumping, all tired and sore. I picked up the camera and felt days of aches running through my body too. The two of us battered and beaten and dodging bullets two weeks running now.

'So. Enough is enough for one day?'

'Jonka, I do not think you know the meaning of those words.'

'Listen, Oleg.'

'No, you listen! I have not seen my family in weeks! Do you know what all this is like for them? Every moment they are afraid. This is Russia and that means I am all they have. I do not just risk my life with you, Jonka. I risk everything.'

The big orange clouds went grey in Oleg's glasses as cool autumn night rolled in with the darkness.

'So, what you're sayin' here is sometimes I'm a complete asshole.'

'*Da*, sometimes you are a complete asshole. But as an American pig capitalist what else can one expect?'

'Right, fuck it. Let's get something to eat.'

'I would like that, Jonka.'

'Then you gotta call Nadya. Let her know you're OK.'

'I would like that too.'

We crossed the river to the Slavyanskaya Hotel and ordered beers and club sandwiches. Five-star service just down the road from the revolution.

'More beer?'

'Is Yeltsin a drunken fool?'

'Let's join him, comrade.'

As we sipped our beers, Ostankino exploded.

The tape rolled again and again out of Reuters' Master Control. Tracer fire, knifelike and blood-red, slashing through the blackness. Bodies spread everywhere, some trying to crawl and others trying to run, the smart ones not moving at all. Killer bullets blasting out from Ostankino into the street.

'I don't believe this! I don't fuckin' believe I missed this!'

'Julian is upstairs for the live shot. Eugene as well.'

'What?'

'And Eugene will shoot the live shot.'

'Then what the fuck am I doing here? Let's get to Ostankino now!'

'Jonka, it's over. Be thankful you are safe. People are dead.'

'But fucksake! Look at the pictures!'

Like I was losing breath. Like something had been taken from me and watching the tape play out once more and wanting the pictures to be mine. Wanting it like a ghoul. Like a fucking ghoul.

And upstairs on the roof Julian speaking into Eugene's camera. 'Gunfire broke out ... dead and wounded ... Yeltsin's troops have defeated the rebels and retained control of Ostankino.'

'Fucksake. Fucksake.'

'Jonka?'

'Get me outa here.'

Downstairs a Russian cab screeched to a stop. A still-shooter pal from way back named Ron Haviv jumped out with a local freelance shooter named Heidi Bradner. 'Jon, man. Where the fuck were you? It was very nasty.'

'Yeah, I saw the pictures. Any shooters hit?'

'Don't know for sure. Place was a fucking mess, man.'

Ron buzzing and me feeling it like a contact high.

'Gotta get this film processed, man.'

He dashed away and Heidi took my arm. 'Jon, have you seen Rory around?'

'No, why?'

'He was at the doors of Ostankino. The rebels ordered us away but Rory was arguing with them to stay close.'

'Sounds like him.'

'Yes. Well, that's when it all blew up.'

And me still wanting and craving the pictures and nothing else.

'Don't worry, Heidi. Rory's one of the best. He'll take care of himself.'

Twelve thirty a.m., back at the bureau for tapes and batteries. Mainly slamming bits of kit round like a madman. Ian Glover James cornered me for a reality check. 'Where are you going, Jon?'

'Cruise the streets. Look for somethin'.'

'Like what?'

'Pictures. I need pictures.'

'Jon, tomorrow is going to be a very big day. You and Oleg have been in the shit more than anyone. Please go home and get some rest.'

'Yeah, yeah.'

Hour later I was still on the streets looking for something. Oleg along for the ride. He knew the lights in my head had gone out again and the black mood was coming down hard.

'You sure you don't wanna go home, Oleg?'

'I think I will stay.'

'You sure?'

Like a bad hit of crystal methamphetamine. All the rough edge and none of the buzz. We tried to get into the White House for the night but were invited to leave at gunpoint by trigger-happy rebels. Down in the streets, boys and men turned trams and trucks and buses into barricades along Novyi Arbat. Another junk-pile barricade was going up across Kalininskii Bridge. Higher and higher. Everyone grinding teeth and riding the same bad trip, knowing it was all going to crash in a flash.

Spears and stones and bars and shields passing from rebel hand to rebel hand. Caps and fur hats pulled down over rebel ears. Pinwheel eyes staring out into the fearful dark. The whole fucking world waiting.

Down behind the barricades a few old men rubbed hands over a small fire. A bottle of homemade vodka passing between mouths, long gulps in sacred communion, nerves ripping to shreds.

'Christ. Few hours ago they had Boris on his fuckin' knees. They had it all, they had Russia. Now look at 'em. Drunk and waitin' for the hammer to fall.'

'I am sure it reminds you of one of your movies.'

'Million of 'em. And they all end the same way.'

A rebel offered us a swig to chase off the cold.

'No thanks, pal. You're gonna need all the help you can get.'

And Oleg watching and thinking and whispering.

'I do not know if I should salute them for their courage or slap them for their stupidity. If only they had stopped at the White House and not gone to Ostankino.'

'We shudda been there, Oleg.'

'Jonka, do you ever think you might want it too much?'

'What's that?'

'To get yourself killed.'

I wanted to say it wasn't like that. That it was something else. More like proving I deserved to be alive. I looked at my watch instead. 'Almost four in the mornin'.'

And feeling a deadness in my soul, like the touch of a ghost.

'Fuck it. Let's crash at my flat. It's gonna be an early one.'

'Da, an early one.'

Round the corner to Ulitsa Zholtovskovo. Let the bulletproof vest fall to the floor and collapse on the bed. Blackness and hurting spinning round in the dark and Oleg's voice drifting down the hall. Calm tones of comfort for the woman he loved, then the sound of the telephone hanging up, then quiet.

And me closing my eyes and floating in the blackness like the forgotten boy from long ago. Smothering in the dark and crying and begging for it to stop. Wondering if this was how it felt to be dead.

Monday. Dawn

'Jonka, wake up.'

Some Russian guy in underbriefs and socks standing over me. Hair with that finger-in-the-electric-socket look. Spectacles hanging from one ear.

'They are shooting.'

I sat up and listened. Nothing.

'Nope. Not yet. More sleep.'

Oleg pouting back down the hall. 'I am very sure they are shooting.'

And I waited there with the taste of fear in my mouth and bile turning in my stomach, knowing Oleg was right, but just hoping it might all go away.

Crack! Crack!

'Uh, well . . . it is like I said.'

'Yup!'

Out the door in two minutes and smack into a line of army trucks three minutes later. I rammed the car up on to the sidewalk and jumped out with the camera. Oleg grabbed the backpack with spare batteries and tapes and a Russian mobile telephone the size of a bread box.

Police held back anyone coming down Novyi Arbat. Me and Oleg hid behind a kiosk and waited till their eyes looked the other way, then we dashed up and round the corner. Hundreds of Red Army troops forming into squads, machine-guns and extra ammo clips, body armour and helmets . . . moving out with orders to kill.

Feet pounding asphalt. Down behind the trees then jumping behind a line of Ladas and Zhigulis and Neva cars. Bullets hitting the high walls above our heads, and us running faster till we fell into a pile of shields behind the rebel barricade at Kalininskii Bridge.

'Ooof!'

''Scuse me.'

Ron Haviv popped up out of the shields with his Canon cameras slung round his neck. He scrunched his back up to the barricade. 'Oh, morning, Jon. Bring any coffee?'

''Fraid not.'

More faces popped out of the shields. Russian teenage boys.

'Who the fuck are these kids?'

'War tourists.'

'Fuck me. Any idea where the bad guys are?'

Ron rolled his eyes. 'It's crazy, man.'

I crawled out under the wheels of a burnt-out truck and stuck the lens out round the wheels. The White House rose from the street against a purple-cloud sky. Ten seconds of tape and crawl back.

'Nice postcard shot, but there ain't much else from this spot.'

Machine-guns cracked and roared like ocean surf. Endless waves of bullets rolling through the dawn. Another peek round the barricade, twenty feet to the concrete stairs winding down to the embankment road where Red Army APCs rolled through smoke and fire.

'Over there. Ready?'

'*Da.*'

Mad dash to the stairs and down along the spiral wall till bullets cut us off. Down and wait, then down a few more steps into a Red Army squad, half kneeling and half hunkering down, blasting their assault rifles up towards the White House.

'This'll do.'

And pulling the camera up for the shot and feeling a full magazine of bullets chopping at the wall above our heads. Dust and concrete falling in chunks. Rebel rifles had the soldiers in their sights and were drilling them into the ground.

'Fuck me!'

The squad commander screamed out orders and the soldiers bolted down the stairs into the smoke and fire.

'Jonka, you are not thinking of following—'

'Not without a fuckin' rifle!'

We dashed back up the stairs and took cover behind a wall of logs and garbage in the middle of the road. A truck commandeered by the rebels edged round the barricades, white flags flapping out the windows. For a moment the bullets eased and faded.

I crawled up the wall and caught the rear end of the truck rolling through the lens. Big lumps under bloodstained cloth. Five or six fresh kills, maybe more. The truck cleared the intersection in about the time it takes to change banana clips in an AK47. Then bullets ripped apart the silence once more.

BOOM! BOOM!

Cannon blasts rolling and rumbling through the streets like a cattle stampede. Black smoke and fire pouring out the Mayor's Office building. Then the roar of rifles louder and louder. And me inches from Oleg's face but screaming through the sounds: 'Oleg, you may be right about all my deep-seated and self-destructive psychological problems! But before I get my ass blown off I wanna get at least one decent picture in the fuckin' can!'

'Shall we go visit the neighbours again?'

The apartment building across the street from the White House, forty yards away, every step open to rifle fire.

'Looks like a long way, comrade.'

And a hail of bullets slammed into our cover. More rounds ricocheted off the asphalt.

'Then again, let's get the fuck out of here.'

Running low to the ground and along the barricade and then down near the doors. Tucked in a corner was Bill Swersey, another stills-shooter waiting for a decent picture between the bullets. 'Hey, Jon. What's up?' He fiddled with his lenses the way stills guys always fiddle with their lenses.

'Oh, not much.'

I reached up and yanked and yanked at the door.

'Fucker's locked again!'

Oleg reached up and slid it open like it wasn't there.

'How the fuck did you do that?'

'Simple. It is a Russian door.'

'And?'

'I am Russian.'

'Oh . . . of course.'

'Where you guys off to?'

'Not sure yet.'

'Mind if I come along?'

'Nope.'

Into the foyer and huffing up the stairs.

'You see, it is very much like the Russian joke. A steel factory in Chelyabinsk receives an order for ten thousand Chinese umbrellas . . .'

Round and round and up and up till things looked familiar.

Bang on the door till it opens just a peek.

Mumbled Russian back and forth.

'Uh, well . . . he says we may come in.'

'Good.'

'But he wants three hundred dollars.'

'You jokin'! I gave him two hundred the last time!'

'He believes there is more of a demand today.'

'Who says you people don't understand capitalism?'

Our squatty hostess in the same sort of green apron waved for our boots to come off as we tumbled in. She arranged them into a neat row under the coats and hats and set out three pairs of house slippers. We put 'em on and shuffled down the hall and ran into the sitting room, throwing back the heavy curtains and pulling open the tall windows.

'Holy shit! Look at it!'

'Not bad.'

The White House gleaming in brilliant light. Hundreds of Red Army troops down by the river, seven APCs rolling up into position at the foot of the White House, 30mm cannons and heavy machine-guns ready to rip.

Zing! Zing!

'What was that?' asked Bill.

'Bullets.'

'Up here?'

'Shit's flying everywhere. Bouncing off the buildings I s'pose.'

'Up here?'

I emptied the backpack, grabbed a cushion off the couch, stuffed it inside, punched the backpack into a ball and tossed it out the window on to the concrete ledge.

'Exactly what are you doing, Jonka?'

'Ain't gotta tripod. Need somethin' to balance the camera on.'

'Out there?'

'Yup.'

I crawled out and settled the camera into the backpack.

'See? Nice and steady.'

'Let's hope you do not look like a sniper.'

And the Red Army let out another round of merciless fire, cannon shells and bullets, thunder and steel. Thousands and thousands of rounds ripping through the dawn and chipping away at Commie rebel dreams. Sparks and flashes on the marble walls, glass shattering and blasting apart.

Red Army soldiers ran out the main doors of the Mayor's Office. Mission accomplished, no more rebels left to kill. They crawled under walls and out of camera shot.

'Fuck . . . can't get 'em!'

And Oleg yelling: 'Jonka! Perhaps you should come inside!'

'Hang on, Oleg!'

He grabbed my belt and pulled hard. I crawled further out on the ledge and leaned out over the street.

'I am thinking, Jonka, when this is over perhaps we can find employment in the Moscow Circus!'

'Got 'em!'

Zoom in and focus.

The commander gathers his soldiers round for orders, pointing to a low concrete wall under the White House. The soldiers lock fresh ammo clips into rifles and take aim. Then thirty more soldiers run out of the building and fall in behind the advance squad. More orders and more fresh ammo clips and more deep breaths before the next attack. The commander nods and thirty rifles lean as one round the corner blasting cover fire up to the White House. The advance squad tears out under the bullets and runs faster and faster down the stairs and out across Konyushkovskaya street and falls behind the low concrete wall. The Red Army was ten metres from the White House.

The roaring guns went quiet and I eased back into the flat.

'Oleg. S'pose it would be rude to ask for a cup of tea?'

'Uh, well . . . tea. Let me ask Babushka.'

Gunshots cracked through the quiet every now and then. Fire and heat blew out windows in the Mayor's Office building, sulphur and smoke drifting into the flat. Down in the street and along Kalininskii Bridge, war tourists crept closer.

'Stupid fuckin' people.'

'See the guy with the dog?'

A middle-aged Russian in the middle of the intersection, a small dog on the end of a leash. The dog pulling at the leash trying to get away and the guy just standing there with a stupid look on his face. Rifles opened up from the White House and bullets screamed across the road. The dog broke loose and ran off. The man following with the waddle of someone who'd just shit his pants.

'Always thought dogs had more sense than most people.'

'Seems so.'

'Good shot over there.'

Twenty-five Red Army troops ran out across Konyushkovskaya and dropped into a tight group behind a stack of concrete blocks and sewer pipes. Quick dash through the trees and they'd be knocking on the doors of the White House. The officer signalled orders. The soldiers checked weapons and ammo and pulled tight the straps of their helmets then jumped to their feet ready to charge when a hundred rebel automatic rifles opened fire. The soldiers fell back in a pile, bullets ripping over their heads. One soldier down and bleeding.

The sitting-room door opened and our hostess in the sort of green apron wandered in with a tray of tea and little salami sandwiches. She arranged the teapot and cups on a little round table draped with Russian lace.

'Oleg. Perhaps she shouldn't be in here.'

'Babushka just wants to be polite.'

'Yeah, but there's a little problem of—'

SCHACRACK! SCHACRACK!

Two wildfire bullets ripped across the window-frame, ricocheted off the ledge and screamed back into the sky. Oleg grabbed the old woman, spun her round and shoved her out the room.

'*Tak*, so much for our polite Babushka.'

Down below, the soldiers rose amid the onslaught of rebel guns, locked eyes down rifle sights and returned fire with steely precision. Endless waves of Red Army bullets exploding from killer rifles. More and more till the soldiers themselves disappeared in a cloud of killer smoke.

Rutskoi's rebels were living on borrowed time.

'Uh, well . . . *chai?*'

'My dear comrade.'

Back out on the window-ledge. A Red Army squad tested the ground near an abandoned rebel barricade, leaning out and drawing rebel fire from the White House. The soldiers sat back behind the barricade, lit up fags, smoked and waited like they had all the time in the world.

Close-up of the White House. Quick shadows dodging and running behind shattered glass and marble walls. Rutskoi's rebels were moving from window to window and floor to floor, dodging Red Army bullets and getting off a few rounds before disappearing into the dark. And then all the rifles and cannon and machine-guns swelling into one sound like something alive and hungry. Screaming and ripping and killing.

'Fuck me! Listen to it!'

And feeling the sounds roar through my body and blast through my brain.

'Jonka! Come back inside!'

'Not yet. There's some great shots out here!'

Out from the trees around the White House, rebels dragging a comrade into the open. They jump up and race through the bullets. The body dangling in their hands and the head bouncing like a puppet. A lifeless head with no face. Just a puddle of blood.

Down in the White House driveway, desperate men running through the ripping and killing. A lifeless body swinging from their hands. They dive behind a barricade and lay their comrade on the ground and tear open his bloody shirt. There's a perfectly shaped hole in the centre of an unbreathing chest.

'Fire! It's on fire!' yelled Bill.

Wide shot. Funnels of black smoke pouring out of shattered windows and drifting up the marble tower and into the blue sky. The bullets and cannon shells ceased fire. Soldiers and rebels and war tourists watching in stunned silence as the White House began to burn.

I slid back into the flat and changed tapes.

'Right, Oleg. Two tapes so far and one battery down, one half gone and one to go.'

'Let me guess, you are about to announce a plan.'

'Yup.'

'Let me guess again, I go back to the bureau with the tapes and bring you batteries and more tapes.'

'I'm dead in the water unless you can do it.'

Oleg ran to the hall and pulled on his boots. 'Don't fall into the river till I get back.'

Then he was out the door. Bill changed film rolls and we sipped tea, waiting for the next round of bullets.

'Tea's cold.'

'Let's complain to the management.'

'So. What did Oleg mean about falling in the river?'

'Hell if I know.'

'Seems like a good guy.'

'Most decent man I ever met in my life.'

'That's quite a compliment.'

'Just plain fact.'

Rifles kicked in and sprayed the air with steel. And me thinking about the entire Mexican army closing in on Davy Crockett and Colonel Travis and a handful of Texans way back at the Alamo, then remembering John Wayne played Davy in the movie but forgetting who the hell played Colonel Travis ... and then hearing and feeling the unmistakable sound of heavy metal crawling and scraping over asphalt.

'Fuck me.'

'What?'

'Tanks.'

We jumped up to the window-ledge. Out across the river under the Hotel Ukraine, three monsters, giant and beastlike, grinding on steel tracks and raising their fire-breathing mouths towards the White House.

'Holy shit!'

'Let's hope they don't fuckin' miss. Couple inches this way and we're toast.'

'Good point, Bill.'

More heavy metal sounds crawling and scraping as three more tanks took positions along the river. Focus down through the long end of the lens. A single tank cannon moving up and down and side to side hunting for just the right spot.

'This is gonna be a great shot!'

BLEEPBLEEPBLEEP.

'Is that a beeper, Jon?'

'Can you fuckin' believe it?'

I pulled back and grabbed the mobile phone, dialled the bureau and heard the voice of our Russian producer Irina. 'Jon! Where are you?!'

'Looks like they're getting ready to fire, Jon!' yelled Bill.

'I'm kinda busy, Ira!'

'Julian wants you to rush over by the American embassy for a stand-up. He can't find Eugene! He wants you to do it!'

'Jon! Better hurry!' yelled Bill.

'Is he out of his mind? You guys seen any pictures? It's a fuckin' turkey-shoot out there. I'd have to fall back to the Ring Road and circle round through a few thousand soldiers! No fuckin' way I'm gonna find him out there!'

'What can I say? He wants you to do it!'

'Bullshit! I've got six T-72s just outside my window ready to blow the fuckin' world to hell!'

'Jon! You're going to miss the shot!'

Out the window, a column of APCs rolling across the Kalininskii Bridge to join the tanks.

'He's gotta find someone else, Ira. I ain't makin' the same mistake as yesterday.'

'Jon, wait!'

I slammed down the phone.

'Fire!'

KABOOM! CRASH!

The sky exploded with deafening thunder. The floor shook and rattled. I jumped back out to the window-ledge and caught another fireflash in my eyes.

BOOM! CRASH!

'Shit!'

Red Army bullets still pumping into the flames. A tiny strip of white cloth flapping from one shattered window of the White House and the lens searching for signs of life but seeing only fire and smoke and terrible darkness.

APCs ploughed into the barricades and split them open. Small cannons and heavy machine-guns blasting into the trees surrounding the White House.

ZZINNG! SHACRACK!

'Yikes!'

'What the hell was that?'

'Fuckin' bullet in the flat!'

'You are shitting me?'

'Nope. Now I really am gonna complain to the manag– fuck me. Where are they?'

I dropped the camera, ran into the hall and searched the bedrooms and behind the chairs, empty. Down another hall into the bathroom, nobody. Round a corner and into the kitchen and there, amid the pots and pans and jars of pickled vegetables, tucked down in a ball on the kitchen floor, the two grey heads of our host and hostess.

'Normalno?'

'Da, khorosho!'

Back down the hall and grab the camera as flames poured from the mouths of the monster tanks and APCs blasted cannons and machine-guns. The final assault of the final kill. Yellow fire and black smoke spread up the marble tower of the White House. And then the camera went dead.

'Shit!'

'What's up?'

'No more battery.'

Tank fire and explosions and rifles and Bill's motor drive winding through a roll of film. He kept working with a concentrated look in his eyes, the kind that said he was getting great shots. I wanted to throw him over the fuckin' ledge. More blasts and booms and non-stop thuds echoing from the hall.

'Is that the door?' asked Bill.

'Oleg!'

Down the hall and yank open the door. Sure enough.

'Oleg! Damn glad to see you! How was it?'

BOOM! CRASH!

'Uh, well . . . tanks.'

'Yup.'

KACRASH!

Tank shells ripped open another floor of the White House.

'How big are those shells anyway?'

'I s'pose big enough to spread a man across a wall like a can of paint.'

An ear-splitting roar and a grey streak through the sky crashing smack dead centre into the White House. And the shell flashing alight in the rebel fortress and exploding with yellow fire and screaming hot death and black smoke, gushing bloodlike into the sky. And the whole world shaking as the sounds vibrated on and on and on till fading into quiet along the Moscow river.

'Fuck me. Avon calling.'

'Holy shit.'

Back on the floor of the flat and another sip of cold tea and a time check. ITN was on the air in less than an hour.

'Oleg. You gotta get this tape back to the bureau. There's some fuckin' great stuff on here.'

'So, you will stay?'

'Yup.'

'In this flat?'

'Nope, done all I can from up here. I'm gonna get down to that field hospital next to the river, then work my way up closer to the White House.'

'How will I find you?'

'Don't know, but you always do.'

Rifles crackled through the quiet and machine-guns opened fire once more and Oleg's eyes locking into mine.

'Don't worry, Oleg. I won't get killed today.'

'Promise?'

'Promise.'

He grabbed the tape and charged out the door.

I sat back and watched black clouds curl up round the White House clock tower. The Soviet flag looking like it was choking and gasping for air.

And the lens panning and zooming and looking for something.

In the streets, an unarmed rebel crawled towards a motionless body. Bullets sparked and ricocheted round him, but the rebel kept crawling and reaching till he could touch the face before him. A long moment of recognition and sadness, then pulling the body near as if to hide the dead man from any more harm.

'That's it, Bill, I'm outa here.'

'I think I'll stay awhile.'

I bade farewell to the old grey-haired couple and told them to stay on the kitchen floor till the bullets stopped for at least one hour. Their arms wrapped tight round each other and their wrinkled faces huddled together, fear in their eyes.

'Trust me, it's going to be OK.'

'*Tam opasno i kholodno v oktyabre! Nye vykhodi na ulitsu byez shapki!*' cried Babushka.

I treated myself to the lift and sank to the ground trying to figure out the old woman's words. Something about October and danger and being outside without a hat. Smoke and bullets and long afternoon shadows over the road. I crouched under a crumpled rebel barricade trying to get a feel for the sounds blasting round my head. A gang of rebels dived into the barricade and hauled in a bleeding body, the eyes rolling white and empty. Quick desperate words and then up and running through the open street. The body scraping over asphalt and the lens following a trail of blood down into the pedestrian tunnel under Novyi Arbat.

Back into the streets and along the barricades and down under a lamp-post in the middle of the road. I peeked out with the lens hoping one more tank shell would blast into the White House. Low-angle shot would suit me just fine. Four men came running into the frame, white bands wrapped round their arms and a heavy stretcher swinging in their hands and running right over the lens.

I spun around and followed them down the wide stairs to the embankment road. A high concrete wall and a patch of muddy grass and another makeshift field hospital working overtime. Doctors in bloodsoaked smocks. Bags of saline solution hanging from trees. Used needles and bloody bandages. Bleeding and screaming bodies shoved into cars and ambulances . . . and some bodies just left in the muddy grass. Someone pulled the breathing tube from the lips of a dead rebel as another body was dragged across the ground and tossed into the bushes. Dead rebel eyes staring up through the trees and into the autumn sky. And me zooming in slow and filling the lens with the dead rebel eyes and then looking up through the trees and into the autumn sky and watching a small cloud drift away and thinking it looked like a camel and wondering if the dead eyes in the lens could still see, till gentle hands reached into the frame and closed the eyes for ever.

The stretcher-bearers tore up the stairs for another load. I followed at their heels and dropped down next to a lamp-post and watched them run through the trees towards the White House. Rifle fire cracked back and forth through the street and the sounds snapped every which way and back again. I checked my watch and counted the minutes till the stretcher crew ran out from the trees . . . three and a few seconds . . . twice in and twice out with no hits. Good odds. I waited for a lull in the bullets and took off towards the White House.

I eased back into the driveway and saw more uniformed troops coming out of the White House.

'Bingo! Red Army!'

I started ripping off pictures as fast as the tape would roll. And from nowhere hundreds of bystanders and war tourists ran up from the bridge towards the White House. The troops sealed the entrance and held back the mob and I slipped back over the wall down to a blown-out window near the ground.

An army of Boris's rifles pointed into the White House, waiting. A young officer marched forward and screamed into the dark. *'Vykhodite! Vykhodite!'*

Then the surrender of the True Believers. One by one they emerged from the dark. A young man with a bloody arm in a sling, a woman with a shopping bag, a teenage boy and girl holding hands, an Orthodox priest in soiled black robes, a babushka with an icon of St George in her hands, men with hands and caps over faces. Every one of them searched for weapons then forced into the jeers and fists and spittle of an angry mob. Rebel MPs came out under a Soviet flag. More jeers and fists. Then rifles blasted out from over our heads.

Everyone hit the dirt. Somewhere high above in the fire and smoke, the last of the warrior rebels. The mad leftovers unwilling to surrender, choking and drowning in smoke while jamming the last of their bullets into their Kalashnikovs and firing down on to the army of Boris Yeltsin. The Red Army cannons blasted the building again in response.

Bodies crawled through the lens and soldiers screamed for everyone to get the hell out of there.

'Snipers! Snipers!'

Red Army rifles peppered the building with machine-guns and the rebels' guns fell back into the smoky fire. I ran by the soldiers and through the trees and into a stone cove at the bottom of the marble stairs leading up to the White House. A small tribe of stills photographers all had the same idea. We shook hands and slapped each other on the back and generally observed that we were happy to see each other alive. A couple of Russian shooters babbled and pointed over to Ron Haviv. He was sitting on the ground changing rolls of film in his cameras.

'Hey, Ron. Ever get that coffee?'

'Still waiting, man. The locals seem worried.'

The Russians talked faster. We were dead close to the bullets but safe enough, they said. I listened closer trying to gather their concern. 'Shit' ... 'Stupid foreigner'.

'Ah, got it. Seems you've set yourself down in the rebel toilet, Ron.'

'You mean I'm sitting in a pile of shit?'

'That's 'bout right.'

Ron looked down and shook his head. 'I'm way too tired to move, man.'

'Hard day.'

'You get any good shots?'

'Oh. One or two. You?'

'About the same, man.'

KABOOM! CRASH!

A tank shell slammed high into the tower and rocked the ground. The White House Photographers Club all joined Ron in the rebel toilet and waited for the dust to settle.

'Fuck me, that's loud.'

KABOOM! KACRASH!

The vibrations rolled and rolled and pounded in our chests till there was only the crackling and smouldering fire sound high above our heads.

'Seems to have gone quiet.'

'Seems so, man.'

'Care to take a walk?'

'Let's go.'

Seven camera-shooters stepped out on to the marble stairs in full view of the Red Army. No quick movements, let the soldiers see us plain as day.

Heavy steel gears growled behind us as an APC rolled across the grass and twisted over the pavement and stopped at the bottom of the stairs. A 30mm cannon pointing at our collective testicles.

'Oops.'

'Yup.'

The rear hatch popped open and a squad of big green men jumped out and took positions round the steel tracks. Big green helmets with black face-guards. Big kick-ass rifles searching the White House for something to kill, the cannon rising above our heads locking on targets.

'OK, who are the fuck are these guys?'

'No idea, man. Looks like we've been invaded.'

'Yeah, but from what planet?'

The White House Photographers Club ran down the steps and started snapping shots of the creatures from the APC. An officer piled out the hatch and tore off his helmet. Black hair and black eyes. A neatly trimmed black moustache. He snatched the transmitter from his radio man, his voice booming like he'd had enough. Like a man who didn't give a shit about orders. He tossed aside the transmitter, refitted his helmet and barked at his squad. They sank to the ground in a football huddle talking and planning. I squeezed the lens through the pack and focused on hands that'd spent the day killing, now tying white cloth to a wood stick. The officer held it in his grip and gave it a test wave. '*Khorosho!*'

The squad grabbed rifles, raised their black visors, walked into the rebel rifles and moved slowly forward. The small white flag high in the air. The White House Photographers Club followed along.

Crunch. Crunch. Crunch.

To the top of the stairs and on to a small plaza. Rubble and destruction inches deep. We stood twenty feet from the shattered doors of the White House. Wind swirled and whistled through the blown-out windows above. Plumes of smoke drifted from the inner darkness like restless spirits. Somewhere in that darkness, hundreds of rifles were ready to blow our skulls to bits.

I sank down between black boots and framed the soldiers' weapons against the rubble and smoke and spooky dark through the windows. A hand grabbed me from behind and I jumped, spun round, fell on my butt and saw a familiar pair of spectacles peeking through the soldier's boots.

'Uh, well.'

'Jesus! Oleg! Fucksake!'

'I went back to the flat to find you and saw you crawling down here. What are you doing with Group Alpha?'

'Who the fuck is Group Alpha?'

Oleg pointed up to big green men with rifles.

'You mean these guys ain't from outer space?'

'Actually they are a specialist attack group with modified AK74 rifles ... extremely well trained and ... What does the Soviet space programme have to do with them anyway?'

And a heavy boot stomping for quiet.

'*Molchat!*'

And the wind swirling down again and marble dust and smoke hanging in the air like LA smog. Then beyond the shattered glass and wooden barricades, rebel shadows floating across the light. A White House guard emerged from the doors. His uniform covered in dirt and soot. The Group Alpha officer stepped ahead, shared a few words then rejoined his men. The guard turned and called up to the rebels. 'These soldiers have come with a message from the Red Army Command and they beg us to listen!'

A megaphone squealed with a distorted voice from high above. Bitter and willing-to-die tones through the smoke. The Group Alpha officer looked at his men and nodded. Then one slow move as the entire squad laid their weapons on the ground.

'You see? They are unarmed! Now, please! Listen to him!'

I crawled around the front of the soldiers and framed their unblinking faces in the lens. Unblinking faces staring up into the barrels of unseen rebel guns.

Two rebels stepped out of the White House and into the light, kicking their way through the rubble. The warriors stood face to face. The Group Alpha officer and his second shook hands with the rebels. Words and proposals went back and forth. The rebels nodded approval and the warriors turned to enter the White House. Oleg was up and across to the Group Alpha officer in a flash. He pointed to my camera and made all those begging signs.

'You going in, man?' asked Ron.

'Maybe.'

The rebels nodded approval but the officer shook his head.

'Maybe not.'

Oleg ran back and we squatted down near the stairs. The rebels and soldiers disappeared into the White House.

'Nice try, Oleg.'

'The rebels did not seem to mind.'

'How 'bout the guy from Planet Alpha?'

'He said we were lucky not to be shot for being here in the first place.'

'OK, then.'

'OK then what?'

'I got another plan. Take this tape back to the bureau. It's got some bodies and ground-level shots of fighting. Wait there and I'll come in an hour. We'll have some food and regroup.'

'You are talking like a normal person, Jonka. Are you feeling sick?'

'Nope. Just the guns have all gone quiet. I think the fat lady's gettin' ready to sing.'

Oleg peered over the rims of his glasses.

'This means something, doesn't it?'

'Yup.'

'Of course, singing fat women in a war zone – after all, why should I not grasp the wisdom of western logic?'

He hid the tape in his jacket and ran down the stairs. I sat with Ron and we listened to the quiet and the wind and watched the light fade along the river, waiting for the end game. Group Alpha still standing like Stonehenge. Unmoving and eternal. Having no doubts their officers would return . . .

'Seriously big *cojones* on these guys, man.'

. . . even if they had to pick up the rifles at their boots and march in and kill every fucking rebel they could find.

'No shit.'

'It's gotta be over soon, man.'

'Maybe.'

Hands reached for rifles.

'Maybe not.'

I grabbed the camera and crashed the zoom into the doors. The Group Alpha officer stormed out of the White House and slammed the black visor over his burning eyes, like hiding the killer rising once more. He snatched his rifle from one of his men.

'*Poshli!*'

And Group Alpha ran down the stairs towards their APC. The White House Photographers Club stood round with curious expressions.

'Doesn't sound good, man.'

'Nope, it doesn't. Maybe we should mosey down the stairs.'

Shots cracked from the White House tower, rebel guns screaming with the rage of a dying animal. Red Army troops dived for cover and returned fire.

'Shit, man!'

'We're fucked!'

Roll.

Scrambling down the stairs and bullets cutting the air. A flash of fire from across the river and Ron's voice yelling, 'Tank!' and then hearing the outgoing explosion and hitting the ground and pointing the camera into the air and covering my head and feeling the shell howl and roar overhead . . . KACRASH! And glass and dust falling all round and a heavy blast of heat washing over me and feeling like I was rolling in an endless wave of sound tumbling over and over and over again till a shell-shocked numbness echoed through my head.

'Holy shit!'

'You OK, man?'

'Holy shit! I got it!'

'You were rolling?'

'Fuck, yes! I got it!'

'Shot of the century, man!'

We raced away and jumped into the trees. Bullets blasting through the branches. We tucked up under the marble stairs. A Red Army squad broke through the trees. Rifles in our faces.

'*Vyezaite! Vyezaite!*'

'Think he's sayin' it's time to fuck off!'

'See ya next time, man!'

Out across the grass and down the hill towards the field hospital on the embankment road. My heart pounding fast and me falling down in the bushes and smelling smoke and dust and blood. I turned round slowly. Twenty-five dead rebels were starin' me in the face.

I pulled the camera on my lap and focused the lens wide. Somewhere in the stink was a picture, a great picture. I could feel it.

I got to my feet and circled round the bodies looking for the shot.

Look at it . . . don't turn away . . . where is it?

A small hole and a trickle of blood on the side of one face and me circling round and seeing the rest of the head blown to hell. And some other guy's guts hanging out and blood dripping on to the ground in small red pools. Arms and legs twisted and bent and all locked together. Dead faces watching me watching them. I could feel the presence of their still-breathing souls trapped and screaming in terror, unable to escape.

C'mon . . . where the fuck is it?

And some Russian doctor pulling me and telling me to leave.

'What are you doing? Have you no shame?'

'No. Get out of my way!'

And hearing the souls screaming louder in my head. So I walked round the bodies again and again till I heard a voice, one dead voice muffled and desperate. I stopped in my tracks. There, a bloody arm reaching up to me from deep within the bodies like someone trying to dig his way out of a grave. Fingers stretched open and almost moving.

Gotcha.

I looked up to the sun. Soft and low in the sky.

I went down in the dirt and framed the bodies against the light and hit the auto-iris of the lens. The world faded into a silhouette of ghastly shapes against a starlike sun. No smashed heads, no blank eyes, no blood. Just one rebel's hand reaching through a pile of death trying to grab the sky.

I touched the roll button and sucked the screaming souls on to the tape and into my brain. Ten seconds, twenty seconds, thirty seconds.

I got to my feet and saw the hating eyes of the doctor once more.

'That's one great picture. Says it all.'

'Go to hell, you American bastard.'

Down Novyi Arbat and through the troops, round the corner to the ring road and into a squad of Interior Ministry troops. They were using my beat-up Volvo as battlefield cover. Their rifles braced across the bonnet, blasting up to the high windows above the street.

'Snipers,' said one soldier.

'My car,' I said.

The boys politely ceased fire and let me climb into it. I looped round and headed towards Tverskaya Avenue and the bureau. I caught the troops in my rear-view mirror, packing themselves behind a Lada and opening fire again. I sped down the road towards the American Embassy where an APC and thirty Red Army soldiers stood across the road. Fifty Commie demonstrators gathered ahead of them. The soldiers tossed tear gas, the Commies tossed stones. So the soldiers fired bullets over the demonstrators' heads. The Commies tossed more stones.

'Ah, what the hell.'

I pulled over, grabbed the camera and walked over for one more thrill. A soldier was enjoying a relaxing smoke on the side of the APC.

'Hey, comrade.'

He watched me walk by.

Switch on and frame the Commies through the soldiers and roll. Then something rammed into the back of my flak-jacket. I turned round. The soldier was grinning from ear to ear with the cigarette dangling from his lips, his rifle pointing at my heart.

'*Poshli!*'

Fuck me . . . the tape.

He shoved me forward towards the rest of the soldiers. Rifles all turning on me and pushing me into the sweaty fat face of their commander. He wasn't having a good day. He waved his Tokarov pistol in my face.

'*Chto ty delayesh?*'

His breath smelling like week-old vodka.

'*Kto eto?*'

I pulled my press pass from under the flak-jacket. He tried to rip it off. I jumped back into the soldiers and the commander screamed and a pack of rifle butts crashed into my back and I went down on my knees, gasping for air. Boots smashed down on my legs.

'*Kto eto?*'

English . . . English . . . if they think I'm a foreigner maybe . . .

'I'm a journalist!'

'*Ty shpion yobanyi!*'

'I'm a fuckin' journalist!'

Hands snapped at the camera. I pulled it close to my chest and wrapped the strap over my shoulder. Fatso grabbed the collar of my flak-jacket and rammed the pistol into my neck.

'*Davay mne kassetu!*'

Goddammit . . . Oleg warned me.

'Look! I don't understand. I don't speak Russian.'

'*Ty vsyo vyrosh!*'

Boots kicked hard against my flak-jacket, my ribs rattling against the body armour. Couple of soldiers jammed their rifle barrels between my chest and the camera trying to pry it from my grip.

Not this tape, not this tape, please!

Comandante Fatso dragged me to my knees and slapped his fat hand hard across my face. *'Davay syuda kassetu!'*

'Nyet! You fuckin' asshole!'

Slimy vodka spit in my face and the click of a safety flipping off . . . a crack over my head and an explosion in my ears. Spittle frothing from Fatso's mouth. The barrel of the Tokarov pressing against my head . . .

'Kassetu!'

. . . and seeing madness in his drunken eyes. His fat finger barely fitting through the trigger guard and squeezing tighter. My head spinning and a dribble of piss running down my leg.

He's gonna do it . . . he's gonna fuckin' do it!

'OK! OK!'

He dropped me to the ground. I opened the camera and pulled out the tape. Someone snatched it in a flash and all hands went for the camera again.

'No, you bastards! Fuck off!'

The soldiers pulled me to my feet and slammed me into the APC. Rifles pinned me tight. Fatso lunged forward with his pistol in the air. He was gonna hurt me bad.

'Shpion! Shpion!'

'Fuck you! You fat fuck! I fuckin' dare you!'

Then voices calling from the side of the road.

'Ostanovites! Stop!'

'Eto Korrespondyent!'

A small group of Russian women behind a wire fence watching and crying.

'Ostanovites! Vy dolzhny eto delat!'

'Khvatit ubivat!'

'Ostanovites!'

The commander's sloshed brain was clear enough to recognize witnesses when he saw them. His drunken eyes blinking with indecision. His soldiers glanced nervously at each other.

'Osvobodite yevo,' he grumbled.

Rifles lowered and fists shoved me hard. I backed away with the camera still glued to my chest. Fatso's Tokarov following my every move. I turned and headed to the car. Behind the fence, one woman made the sign of the cross, another raised her hands to the heavens.

'Yeah. Me too, sister.'

A shot cracked behind me but I didn't turn round. I just kept walking with visions of one ITN cassette laid upon the ground and executed by firing squad.

Into the bureau.

Me looking like dog meat and stinking of piss. Everyone was crammed into the edit suite crashing the story together. I threw my bulletproof vest on to the floor and locked myself in the toilet to wash. Water and soap and rubbing and rubbing harder till the skin turned red and raw. The piss smell wouldn't go away. 'Fuck it! Goddam fuckin' bastards!'

A knock on the door.

'Jonka?'

I walked out. Oleg looking into my eyes. 'What has happened?'

'I fucked up, Oleg. I fucked up big-time.'

'Uh, well . . . listen to me. It is all right, it is over. Everyone has now surrendered. Rutskoi, Khazbulatov, everyone. It is over.'

'It can't be! Not yet. There's this picture, Oleg, I just need some tape. We can go back. It can't be over yet!'

'Jonka, please hear me.'

'These soldiers were playin' this game, like they were gonna kill me and now I can't remember. All these bodies. This fat fucker took all these bodies from me!'

'Try and calm down. There is something I need to tell you.'

Irina stepped between us and put her hands round my arm. 'Not now, Oleg, he must have something to eat. You must be starving, Jonka. Come with me.'

She walked me into the small kitchen and fussed like a Russian wife. Warm tea and a plate of food. Potatoes with some kind of meat. 'Jonka. Eat.'

I wolfed it down fast. 'What did Julian do about his stand-up?'

'He found an agency cameraman to shoot it.'

'*Spasibo*, Irushka.'

'*Nyet problemy*. Now eat.'

'What's up with Oleg? Says he needs to talk.'

'Oleg is fine, Jonka. But there is something else.'

Eugene Campbell stepped into the kitchen to grab a cup of tea. 'Have you heard about Rory?'

'Nope. Where is he?'

'Dead.'

The plate fell from my hands and crashed into the sink. I grabbed the counter top and held on.

'Last night at Ostankino. One shot to the head.'

I sank to the floor. Not believing, not hearing, barely able to speak. 'Jesus. No.'

Irina knelt near me and touched my hair and laid her head on my shoulder. 'It is a such a terrible day, Jonka.'

'But I saw him. He was alive. He's been through a million fuckin' wars.'

Water dripping in the sink, sounds of the city through the open window, cool night air and feeling it all slip away . . . all the buzz and all the rush. Now there was only emptiness. Not even tears.

Out in the newsroom, Oleg was watching three TV screens at once. Pictures of the day's battle rolling over and over again . . .

'Uh, well. You know about Rory.'

'Yeah.'

. . . bullets and tanks and fire.

'I don't get it.'

'How do you mean, Jonka? Hundreds of people were killed. You filmed many of them. What do you think you were seeing in your camera?'

'But Rory, he's one of us.'

'Seven journalists are dead, Jonka. Seven.'

'Jesusfuckin'Christ.'

And not knowing what to do but stare at the screens and watch the pictures again and again.

'Cram it into a television and it all looks so fuckin' harmless.'

'Perhaps if pictures could bleed, Jonka.'

And me remembering the bodies and the faces.

'Maybe they do.'

I stared out the high windows. Night falling on Moscow, long trails of smoke and crimson clouds above faraway trees, the White House in flames like a beacon of vengeance.

'So what shall we do now?'

'I think you should go home.'

'And you? What will you do?'

'Gonna get drunk most likely.'

'Perhaps I should stay with you.'

'Nope. This is a solo drunk. Something I gotta do.'

'What is that?'

'Don't know yet.'

Oleg wrapped up in his coat and scarf and pulled his cap down on his head. He gazed at the screens once more and sighed. 'Sometimes, Jonka, you seem lost like a little boy.'

He headed down the hall towards the lift . . .

'Hey, Oleg.'

. . . and him stopping without turning, waiting quietly.

'Sometimes when I'm lookin' down the lens I can't tell if it's real.'

He waited a moment longer, then he stepped into the lift and the door scraped shut.

NOWHERE ROADS

Moscow, 1993

How long has it been like this? Two people at the end of the road. But it wasn't even that, was it? We never stopped loving each other. More like hiding from the pain of a shared loneliness deep within ourselves. Holding on and letting go then holding on again. Hearts trapped in no man's land.

Started when I left for Russia six months before you. I was going on ahead to get settled, but things were bad between us and I didn't want you to come, remember? You were off in Nicaragua or Haiti covering some big story. I remember your voice over a crackling phone line. Sounded like you were calling from the other end of my life.

'Jon, we've made a lot of mistakes but we can't end it like this. You have to try and hang on to something in your life. Trust me, Jon.'

And me thinking, I have to go, Kate . . . I just have to go.

Do you remember that first night we met, long ago? Some Italian restaurant with a Korean name on Second Avenue in Manhattan. Rocky Lee's, that was it. Decent food, cheap wine. I was sitting across the room watching people and framing pictures in my head when I saw you. You were having dinner with friends and family. You were sitting in the middle of the group, a glass of white wine in your hands. Blonde hair, blue eyes, gorgeous and classy. One of those Irish Catholic New York babes who could cut the big boys to shreds with her sharp-tongued wit. You were doing a pretty good job of it as I eavesdropped on your conversation. Always had a feeling you knew I was watching you – you'd look my way and smile every once in a while. I sent a note to your table saying you were beautiful. One of your pals got a hold of it and read it aloud. There were lots of 'umhmmms' and curious eyebrows all round. You walked over to my table, sat down and looked me straight in the eyes.

'You were saying something?' you asked.

My heart was pounding with excitement like I'd never felt.

'I'm Jon Steele.'

'I know that. I've seen you around. I also know you're twenty miles of bad road.'

'How the hell you know that?'

'Take a good look at me, buster. Do I look stupid to you?'

Few hours later we poured out of some fine Irish bar called Kennedy's and stumbled down the street. Our voices laughing through the chilly September night. Seemed like everything I said to you and everything you said to me was funny as hell. We read the same books, loved movies, lived and breathed our TV news jobs. And me watching you again and thinking you were more beautiful than the last time I looked you over. I reached out and put my arm around your shoulders.

'Why are you touching me?'

'Your perfume, it's nice.'

'Thank you. Now back off.'

'Sorry.'

'No, I just need to tie my shoelace.'

You knelt down and lashed your shoelace tight, then you popped back up with a wonderful smile. Your face so very close to mine.

'OK, you can kiss me now.'

'How do you know I wanna kiss you?'

'I see. You're cute, but not too bright.'

'Well, why couldn't I kiss you before?'

'I told you, I had to tie my shoelace.'

'I think I'm fallin' in love.'

'Don't be stupid.'

''Scuse me?'

'Number one, you've had only one conversation with me and that was tonight. Number two, I was only tying my shoes. Number three, I've been a network television producer for ten years.'

'What's that got to do with it?'

'I know bullshit when I hear it.'

'OK.'

'So there.'

'So there what?'

'You were saying something?'

'Nope.'

'Are you going to kiss me or do I stand here gazing endlessly into your eyes till you get the hint?'

And we kissed till the world got dizzy. Traffic lights must have changed two or three times during that kiss. Yellow cabs speeding by, horns honking, cabbies calling . . .

'Olé!'

'Give her one for me!'

'Get a room!'

. . . and you still kissing me within an inch of my life.

You pulled away, looked into my eyes and smiled. 'So how was that?'

'You have a very sexy mouth, Kate.'

'You don't know the half of it.'

'That's it, I'm in love.'

'Men, they're so easy. Now let go of me.'

'Sorry.'

'Relax. I just need to tie my other shoelace.'

And you knelt down on the sidewalk and lashed the other shoelace as fast as the first one and you popped back up again.

'OK, you can kiss me again.'

'What makes you think I wanna kiss you again?'

'Because you just might get lucky, you big stupid.'

And you smiled with that same wonderful smile.

But by the time you came to Russia, I was gone from you. At least, that's how it felt, you said. After a few months we took off to Florence for one of those pretend-everything-is-OK holidays. We stayed at the Regency Hotel just across from the shady square where old men talked in the day and young lovers caressed in the night. You sat on the edge of the bed and you looked into my eyes. 'Jon, there's something I want to ask you.'

'What's that?'

'Your producer in Moscow. The English girl I met, Bridget. You're in love with her, aren't you?'

And wanting to tell you the truth . . .

I'm sorry, Kate, I just gotta go.

. . . but not knowing what the hell the truth was.

T'bilisi, Georgia, November, 1993

There was this small sign. One of those clever Eurospeak symbols. A red circle with a red line crossing through it. In the middle of the circle was a handgun. A gang of goons in combat gear stood at the door, their beady eyes giving us the once-over.

BEEEEP!

'Swell. A metal detector.'

'Uh, well . . . the better to protect your capitalist ass, Jonka.'

The beady-eyed goons rushed over and inspected the camera gear.

'Bomb?' they asked.

'Only sometimes.'

Check in and up to the rooms and pry open the metal cases stuffed with provisions. It was one of the pleasures of travelling throughout former Commie land, packing your own food and water and booze like a tribe of gypsies. Oleg loved to sift through the imported goodies I'd bought from the western food shops in Moscow.

'Oh, look! French cheese! Good French wines! Toblerone chocolates! Swiss meats and such excellent quality caviar! And a jar of . . . peanut butter?'

'Should be some strawberry jam in there too.'

'With caviar?'

'No. PB&J.'

Oleg looking confused.

'Peanut butter and jelly sandwich, you know?'

'This is one of your American things, isn't it?'

'Oleg, you tellin' me you never had a peanut butter and jelly sandwich?'

'Uh, well . . . well, not really.'

'Stand aside, comrade.'

I reached down under the bottles of good French wine, enough to choke a company accountant.

'Hand me a corkscrew, Oleg. Let's have some wine.'

'Red or white?'

'Don't matter. Just need somethin' to loosen up the peanut butter when it gets all gummed up on the roof of your mouth.'

'Perhaps I'll just have some Brie, Jonka.'

'Oleg, who the hell's ever heard of peanut butter and Brie?'

I found a loaf of rather squashed bread and laid out a couple of slices.

'Now, a glob of peanut butter here, a dab of jam here, spread evenly.'

'*Pozhaluista*. But please don't trouble yourself, Jonka.'

'*Nyet problemy*. Of course, back in the USA this would be considered heresy. Most Americans hold PB&J can only be made with grape jelly.'

'You don't say.'

'But, you will note, I'm usin' the real all-American white bread.'

'Fascinating.'

I slapped the slices together and handed Oleg one perfectly formed PB&J. 'I was raised on this stuff.'

'Jonka, I have often wondered what happened to you as a young boy to make you turn out the way you did. This explains a great deal.'

Flop, flop, flump.

Heavy feet down the hallway.

'Hahaha! Hohoho! Heeheehee.'

Julian's laughter bouncing down the corridor and coming closer.

'Jon! Oleg!' And he flopped through the open door. 'You won't believe it! I was down in the lobby and guess what?!'

He reached out into the hall and hauled in Eddie Parker. Same Croatian-army trousers, same Russian naval T-shirt, same war-crazed grin on his skinny face. I shook his hand and gave him a big hug. Oleg quickly stuffed the PB&J into Eddie's hands. 'Uh, well . . . Eddie. You must be hungry, eat this most interesting American food.'

'Thanks! Fucking great! What the hell is it?'

We guzzled some wine and Julian opened another bottle.

'Not bad plonk,' slurped Julian.

Oleg picking through the food box like a kid at Christmas and Eddie wolfing down the leftovers.

'So, Eddie. Ever find that Georgian gal with the moustache you were hopin' for?'

'Jon, let me tell you. I was working on this one little thing when Julian found me downstairs. I always come here to chat up the birds behind the front desk.'

'How goes it?'

'Jon, you wouldn't fucking believe it! All the women in this fucking country want to get fucking married *before* you fuck them!'

'Fuckin' outrageous.'

'Yeah, but I think I'm really close this time. I keep asking this tiny one with big tits to join me down the sauna baths.'

'And the moustache quotient?'

'You could run a fucking comb through it.'

'Calls for a toast.'

Julian filled the glasses to the top and the evening sank into jokes and laughter and more wine. Outside, the T'bilisi night snapped with gunfire.

'Shit goes on all the time. Gangsters and fucking kids get stoned and shoot it out. Place is going to hell,' said Eddie.

'What happened in Sokhumi, Eddie, after we left you?'

'Fucking incredible. Last few days I was up at Shevardnadze's house. Everyone had run away except for a few doped-out soldiers. I had to tell them what to fucking do!'

'So you made general after all.'

'Didn't take much with those bozos.'

He talked about bodies and fire, screams and panic. There wasn't a shred of food in the city.

'Then there was this cuntface from Médecins sans Frontières sitting in his truck with a big slice of cheese and a loaf of French bread. I asked him if I could have a small piece.'

That seemed to make Eddie hungry all over again. He found another leftover something from the provisions box and gulped it down, his hands shaking. 'Fucking guy looks at me and says, "Geet fucked!"'

'You're jokin'.'

'Fuck no! So I grabbed the cheese and ate it in front of his ugly frog face! I should've shot him!'

'You had a gun?'

'Czechoslovakian issue AK47.'

'You had a fuckin' machine-gun?'

'Yeah, why?'

'Eddie, we gotta talk about the rules of this job.'

'Good Lord, I can see the headlines, "ITN Stringer Slays For Food!"'

'Fucking great, Julian! Can we do that? I got a photo if you need it!'

'Eddie. Please, read my lips, no guns.'

'C'mon, Julian. You guys could do the whole story. Me walking four days through the mountains. Georgian soldiers everywhere looking for morphine. I could have made a fortune selling dope. Maybe I should do that next. Anyway, I jumped on a bus full of refugees back to Sokhumi. You guys want to see my bayonet from the AK47? I had to give back the rifle.'

'Perhaps we could use another bottle of wine,' offered Julian.

A cool breeze drifted down from the Caucasus mountains and over the balcony and into the room. The rifles gone quiet, just a few dogs howling at the moon. Julian laid out the plans for the next day. Eddie listened between gulps of food.

'Now, then. Two Georgian taxis will drive us over the mountains towards the front lines.'

'Sounds fucking great so far. Can I have more food?'

'*Pozhaluista*, Eddie.'

Seems since 1992, Mad-as-a Hatter Professor and Former President of Georgia Zviad Gamzekhurdia had been sitting across the border in Chechnya listening to his Lady Macbeth wife moan and groan about Eduard Shevardnadze taking over her Georgia. Gamzekhurdia listened to the old bat till he decided it'd be a good time to get out of the house. He assembled an army of like-minded fruitcakes and crossed the border back into Georgia. In a matter of days, much to his own surprise, madman Gamzekhurdia was half-way to T'bilisi with a big chunk of the country in his pocket. There was another civil war in Georgia. Gave me a chance to get out of my own house and back on the road chasing some far-off war. I was happy as a bullet in a gun.

'Want to tag along, Eddie?'

'Fucking great!'

'We'll pay you, of course.'

'That's fucking great too!'

'But no guns.'

'How about the bayonet?'

'Eddie!'

'Okokokok.'

Julian poured out the last of the wine and he and Oleg packed off to their rooms. Eddie rushed downstairs for another go at the girl with the moustache.

'Stop being such an American!'

'I am an American.'

'You are not! Not really, anyway. I should like to think of you as a citizen of the world.'

'Bullshit.'

'Don't be so crude. I am not having dinner with a crude American.'

And you giggled and laughed the same way you giggled and laughed when we first met, months ago.

'Hallo. My name is Bridget,' you said, with very proper English tones, as you held out your hand for a very proper English handshake. You standing there in riding boots, black jodhpurs and some kind of beige furball sweater, long brown hair falling round your face. You'd been riding through the snowy forests outside Moscow that day. Your cheeks glowed red from the wind and you smelt of pine and snow and cold.

You were twenty-six, with little experience in television, but you had all the desire in the world. You walked off the Moscow streets from a broken love affair and landed one of the best jobs in the business. You worked as hard as anyone. You adored Russia, spoke the language, treasured every moment of the Russian winter. The wondrous cold and the moody dark.

'Isn't it the best? Look around, you stupid American, isn't it the best?'

You were my guide walking through the streets of Moscow, the forests and woods, teaching me the language of the most passionate country in the world. And that first Christmas when all the journos deserted Russia in droves, it seemed like it was just me and you in Moscow. I'd come to your door in a jacket and tie.

You stood there in blue jeans and that same beige furball sweater.

'Ah, I see. You meant that kind of dinner.'

You dug through the piles of clothes scattered over the floor and pulled out a black dress.

'This one looks as if it could stand up and walk but it'll do.'

I watched you brush your hair. Like watching a secret.

And you laughed across the table of Stanislavski's restaurant. Small place around the corner from the Kremlin run by three mad Polish women who slammed the door in the face of anyone they didn't like the look of. There was a lot of door-slamming that night, we were the only ones in the place. Christmas Eve in Russia. Caviar on warm blini, a small tree in the corner wrapped in red ribbon, chandeliered light bouncing off baroque mirrors and twinkling fairylike through streams of good Russian champagne pouring into our glasses again and again. One of the mad Polish women walked over and set another bottle of champagne on the table. 'On the house, Happy Christmas,' she said.

Outside, snow was falling through the glow of street-lamps, flakes like tiny pieces of Russian lace. You touched the frosty glass and felt the cold.

'It really is the best, isn't it?'

'Jon, I was thiiiis fucking close!'

'It's a cruel fuckin' world, Eddie.'

'I mean, what does it take to get laid in this fucking country?'

'Can't help you, Eddie. Got my own problems back in Moscow.'

One bleary-eyed cameraman cleaning the zoom lens, Eddie packing the two Ladas with camera kit and bulletproof vests, Oleg arguing with the drivers as they smoked and grumbled. All of us waiting for Julian Manyon.

'It seems the drivers are a bit nervous, Jonka.'

'At two hundred dollars a day they'll get over it.'

'Do all Americans define life in terms of dollars per day?'

'How we won the Cold War, ain't it?'

Our correspondent finally spilled out from the revolving doors.

'Oh, I'm terribly sorry I'm late. I'm feeling a bit nasal today.'

And with that he jumped into the lead car and rocked back and forth, ready to roll. The Lada bouncing on its springs and me and Eddie and Oleg wondering about the general weirdness of the last comment.

'Anyone here wanna guess what the fuck that means?'

'Uh, well . . .'

'. . . not me.'

'Oleg, you ride with Julian. I'll take Eddie.'

'Because?'

'You heard him. He's feelin' nasal. Man needs help.'

The Ladas sputtered through the early-morning light of T'bilisi, my eyes grabbing the images flashing by. Hungry-eyed kids, a crowd of old men and women huddled near a wooden doorway, their hands rubbing over a small fire of twigs and fallen leaves, smoke rising up to faded letters above the doorway, 'Khlyeb'.

'Nothin' in the bread shops?'

'Fucking riots here last week, you should have seen it. Old ladies kicking the shit out of each other for a loaf of bread. But, hey, Shevardnadze's got an army to feed. You know what that means.'

Winding round St David's Church and on to a two-lane road hugging the cliffs above the Kuba river and rising slowly into the Caucasus mountains. The water running fast over stones. The hills brown and rocky. Pine trees stretching up towards the sun. It was good to be on the road, any road.

'Yup. It's a cruel fuckin' world, Eddie.'

'Do you realize you're never home?'

'Just busy all the time.'

'I think it's more than that, Jon.'

'Kate, it ain't what you think.'

'Why don't we talk to someone, a marriage counsellor?'

'In Moscow?'

'I called the embassy and got the number of an American woman, a therapist.'

'Kate, I'm always travellin'. I can't commit to a schedule.'

'Jon, look at me. It's me, Kate. Is there anything more important than our marriage?'

'I'm out there runnin' round in dangerous places, I'm doin' the best I can.'

'Jon, you're out there because you don't want to be here.'

'Sorry, I don't mean it to be like that.'

'I wish you could just talk to me. I wish you could just express how you feel. It seems the more I try to hold you close, the more you slip away.'

'Kate, you're a good woman.'

'I don't want to be a good woman, I want to be the woman you love.'

'Kate . . . I never . . .'

'What is it, Jon? Please tell me.'

'Sometimes I feel like I'm kinda broke emotionally and no matter how much I wanna feel things like everyone else, I just can't.'

'Oh, Jon, let me help you. Please let somebody help you.'

'I don't need a shrink.'

'C'mon, you big stupid. You can't keep running away from your life.'

Midday. Kutaisi, Georgia

A pleasant warm afternoon in a provincial town of the former Soviet Union. Palm trees and evergreens, with the remnants of battle in the town square. Men and women in battle fatigues scraping a 'Death to Shevardnadze' paint job off the turret of a captured tank. A can of paint nearby to slap on 'Death to Gamzekhurdia'.

'Thought they could just switch the names and leave the rest.'

'Some aspects of Soviet manufacturing policy are hard to forget, Jonka.'

Little boys in woolly coats scampered up the steel tracks and swung from the cannon like monkeys, crawling up the turret and peeking down the hatch and dreaming of being soldiers.

'So,' mused Julian, 'where's the fucking war?'

'Lots of Kalashnikovs,' I said.

'Always a hopeful sign,' said Oleg.

Julian and Oleg disappeared into a nearby police station looking for news and I looked around for pictures. Eddie twitched with disbelief. 'This is absolute bullshit!'

'Oh, I don't know, Eddie. Kinda colourful.'

Some guy sitting on the ground with a Second World War vintage helmet on his head, prayer beads in his hands, a gang of war buddies gathered all round. Some jamming bullets into magazines, others wiping down well-oiled Kalashnikovs. All eyes watching a young woman in battle fatigues saunter by in a sexy killer sort of way. White bandana wrapped round her long black hair, candy-stripe socks over the leggings of battle fatigues, automatic rifle slung low across her round ass. She jerked her head at one of the boys. He jumped up like a horny dog and followed her across the road and into the trees. Hand in hand, rifle butts bumping tenderly.

'That is one fucking lucky soldier,' groaned Eddie.

'Don't even think about it, Eddie. Far too painful.'

APCs rumbled through the streets, swerving round bundles of old women dressed in head-to-toe black. Buses of Shevardnadze's soldiers cruised down the street and back again and then back again. Clouds of bad Russian tobacco pouring out the windows and following the buses like smoke signals from the desperately bored. Eddie edged close to me and whispered.

'Jon, listen. I'll grab a rifle, run around the corner and let off a few rounds, just to get things going.'

'Eddie, remember what we said about the rules.'

'Jon, they'll be killing each other for a fucking week before they realize it was all a mistake!'

'Eddie, listen carefully. *No!*'

I leaned up along the tank thinking maybe this was all bullshit. Then again here I was surrounded by rifles and bullets and all kinds of killing things. It was the best buzz going for the moment.

'Well, it seems the war has already left!' Julian barking down the stairs. 'Gamzekhurdia has done a runner!'

'You're shittin' me.'

'Not at all. Shevardnadze's not only stopped the advance, it seems his army can hardly keep up with the rebels.'

'You are shittin' me.'

'Uh, well . . . they're heading towards Abkhazia. Perhaps to join up with the rebels in Sokhumi.'

'Now you're shittin' me.'

'No, Jonka.'

'Can we hook up with one of Shev's units and get after 'em?'

'Except by the time we find them they may be back across the border. Unfuckingbelievable . . .'

Julian squirming round like a kid ready to skin a cat.

'. . . I mean, what kind of country is this?'

'Sorta confused, I'd say, and we're runnin' out of time.'

One o'clock. Ten hours till the programme went to air. We tossed round plans and ideas like ping-pong balls, none of them good. On top of that it was Friday, last day of the week for the regular newscast. The story was already half-way down the drain and if we didn't make air tonight we'd be lost in the land of weekend programming.

'As things stand right now we can't get back to T'bilisi in time for the bulletin.'

'Seems we're screwed.'

'Won't look good on our résumés.'

'Jon, sure you don't want me to grab that rifle and shoot someone?'

'No, Eddie. Not yet, anyway.'

'Uh, well . . . our German friends from ZDF do have an edit pack here in the police station . . .'

'. . . and we could borrow it . . .'

'. . . and hook up a microwave feed to Moscow . . .'

'. . . and feed it on the satellite to London.'

'All we need now is a war,' said Julian.

'There's gotta be one somewhere down that fuckin' road.'

We jumped back into the Ladas and sped out of town. Mountains opening out on to a wide plain of wheat growing tall and brown. Winds combing through the grain and the grain bending and twisting in shadowy waves of rolling light. A daylight moon low on the horizon and me thinking how it looked so much like Montana . . .

'You thinking about something, Jon?' asked Eddie.

'Nope.'

. . . a lifetime ago . . .

'Can I ask you something?'

'Yup.'

'How did you ever get into this job?'

'Lucky, I guess.'

. . . walking through a field of endless wheat. Tall scratchy stalks brushing my eyes . . .

'Driving down a road in the middle of fucking nowhere?'

'Just now, no place I'd rather be in the world.'

. . . further and further into the field then running till the stalks caught round my legs ropelike and pulled me down under waves of grain. My face in the dirt and me hating my twelve-year-old life and wanting to stay there for ever and die and be eaten by animals so no one'd find me, or touch me, again.

'Why does he do that?'

'Why does who do what?'

'Up in the lead car, see Julian? His head just rocks back and forth. He's been doing it since we left T'bilisi.'

'Julian may appear a little weird to the untrained eye. He's all right . . . hardest-workin' reporter I ever met.'

'You're a funny team. Like cats and dogs you are.'

'Yeah, maybe. But Julian has the quality I admire most in a good dog.'

'What's that?'

'He ain't gonna leave me bleedin' to death in some ditch.'

'Huh. Look, he's still doing it. Rocking back and forth.'

'Makes the car go faster, Eddie. First thing you learn in TV.'

'Where do you come from, Jon?'

'Lots of places, mostly a place called Montana.'

'How do you find this Montana?'

'Walk out this restaurant, head towards Denver then make a right, just keep goin' till you find a place with more cows than people. Champagne?'

'I mean, you ignoramus, is it pretty?'

'Well, actually, you snooty Brit, it's wide and open and lonely.'

'Sounds moody.'

'Yup. Blackfoot Indian tribe out there called it "Big Sky Country" when it was nothing but mountains and prairie grass and a million head of buffalo.'

'Do you have a familial home out there still?'

'My familials kinda got scattered.'

'And what sort of people are they?'

'One drunken warrior father who's been through more wars than Genghis Khan, one rather odd earth-mother not quite of this earth, four abused boys who sorta survived the both of them, one dog that got rolled over by a semi-truck, one dog that died of old age, and one parakeet I accidentally stepped on and squashed when I was ten years old.'

'I see.'

'Need more champagne yet?'

'I think so. Tell me about your boyhood. What games did you play? What were your little-boy dreams?'

'Why the hell you askin' me all this, Bridget?'

'Because, Jon, it's fascinating to think you might actually have a past.'

'Bridget, stop and listen to me. My past ain't something I care to talk about. I can't remember most of it, and the rest I'd rather forget.'

Kilometres rolling under the wheels and still no war. Another three hours gone, five to deadline. A crossroads up ahead with a small village shimmering in the light. Our caravan cruised up to a guard post once used by the KGB to spy on the comings and goings of Soviet-loving Georgians. Men in ragged uniforms spread out across the road, Kalashnikovs inviting us to turn round and get lost.

'Oleg, what do you mean, we can't go on?' demanded Julian.

'Uh, well . . . he says it is too dangerous. There are snipers in the fields.'

'What do you mean, snipers in the fields?' demanded Julian again.

And Oleg's eyes wiggling in his head.

'Julian, this man with the rifle is telling us we cannot go on because . . . well . . . there are snipers in the fields ahead on the roads, and well . . . I cannot think of any other way to say it.'

'Christ, at this rate the war will be over before we ever get there! Let's go see the commander and sort this out. I am not being told where I may and may not go by some brandy-swilling idiot! Oleg, follow me! Jon, remain here and take pictures!'

I clicked my heels together.

'Yes, *mein Führer*.'

'Yes, right. Whatever.'

Julian stormed across the road towards the guard post. The Georgian soldiers jumped out of the way. Oleg waited for the dust to clear and hustled along, his voice trailing behind. 'I thought it was very clear . . . I mean . . . well . . . snipers in the fields seems obvious . . . but then . . .'

A yellow straw mountain eased slowly over the rise. Two oxen pulling a heavy load of hay up the road. Hoofs pounding and rusty wheels creaking and an old man atop the straw reaching down and snapping a long whip against the sweaty haunches of the dumb beasts, nudging them past the guard post.

'Nice picture,' I said.

'Yeah, but it isn't a war. I mean, what are we working for? That magazine with all the African chicks with big tits?'

'Eddie, you don't mean *National Geographic*, do you?'

'Yeah, that's it.'

Along the dirt track from the village. A dusty peasant pushing his bicycle out of the heat haze and up the hill towards the crossroads. A dusty black hat pulled down low on his dusty head. He eased through the frame and out of the lens, and since he wasn't being followed by a tribe of African women with big tits, I decided that was about it and switched off the camera. And I lay across a big rock and closed my eyes, the autumn sun warm, so very warm.

'There isn't a day that goes by that I don't think of him.'

'Steve?'

'Yes. Steve.'

Long before me and you there was Kate and Steve. Husband and wife for six months. Everyone liked Kate and Steve. Then driving to work down that same everyday bending and turning road through Rock Creek Park, the car slipped from the road and span out of control and rolled down into the stream. Steve screaming for help and pounding the windshield. He was trapped, feeling the cold dark water rush in round his legs and higher and higher till his face went down. When the rescuers pulled him out he was alive . . . but all his thoughts, his memories, the man you loved . . . gone. He lay in a coma for eighteen months before he finally died.

'I've lost my father to alcoholism, Steve to an accident . . . God.'

Your voice echoing through the dark room. Your Russian Blue kitten chasing a rubber band across the floor. Dim light pouring through the door.

'Kate . . .'

'Jon, I love you so much. I'm trying to tell you I need you to help us make it through this. I can't do it alone. I don't want to lose you too.'

'I ain't gonna die in Russia, Kate.'

'It isn't about you dying in Russia, Jon. It's about our life together. That's what's dying in Russia.'

*

Crack! Crack!

AK47s. Five, six rounds. Rapid fire.

And me down and rolling on the ground. Open my eyes and grab the camera. Eddie kneeling nearby. Shots ripping through the wheat-field.

'Hang on a minute,' said Eddie.

'What?'

'The soldiers. They're just sitting there.'

Up at the guard post, Shev's boys smoking and pointing and laughing. One of the gang taking aim and letting off another burst into the field.

'What the hell's he shootin' at?'

Eddie followed the target line above the grain and peeked over the edge. 'Looks like they're shooting at that guy with the bicycle.'

'What the fuck?'

'Maybe they think he's Gamzekhurdia.'

'With a bicycle?'

'Yeah, but these jerks have been drinking plum brandy since break-fast. Probably was breakfast. Maybe they think he's got a tank.'

'Oh, swell.'

We came out of the dust and peered down the dirt track. The peasant with the bicycle was half buried in the ground. One hand scrunching his dusty black hat down on his head and the other waving a small white handkerchief in the air. The soldiers laughed and con-gratulated themselves in slurred Georgian. One tried to slap another on the back in drunken camaraderie. He missed and spun round and flopped down in a chair.

'And we're s'posed to worry about Gamzekhurdia's snipers?'

Then a thunderlike roar came up behind us and billowing clouds parted to reveal a stampede of beat-up cars and dented buses with hundreds of men hanging from windows and the sides of trucks, everyone screaming their head off and waving automatic rifles and pistols and knives . . .

'I don't believe it. It's fuckin' *Road Warrior*!'

. . . and swooping past the guard post and roaring on down the road.

'Now this is more like it!' howled Eddie.

And Julian's voice calling from across the road, 'Jon, Eddie! Let's go!'

. . . and running with Oleg in tow. We jumped into our cars and sped thataway. Julian waving his arms and ordering his driver to slip ahead of the charge as ITN's Lada division of the Georgian Army dashed from the rear and past the centre with the drunken Georgian road warriors cheering us on like brothers. The head of the stampede moving just round the bend and into a small village.

CRACKCRACK! CRACK!

The stampede screeched to a halt. Twenty of Shevardnadze's men spread out across the road, blasting machine-guns into the fields. Our drivers found religion fast, ground their gearboxes into reverse and slammed down on the gas.

'*Nyet!* Stop! Fuckin' stop!' I grabbed the camera and threw open the door. 'Eddie, you stay here and make sure this driver doesn't leave us!'

'Don't worry, Jon! He moves an inch and I'll cut his fucking throat with my bayonet!'

'Eddie, listen to me carefully. Take the keys, just take the keys.'

'Ohyeahallright.'

Oleg and Julian and me ran up behind the firing line for a peek.

'What do you see out there, Jon?'

'Don't really know what I'm lookin' for.'

We crawled through the road warriors and knelt down alongside the rifles. One soldier debated whether to fire or take another shot from his bottle of slivovitz. He opted for a swallow of booze then fumbled with the safety of his Kalashnikov, the barrel pointing point-blank at Oleg's head.

'Oleg, maybe we should ask what the hell's happenin'.'

'I suppose, but from which one of these strange characters?'

'How 'bout the one ready to blow up your head?'

'*Da*, perhaps he would be a good start.'

Oleg eased the rifle barrel to the side. '*Izvinite*, comrade, *v kovo vy strelyayete?*'

The soldier was suddenly confused. He shrugged and tapped a comrade on the shoulder and yelled a few words between the gunfire. His comrade thought a moment, shrugged his shoulders and let off a few more rounds.

'Jon,' called Julian, 'I think you should look at this.'

'What is it?'

'Trust me. Words cannot begin to describe what is coming up the road.'

A large goods truck snaking through the traffic jam. Soldiers and rifles punching the air with cheers of victory. And towering over their heads something big and shiny and pointy. 'Fuck me.'

'Jon, I thought you might say those very words.'

The truck bed had been ripped away. And there, mounted and sort of balanced over the rear axle, one slightly used B8 85 air-to-surface missile launcher. Oleg's glasses drooped down his nose in disbelief. Julian chuckled and roared like he was being tickled to death. And me too dumbstruck to shoot a picture.

'Correct me if I'm wrong, Oleg, but hasn't that weapon been removed from a helicopter gunship?' laughed Julian.

'It does not seem logical . . . but, then, well . . . only Georgians would take the gun and leave the helicopter.'

The truck hit the brakes and the road warriors held their breath as the gun bowed ahead and rocked back like it was going to fall over and take the whole truck with it. All of us watching and wondering if we were about to die in a flash of fire.

'I wanna picture of that fuckin' thing when it launches a few rockets.'

'Jon. Might I humbly suggest that if that mutant beast does release a single rocket, the entire thing will most likely explode killing anyone close to it? Oleg?'

'Uh, well . . . da.'

'Yeah, but what a shot.'

I wandered round the back of the beast and rolled a few pictures. Couple of soldiers tossing spent shell casings the size of rubbish cans on to the road. Clangs and clongs ringing like the chimes of doom. New shells lay heavy and sparkling in the sun: 80mm of killing steel loaded into a firing tube one after the other; 80mm times the power of twenty. Whatever was out in that was about to be blown to kingdom come.

A gang of soldiers stumbled by, lifted me up and carried me back to the firing line. They wanted me to take their picture. Ray-Bans and bandanas, fags on lips and guns on hips, slivovitz passing from hand to hand and draining in deep gulps. Drunk as skunks to the last man.

'OK, say, "Cheese"!'

'CHUZZEZ!'

They gathered round and offered me a drink. The homemade stuff. Three sips and you go blind.

'Swell.'

Went down like fire.

'*Khorosho!*'

And lots of back-slapping and macho handshakes like we were best pals. My eyes looked down and caught a 1945-era revolver swaying in one wobbly hand. Pan up to a very drunken face then back down to the revolver. Hammer cocked, ready to fire, fingers twitching at the trigger. One hiccup and the son-of-a-bitch would blow my balls off.

'OK, gotta go.'

'CHUZZEZ!'

'Let's try this again . . . Cheese!'

'CHUZZEZ!'

'Jonka, I have been looking for you. Actually over there, but of course you seem to be here now and, well . . . didn't we have our pictures taken with these same boys in Sokhumi?'

'Nope, these guys are far more drunk. Why's everybody so excited over there?'

'There is an enemy tank in the field.'

'Christ, people round here got tanks on the brain.'

'Well, one of them says he saw it, so now they all do.'

'If it was a fuckin' tank, we'd all be dead by now. I mean, it's not like this circus is actually sneakin' up on anybody.'

'I agree. But they say something is definitely out there, by that copse of trees.'

'What the hell's a copse?'

Two hundred yards past the village. A clump of bushy trees sticking out above the summer wheat. Seemed harmless enough.

'I don't see anything.'

'They say they can see it shining. Actually, there are two schools of thought here . . .'

And Oleg glancing round at the drunken road warriors itching for something to destroy.

'. . . perhaps school is not the correct word . . .'

'Nope, maybe not.'

'. . . but some say it is a tank and others say it is a sniper.'

'Pretty hard to confuse a sniper with a tank, ain't it?'

We both glanced round the drunken mob once more. Everyone reloading and drinking and arguing and shouting orders to everyone else all at the same time.

'Then again, maybe not.'

Voices called to the rear for something or someone. A few hushed moments, then from out of the mob came Goliath, as if risen from the past to stomp through the world of mere mortals once more. His massive Goliath chest pumped and swollen under a striped muscle-man T-shirt. His huge Goliath arms rippling with power as he swung a rocket-propelled grenade launcher across his shoulder like a tinker toy. And popping out of the top of his trousers, one spare Goliath 30mm RPG shell, erect and ready.

'Oleg, this is now officially weird, real weird.'

Goliath took careful aim out towards the trees. Soldiers stepped back giving him room to swing to and fro, searching for the target.

'Ah, Jon, Oleg. Anything happening?'

'Not sure, Julian. They wanna destroy somethin' out there.'

'They could use a pair of binoculars.'

'Hell, Julian. Good idea.'

And up next to Goliath. Camera on my shoulder and flipping the lens-extender into 320mm of long vision. Goliath looked down with a smirk on his Goliath face.

'Jon, I hate to disappoint you but his is definitely bigger. Wouldn't you agree, Oleg?'

'*Konyechno*.'

Zooming the lens out across the field and into the trees towards the mysterious soon-to-be-dead whateveritwas. Turn the focus ring to reveal . . . a huge sheet of plastic tied tentlike along the branches of a tree. A herd of goats grazing in the tall grass nearby.

'Shit! Stop! Stop!' I yelled.

The road warriors stared at me with contempt. Goliath's smirk melted into scorn.

'Oleg! It's a tent! A big plastic tent!'

'What?'

'Tied on to tree branches. It's a fuckin' tent!'

'What?'

'It's a tent. Plastic tent. Out there.'

'Uh, well . . . what?'

'I think you'd better say somethin' quick.'

And Oleg panning quick across the glaring faces.

'Jonka. They will be very disappointed.'

'Well, how 'bout that old lady or some kid out there watchin' their fuckin' goats? One minute it's "home, home on the range" and the next minute they're all blown to shit by a bunch of drunken road-warrior crazies!'

And Oleg taking a deep breath and standing up about eye level to Goliath's belt.

'This should be entertaining,' mused Julian.

'Yup,' I said.

Oleg coughed and explained that Comrade Cameraman, from Kompaniya Televideniya Britanskaya, ITN, had a very good lens mounted on a very good camera, and after careful study Comrade Cameraman could see that the offending object was neither a tank nor a sniper but was, in fact, some insignificant village shepherd tending goats.

Silence.

Much shrugging of shoulders.

Soldiers shuffling back to buses and trucks.

And Goliath looming low into my face and coughing up a big glob of brown spit and me watching it bubble over his lip and hang there for a half second before it rolled free and fell down and went splat! near my boots. He stuffed the RPG into his armpit and swaggered back to his bus. The whole thing leaned to one side as he climbed aboard.

'Congratulations, Comrade General Jonka!'

'Huh?'

'You have just given the order to advance!'

'I have?'

Trucks and buses started up and the road-warrior stampede began to pull away.

'*Da!* And may I say, Comrade General, I hope that there is *nyet* tank out in the copse of trees.'

'Could be a minor source of embarrassment.'

'It would be your ass, Comrade General Jonka. But I'm sure that your large friend with the exploding vibrator will be happy to hear your explanation.'

'I shall address the troops!'

'*Da, moi general!*'

Up on the side of the road, camera on my shoulder and the lens watching the drunken faces roll by.

'Always cheers the boys to put 'em on TV.'

'*Da, moi general!*'

Rifles and brandy and road-warrior hands waving furiously over-head . . . believing and hoping that somewhere along this road there had to be someone to kill.

'*Urah!*'

We ran back to our cars, passing six Georgian soldiers busily cramming themselves into a small white Lada like a troop of circus clowns. Kalashnikovs and arms and legs poking out the windows . . .

'*Oye! Allo! Snimitye nashu gruppu!*'

. . . and smiling through yellow teeth and posing for the lens.

I laughed and waved them away. 'Ah, fuck off! Get to the front, then I'll take your picture.'

They laughed loud and hard. One pretending to threaten me with his rifle, another inviting me along for the ride. The driver revving the four cylinders like 'Hi, ho, Silver!' and speeding off to take the point. Arms and rifles waving goodbye.

'*Urah!*' I yelled. 'Go for it!'

And holding the camera high above my head and shaking it like a prize. And hearing their voices cheer and laugh as I watched them fade into the dust.

'Jon, do you not wonder what all these pictures might be doing to you?'

'Nope.'

'Why not?'

'You ask a lot of questions, Bridget.'

'I'm a budding journalist. Pretend you're being interviewed and pour me some more champagne. Do you ever think there could be more to life than taking pictures, these kinds of pictures?'

'Maybe, but takin' these kinda pictures is the only thing I'm any good at just now.'

'Doesn't it get to you?'

'Can't really think about it.'

'Why not?'

'Just can't think and take pictures at the same time. Doesn't work that way. Kinda have to disconnect one side of the brain from the other.'

'Need I point out the general disconnectedness of your brain in the first place?'

'Guess that's why I'm good at it.'

'What does it feel like? C'mon, you can do it. What does it feel like?'

'Sometimes it's fun, sometimes it's scary. Sometimes it's like I'm ridin' this weird merry-go-round that I can't get off. All the horses and giraffes and everything else goin' at a dead run in opposite directions. One hoof outa step and wham.'

'Maybe you should slow down.'

'Slowin' down ain't the problem.'

'Enlighten me.'

'It's tryin' to remember why I climbed on in the first place.'

'Oleg! What do you mean, "The drivers will not go on"?'

'Julian, I am telling you they simply do not wish to go on.'

Down the road, gunfire crackling like popcorn.

'I'm sure the sight of us puttin' on flak-jackets ain't very reassuring.'

Crunch time. One more hour and we'd be off *News at Ten*.

'Judas Priest.'

'If it takes money, Oleg, do it.'

Whatever Oleg offered took about a half second to register in the drivers' bandit skulls. They jumped behind the wheels and took off after the stampede, racing through long tree shadows across the road. The sun sinking down into golden fields. A railroad yard tucked nearby the trees. An overpass beyond the tracks.

'Great place for a fuckin' ambush, ain't it?'

Brakes and screeching tyres as machine-guns exploded on both sides of the roadway.

'Shit!'

'Bingo!'

Road warriors dived from their vehicles and hit the deck. They opened fire in a wide arc. We jumped out of the cars and into a ditch, pinned up next to an abandoned house. An APC blasting shells towards the overpass. The road warriors keeping low to the ground and crawling through tall grass, rifle barrels peeking over railroad tracks and firing double taps up the road.

'Can't get a decent shot from here! Shit!'

'Stay here, Jonka!'

Round the corner of the house, road warriors spreading out in a cemetery, crouching for cover behind gravestones, bullets smashing into the slabs and stone chips flying like broken glass.

'That's it. That's the one.'

'What are you thinking, Jonka?'

'Guys firing over the gravestones. Just need to run twenty yards.'

Down and ready to dash. Oleg eyeballing the soldiers and seeing the crossfire from the fields and railroad yard.

'No, Jonka!'

'Bullshit! It's a great shot!'

I threw the camera on to my shoulder and crouched ready to run. Oleg's hands grabbed the back of my body armour and pulled hard. 'Jonka! What is the matter with you? You are being stupid!'

Gunfire whipping through my head and the blood pumping faster and feeling the purity of the rush burning away every care of life and a voice wailing sirenlike in my head, DO IT! DO IT! DO IT!

'It'll be OK! C'mon, Oleg!'

Oleg pushed me up against the house, anger flashing in his eyes. 'Jonka! You will be killed!'

'Fuck sake, Oleg!'

'Listen to me, Jonka!'

'Shit!'

'It is too dangerous!'

'Fuck you! That's not the fuckin' point!'

'Fuck you, Jonka! What *is* the point?'

'There's nothin' I can do, Kate.'

'That's it? Jon, you can't be this cut off from everything. It's like you're crawling into a shell and I can't reach you any more. We can't go on this way.'

'What am I s'posed to do? Quit? I finally got somethin' I'm good at in my life. People respect me. Don't you fuckin' get it?'

'Look what it's doing to you.'

'It's given me a life!'

'Losing our marriage isn't life, Jon. Let's just go home to America. Let's leave all this. Is there anything more important than us? This isn't worth it.'

'Kate, this is what I do.'

'How can it be worth it? I'm your wife and you're treating me like a stranger in your life. Look at me, Jon, look into my eyes. It's me, Kate.'

'You don't like it here, you leave.'

'Come on, Jon. This isn't fair.'

'I don't need this.'

'You need some help.'

'I don't need help! I don't need anyone!'

The rifles went quiet. Stood there breathing hard and fast, like the rush was fading away and there was nothing left but the gnawing hunger for more. Up on the overpass a road-warrior shadow waving a rifle. All clear.

'Fuck it. Let's see if there are any pictures on the road.'

'Uh, well . . . yes.'

Soldiers crawled out from cover and eased on to the road, their rifles pointing and searching, wanting to kill some more. One of Gamzekhurdia's rebels splayed out on the road like Christ. Hands as if nailed to the asphalt, big hole in his side. The road warriors leaned over for a slow gaze into the still and open eyes.

Pan right. Another trail of blood leading out of frame. The lens following like a bloodhound, sniffing and sucking at the scent of images pouring through the glass. Motionless legs and more blood, a rifle in the road, blood on the trigger. Pan up and pull wide.

'Oh, fuck.'

A small white Lada blown to hell. The bonnet cut open by a hail of bullets. The windshield shattered to bits and the doors full of holes, blood smeared down the side like paint. On the ground, the soldier who invited me along for a ride. He was bleeding the last of his life on to the road. Another body pulled from the car, dead hands and dead eyes. The road warriors laid him on the ground and covered his dead face with a cloth. Two men, two fathers, two husbands. They'd stuffed themselves into a Lada like clowns and raced to the front because they wanted to be on TV. And me standing over their bullet-ridden corpses, camera in my hands, like a weapon.

'Fuck me, just in time for *News at Ten*.'

'What did you say, Jonka?'

'Nothin'. Forget it. Just fuckin' forget it.'

'You must remember you are a kind person. You've been kind to me. You're kind to everyone around you. You would not deliberately hurt anyone. Are you listening to me, Jon?'

'Yup, nope.'

'You just need to be kind to yourself.'

'Fucksake, Bridget. This from a woman who can never find her fuckin' house keys.'

'Oh, don't be horrible, you horrible man.'

'Ain't horrible, just sayin' the truth.'

'You are a mystery, Jon Steele.'

'Only mystery round here is gettin' more champagne in my glass.'

'I may be slightly intoxicated but I can still see through you, Jon Steele. A man like you needs the love of a good woman.'

'Funny, I thought the same thing for a while. Turns out the entire art form is sorta beyond me.'

'It can't be that difficult to let someone close to you.'

'Bridget. I ain't very good at it. I tend to fuck it up.'

Walking along the road looking for another dose of war but it was all gone for now. Time to move on. Me and Oleg and Julian and Eddie jumped in the Ladas and eased through the rail yard back towards Kutaisi. A group of men were loading the bodies of the dead road warriors on to the back of a small truck, the bodies now wrapped in bloodsoaked sheets. Another group of men dragged the bodies of the rebels across the asphalt and tossed them into the weeds along the side of the road. A pack of wild dogs circled nearby. They sniffed the air and licked their muzzles and crept hungrily towards the feast.

'Great fuckin' shot that one, ain't it?'

'Jon, please . . .'

I pulled the door closed behind me and stood in the dark stairwell, listening to the sounds of your voice calling from far away.

'. . . don't run away. Don't do this to yourself. Don't do this to us.'

I just have to go, Kate . . . and I don't even know why.

POSTCARDS FROM A TRAIN

December something, 1993

RINGGGGGGGGG!

   RINGGGGGGGGG!

   'Fuckin' hell. *Da?'*

   'Do not for one moment pretend that you speak this most beautiful of languages.'

   'Jesus . . . Bridget, it's dark outside.'

   'What time did you get home?'

   'Dunno. It was dark then too. Can't this wait till the sun comes up?'

   'The sun has already come up and gone down again, you stupid git.'

   ' 'Scuse me?'

   'It is winter in this most glorious of countries. That would be Russia as your memory is most probably still soaking in alcohol. And you have missed all the sun there is today.'

   'Oh.'

   'Is there a woman in your bed?'

   'None of your business.'

   'Of course. How silly of me. That business, I assume, would be hers.'

   'Bridget . . .'

'Now, listen, you worthless pile of poo.'

'What is it with you Brits and number two?'

'I have told you before to stop acting like such an American. *Number two*, as you reprovingly call it, is in fact a perfectly normal function of the body for all members of the human race except Americans, where it seems the first sign of turtle head is cause for a declaration of national emergency.'

'What the hell's turtle head?'

'Think, Jon, a little turtle pokes his little head out of the—'

'OK, never mind. I'm hangin' up now.'

'How nice for Olga.'

'How'd you know her name?'

'Oh, for God's sake, Jon. Fifty-five per cent of the women in this country are named Olga, the other fifty-five per cent are named Natasha and the other fifty-five per cent are named Svetlana.'

'Fuck me.'

'Speak to Olga. I'm way out of your price range.'

'Tart.'

'Bastard. Now, listen. Stinky James Mates phoned from London. You may recall there is an important election in Russia three weeks from today.'

'Yeah, yeah.'

'Do not be smug while addressing your producer. By the way, you do drop to your knees at the mere sound of my voice, don't you?'

'Yeah, yeah.'

'Oh! You are worse than that worthless pile of poo. You are lower than a worm. You are beneath contempt. You are—'

'Sayin' there's an election.'

'Ah, yes, the election. At any rate we have decided it's time you stopped being such a show-off, running from this war to that war. You need some real work for a change. Now, London wants a preview piece before the big day. Get out there and see what Ivan and Olga are thinking.'

'Just a second, I'll ask her.'

'Not *that* Olga, you disgusting pervert. I speak of the millions of other Olgas in this glorious land.'

'What the hell you talkin' about?'

'What we are talking about is a little trip across Russia.'

'What kind of little trip?'

'The Trans-Siberian Express! Can you believe it? From Vladivostok to Moscow! You and me and stinky James Mates!'

'The train.'

'*Yes!*'

'Across Siberia.'

'*Yes! Yes!*'

'In the middle of fuckin' winter.'

'*Yes! Yes! Yes!*'

'You sure 'bout this?'

'*Yes! Yes! Yes! Yes!* Isn't it the best?'

Click.

Midnight. Domodedevo airport, Moscow

'No, that is the flight number. Aeroflot 007. Why?'

'Just sounds weird, don't it? Russia . . . 007. The licence plate on my fuckin' car is 001. James Bond was . . .'

'You're not going to babble on about life and movies, are you?'

'Well, then, you explain it.'

Me and Bridget marching down the stairs of the unheated terminal building, icicles hanging from the ceiling. We were being herded on to an unheated bus stuffed with a bunch of Russians in mangy fur hats and smelly old coats. Blasts of snow gushing through squared-out holes where the windows used to be.

'We're doomed.'

'Oh, stop acting like such a coward. It's only a little snow.'

'It's a fuckin' blizzard.'

'My God, how did you Americans end up as the last remaining superpower on earth?'

'Whaddaya mean? Look around. It's like the crash scene from some airplane flick and we haven't even taken off yet.'

'Oh, stop whining, you silly old git. This is the most fun you've ever had!'

Her eyebrows wiggling like caterpillars, a giggly smile on her face.

'Swell. I'm travellin' round the globe with a two-year-old.'

'No, that would be stinky James Mates. He will join us in a few days.'

The bus driver wandered blind through the storm till he spotted a Tupolev jet planted in a faraway snowdrift. He spat and kicked open the bus doors and pointed into the storm.

'Get out!'

We obeyed and trudged through the blizzard like Napoleon's army, lost in a howling whiteness, till ploughing up near the threadbare tyres of the jet's nose gear. Baggage-handlers under the fuselage sorted through gargantuan bundles wrapped in the same knitted red and blue and white plastic you see all over Russia and China and the third world. They hammered and crushed and crammed the bundles into an already overstuffed cargo hold.

'S'pose the pilots have any idea how much stuff is gettin' loaded on to this thing?'

'Of course not, you fool. The pilots are far too busy stuffing their families and friends into the cockpit.'

'You don't say.'

And over there two men on a fuel truck jamming the nozzle end of a long hose into the portside wing tank. The nozzle popped off and jet fuel splashed down the truck and on to the snow. One man thought it a good idea to turn off the fuel flow. The other thought it a good idea to light a cigarette.

'I need a joint.'

'Don't be ridiculous. This is all perfectly normal for Aeroflot Airlines.'

'Then I really do need a joint.'

Up the gangway, a fat but shapeless woman in an even fatter and more shapeless coat stood at the top of the stairs. She greeted us with that official Soviet scowl. Annoyed as hell to be taken away from her foot-heater and warm *chai*. She pointed a finger towards the jet door. 'Get in!'

Tattered seats, most of them broken. A shredded carpet over a floor of rusting metal, toilet stench that could choke a horse. Baggage stacked in the aisle and seats jammed with a few hundred Russians, all staring at us with that 'Abandon Hope All Ye Who Enter Here' gawk in their eyes.

'Fuck me. It's the gulag express.'

'Nonsense. Just the huddled masses of happy comrades.'

Took a few acrobatic moves to pull off our coats and hats without bashing some poor babushka in the gums. We squeezed into our seats.

'Very comfy.'

'Do not insult the national airline of this once glorious empire. You know perfectly well that the seating arrangements were designed in accordance with the Soviet ideal of a classless society.'

'Meaning the seat in front locks your legs into a vice so the knees behind you can dig through the back seat and grind your kidneys to pulp.'

'Of course. It keeps one in one's place, for ever. Perfectly logical.'

The fat woman in the fatter coat slammed the door closed over and over again trying to make it fit. Clouds of snow rushed by her fat red face.

'Urrummmppf!'

Clunk! Clunk! Clunk!

'We're fuckin' doomed.'

Her distorted voice squealing through the speakers . . .

'*Uvazhayemye passazhiri! Dobro pozhalovat . . .*'

'Ah, I shall translate. The nice woman has just welcomed us as the "Dear Passengers" . . .'

'Oh, swell.'

'. . . and that the flight will take sixteen hours and do not even think about disturbing her or any other members of the crew as they will be sleeping throughout most of the trip.'

The dear passengers quickly set out their supplies of breads and meats and a blinding array of alcohol. A few fast belts down throats and Aeroflot 007 roared down the runway. Bottles rattling and glasses shaking, but not a drop was spilled.

Bridget opened our own bag of goodies. Smoked salmon, bread, cheese, apples and red wine. The burly guy with his knees in my kidneys passed up two glasses of homemade brandy. We passed back some wine.

'How can you foreigners drink such *ochen plokho* piss-water?'

'Funny. I was gonna ask you the same thing, Boris.'

'How you know my name ees Boris?'

'Easy, fifty-five per cent of the women in this country are named Olga.'

'You clever foreng man! Let us toast and drink!'

'OK, comrade. Cheers!'

A bottle of vodka from across the aisle and apples in return.

More heartfelt toasts.

A rather green salami from somewhere overhead.

'How kind. Salmon?'

'To international co-operation and friendship!'

'To understanding between peoples!'

'Legalize dope!'

'*Kto?*'

Bridget poured out more wine. 'Dearie me. One would have taught . . . I mean . . . thought . . . thish bottle of fine *vino* was just fullish a minute ago.'

'Bridget. You're fuckin' pissed.'

'Of course I'm pissed, you idiot. Who in their right mind flies Aeroflop while shober?'

A drunken stupor settled through the jet. Heavy snores in harmony with the hum of the jet engines. Bridget shoved me up against the fuselage and fluffed me up like a pillow. She threw her big down coat over her legs and dropped her head on my chest.

'Arm.'

'No thanks, I'm full.'

She rolled her eyes and grabbed my wrist and pulled my arm round her shoulders. 'You are such a silly old git.'

She fell asleep somewhere over Siberia.

On the edge of Russia

Ice-blue light. Ice-blue clouds. Twenty below zero. An endless frozen horizon of ice and sky. I stared in silence, holding my breath and feeling the cold wind on my face.

'Shall we?'

'Shall we what?'

'For fucksake.'

And I pushed Bridget on to the ice and she skidded out on to the Sea of Japan like Jesus on the water.

'Good. You didn't fall through. Now let's hike over towards those fishermen.'

'What fishermen?'

'Out there. Look like little ink spots on the ice.'

'Those "ink spots" seem a very long way "out there" on the ice.'

''Bout one kilometre. Here . . . catch the tripod.'

'Jon, I am the producer. And as such one should not expect—'

'Here.'

'Hallo! This fucking thing is heavy!'

'Yup.'

'One could fall through the ice and drown.'

'Precisely. You go first.'

'Charming and desirable, yes. Stupid, *nyet*. You first, spiky monster.'

Thick winter boots slipping and sliding with babylike steps. Arms this way and that way trying to find a sense of balance. We circled round shallow spots and followed dog tracks further and further and further till the village back along the shoreline fell below the horizon and there was nothing left but thin curls of woodsmoke and the tops of faraway trees . . .

'My, my. We are a long way from anywhere.'

'Yup.'

. . . and turning towards the ink-spot dots way out on the ice. My eyes panned and zoomed and settled on one solitary spot just a bit left of a low-hanging sun.

'Let's go talk to that guy.'

'Why?'

'Dunno. Looks good in the light. Kinda like the lone ice fisherman.'

'Oh, yes, please. Let us follow Jon Steele's crazed visions of light across the endless realms of frozen waste.'

''Scuse me?'

'Nothing. Lead on, Picasso. Then, given the grandeur of the scene, perhaps Monet or no, no . . . Turner. And one day our bodies shall be found clutching hold of each other and people will write poems about the beautiful young producer who followed her idiot cameraman to the ends of the earth and—'

'Fuck me. Look at it.'

'Look at what?'

'That. All of it.'

Turning round and round in a circle. Ripples and waves of the Sea of Japan caught and frozen in mid-swell as if time and motion just stopped and the world would stay frozen for ever.

'Don't think I've ever seen anything like it before.'

'It isn't bad.'

'Nope.'

Half-hour later we came close enough to make out the lone ice fisherman. He was sitting on a small wooden crate. He was wrapped in a coat that might have been warm ten or twelve years ago. Now thinned out and winter-worn. Raggedy mittens over his hands and a plastic line dropping from his grip and bobbing up and down through a small hole carved in the ice. Ice as thick and solid as concrete. The fisherman looked up from under his fox-fur hat and caught sight of two half-frozen foreigners with a television camera. He smiled with a face so cold I thought it might crack.

'*Ochen kholodno*,' he said.

'Yup, cold.'

'Actually he said "very cold".'

Clear green water lapping and slurping through the ice hole. Small splashes rising and freezing and the lone ice fisherman's Russian words mixing with Bridget's English words in the very cold.

'I saw you walking across the ice. I wasn't sure you were real. You see a lot of things out here on the ice. Some things are real and some things are only in your mind. It's difficult to tell the difference sometimes. You are real, aren't you?'

'*Da*. We are real.'

'*Khorosho*. Are you from Japan?'

'*Nyet. Britanskoye televideniye.*'

'Ah.'

The fisherman was from the Ukraine. He had come to the Soviet Far East a long time ago. Something about a job or a woman, he couldn't remember . . . they were the dreams of a young man. One day the dreams wandered off across the ice and never came back. Now he was just an old man wanting to go home before he died. 'But I don't have any money and, anyway, there is no work in the Ukraine. So I can only sit out here on the ice and fish for my supper.'

The line jerked and the fisherman yanked a small silver fish from the ice hole. The fisherman's hands coming out of his mittens. Old hands cut and cracked from the cold. He worked the fish from the hook and tossed it on to the ice. The fish jumped and flipped till it lay frozen as the Sea of Japan. The fisherman lit a cigarette and let hot smoke sink into his lungs. He exhaled with a slow sigh.

'I'll have to catch a lot more if I'm going to eat today.'

Fresh bait on the hook and the line back down the hole. Mittens over freezing hands.

'*Ochen kholodno.*'

'And what do you think of the election next month?'

'Is there an election?'

'*Da.*'

'For what?'

'For the Russian parliament, then for president.'

'Ah, *konyechno*. Will this election make any difference to this place?'

'What place?'

'This place on the ice. We are a long way from Moscow out here on the ice.'

'Will you vote?'

'What is voting? We are Soviets, I think. Nobody knows what we are any more. But we know nothing of democracy. It's only a way for corrupt fat men to grow more fat.'

'So you will not vote?'

'*Nyet*. I'll stay and fish. You can't eat democracy, can you?'

I walked away with the camera looking for a picture. A picture to show how small and alone he was out there on the endless ice. I framed him against the sun and set him low and off centre in the lens. Pale light wrapping all round him. A tiny shadow on an Impressionist canvas of ice blues and steel greys, frozen in the cold wind.

'Getting what you need?' asked Bridget.

'Your lips are blue.'

'You try speaking Russian in this cold.'

She pulled the hood of her coat tight round her face. Her eyes peeked through the fur. 'Yes? What are you looking at?'

'You look kinda Russian just now.'

She stomped her feet on the ice and shivered, trying to get warm. I put my arms round her and pulled her close against the wind.

'Don't get any ideas, you stupid old git. Just take the pictures.'

'Don't think I can do any more.'

'How do you mean?'

The sun slid down on to the ice and spread an orange glow across the frozen waves. The sky faded into a deeper shade of blue. Off in the distance, the spark of the first night star.

'Christ. Look at it. Just about the most beautiful place I've ever seen. How am I s'posed to stuff all this into a lens? Picture's just too damn big.'

'You're enjoying yourself, aren't you, Jon?'

'S'pose I am.'

'Good. Now, take your hands off me and let's get the fuck out of here. I can't feel my feet.'

We said goodbye to the lone ice fisherman and wished him well. He waved us off with another frozen grin. 'I'm not sure you strangers are real. You might be one of those things I see on the ice at times.'

'Nope. We're real.'

'And you're not from Japan?'

'Nope. Not from Japan.'

'*Tak*. Real or not it was nice to talk to someone. *Do svidaniya*.'

Vladivostok

The Soviet national anthem blares from tinny speakers at midnight. The conductor waves a lantern and the engineer opens a switch and two powerful diesel engines huff and puff and the Trans-Siberian Express surges ahead on two steel rails. Two steel rails that stretch ten thousand kilometres across Russia. The last celebration of an empire long gone.

I knelt on the ground and let the massive steel wheels churn slowly through the lens. Steel and steam and ice in my eyes. The conductor leaning out the last rail car and looking down as he floated by. Happy as a kid in a candy shop.

CHOOOOOOOOT! CHOOOOOOOOT!

'Now, listen, Jon. One of these days we are actually going to have to get on this train!'

'Soon as I get all the shots I need.'

'How many shots of trains and people getting on trains and people getting off trains do you need?'

'Lots of 'em.'

'You're lying.'

I'd been dragging Bridget from one location to another. Daytime, night-time, anytime. I was shooting miles of tape and loving it. Standing in a small village watching the train snake through the trees and around the bends, the Red Star of the Soviet Union still anchored across the grille of the gigantic locomotive, leading the way. Watching it race faster and closer till just when it felt like it would rip through the picture and roll over me, the locomotive'd veer off and pull the train away like a toy. Must've done that shot twenty times already. And once lying in a snowbank under the moon and the stars, on-coming train light pouring over the sleepers and steel rails, glistening and humming and then ... WHOOOOSH! A ribbon of light flying through the lens and seeing all the faces of Russia through a cloud of snow. And, in the blink of an eye, the red tail-lights slipping away and fading into the dark.

'Kinda nice to take pictures without dead people in 'em.'

'You certainly know how to talk to a girl, don't you? I'll get some tea.'

I wandered into the train yard looking for more pictures. Lots of low-angle shots from the ground. Old women dragging bundles, beggars praying and crossing their hearts, a train worker smashing ice from steel wheels. All good fun, till a pair of scruffy boots plopped down in front of the lens. I looked up at a stern Russian face under a stiff Russian hat. The hat had a badge.

'*Vy arrestovany!*'

'Oops.'

'*Vashe dokumyenty!*'

I got up and showed Comrade Traincop my press credentials. He was unimpressed. He sputtered in nasty Russian about not taking pictures of trains and violations of national security and what the hell was I doing in his train yard anyway, foreign pig?

'Uh, Bridget!'

She sauntered over in her own good time. 'Getting arrested already? I cannot believe you've spent so much time in this great and good land and you still cannot speak the language to any level of comprehension. Instead you insist on taking endless pictures in direct violation of Russian law. I told you so, but would you listen? *Noooo.* I should just let this worthy official drag you off to prison where you would be buggered by large men with colourful tattoos. Yes, that's what I should do.'

'OK. We get on the fuckin' train.'

'I thought so. Step aside, you American imbecile.'

A slow turn to the cop. A warm smile. A well-poised and cultured hand. Lights, camera, action!

'Hallo. My name is Bridget.'

Somewhere on the Trans-Siberian Express

Clickityclak, kaclickityclak.

Hot tea swirled in the glass. Slow and easy circles. The cup was steaming and the steam fogged the window near my face. I traced squiggles in the fog and peered through the looking-glass to see Russia. Vast fields of snow, patches of silver birch trees, sleeping fields waiting for the sun. And just on the edge of nowhere, a village of painted wood cottages with yellow lanterns in frost-flowered windows. Windows lined with delicate old lace. Faraway places where villagers huddled close to their samovars and told stories and sipped hot black tea and listened to the sound of the train rolling by in the night.

Clickityclak, kaclickityclak, clickityclak, kaclickityclak.

The door pulled open and James Mates piled into the compartment with two bottles of Châteauneuf du Pape.

'Right, let's have some wine.'

'Sounds good.'

'I mean, it isn't often one can drink a fine wine on the Trans-Siberian Express in the middle of winter.'

'S'pose not.'

'Good trip so far?'

'Been fun at times.'

'Good. The most important part of this story is to have fun.'

'Nice wine.'

'Yeees. We just have to hide it from you-know-who.'

'You mean *her*.'

The door pulled open again and Bridget barged in with an empty glass. 'Right! I'm not having it. None of this *Boy's Own* nonsense.'

'On the contrary, my dear, we were just speaking of you.'

'Yes. I bet. Pour me some wine, darling.'

'Which one of us is "darling"?'

'I don't give a poo jab. Just pour.'

'Speaking of which, terribly difficult to have a poo on this train,

don't you think? Rocking from side to side over a hole in the flo
feel like a bombardier in the RAF.'

'Yes, how true. One must gauge the trajectory and proper wind
speed for a successful drop.'

'For fucksake.'

'Oh, there goes our American friend again. All squirmy at the mere
mention of poo.'

'Indeed, squirmy.'

'Silly American.'

'Indeed. More wine, Bridget?'

'Thank you, darling James.'

'Christ. I'm sittin' here in the quiet watchin' the world go by and you
two Brits stumble in with visions of number two in your heads.'

'See, James? He can't even say it!'

'Well, he is an American, after all.'

'Come on, Jon, say it . . . "poo".'

'Fuck off.'

'Come on . . . poo, poo!'

'Yes, say it!'

The door pulled open again and a fat Russian in a sleeveless T-shirt
tumbled in with a bottle of vodka.

'*Dobryi vecher! Menya zavut, Anatoly!*'

'Good evening, my dear Mr Anatoly. I am James Mates and these
would be my colleagues.'

'Te foreeng people!'

'Indeed. We were just discussing your toilets.'

'Toilets in Russia shit!'

'Well, actually, we believe it to be a matter of trajectory and wind
speed.'

'*Nyet problemy*. We drink!'

'And how do you feel about the upcoming elections?'

'Elections in Russia shit!'

'Will you be voting for Mr Yeltsin's party?'

'Yeltsin! Bolshoi shit!'

'Ah, a Communist.'

'Communism shit!'

'Most insightful. Perhaps we should interview this chap.'

'I want buy woman.'

'Now we're talkin'.'

'Did our beastly friend just say, "buy woman"?'

'Stay out of this, Bridget. James, open another bottle?'

'My dear chap.'

'How much woman?'

'Oh, let me think.'

'I give two hundred roubles.'

'Two hundred roubles!'

'Stay out of this, Bridget. More wine, James?'

'What do you mean, "Stay out of this, Bridget"?'

'Well, I am afraid, my dear sir, that is a ridiculous offer. I mean look at her. She is of prime British stock . . .'

' "Prime British stock"!'

'Stay the fuck out of this, Bridget.'

'. . . and as ITN correspondent, and leader of this team, I must insist the price be no more than one hundred roubles!'

'One hundred roubles!'

'Stay the fuck out of this, Bridget.'

'*Nyet problemy. Mnogo* drink!'

'Listen, you cretins! I am not a piece of meat to be bartered on a train!'

'Course you are. We got all these excess-baggage bills to cover.'

' "Excess baggage"!'

'Indeed. Just lie back and think of England.'

'That was Queen Victoria, you twit! Pour me some more wine. If I'm about to be ravished by this beast I'd best be well pissed.'

'Woman mine, *da*?'

'Well, actually, no. As much as it would please us to accommodate you, I'm afraid we must decline. You see, for some inexplicable reason, the woman is in love with our American cameraman here.'

'America *ochin* good! Want go America! USA! USA! USA!'

'Hang on. What about Great Britain?'

'Greet Britain shit!'

'I'll fuckin' drink to that!'

'Excuse me!'

'You love woman?'

'Well, not really . . . ouch!'

'Choose your next words very carefully, Mr Steele, or the next kick shall land in the midst of your testicles.'

'Yeah, yeah . . . it's love.'

'My hero.'

'Love *v* Russia shit!'

'I'll drink to that!'

'Me too!'

'*Da!* We drink!'

The door pulled open again and the conductress stood glaring in all her one hundred and ten kilos of uniformed authority.

'*Chto eto takoye?*'

'Yikes!'

'My God. It's the fuckin' Wicked Witch of the East.'

'No, Boris Yeltsin in drag.'

'Fifty roubles!'

The conductress's eyes narrowed at the booze and general immorality of the scene. 'Sleep! Now!'

'Well, I guess that's that.'

'Indeed.'

We poured one more for the rails and locked ourselves in our compartments. The booze and the laughter and the rhythm of the train mixing with dreamy sleep.

Clickityclak, kaclickityclak, clickityclak, kaclickityclak.

Irkusk. Twenty-nine below zero

Standing in the freezing snow staring at the monster. It wasn't pretty. A Leontyevich Mil Russian helicopter with steaming oil leaking from the engine and dripping over the word 'Aeroflot' painted along the side. This because our Cheery Pilot was on top of the thing, banging away at the rotor mount with a monkey wrench. He was having some trouble getting the monster to start up in the cold. He looked over and waved and smiled and nodded with confidence, dirty blond hair poking out from his leather flying helmet.

'Correct me if I'm wrong, but that fuckin' guy is cross-eyed.'

'Oh, don't be such a baby,' said Bridget.

'Whose dumb-ass idea was it to get aerials anyway?'

'That dumb ass would be the deputy editor of ITN in London.'

'You were saying, Jon?'

'I was sayin' damn good idea. Solid management thinking.'

'Yes. I thought so.'

We tossed the camera gear behind the seats and climbed in.

Kachugga, kachugga, kaphew, karrrrrrrrunnnng!

Lift-off.

'*Urah!*'

Me sitting up front with Our Cheery Pilot, James and Bridget in the rear. All of us wearing big-eared headsets with microphones to communicate through the screaming noise of the engine. I looked back through a maze of wires and cables and switches. James and Bridget were shaking from head to toe . . . both of them with goofy grins on their faces like they'd been sucking on laughing gas most of the morning. The chopper floated higher and higher and cleared the trees. Quick bank left and head for the railroad tracks. Ten minutes into the flight I noticed ice forming in the corners of the windows.

'Bridget, could the pilot kick on the heat.'

Moments of squelched Russian through headsets.

'The nice man says, "It *is* on." '

'My toes are numb.'

'Oh, don't be such a baby.'

We flew at three hundred metres above the rails looking for the Trans-Siberian Express. Soon the road next to the tracks vanished under the snow and villages became few and far between. The chopper vibrated like a kitchen blender. Nuts and bolts holding the monster together seemed to come unglued. I glanced at Our Cheery Pilot; he winked with his good eye.

James tapped me on the shoulder and pointed down through the trees. 'There's the train. Roll, please, cameraman.'

I looked back at the faces in the rear. Goofy grins getting bigger and James turning to Bridget.

'Oh, I do so love being boss!' said James.

'No, I want to be boss. You there! Cameraman! Take that picture!'

'No, I'm the boss!'

'No, me!'

The two of them pinching each other's arms like kids.

I twisted in the cockpit and put the camera on my lap trying not to knock out the flight controls. Focus through the windows and seeing nothing but an icy blur. 'Anybody notice anything funny about the windows?'

James rubbed the plastic and scraped away a few chunks of ice. 'Hmmm. Slightly worrying.'

'Bridget. Ask the pilot if everything is OK with this fuckin' thing.'

More squelched Russian.

'The nice man says everything is *normalno*.'

'Fine. Then can I open the door for a shot? I can't see shit.'

Squelched Russian again.

'The nice man says, "*Pozhaluista*." '

We tied down anything loose and I tightened my seat-belt. Our Cheery Pilot stretched across the flight controls and threw the locks. The door flew open and a blast of snow rushed into the cockpit. I leaned out into the wind.

'OK! Get him to hover above the train!'

Bridget talked Our Cheery Pilot through the moves. My face burning in the cold and a weird fog filling the cockpit.

'Jon, the nice man wants to know if you're finished.'

'He worried 'bout this fog?'

'Well, actually the nice man says it's smoke.'

'SMOKE?'

I pulled the door shut and secured the locks. Suddenly Our Cheery Pilot wasn't so cheery. He was flying blind and the chopper was drifting from side to side. The engine coughed and sputtered and the rotor blades groaned. He spoke in clipped Russian and his good eye twitched.

'Jon, he wants you to crawl into the back of the helicopter.'

'What? Now?'

'It seems he's lost control of the helicopter.'

'LOST CONTROL?'

I ripped off the headset, threw the camera over the seat and climbed over the comms panel. James and Bridget pulled me through and tossed me in the back with the baggage. The chopper's engine screeching and grinding as the Pilot struggled from one seat to the next, grabbing hold of the controls and pulling hard. We were spinning and falling through the sky.

'Oh, this is so fuckin' swell!' I yelled.

'Don't be such a baby!'

'Yes! Everything should be fine till we hit the ground!'

Our Not So Cheery Pilot pumped at the pedals and steadied the chopper as best he could. He pushed open the door and looked below. No doubt about it. We were going down. Like living in a fuckin' cartoon.

VUUUMPH!!!! GABOOF!!!

Silence.

'I told you I should have been boss,' said Bridget.

'Oh, bugger off.'

And me lying there thinking about my air-force air-jockey father a long time ago, stumbling stone drunk through the door and slapping me on the back and saying, 'Son, any landing you can walk away from is a good one.' Then he passed out cold.

'One of the few times the drunken bastard ever made sense.'

'Say something, Jon?'

'Nope.'

I kicked open the rear hatch and we jumped out into Siberia, right up to our hips in virgin snow. We'd come down in a small mountain meadow surrounded by tall green pine trees and white powdered hills. Four beat-up cabins sat half buried in snow.

'Well,' announced James, 'here we are.'

'Yes, isn't it lovely?' gushed Bridget.

'See how the sunlight sparkles on the snow?'

'Oh, it *is* so lovely.'

'Excuse me! I hate to interrupt this nature-fest, but did we even want to be here?'

A considered pause.

'Doesn't really matter, does it?'

'Yes. What does that have to do with the price of fish?'

More goofy grins.

Up on the ridge, the Trans-Siberian Express rolled round the bend and chugged on across a meadow of perfect snow. We waved.

Achinsk

Lamplight was gold and warm on his silver hair. He lit one more Cosmos cigarette and stared out over the endless Russian steppe. His sharp eyes locked on to that one faraway point on the horizon where a single black line in the snow spread into two impossibly small steel rails. His hands moving over the controls then pushing forward on a brass lever. Easy, easy till he found just the right rhythm for this stretch of track.

'Thirty years of my life I have been studying these rails. I know them like a musical score. I am the maestro. This train is my orchestra.'

Eight hundred tonnes of iron and wood and fragile Russian souls under the baton of the Maestro Engineer.

'Now we play *molto allegro.*'

And his fingers touched a red button and the locomotive's horn blared a solo note loud and for ever through the Siberian forests. A symphony for steel at seventy kilometres per hour. James and Bridget and the Maestro had been talking and laughing for hours. About his train, his home, his family… but mostly about his train. I was busy with pictures. Focusing through the windscreen and watching the lens swallow the rails with blinding speed. And ahead in the distance, tiny shadows in the snow and then *whoosh!* Close enough to touch as the train flew by. A peasant with a cow, a babushka with a bundle of firewood, rail workers swinging sledge-hammers, children with happy and dreaming eyes. Eyes and faces that smiled and disappeared like a flash of light. Maestro Engineer raised his hands and waved to each and every one.

'All the people love my train.'

'Do you know them?'

'*Konyechno.* I watch the men work in the fields and the women gather water and wood. I see their children play and grow and fall in love and make their own families. And one day they bring their own children to see my train. I am part of their life, they are part of mine.'

We swayed in time to the rhythm of the train and listened to the wind slap at the windscreen. The Maestro moved his hands once more and the locomotive followed his cue, slowing and curving through the trees. A gentle push on brass and the diesel engines pulled hard again. And the symphony for steel played to the south-west. *Allegro non troppo.*

'That is why it is hard to see them suffer.'

'How do you mean?'

'Life is hard now. Very hard. I see their clothes and their boots. Nothing is new, everything is old. People still smile but I can see the pain in their faces. Not enough food or medicine. The schools are run down. And there are more and fresh mounds of dirt in the graveyards.'

'Will you vote?'

'I will vote for Zhironovsky and the Nationalists.'

'Really?'

'Yes, but it will not matter. Yeltsin will win even if Zhironovsky gets more votes. The West will make sure of it.'

'Was it better under Communism?'

'Better? I don't know. But at least we were a nation, the Soviet Union. We had strong leaders and were respected throughout the world. Yeltsin has sold us to the West and the Russian Mafia. And now the people out here along these rails, they are all forgotten. That is why my train is so important to them.'

Another village in the distance and another solo from the horn. Smiles and faces and waving hands then gone again.

'My train is a symbol that somehow life will go on.'

'Like hope.'

'You must read more Russian literature and listen to more Russian music. Hope is not something you find in our nature as Russians. We do not hope. We survive.'

'And the Nationalists would be better than Yeltsin?'

'Perhaps, but it doesn't matter. We survived the tsars and the Tartars. We survived Fascism. We survived Stalin and the Cold War. And we will survive under Yeltsin and the West and whatever else God has planned for us. To be Russian is to survive.'

He lit another cigarette and drew the smoke deep into his Russian soul.

'Enough talk. Listen to my train,' he said.

It'd been a day of heavy clouds, the sun throbbing behind a curtain of grey. But now the light went soft and blue as evening spread across Siberia. The train pulled over a small hill and rolled into a wide valley of birch and snow. And dead ahead, a giant pale sun hanging just above the steel rails.

'Oh, my,' said Bridget.

Maestro Engineer smiled.

'Closin' shot.'

'Bit of a cliché, isn't it?'

'Nope. Not the way I'm gonna do it.'

I wobbled out of the control compartment and stumbled through the ear-splitting roar of the engine room, pulling open a side door and leaning out of the platform just behind the locomotive. The freezing wind scratching my face like pine needles. Quick look down the tracks. Speeding train on icy rails, trees brushing close to the train. A good shot getting better by the second and then it would be gone. Back into the locomotive.

'How long is this stretch of track?'

'Three kilometres.'

'Good enough. Bridget, care for some fresh air?'

'What are you babbling about?'

'C'mon, let's have some fun.'

I grabbed the camera and led the way through the engine room. I looped the shoulder strap round my neck and switched on the camera. Set the iris and locked the focus just shy of infinity.

'What are you planning to do?'

'Told you. Have some fun.'

I peeked down the tracks again. Blue light breaking through the clouds and spilling over the snow all surreal and magic-like. The sun shimmering and shivering like a giant neon snowball. I leaned back, took Bridget's wrist, lifted my coat and stuffed her hand down my trousers. 'Hang on!'

'Hang on to *what* precisely?'

'The belt, stupid, the belt!'

'Ah! Of course!'

Anchoring myself as best I could on the icy platform. Trees whipping by the train in a blur. Waiting, waiting.

'Are you planning to shoot anything or is this just some ploy to get a beautiful girl's hands in your pants?'

'Don't flatter yourself!'

'I beg your pardon!'

I pressed the roll button, leaned far out into the icy wind and lowered the camera down alongside the train. Maestro Engineer opened the throttle for the crescendo. Faster and faster, steel wheels spinning above the rails. The locomotive howled and the Trans-Siberian Express raced for the sun.

Ural mountains

The Elektrichka rattled through the village and turned up the hill. This was the local train. Wood benches, snow-slushed floors, sixteen babushki all in a row. All in the same dark coats and grey scarves and heavy felt boots. A small boy sat squashed up next to the frost-covered window. His little sister was kicking and pinching him into submission.

'Nyyyeeeet! Irushka! Nyyyeeet!'

Few benches back two more kids kicked and pinched themselves silly.

'But, James, you've been boss for two whole days!'

'Yes, Bridget. That's because I'm more important.'

'Oh, poo jab! Poo jab!'

And me doing sums in my head. Three salaries and the costs of the trip. It was inconceivable that ITN was paying out this kind of cash for one big goof across Siberia. One day the accountants would figure it out and demand the money back.

The train slowed to a stop in the middle of nowhere. Out in the snow a babushka stood with a few bulky bags. She waddled up the ice-crusted stairs and stomped her boots and took her place with all the other old women in dark coats and grey scarves and heavy felt boots. The train eased ahead once more. That's how it worked in Siberia. You need a lift, you stand next to the railroad tracks and wait. Sooner or later an Elektrichka will pass by and you wave your hand and the train stops and you climb on. When you get somewhere in the vicinity of your destination, you pull a half-worn piece of rope along the windows and the train slows to another stop and you jump off into the middle of nowhere again.

A ruddy-faced conductor shuffled through the benches collecting ten roubles here and four roubles there. He stuffed the money into a bag and gave a thin paper coupon in return. After each transaction he coughed up something gooey in his throat and pulled down a window and spat into the wind. Then he'd wipe his mouth on the sleeve of his thick blue conductor's coat and move on.

Thump, thump, thump, thump.

In time with the rhythm of the train, a little boy tapping his boots on the side of the wooden bench. He was wrapped to the gills in a scratchy wool scarf. His eyes dazzled by the camera in my lap. He'd been watching me for a while . . . my coat, my boots, my hat. He liked the camera best.

I set the camera upright and flipped on the power. His eyes got bigger. I looked down through the viewfinder and focused on his babushka and invited the boy over for a look-see. He jumped over like a frog and pressed his face to the eyepiece. He broke into giggles looking through the lens, then up to his babushka, then back through the lens, then back to his babushka . . . and the old woman arranging the three strands of hair hanging from her wool hat and giggling just like the little boy.

'Ah, a new cameraman,' said Bridget, sitting down with the babushka. 'Good, because I'm sure your material is absolute crap, Jon Steele.'

And the little boy turning and twisting the camera this way and that way and me trying to keep the camera from falling on the floor and breaking into bits and him giggling and laughing even harder and me saying, '*Nyyyeeet!*'

'You're so good with children.'

I looked at the little boy's head. Same colour hair, same little-boy smell. And then I remembered another little boy standing at the top of the stairs. Tears in his eyes and his tiny hands clutching at the air and his little-boy voice crying, '*Daddy, Daddy!*' I walked out of his life for ten cocaine-fuelled years.

'Nope. Not really.'

'Ah, a new cameraman,' said James, sitting down next to the little boy. 'Good, because I'm sure your material is absolute crap, Jon Steele.'

'You two are real fuckin' spooky.'

'Why's that?'

'Trust me.'

Out through the windowfrost the hills rolled higher and further through deep forests and higher still into the middle of another nowhere.

'Well. We seem to be getting closer.'

'How can you tell?'

'Oh, do pay attention! We were told the obelisk stands on the railroad pass through the Ural mountains where one crosses from Asia into Europe. At present one must simply look out of the window to see one is going up the mountains. Therefore the obelisk must be very near.'

'These ain't mountains, they're fuckin' hills.'

'Oh, yes, Mr Cowboy from Montana. Nothing could possibly equal the grandeur of his beloved Montana. James, you may offer me your support.'

'I would say your precious obelisk may be hours away yet,' he said.

'Beast!'

'And I'm just sayin' these ain't mountains. They're fuckin' hills.'

'Listen, you vile creatures! I am the Russian expert. I am the one who understands the wonderful mysteries of this glorious land. I am full with her many stories and legends.'

'You're full of horse shit.'

'And, besides, I asked the conductor.'

'Hear, hear.'

'Thank you, James.'

'No, I agree with Jon. You are full of horse shit.'

'Oh! Beasts! Both of you!'

The air brakes hissed and the train grunted to a stop. The conductor stood over us coughing and snorting, signalling this was our stop. Then he opened a window and fired off a big glob of spit into the thirty-five-below-zero cold.

'Stunning performance, don't you think?'

'Olympic material. Silver medal at least.'

We gathered the kit, wrapped scarves round our necks, closed our coats and pulled big fur hats down on our heads.

'When does the return Elektrichka come by?'

Russian, Russian, Russian.

'Actually, comrade conductor doesn't know.'

'Hold it. There's gonna be a train back down this fuckin' hill, isn't there?'

Russian, Russian, Russian.

'Comrade conductor says, "Da, there will be a train . . . probably." But he says not to worry because the worst that will happen is we will freeze to death and he says to tell you this is a mountain not a hill.'

We climbed down the steps and watched the Elektrichka roll through the ravine and struggle over the hill and slip out of sight. We dug through the snow and scrambled up on to a ridge of deep powder and powerful cold. And there it was, the long-lost obelisk. A sharp-edged and pointy-tipped chunk of ice-cold concrete ten metres high. 'Asia' carved on one side and 'Europe' on the other.

'Looks like it.'

'Indeed.'

'Now you foul cretins. I calculate a Trans-Siberian Express will pass this way in less than an hour using a rather complex mathematical formula devised while travelling across this most inspirational of lands. Pay attention. A Trans-Siberian left Vladivostok at midnight three days ago. At an average speed of fifty-three kilometres per hour, and given the difference in time zones and allowing for stoppage and dividing that by a factor of twelve, one may then assume—'

'Stop!'

'I beg your pardon, James. I haven't finished.'

'This *formula* of yours is an absolute disgrace to mathematics.'

'James! How dare you!'

'Factor of twelve! What in God's name has "factor of twelve" got to do with the Trans-Siberian Express?'

'Don't you begin to assume a superior intelligence to me.'

'Don't worry. I don't assume it. Not one bit.'

'Good. Hey! You've just insulted me!'

I stood in the freezing cold, watching James engage in his favourite sport of ripping apart the thinking processes of lesser humans. The game was on. Bridget feigning shock and horror, James laughing his way to her jugular. Bridget stomping off through the snow, James resting a boot on the obelisk and striking a pose like Wellington at Waterloo.

'Superior firepower through good breeding. I await her surrender.'

Bridget wandered to the edge of a cliff and pulled the hood of her coat away from her face. She looked out over the Ural mountains and all the Russias beyond. Stretching her mittened hands into the sky and breathing in the pure Siberian air. 'Oh, it is *sooo* beautiful!'

And she kicked her way back through a flurry of snow.

Over on a nearby hill, one dark wood cabin. Woodsmoke puffed from a pipe hanging out of an ice-frosted window.

'Ah, civilization.'

'Sort of, I s'pose.'

'Come on, Miss Mathematical Genius. Let's see if we can learn anything about the return train from that cabin.'

'Oh, don't be so stupid. Who has ever heard of asking a cabin for information?'

'Bridget, if there is smoke emanating from the cabin, then most probably there is someone inside the cabin.'

'Yes, of course. I knew that.'

And them struggling up the hill and me alone amid deepest winter. Arctic wind whooshed through the pine and for a moment I felt the white hills stir from their hibernation. Clouds of fine powder swirled across the ridge and twisted into white funnels then faded away spirit-like. And me thinking back to all those winters in Montana. Quiet and untouched and alone. And not knowing if the aloneness in my life was who I was or who I'd become. And being terrified of the aloneness and wishing it could be different. But knowing that no matter what happened or who crossed through my life, I would always run to this place and hide in this moment. Alone on a hill in deepest winter. The world so very far away.

'Fuck me. I really do need a joint.'

I set up the tripod at an angle to catch the Trans-Siberian Express with the obelisk in the foreground. Big wide shot of the train crossing from Asia to Europe. I looked through the lens imagining the train and setting the shot. I yanked off the camera battery and stuffed it down my coat to keep it warm. For some reason I thought it a good idea to cover the camera with my fox-fur hat and pull the hood of my coat over my head. Then I waited for a train.

One freight train, two freight trains, a slow-moving Elektrichka full of Russian villagers heading into Asia. I waved and they stared back in horror. Not every day they'd hop a train through Siberia and see some crazed foreigner ass-deep in snow and deathly cold, standing next to a TV camera with a fur hat on top of it. So I waved again and they stared back in horror some more.

Thwack. A snowball hit me in the back. James and Bridget struggling back through clouds of white powder.

'There is someone in the cabin,' called Bridget. 'A woman. But she's barking mad.'

'How 'bout the Elektrichka?'

'She doesn't know for sure. She thinks there may be one.'

'Swell.'

The low sun edged closer to the horizon and long shadows spread across the snow. Then the wind kicked up and the air felt like little bits of sharp glass.

'Oh dear, seems to be getting a bit nippy.'

'S'pose we could stay in the woman's cabin if night falls?'

'I would think we'd have a very good chance of ending up as stuffing in Siberian sausage.'

'So we're talkin' barkin'.'

'Woof, woof,' opined ITN diplomatic correspondent James Mates.

We ran in circles for warmth, threw snowballs, made angels in the snow and posed for happy snaps under the obelisk. Still no train.

'So much for you and your complex mathematical formula.'

'One moment, James. I believe the operative word in my sentence was "complex". I said nothing about being correct.'

'Yeees, well, I need a pee.'

He trudged down the hill and ducked into a clump of trees.

'Forgot to tell him never eat the yellow snow.'

'I beg your pardon?'

'First thing an Eskimo teaches their young.'

'Is that some crude example of Montana humour?'

'Alaskan, actually. But close enough.'

'How revolting. Absolutely repulsive. Oh, James! Never eat the yellow snow!'

And we stood around stomping our boots and watching the sun fall behind the trees.

'Do you hear something?'

'Little far away, ain't he?'

'Not that, you disgusting pervert. *That.*'

A fast-moving rumble and then coming through the trees . . . the Trans-Siberian Express. Slap on the battery, kick on the camera, pull the hat off the lens. Peer down the eyepiece and check the framing. Nice shot. The train clears the trees and races towards the obelisk. Roll tape and check the shot and there, in the lower right corner of the picture, was ITN correspondent James Mates, jumping out of the trees in mid-urination waving his free hand and yelling, 'There's a train coming! There's a train coming!'

'Fucksake, James! You're pissin' in the fuckin' shot!'

'Oops!'

And he jumped back into the trees just as the train charged up and over the hill and roared past the obelisk.

'Well. That's a wrap.'

'All we need is an Elektrichka.'

We slid down through the snow and waited near the tracks. Freight trains rolled by, practically knocking us over with the backdraught.

'Think I'll cross over and get the next freighter. Tight shot of steel wheels spinning through the snow might be good.'

'Oh, how artsy.'

'Yes, more of Jon Steele's crazed cinematic visions of the Siberian wastes.'

'Fuck off.'

I crossed over the two sets of tracks and set the tripod in a snow-filled ditch for a low angle shot in the snow. Just as I locked the camera on the tripod a freight train rolled over the pass. And out of the corner of my eye, an Elektrichka coming the other way on the far set of tracks.

'Oh, shit.'

'Jon!'

'I know!'

I broke down the kit and climbed out of the ditch. Up to the tracks a hair too late. The freighter cut me off and blew me back down into the snow ditch and I was lost in a white-out blizzard.

'Oh, just fuckin' wonderful!'

I crawled back up the hill, keeping my head down, waiting for the endless line of cars to whip by till . . . zzzzunnnggg! The last car gone in a flash. Across the tracks James and Bridget were climbing aboard the Elektrichka. I jumped on to the tracks and ran like hell. Twenty metres, fifteen. James hanging off the end of the train, Bridget signalling for me to run faster. 'Come on, Jon! Hurry!'

'Yeah, yeah!'

The Elektrichka started to pull away . . .

'Yikes!'

'Faster!'

. . . and roll down the hill.

I watched in disbelief. Quick pan back towards the lone cabin. The Madwoman of Siberia was standing on the porch with a knife in her hands, watching and drooling with lust.

'Great! I'm dinner!'

The train gathered speed. Bridget leaped into the train and suddenly the entire eight cars of the Elektrichka screeched to a halt.

SCRRREEECHHH! KACLUNK!

I caught up to the last car, tossed the tripod up to James and the train pulled away again.

'Fuck me!'

'Come on!'

I jumped and grabbed hold of the side handles, the camera sliding off my shoulder and pulling me down. James grabbed the back of my coat and held on tight. My boots dragging along the sleepers.

'Hang on, Jon!'

And the train speeding ahead and me knowing I couldn't hold on much longer.

'I'm fuckin' tryin'!'

And looking up and seeing Bridget grabbing the emergency stop and pulling hard.

SCRRREEECHHH! KACLUNK!

The train hissed like a pissed-off bull. I scrambled aboard and we plopped down on a bench in the last car. Empty and no heat. My legs pulsing with pain. The train chugged away one more time.

'Well! That *was* fun!' chirped James.

'Oh, yes! Bags and bags!' twittered Bridget.

'Fun? *Fun?*' I yelled. 'So far on this trip I been arrested in Vladivostok, then I'm fallin' out of the sky in a chopper, now I been dragged through Siberia by a train! This is not fun! Being with you two is like being in a fuckin' war zone!'

'Oh, don't be such a baby! Think of it as a wonderful holiday!'

'Yes! You should be sending out bags and bags of postcards!'

'You two are definitely spooky.'

'Besides, I saved your life, Jon Steele. Did you see me, James? Yes, I saved his life. I stopped the train twice to save his miserable life, didn't I, James?'

'Oh, yes. Indeed.'

'And wasn't I the most fabulous, James?'

'Oh, yes. Absolutely the most fabulous.'

'Let's see, what would be a nice thank-you gift? Dinner at the Metropole in Moscow? No, I think this calls for something special. Jewellery! I think jewellery would be nice, don't you, James?'

'Oh, yes. Me too.'

'"Me too" what?'

'I want a prezzy too.'

'Don't be ridiculous. Jewellery doesn't suit you.'

'And why not?'

'I don't fuckin' believe this.'

The far door crashed open and a very official-looking man with a very official pissed-off look on his face marched down the aisle spewing Russian words clear enough in any language.

'Who pulled the emergency brake? It is a very serious offence to pull the emergency brake! Who did it? And you with the camera! You are under arrest!'

'Fuckin' hell. Not again.'

Ekaterinburg

We piled through the doors of the Intourist Hotel. A frozen brown mass of ugly concrete. There was the usual welcoming fragrance of Russian cigarettes and bad plumbing mixed with the slightest hint of heat. Russian Mafia gangs in leather jackets and mink hats sat round plastic tables smoking Marlboros and drinking Turkish coffee. Hookers lounging on leather sofas, various shades of lipstick on their beat-up faces. A glass counter offered a variety of useless items for sale. And, of course, the snarling desk clerk with that Soviet hatred of westerners.

'*Nyet* rooms! Geet out!'

'Oh, yes, I see. Of course. It is the height of the tourist season in your fabulous city and the jet-set is flying in from all over the world to experience the wonderland of Ekaterinburg, aren't they? What do you mean "no rooms", you idiotic little man?'

'Allow me, James. Hallo, my name is Bridget.'

'Geet out!'

'How dare you!'

'We have conference! Geet out!'

'What kind of conference?'

'Important people! Geet out!'

And me looking round the lobby at the goons in leather jackets and mink hats taking intimidating sips from their glasses. A quick pan over the babes with the many-coloured lips winking and squirming in their seats with that certain itch.

'How 'bout our reservations?'

'*Nyet* reservations! Geet out!'

'How 'bout these fuckin' reservations?'

Thud.

A stack of roubles the size of the ancient Pyramids hit the counter. Mafioski and hookers licked their lips. The snarling desk clerk swept up the cash and dropped room keys on the counter.

'Welcome to conference, comrades!'

Upstairs and into the rooms. Ten seconds later a knock on my door. Open to a hooker standing in the doorway rubbing her tits.

'I love you.'

'How nice.'

And slam the door and jump in the bathroom and turn on the shower.

'Yes! Hot water! Thank you, Jesus.'

Another knock on the door and another hooker standing in the doorway rubbing her tits.

'I love you.'

'Of course you do.'

And slam the door again and strip off my clothes and let the water pour down my head. Six days on the train washing down the drain. A clean pair of boxer shorts and clean socks. Friendly old blue jeans and a baggy sweatshirt. Steam heat hissing through the radiator. Dim light, quiet room. Life was good.

I took apart the camera and laid out the bits and cleaned the lenses and filters and gears. My mind rewinding a thousand pictures in my head. Blue light on endless fields of snow, seas of ice and forests of silver birch, small wood villages on the edge of nowhere, Russian faces peering through frost-covered windows. My eyes felt rich.

Another knock at the door.

'Fucksake.'

And pulling open the door . . .

'I don't wanna see your fuckin' tits!'

. . . and Bridget standing in the doorway with a small bag over her shoulder.

'I beg your pardon?'

'Oops. Thought you were someone else.'

'I should hope so.'

She walked into the quiet and dim light and scanned the room with disapproval. 'Oh dear. You've not gone all moody again, have you?'

'Actually I was just cleanin' the camera and thinkin'.'

'Yes, thinking. That's good, Jon. Exercise the grey matter. At your age the brain needs all the exercise it can get. Now, I'm here for a shower. My bath has no hot water. You have hot water, don't you? Good. Now sod off so a girl can make herself beautiful.'

'Can't you bother someone else?'

'Wouldn't be as much fun.'

'So what am I s'posed to do? Wander the fuckin' halls?'

'Good thinking. See? All that mental exercise is helping your feeble brain already.'

She stepped into the bathroom and turned on the taps. The light cast a shadow into the room. The shadow letting clothes fall from its shape and, for a moment, the soft curves of a woman moving across an open door. The shadow wrapped the curves in a huge towel and Bridget stepped back into the room and opened my backpack. 'One more thing, spiky monster, I need some socks.'

'Nope.'

'Excuse me?'

'You've already stolen three pairs of socks, one pair of jeans, my favourite shirt and two sets of thermal underwear.'

'Yes, yes. And what's your point?'

She rifled through the bag and pulled out a black wool sweater. 'Ahh! You've been hiding this.'

I ripped it from her claws. 'Nope! My dead grandmother knitted this with her very own hands!'

'Well, unless your dead grandmother was named "Timberland" I suggest you hand it over or say goodbye to our friendship for ever!'

'Don't tempt me. You know what this fuckin' friendship has cost me in clothes alone?'

'How can you be so crass?'

'How can you be so stupid?'

'What? May I remind you that *I* was a secretary to His Royal

Highness Prince Philip, the Duke of Edinburgh. In Buckingham Palace, no less!'

'Yeah, yeah, and tell me again how you scolded that woman for runnin' around the Palace in a frumpy dressing-gown.'

'How did I know the frump was Princess Anne? It was dark!'

'I rest my case.'

'Oh, you are so cruel. You think you are so good and brave. Don't forget, you worthless pile of poo, it was *I* who was wounded in Bosnia!'

'You broke your toe jumping over a couch tryin' to get a good spot in front of the TV.'

'Beast!'

'Tart!'

'Bastard!'

'Bitch!'

'Pig!'

'You look fuckin' great in that towel!'

'Don't I just!'

And we fell into each other's arms and squeezed our bodies together in the dim light, our hearts racing like runaway trains.

'What the fuck are we doin'?'

'I have no fucking idea.'

Knock, knock, knock.

'Jon, it's James.'

Bridget's face twisted into that 'oh, no!' look. I pointed to the shower and she ran for the closet. We smashed head on into each other's noses.

'Shit!'

'Fuck!'

Another knock, harder.

'Hallo! What'sgoingoninthere?'

Bridget jumped into the bathroom and slammed the door on my foot.

'Fuck! Uh . . . hi, James, what's up?'

'Whatdoyoumeanwhat'sup? Openthedoor!'

'I was just having a shower.'

Bridget slipped and fell against the tin walls of the shower stall . . .

'Shit!'

. . . banging around like a drunken cow.

'Whatwasthat? Whoisinthere? Openthisdooratonce!'

I opened the door to two terribly British eyebrows perched high on a prominent forehead. James Mates standing like a Scotland Yard detective, eyes darting across the scene of the crime, nose sniffing the air for clues. He strolled in, slow and curious.

'Yeees. I see.'

'James.'

'Jon.'

'Need somethin'?'

'I came for loo roll.'

'Loo roll.'

'Yeees. You Americans refer to it by the rather vulgar term "toilet paper". We call it loooo roooll. You did pack extra for the trip. Didn't you?'

'Think so.'

I dug through the travel cases, found the stash and laid it in his hands.

'There ya are, James. Loo roll.'

I squeezed the plastic packaging to certify freshness.

The water stopped running in the shower. Detective Mates's ears twitched and locked on to the sounds of something or someone stumbling around in the bathroom.

'Yeees.' He peeked over my shoulder, his keen eyes ready to pounce. 'Weeell. Thank you.'

'Any time, James.'

His eyebrows crawling higher and higher up his forehead. Any second now his face was going to rip apart.

'Weeell. Thank you.'

'You just said that.'

'Good . . . bye.'

'See ya.'

'Yeees.'

The door swung open and Bridget emerged dressed in her ensemble of stolen clothes. Strands of wet hair dripping round her not-so-innocent eyes.

'Ah. Hallo, James. I was just having a shower.'

'Yeees. Seems to be a lot of that in this room.'

'That's because there's no hot water in my room.'

'Yeees . . . I see. "No hot water".'

'James came by for some loo roll.'

'How nice.'

'Yeees . . . loooo rooooll.'

'Are you feeling unwell, James? You have this rather curious expression plastered on your face.'

'Yeees . . . loooo rooooll.'

He turned and stepped into the hall. He stopped and looked back into the room. Then he tossed his chin in the air, broke into a loud laugh and whistled his way down the hall. Bridget gathered her stuff, laughing to herself.

'He knows.'

'Knows what?'

'He just knows.'

'Knows what?'

She walked through the doorway, spun round and grabbed me by the collar. She yanked me across the threshold and kissed me on the mouth, soft and warm. 'That you're in love with me, you silly old git.'

And she tossed me back across the threshold and closed the door. I walked over to the camera and looked at all the bits and just stared for some time, not remembering how to put them back together again.

Moscow

One of Stalin's nightmare skyscrapers looming over one of Moscow's busiest intersections. A crescent moon drifting low through a daylight sky. I flipped in the lens doubler and compressed the shot so any second now it looked like the crescent moon might drift over and get itself stuck on one of the spearlike towers.

'You can do the same trick at sunset. Compress the picture on the horizon and focus and lock down the shot. What's weird is the sun isn't moving at all. What you're seein' is the ground under your feet turnin' away from the sun.'

'Fascinating. But would you mind getting on with it before we are both killed?'

Bridget in the middle of the street directing rush-hour-crazed Russians round me and the camera.

'Just waitin' for a train.'

'Well, if you'd stop gazing at the moon like the village idiot you'd see one coming! God! Americans!'

'Relax, kid.'

'Jon Steele! I did not spend my university years at St Andrew's to end up as a traffic warden in the former Soviet Union!'

Two Ladas swerved close, almost crashing into each other. The drivers yelling and screaming and waving their fists at Bridget.

'You're damn good at it, though.'

'Oh, sod off! You too! You Russian twits!'

Pull out the lens and roll. An elevated railtrack cutting midway through the picture, just above the tops of cars and trucks. And over in the right edge of the frame, a bug-splattered Red Star pulling a dirty green locomotive and thirty cars of passengers through the shot. The Trans-Siberian Express at the end of the line. Clanking and clunking tired and slow. Ten thousand kilometres of tired and slow.

'How is the picture?'

'Great. Got cars goin' this way and the moon goin' that way and a big fuckin' train rollin' on through, lookin' like it made a wrong turn somewhere back down the road.'

And stopping the tape and switching off the camera.

'That's a fuckin' wrap.'

Bridget dropped her arms. She stomped over through the slushy snow and planted herself in my face. She scowled and rolled her eyes. 'Where in God's name did you learn to speak the English language?'

'The nuns at St Francis de Sales School.'

'They should be crucified.'

''Scuse me?'

'Buy me breakfast, you despicable pig.'

'OK, then.'

We drove round the ring road over Krasnokholmkii Bridge and looped off on to the embankment road. Chunks of ice floated down the Moscow river like small icebergs. Ice-cold air skimmed the river and rolled into steam clouds then rose into the grey sky. And on the far bank, street-cleaning trucks pulled on to the sidewalk and dumped tons of filthy snow on to the river.

'Kinda looks like mountains of frozen horseshit, don't it?'

'You're quite sure it was nuns who taught you the English language?'

'Why you keep askin' me that?'

Under Bolshoi Bridge and ram the car over a snowbank next to the Kempinski Hotel.

'How 'bout a five-star breakfast?'

'That would be nice.'

Sunlight slipped from behind the clouds and glittered across the gold spires of the Kremlin cathedrals. The red-brick walls of the Kremlin glowing deep. The onion domes of St Basil's swimming in splashes of colour.

'Nice shot.'

'Forget it. I'm starving, you beast.'

I climbed out of the car, slung the camera on my shoulder and walked towards the hotel. I turned round and saw Bridget standing near the embankment wall, staring out over the river. Like dreaming. 'Hey! I thought you were hungry.'

Silence.

'Bridget?'

She turned and looked with a faraway gaze.

'What's wrong?'

'Come here, spiky monster.'

I walked over and watched her eyes look all around and down.

'I guess the trip is over, isn't it?'

'S'pose it is.'

She kicked a clump of snow down into the river and watched it bob up and down and float away. She looked back out across the river. 'Did you know someone once asked Michelangelo how he carved David from a piece of marble? Michelangelo said David was in there all the time. All he had to do as a sculptor was remove the bits of stone that were in the way.'

'That a fact?'

'I have no idea but is sounds good, doesn't it?'

'Yup.'

'I just saw how you do it. How you see things.'

'S'cuse me?'

'You said, "Nice shot," and I looked over there and all I saw were these same old buildings I've seen a hundred times, till I looked again. I started removing things, then I saw streams of light and colour and shapes. A little like seeing the world for the first time.'

'Sorta how it works.'

She breathed and sighed like breathing and sighing that first night on the plane somewhere over Siberia. 'You are actually quite an artist, Jon.'

'I just take pictures.'

'My God. Do you run from everything good in your life? Soon as someone says a good word or comes close to you, do you always pull away?'

'You goin' somewhere with this?'

'You have taught me so much about this job. You have opened me to an entire world. Look at me. I'm a television producer who travels the world. A year and a half ago I was out of work and out of love and now I've got a wonderful job and I'm falling in love . . .'

'What?'

'Oh, for heaven's sake, Jon. How can someone like you not see it? It's not just you. It's me too.'

Silence again.

'And I can see what will happen. Because I can remove all the bits around you and I can see you for who and what you are . . .'

'Bridget.'

'. . . and I can love who you are but most of all I'm terrified of what you are.'

'And what's that?'

'Dangerous. Very dangerous.'

And me pulling away seeing something hurting in her eyes and not wanting to look.

'Rather difficult gift to see things. You taught me that as well, Jon.'

'See anything else?'

'Yes. You're going to break my heart. Badly, very badly.'

'Hey. Slow down a second.'

'Too late, it's already happening. You shall make a thousand promises but in the end you'll just break my heart.'

'Fuck me. I can't be this bad.'

'Not bad, just dangerous.'

She tucked her arm through mine and looked into my eyes. 'Now. Buy me breakfast, you cruel bastard.'

7

CHRISTMAS EVE

Upstate New York

Snow fell in the afternoon and the road was slow. It'd been a long day from Moscow to New York. Eleven hours round the world till coming through US Immigration and Customs.

'Welcome home, sir.'

'Just passing through.'

'Where's home then, sir?'

'No idea. Where's yours?'

'Little too much Christmas cheer on the plane, sir?'

'Yup. Well oiled.'

''Tis the season, sir. Happy holidays.'

And now the slow winding road up the Hudson valley with nothing but tidings of comfort and joy on the radio. Kate looking out the window lost in a telephone conversation from days ago. Her mother called and said she wasn't feeling well. Something in the sound of her voice, like the woman *knew*. Kate heard the sound and was worried. We shoved our broken marriage into the closet and made the trip.

'Kate. It's gonna be fine. She's gonna be fine.'

'She sounded so scared.'

'We'll get there. I'll go buy a tree and we'll decorate it and have pizza and drink wine and get pissed. Just like always.'

'I can't believe it's Christmas.'

'It's hard.'

'I just don't know what I'd do if she . . .'

'It's gonna be fine.'

A quick exit off the Taconic State Parkway to Pleasantville Road and straight ahead into Briarcliff Manor. Small-town USA right off the movie lot. The taxi turned on to Maple Drive and found the neat house surrounded by tall evergreen trees. Kate's home, the place of her childhood.

'Well, here we go.'

'It's gonna be fine, Kate.'

She held back tears, her hands clasped in fear.

And me watching her and thinking I should reach out and touch her . . .

'I can't believe it's Christmas.'

'I'm sorry, Kate.'

'I'm sorry too.'

. . . but unable to move.

'Look, whatever's goin' on with your mother, I'll be with you. I promise.'

'Don't say it, Jon.'

'Kate, I'm tryin' to say . . .'

'Don't say it. Listen, I know you mean well. But you and I both know some things in this life are just beyond you. You're so locked up inside, I don't think you're aware of how far from me you've gone. It's like you disappeared from our life. I miss you so very much and I love you. But we both know you never kept a promise in your life. Not to me, not to yourself, not to anyone. That would mean letting someone get close to you, and that's not something you can do. It breaks my heart, Jon. I can't imagine anyone so lonely in their life as you. Now I have to go inside. Stay as long as you want or as long as you can. But please, no promises.'

She ran into the house and I paid the driver and gathered the bags. A weird feeling running in my head. Like crossing some kind of front-line. My eyes panned the trees for danger. Nothing but snowy branches and houses with Christmas lights and a big plastic glow-in-the-dark Santa Claus all down the street. Few minutes later I was in the living room dropping the bags on the floor and looking at Kate in the arms of her mother.

'Hi, Jon.'

'Hi, Bernadette. How are ya?'

'Oh, I think something's wrong with my stomach, but I'm getting over it.'

And Kate holding her mother's arm and helping her sit down. 'Why don't I make you some tea, Mom?'

'Not for me, but help yourself.'

And me looking at Bernadette and seeing the colour of her skin and the pain in her eyes and *knowing*. I walked slowly through the house towards the kitchen. Something lurking in the shadows. Like it was already *here*. I could smell it.

Not here. Fuckin' hell, not here.

Kate was standing over the stove watching the water boil.

'Kate. We gotta get her to the hospital.'

'What?'

'Your mother. Now, right now.'

And seeing panic in her eyes.

'What are you saying?'

'Kate, I'm sorry. Get her dressed, get her coat. We have to go.'

That night Bernadette was diagnosed with a vicious cancer. No cure, no hope, only the torture of chemotherapy to extend her life by a few months. And Kate was condemned to watch her mother die. Slowly, very slowly. The same way she watched her father and her husband Steve and then her marriage to me.

I stood in the corner of a hospital room full of hospital smells and hospital fears. There was a television hanging from the ceiling, the black screen reflecting the shapes and forms in the room. Forms so reposeful and quiet. A daughter holding the hands of her dying mother and stroking her mother's hair.

'It'll be all right, Mom. It'll be all right.'

And then hearing the sounds of Kate's tears.

And me thinking I should move closer and touch her. Kate was good and she was kind and she needed me and I'd loved her deeply once before and even now. But staring at the picture of her suffering, I couldn't move.

Do something! Fuckin' do something!

Two days later, I flew back to Moscow.

8

NEARLY AFRICA

Moscow. Spring, 1994

Warm night on Tverskaya Avenue. Blue neon mixed with the dim headlamps of midnight traffic. Ladas and Zhigulis splashing through puddles of melting snow. My head fuzzy with dope and beer and listening to Pavarotti wail through 'Nessun Dorma' eighteen times full blast. Inspired me to get out of the flat and stroll downtown. Get lost, maybe. Got as far as Pushkin Square. Not very lost at all.

Down through the pedestrian tunnel and under Tverskaya Avenue. Place was stuffed with homeless bums guzzling vodka and street kids huffing on bags of glue.

'Ughfluggyanadski!'

'And a glorious May Day to you, young comrades!'

'*Chto?*'

'OK. Few days early but I figure by then ya'll be dead.'

One drooling-faced kid held up a plastic bag dripping with saliva and snot and the finest mind-meld glue available. His filthy street-kid hands offering me a blast.

'*Skolko lyet*, kid?'

'*Dvenadtsat.*'

'Twelve years old? Christ.'

I grabbed the bag and threw it half-way across the tunnel. The drool-ing faces went blank, then a smudgy flash as six grubby kids flew after the bag. They punched and kicked each other for a huff. Each kid breathing long and slow. Dumb-ass smiles spreading over their faces.

I dropped some roubles on the ground and stepped over the kids. 'Save me a spot in rehab.'

'Fuckink you, Amerikanski!'

And then up the stairs and on to the street. I stood there looking for something. I was bored. Just spent a month in Bosnia watching people hate each other big-time. Lots of guns and shells. Lots of booze and dope. Lots of European politicians not knowing what the fuck to do. Lots of destroyed lives. Lots of wondering if I was going to get out in one piece. Nerves edgy and fierce. But three days back home in Moscow had me wanting more. Didn't like the aloneness. Didn't like the shakes in my hands. Needed a little something to tide me over till the next job.

So I paid my thirty-five bucks at the door.

'Welcome to Nightflight, sir.'

'Busy tonight?'

'Not so much. But the scenery is still very good.'

And into Moscow's most expensive candy shop.

Spinning lights, loud music and the hungry prowl of gorgeous Russian girls. The kind your babushka warned you about. They moved through clouds of cigarette smoke, sniffing for hard currency. Their hungry fingers rubbing and searching along trousers, their eyes gazing deep into the googly-eyed faces of western businessmen far from home. I worked my way to the bar and ordered beer with a tequila chaser. An easy blonde with tempting curves swooned over ready to lick the salt off my glass.

'Allo. I Svetlana.'

'Hello, Svetlana.'

'This name means "flower".'

'I know.'

'What hotel you stay in Moskva?'

'*Nyet* hotel. I live here.'

'You have wife?'

'Don't think so any more.'

'You have girlfriend?'

'Don't think so any more.'

'You want to fuck?'

'Don't think so. Just came to watch.'

'You strange man.'

'So I been told.'

Out on the dance floor, the pictures were good. Dressed-to-kill hookers swaying and humping the air and watching themselves in floor-to-ceiling mirrors. Pouty lips and lusty glances. Russian babes hypnotized by the images of their own reflections. The fuzzy lens in my head zoomed into the hips. A slow pan across the swing and the grind and the soft push. Wanting to feel it burn in my guts like some purifying fire, but there was nothing. And the more I watched, the more nothing I felt.

Another beer and tequila. More pictures flickering in my head . . .

'Hello.'

. . . and there she was.

'Howdy.'

'Ah, American. What is your name?'

'George Washington.'

'Of course it is. I am Natasha.'

'Of course you are.'

She laid her arm on the bar and rested her face in her hand. Pale white skin and the darkest hair, long red nails. Killer grey eyes.

'You look very sad, Mr Washington.'

'Nope. Just very drunk.'

'Men do not come to Nightflight to get drunk.'

Small hips wrapped in tight black leather pants and easing from side to side. Round breasts covered with cream-coloured silk.

'OK. Let's say I get drunk and watch.'

A red nail on red lips.

'Maybe you watch me, Mr Washington?'

'Dunno. Whattayado?'

'I light the candles and play with my friends.'

'What kinda friends?'

'Oh, friends. Wonderful friends. Friends to make you feel very good.'

'How good?'

Her killer grey eyes glowing warm.

'All the way to heaven, Mr Washington.'

'Sounds dangerous.'

'*Konyechno.*'

And the music pounding in my chest and Natasha leaning close, very close. Dewberry perfume filling my lungs. Long dark eyelashes brushing my face.

'You like dangerous, Mr Washington?'

Her hand slipping from the bar on to my leg. Long red nails tracing up my thigh. Her fingers caressing the lump in my jeans. And me watching her blouse open just a peek. Soft white skin. A long red nail sliding beneath cream-coloured silk and tracing secret circles somewhere inside.

'I take you to beautiful place, Mr Washington.'

'You are very good, Natasha.'

'Darling, tell me what you want.'

And watching something rush through her killer grey eyes and feeling the heat and wanting more.

'I just wanna get lost.'

'How much lost?'

'Very, very lost.'

'Oh, my darling, come with me. I fuck you to death.'

9 May 1994

'Listen up! We're trying for a landing in three minutes! Flak-jackets and helmets on! Now!'

The flight sergeant's voice screaming over the engines of the Canadian air-force Hercules as the giant plane banked through the sky. Me and James Mates pulled our body armour from the deck and suited up. The flight sergeant secured the cargo lines then strapped us down into webbed seats along the fuselage.

'Hang on, guys! It's gonna be a rough one!'

Pulling the flak-jacket tight and holding the camera close to my chest.

'Well! This must be it!' yelled James.

And me twisting round and looking out the small round window. High speed, low-angle approach. Second attempt of the day. First shot was scrubbed as we were coming in when the runway came under heavy shell fire. The Canadian pilots were brave but not stupid. Sixty tonnes of airplane was one big target. Each trip back to base found one more bullet hole in the fuselage. One day some bastard might get lucky down there.

'Down there' was Rwanda.

Thick and green and hell hot.

'Seems like the place, don't it?' I yelled.

Few weeks ago, while I was getting lost and more lost in Moscow, the Rwandan president was blown to bits when a bomb blew him and his presidential jet out of the sky. That was the beginning of the madness in this place of blue lakes and jungle hills. Place I'd never heard of before. Rwanda was a small country occupied by the Hutu and Tutsi tribes. Two tribes with long and unforgiving memories. Once the Tutsi ruled the Hutu, now the Hutu ruled the Tutsi. Hate festered like an open sore. And now, with the Rwandan president scattered over the countryside, Hutu-controlled Radio Milles Collines screamed and howled for vengeance over the airwaves.

'Kill the cockroaches! Kill! Kill the cockroaches!!'

Hutu militia understood the coded word. Cockroaches . . . Tutsi.

And the open sore ran with blood.

Days later, tens of thousands of Tutsi lay dead. Men and women and children. Hacked to death with machetes, gunned down at point-blank range, heads smashed open with clubs. A truckload of Belgian soldiers were slaughtered trying to evacuate their nationals and save the lives of a few Tutsi. The Belgians had had the bad luck to be wearing the uniform of Rwanda's colonial masters.

The numbers of dead just kept climbing, but the Rwandan government forces did nothing to stop the madness. Each killing was one less Tutsi to worry about. The Final Solution to rid Rwanda of cockroaches. Mountain streams ran fat with spring rain and rotting corpses.

Meanwhile, in neighbouring Uganda, Tutsi men and boys in simple clothes and flip-flop sandals gathered their weapons. They called themselves the Rwandan Patriotic Front, they were armed to the fuckin' teeth. They'd been training in exile and waiting for years. Now, they were ready. And they charged across the border and cut their way through the jungle and surrounded the capital city of Kigali in a flash. Stage set for the final scene.

Hutu army holed up in the vicious heat.

Tutsi rebels closing in for the kill.

Hutu militia still roaming the streets of Kigali looking for kicks.

Everyone terrified.

Whole place had me buzzing.

And now, me and James Mates on Canadian air force 232, *en route* for the middle of the madness. The giant plane loaded with food and water for the besieged UN garrison in Kigali.

'Listen up! We may get hit at any time from now! If you hear a siren when we're on the ground, head to the nearest exit, get out and run like hell for the terminal building!'

James Mates's eyebrows curling into that how-interesting look.

'And if you hear the siren while we're airborne, hang on! Means we're going to land on something other than the runway!'

''Scuse me?'

'I think that was a euphemism for "crash"!'

'Oh. What's a euphemism?'

Wham!

Hitting hard and rolling fast. Reverse engines, taxi over near the terminal and hit the brakes. The flight sergeant dropped the loading platform and hard white light poured into the darkness of the cargo bay, then the rush of heat. Christ, the heat.

'Sit tight till we offload the cargo!'

Slats rolled down the ramp and slammed on to the tarmac. The plane vibrating at high throttle.

'Doesn't seem like the pilots are gonna waste much time!'

'Probably lots of artillery pointing our way!'

'Kinda like sittin' in a fuckin' bomb, ain't it?'

'A very big fucking bomb indeed!'

The flight sergeant loosened us free from our harnesses and pointed into the blinding light. 'Go! Go!'

Me and James looked at each other for a reality check. Quick breaths and quick smiles. We grabbed the camera kit and the satphone, two sleeping-bags and a backpack, one rather beat-up leather briefcase.

'James, you brought a fuckin' briefcase to the war?'

'Of course! You brought your camera, didn't you?'

'Go! Go! Go!'

The light slicing into my eyes, backwash from the Hercules blowing like a blast furnace. My shirt was sweat-soaked in seconds. A line of

UN troops stood by in parade formation. Blue helmets, green uniforms, black faces, Ghanaian flags on sleeves.

'S'pose this is all for us?'

'I'd like to think so! But I think they're probably here for him!'

And James pointing towards the shot-up terminal building.

Six UN soldiers carrying a stretcher covered in a UN flag. The sky-blue flag shaped over the form of someone dead. A voice shouted through the engine roar and the line of Ghanaian soldiers snapped to attention.

I switched on the camera and pulled the zoom wide.

Arms and hands folding in salute as the body was carried before the soldiers. All eyes straight ahead in that soldier sort of way. Or just maybe not wanting to see what was passing before them. The flight sergeant directed the cortège into the cargo bay and they laid the body on the deck and pulled two cargo straps tight cross the heart of the dead form.

'James! Let's do a stand-up and get these Canadians to take the tape back to Nairobi. Phone in later over the satphone and we'll have a piece on the air tonight from Kigali!'

'My dear chap! What a good idea! Just let me ask someone what the hell's going on here.'

'Better be fast!'

I kept rolling tape, filling the lens with soldiers' faces, the blown-to-hell airport, the flight crew making last-minute checks and pulling chock blocks from under the giant wheels.

'Right! UN soldier killed yesterday! Fourth one this week! Seems they're being targeted!'

'By who?'

'Everybody! And it's *whom* not *who*!'

'Yeah, yeah!'

The Hercules wound up ready to roll.

'OK! Let's do it!'

I tossed the microphone to James and he lipped off the words in fifteen seconds with one take. I popped the tape from the camera and scribbled 'ITN, Norfolk Hotel, Nairobi ... ASAP' and ran after the plane.

'Hey! Hey!'

The flight sergeant saw me coming. He looked a bit amused.

Probably thought I'd come to my senses and wanted the hell out of the place but it was too late. I ran faster waving the tape over my helmet. 'Norfolk Hotel! Norfolk Hotel!'

He signalled me to throw the tape and I gave it a wind-up and let it fly through the plane's backwash. It sailed into the cargo bay, bounced off the deck and skidded up on to the dead soldier. The flight sergeant stared at the tape atop the honoured dead, then looked at me with a nod and a wink and thumbs-up. The Hercules roared like a lion and sped down the runway. And then there was just the quiet of the jungle and the report of rifles in the distance.

James was standing over near the terminal with a tall white-skinned soldier. Green flak-jacket over a green uniform. Red and white patch over one pocket, the Maple Leaf of Canada. A friendly round face topped with a baseball cap. He looked like a relief pitcher in the Canadian Semi-Pro Baseball League.

'Jon, come over and say hello to our minder, Major Jean-Guy Laplante.'

He held out a wide hand. His words rolling through a thick *québecois* accent. 'Allo. I'm very glad to 'ave you guys here. I was telling James we need help in this place.'

'Thank you, sir. You from Montreal?'

'Just outside! You know Canada?'

'Sure do, sir.'

'Great. By the way, forget the "sir" crap.'

'Yes, sir. No more "sir" crap, sir.'

'Great. I 'ave a couple of clowns. Let's go.'

We climbed into a white UN jeep and drove off the tarmac and round the terminal. Haggard soldiers emerged from the bushes and surrounded the car. Black berets with blue ensign. Black faces with suspicious eyes.

'Hutu. I suggest you do not take their picture.'

'Wasn't even gonna think it.'

'And it is best only I should talk.'

Jean-Guy lowered the window and held out his wide hand. '*Ça va, mes amis!*'

Their suspicious eyes searching over us, the camera, our white skin.

'*Qui sont ils?*'

'*Oh, lui est américain et lui est anglais.*'

'*Pas belgique?*'

'*Non. Américain et anglais.*'

Their rifles ten and twenty years old, deadly enough. Their faces looking worn and underfed and nervous. Jean-Guy told them we were from the international press and wanted to tell the world of the Rwandan government's brave struggle against the Tutsi rebels. The soldiers waved us through.

'Gotta be friendly with both sides?'

'Let me tell you something, in this place any guy with a rifle is my friend. My very good friend.'

Down on his hip. One black polished .45 automatic. Loaded and ready.

'That for the odd friendly argument?' .

'So far I 'ave luck.'

James gazed out the window into the jungle. His reporter brain spinning for facts. 'What is the situation in Kigali, Jean-Guy?'

'Bad. This place is a free-fire zone. Anytime, anywhere. Rebels 'ave this place surrounded. Government forces hold the airport and the city centre. That was five minutes ago, hard to say what is happening now. We're here on a peacekeeping mission with a detachment of Ghanaian and Tunisian soldiers under the command of General Romeo Dallaire, another French Canadian.'

'Good man?'

'A great man.'

'So how goes the peacekeeping, Jean-Guy?'

Shots and bullets ripped from the trees.

'Oh, you know. Goes on all the time.'

Jean-Guy slammed the accelerator to the floor and swerved round a pile of junk in the road. Crates and wagons and concrete blocks and a mound of purple-black flesh, swollen with rotting gas and maggots. The smell grabbed my throat and squeezed tight.

'A lot of that smell everywhere too. New bodies every day.'

And shots ripping again.

'Dammit! A lot of that too! This airport road is very hot.'

'Well. So far so good, I s'pose. Course, we just fuckin' got here.'

'Indeed. You don't think they're shooting at us, do you, Jean-Guy?'

'Unfortunately they are.'

And me looking at James, and James looking at me, and both of us looking at Major Jean-Guy Laplante as he refitted the cap on his head, rubbed his chin, and slammed down on the accelerator one more time.

'You know. I don't do this work with the press all the time. I am actually a military policeman.'

'How the hell'd you end up here?'

'That is an interesting story . . .'

Cruise through a maze of barbed wire and sandbags. UN troops posted at a flimsy gate. APCs and jeeps surrounding four floors of what used to be a Kigali tourist hotel.

'. . . for another time. This is Headquarters. No electricity, no water. Supplies are running low and relief flights are down to one a day. Maybe.'

All over the place. Ghanaian soldiers in trenches and digging deep into the African earth and filling huge bags with red African dirt and tying them off and stacking them like a wall round the compound. Rifles and artillery rumbling in the hills.

'Fuck me. *Fort Apache.*'

'Pardon?'

'Henry Fonda, John Wayne, lots of Indians.'

'Oh. That makes sense.'

' 'Nother movie in the sixties by the same name but set in New York City. Wasn't near as good.'

'Jean-Guy, you must excuse Jon. Everything reminds him of a movie.'

'It's OK. Nice to know I'm not the only crazy person in this place.'

The building scarred with bullets, sandbags stacked by the doors. Inside we got a briefing on the situation in official UN-speak. Came down to two facts. One: Kigali was going to hell in a hand basket. Two: both armies were saying if the UN wanted to get caught in the middle, so be it.

We wandered back outside and watched the Ghanaian soldiers in the trenches, still digging and filling the sacks and building the sandbag walls higher and higher. Place was sure as hell lookin' like the last outpost.

'When will we have the opportunity to meet your General Dallaire?'

'Oh, like most generals. When he's damn good and ready. Two things keep him busy. Saving the lives of innocent civilians and saving the lives of his men.'

'Gettin' much help from the UN bureaucrats in New York?'

Major Laplante looked up with the unreadable face of a seasoned cop. He dropped two cardboard boxes and two litres of water on the back seat of his jeep. 'This is what you will get each day. Two meals in each box. And I would go easy on water. God knows when we will get more.'

'Seemed to be a pile of food and water on the flight.'

'Where do you think this came from?'

Rifles and outgoing shells punched the thick, humid air like stones hitting a pond . . .

'That sounded rather close,' said James.

. . . and me feeling the ripples flow by my head.

'And gettin' closer.'

'Jump in the jeep, you two. We 'ave the tour.'

'S'pose we'll see any elephants?'

'Pardon?'

'Africa, ain't it? I wanna see an elephant.'

'*Non.* No elephants in this place.'

'James, you lied to me.'

'Just a little white lie. Plenty of elephants waiting for you back in Kenya. Be a good boy and get in.'

I jumped in the front passenger seat and Jean-Guy slid the jeep through the sandbags and barbed wire and stopped to look both ways. Burnt-out cars and rubbish and the scattered forms of rotting bodies down the road. He took a deep breath and hit the gas. I hung the lens out the window and caught a blur of green jungle . . . and then passing a dead zone of smashed homes and burned-out buildings and bloodstained walls . . . then more bloated bodies baking in the sun.

'Christ. Forgot how that smell gets into your nose,' I said.

'I don't think you ever forget the smell. You just don't ever want to remember it. It is that awful,' said Jean-Guy.

Over near the edge of town and down a hill. The Kigali sports stadium standing on the edge of the jungle. Jean-Guy raced ahead and sounded the horn like he wasn't going to stop. Two Ghanaians yanked open the gates and we flew through a tunnel and on to the pitch and touched down in the end zone.

'OK. You can get out now and take pictures if you want.'

Hundreds of Tutsi refugees packed into a makeshift village of plastic tents and campfires, all surrounded by rolls of barbed wire. Up in the stands, a squad of Ghanaian soldiers with automatic rifles.

'Only a handful of our UN troops separates these refugees from the Hutu machetes outside.'

'Where are they from, Jean-Guy?'

'We find them hiding in the city and we bring them here. Look at the faces. I 'ave never in my life seen such fear.'

'Shots, Jon?'

'Think so.'

The sun poured firelike into the stadium and the sweaty air boiled into a rancid soup. Stinking wet dripping down the brown faces. I moved through the woodsmoke looking for fear. Then I smelt it, then I felt it drip down my own back, then I tasted it on my lips. Wet and sour. And me thinking fear always tasted the same. I switched on the camera and sucked it into the lens. Men and women and children stepping quietly as if not wanting to be found. An old man chopping wood almost without sound. A woman reaching into a bucket and scooping out a handful of filthy brown water and pouring it over the face of her child, the child not making a sound, the woman's panic-stricken eyes darting from side to side.

Kacrack! Crack! Crack!

The woman stopped and the child clutched her breast. The man stopped chopping the wood. The entire camp not moving and holding its breath like some terrified animal, listening to the killer sounds echo round and round the stadium, knowing that at any moment Hutu militia might rush in and cut them to pieces. But the killer sounds faded into stillness and the Tutsi refugees breathed once more.

Jean-Guy passed out some military-ration high-protein biscuits to the hungry kids. There weren't enough to go round. His round face trying to smile and promising he would come back. He walked over and nodded towards the jeep. 'Listen, I do not like to stay in one place too long. I want you to see the King Faisal Hospital before it gets dark.'

'Looks like this place?'

'Oh, you know. Worse.'

'OK, then. Let's go.'

Another run through the streets. Long shadows crossing the road, the sun sinking into the jungle, night coming soon. Round a curve and into another roadblock. Machine-guns in the trees following the jeep.

Tall, slim soldiers rising from unseen trenches in the bush. Flip-flop sandals and dusty clothes. Brown skin, determined eyes.

'These are Tutsi rebels.'

'Friendly?'

'Depends. Many 'ave lost relatives in the killings and many more suspect we are protecting the Hutu soldiers. *Ça va, mes amis!*'

The rebels looked through the car and checked our credentials. Jean-Guy glanced down to the camera on my lap, the lens up and pointing out the window.

'Please, be careful with that thing.'

'Yup.'

The rebels opened the roadblock and Jean-Guy hit the gas and drove on. A thin column of smoke floated up through the trees from just around the bend. Another roadblock of wood logs and tin roofing spread across asphalt. Hutu government soldiers within a hundred yards of the Tutsi.

'Seem awful fuckin' close to each other, Major.'

'It is 'ard to keep track of the checkpoints. And you do not want to be on the wrong side at the wrong time.'

The Rwandan government troops sat around a small fire and smoked hand-rolled cigarettes and just watched us. Whispers and grunts and pointing our way. Then out of the trees, thirty Hutu in civilian clothes. They walked towards the soldiers and squatted next to the fire. Machetes in hands. Firelight reflecting on steel.

'Yikes.'

'Yikes, indeed. Can you get a picture?'

'Maybe.'

'No, do not move. These are Hutu militia.'

'Double yikes.'

Dead-flesh smells flowed from a nearby ditch and drifted through the jeep. The Hutu just kept watching as if stoned on the dead-flesh smells and getting more stoned with every sniff. Finally, one of the soldiers stood and smiled with big white teeth. He waved us through, like a cat playing with three blind mice. Jean-Guy pulled ahead and rounded a turn and refitted his baseball hat and rubbed his mumbling chin.

'OK. I think that went OK.'

'Fuck me.'

'What would happen if Jon and I showed up at one of these road-blocks without a UN escort?'

'They would kill you in a second.'

'S'pose we can rule that one out, James.'

'Yes, I suppose so.'

Jean-Guy's hands tapped the steering-wheel, tense but cool, very cool. His eyes squeezing tight and scanning the trees for any sign of danger. His boots touching the brakes and the jeep bouncing through blast holes in the road. 'I hate to slow down in this place. But some-times the mortars hit the road and don't explode. We lost a truck just a few days ago. See anything?'

And James leaning out his window behind Jean-Guy . . .

'How about something like this?'

. . . and Jean-Guy hitting the brakes and twisting round and me scooting over for a look-see. Down under the jeep, just next to the rear wheel. One slightly dented but unexploded mortar round.

'Oops.'

'Yeees.'

'Gentlemen, welcome to Kigali.'

Jean-Guy manoeuvred round the shell and raced away like a bandit.

Few minutes later we were standing in the middle of King Faisal Hospital. Four floors built around two courtyards with five thousand Tutsi crammed into every inch of space. Place was a stinking pit of squalor. Mounds of human shit under every other step. Pools of rain-water mixed with green slime in the courtyards. At the edge of one pool, a woman dipping a cup into the slime and touching the cup to her baby's lips for a drink.

'This their drinkin' water?'

'Yes, I'm afraid so.'

Up a dark stairwell. Stepping over deadlike forms sleeping on piss-soaked blankets. Yellow eyes, unfocused and blank. Coughing and choking sounds echoing in the dark. Babies screaming like lunatics. A crooked old woman stumbling near the lens, vomit dripping down her half-naked chest. She collapsed in a heap of mad tears.

The camera followed Jean-Guy down another stairwell. A darker room stuffed wall to wall with the deathly sick. Sweat and piss and shit smells strangling what was left of life.

'There are no doctors or medicines here. So there is nothing for these people to do but die. A few days ago a shell landed inside the hospital. It killed fifty people. I sometimes think they were the lucky ones.'

James leaned up next to a wall. He was seething. 'That happens in Bosnia and NATO calls in air strikes.'

And we stood there breathing in the stench and listening to the sounds, watching human lives fade away.

'Shoot the hell out of this, Jon. Shoot the fucking hell out of this.'

'No problem.'

Through the halls stuffing horror after horror into the camera. Putrid sweat burning my eyes, a glob of stinking filth stuck in my throat. And me gagging and crawling on the ground framing shots and picking off pictures one by one. Each picture looking into the lens and begging for help . . . so I hit the roll button and let the pictures beg.

'Quick interview with the major?'

I put Jean-Guy against a rail and framed the scene over his shoulder. I watched his round face in the eyepiece.

'Look at these people. They are suffering and they need food. And we 'ave food stored around the city. But now fighting is getting close and we are constantly blocked by this side and that side. And each time that happens . . . that is one more day these people do not eat. And there has been no food delivered here for three days.'

'What would happen to these people if the UN garrison pulled out of Kigali?'

Zoom into the round face and see twenty-five years of military discipline on the line. Biting his lip trying to speak, the suffering around him ripping his heart out.

'You 'ave been around the city. You 'ave seen the roadblocks and the bodies. We cannot leave this place.'

Cut.

We wound our way out of the dark and into the sweaty sundown. I bent over and spat globs of filth from my throat and drew in air like a drowning man. Into the jeep and one more race down narrow jungle lanes.

'You gentlemen will be staying in the Meridian Hotel. But don't expect much, it's pretty bad. There's a company of Tunisian soldiers on the ground floor guarding the place and a few hundred refugees hiding on the upper floors. You can 'ave a room in the middle, I hope.'

Trenches all along the road and fortified positions mounted with heavy machine-guns. Small fires and the smell of roasting meat. Tall forms of Tutsi rebels amid the trees, AK47s in their hands ready to rip.

'Two days ago this was held by the Hutu. Now the rebels have control. Tomorrow, who can know? Lots of action around this place at night. So keep your heads down and away from the windows.'

'Hotel near the front-line, then?'

'Uh, sort of.'

A sharp turn between two rebel foxholes and presto . . . the fabulous Meridian Hotel. Twelve floors of target smack dab *on* the front-line. Tutsi fighters crawled from their foxholes and watched us pile out of the jeep.

'So do these chaps help with the luggage or what?' said James.

'S'pose it wouldn't hurt to ask.'

'Inside, you clowns. I 'ave to get back to Headquarters before dark.'

We grabbed the kit and ducked into the hotel. Dark and full of smoke. The Tunisians cooking up a meal over camp stoves in a corner of the lobby. Handshakes and *salam alekum*s all round and upstairs to Room 317. Blown-out windows and bullet-scarred walls. Chunks of masonry and shards of glass over the floor. Beat-up TV in the corner. Small door leading to a balcony just above the rebel trenches.

'Yeees. One was expecting a bit more from the travel brochure.'

'Uh-huh.'

We crawled over the floor, sweeping away bits of glass, laying out our sleeping-bags and opening the German army-issue Meals-Ready-To-Eat. All function, no taste. The door opened and a couple of white guys crawled in with a bottle of good whisky.

'Hello, lads. Welcome to Rwanda. How about something to wash down the MREs?'

Ken Harron and Jonathan Cavanaugh, WTN producer and camera-man out of Nairobi. Veterans of famines and wars throughout Africa. We offered some protein biscuits and they poured out generous portions of booze. Down in the trenches, Tutsi rifles cracked and zinged. Me and Jonathan set our cameras on tripods and let them roll on autopilot.

'More whisky?'

'Think so.'

'Get any shots today?'

'One or two.'

'Tough going, isn't it?'

'Yup.'

'Hear, hear.'

Crack. Crack. Kacrack.

'Doesn't seem very sensible to waltz off into the jungle looking for a battle.'

Shoosh . . . BOOM!

'Then again we may not have to go looking very far.'

'Ever wonder how it's always the same? Good guys, bad guys. Lots of innocent people killed in the middle.'

'Ah, yes, but this seems like much more than your average shithole.'

'How 'bout callin' it a seriously fucked-up place?'

'Way beyond fucked up, Jon. Nightmare City.'

'That bad?'

'Indeed it is.'

'Then how 'bout another drink?'

Rifles and shells popped in the jungle. Darkness fell and tracers sailed by the balcony. Then a single lightbulb hanging from the ceiling flickered till sixty watts of white light filled the room.

'Well, that adds a nice torture-chamber feel to the place,' said James.

'The Tunisians have a generator and kick it on for a couple of hours a night. If there's enough fuel.'

'Helps keep the bogeyman away I s'pose.'

'You guys been in any of the the loos yet?'

'Nope. Why?'

Then the TV sputtered and sparked and CNN appeared as if by wizardry.

'Fuck me. Big Brother lives.'

'And right at the top of the hour.'

'Big Brother! Big Brother! Give us the news!'

Top of the bulletin. Rwanda and more Rwanda, using a whole lot of dated footage. Then a bunch of other stuff followed by some boyo screaming sports scores followed by some woman telling us about all the interesting weather in Brazil. Then some commercials for forgettable products, then a serious voice booming through the bullet-scarred room . . . 'Crisis in Rwanda.'

'Indeed. We're running out of whisky.'

'Say it ain't so.'

Slow motion dissolves from one dramatic shot into another. Then a lanky guy in a bush jacket on the screen: 'And CNN will bring you the story!' We looked at each other and around the room. We crawled out into the hall and looked around some more.

'Hello!'

'Anyone here from CNN?'

'Doesn't seem to be here.'

'Too bad. We could have offered them a drink.'

'Oh, well. Nighty-night.'

The WTN crew crawled off to their room. Me and James peeled off our sweaty clothes down to our boxer shorts and sprayed every inch of exposed skin with anti-mosquito goop, grabbed our toothbrushes and opened the door to the bathroom. A foul smell slapped our faces. The toilet overflowing with a brown Matterhorn sculpture of aged and crusty shit. We slammed the door.

'That was fuckin' weird.'

'Yeees. Though one must admit to a certain degree of creative effort.'

'So was *The Blob*?'

'Pardon me?'

'Sci-fi flick in the fifties. Gooey monster from outer space.'

'I am not moving my bowels in this country. Ever.'

'Me neither.'

We crawled on to the balcony, brushed our teeth and spat over the low concrete wall.

'Right. One problem remains. I must drain the whisky.'

'Me too but I ain't goin' nowhere near the Blob in the toilet.'

'That appears to leave but one answer.'

'S'pose so.'

On with the helmets and flak-jackets, turn off the lights and out to the balcony again.

'Ready?'

'Indeed.'

We stood and dangled ourselves over the side. Two whiskied water-falls trickled down into the African jungle as rifles cracked twenty yards below. We hurried along as fast as we could.

'Jon, you do realize if we are killed at present . . .'

'And they find us like this . . .'

'. . . dressed in helmets and flak-jackets and boxer shorts . . .'

'. . . not to mention our dicks in our hands . . .'

'. . . it will not look good.'

'Nope, sure won't.'

The jungle rose and fell under a wide Rwandan sky. My eyes dozing on greens and blues and lazy puffs of white clouds. I was watching it all from the back of a UNHCR pick-up truck speeding through Kigali. Two UN trucks packed with protein biscuits following close behind. A relief convoy headed west for some place called Camp Runda. Seemed there were thirty thousand Hutu civilian refugees living on a stove-top plateau. They fled Kigali ahead of the Tutsi onslaught only to find themselves trapped in the middle of nowhere. The Hutu government asked the UN for food and water. Hutu children were starving, they said. Me and James asked to go along for the ride. The convoy leader was a square-headed guy named Roger Cormack. He looked us over from head to toe.

'Well, OK. As long as you guys understand we're going into a hostile area and we're unarmed.'

'Fine. Besides, we figure travellin' with the UN means there won't be much of a problem,' I said.

Roger checked us out from head to toe one more time. He tapped the ceramic plate of my bulletproof vest.

'Out here, it doesn't mean shit. Get in the back.'

A German stills-shooter jumped in as well.

'Hello. I am Fritz.'

'Welcome aboard, Fritz.'

'Where do we go?'

'Somewhere out there.'

'Sounds good.'

Hutu roadblocks every five minutes. Every car and truck and mule-drawn wagon searched by Rwandan government soldiers. Bad-ass pick-up trucks cruised the streets, Hutu militia goons with automatic rifles and machetes piled in the back. Black shapes darted through the back-streets from building to building. Maybe hiding, maybe searching, couldn't tell which. Corpses in the road and dead smells in the air. I held the camera under my arm grabbing pictures as best I could. Happy snaps from the city of the dead. Up a hill and round a bend to a church surrounded by Hutu militia. Hutu soldiers blocking the road.

'That's the church where God knows how many Tutsi were murdered.'

'Fuck me. I want that shot.'

'If you can get it without us getting killed.'

A mass of drooling evil swelled up over the back of the pick-up. His nostrils flared like smelling our white skin.

'*Belgique?*'

'*Non, non.*'

His eyes saw the cameras and he swung a machete at our heads.

'*Ne filmez pas ici! Ne filmez pas!*'

Roger leaned out the window and talked to the Hutu in a calm voice. The Hutu stepped away and let us through. I looked back and saw Hutu machetes gleaming in the sun.

The convoy rose over the hill and out of town. The trucks dropped into low gear and climbed higher. The jungle canopy shading us from the hot sun. We settled back and watched the world go by. Villages and farms burned to the ground. Blood-red graffiti painted on empty shacks. Some fresh graves, some bodies rotting in the open. All the murderous signs of Hutu militia.

'Quiet up here, ain't it?'

'Certainly is that.'

'I hate it when it gets this quiet.'

Wind blowing hot.

'Yeees. I suppose the good news is the boys with the machetes must know we're coming.'

'What's the bad news, James?'

'The bad news is the boys with machetes must know we're coming.'

Fritz didn't like the sound of that. Me neither. We looked around at the blurry wall of green jungle whipping by.

'Man, oh, man. This ain't right.'

Kacrack!

Our heads spun round and we saw it coming.

Swooosh!

A screaming ball of rocket-propelled grenade heading for the truck.

'Fuck!'

Slam on the deck as the shell ripped over our heads and exploded in the trees. Switch on the camera and point the lens towards James and

Fritz squashing together like a couple of sardines. The convoy raced ahead.

GTTTTTTRRRUPPPT! GTTTTTRRRPPP! GTTTTTRRRRRUPPT!

Heavy machine-gun fire cutting through the trees and me trying to claw through the truck bed. Another round and then just the rush of wind and the buzzing of rubber tyres on a jungle road.

'You forgot to mention the part about the boys with the fuckin' machine-guns, James.'

'Were you actually rolling on that?'

'Yup, most of it.'

'The shots came from that grass verge on the hill.'

'You don't say?'

We unpacked ourselves from the deck. Fritz looking at my head and out to the leaves brushing close by and back to my head again.

'You know, the leaves of these trees were shot to pieces, just about where your head is sitting.'

'You don't say?' My voice cracking.

I spun back the tape and rolled the last thirty seconds through the viewfinder. We all got a chance to see ourselves digging through the steel flooring trying to get lower and lower.

'Yeees. Suitably heroic, I think.'

'Or incredibly stupid for bein' here in the first place.'

The convoy passed through a roadblock of young Hutu and the jungle canopy gave way to a big hard sun and a wave of hellish heat. A slow line of skinny shapes with huge bundles on their heads moved along the road, Hutu refugees melting in the sun. Ten, fifty, hundreds. I pulled up the camera and rolled tape along the line of struggling Hutu and up the hill and on to a wide plateau. And there, shimmering in the heat, a massive jumble of grey smoke and thatched huts.

'Camp Runda, I presume.'

'S'pose we're safe now.'

'You don't really believe that, do you?'

'Nope.'

We followed a dirt track off the road, passed a broken-down bus in the grass, the windows stuffed with sweaty black faces. Roger Cormack pulled over and popped out of the truck for a stretch.

'Hey, Roger. You hear the gunfire back there?'

'Yeah, but I sure as hell wasn't going to stop.'

'Nope. S'pose not.'

'You guys OK?'

And us checking all our bits and seeing things were still attached.

'Yup.'

'Let's go, then.'

I climbed on top of the first lorry for high shots. The dirt track opened on to the plateau and we followed the melting Hutu refugees into the camp. The camera drinking in a sea of desperate black faces, black feet walking through mud and shit, children wandering alone and parentless. And coming through the crowd, Hutu soldiers with automatic rifles, then more soldiers. Far too many for a refugee camp. Fritz leaned over grabbing shots of hungry kids.

'Look out there. See those guys?'

'I have seen them. Strange.'

'This ain't good.'

A crowd circled the trucks and hemmed in the convoy. Not talking, just watching. I jumped down for some close-ups. Roger walked up, talking in a clip as square as his head. 'I'm going ahead to find someone in charge. Be back as soon as I can.'

'Problems?'

'Maybe, maybe not. Place has a nasty feel about it.'

'Yeah. Soldiers all over the place.'

'Yeah. Don't get lost in the crowd.'

I set up the tripod and compressed long shots into a series of smoky mirages. Packing the faces close together, feeling them sweat in the lens. And then picking out the soldiers in the crowd and hoping the soldiers didn't notice me noticing them. All the time feeling Hutu faces coming closer and watching my skin. Something hit the side of my face. Wet and warm. I wiped my cheek. Blood smeared on my hand.

Thwack! Thwack! Thwack!

On a table, under a tree. A machete chopping down hard and my eyes zooming into a mass of blood and meat and intestines. My stomach reeling and the machete chopping down again and blood splattering on the lens and into my mouth.

'Shit!'

I turned round and spat. Hutu faces laughed and giggled.

'Ce n'est qu'une vache!'

'What?'

'*La vache! La vache!*'

'Glad it's so fuckin' amusin'.'

I walked away, pushing through the laughing crowd, wiping the blood from my face. James was leaning on the pick-up.

'James, what the hell's a fuckin' *vache*?'

'That would be a fucking cow, Jon. Why?'

'Forget it.'

Roger came back with three Hutu officers and a pack of civilians. The civilians carried machetes. They greeted us with sneering smiles.

'OK. Here's the deal. We'll drive ahead through the camp. There's a storage house on the far side. We'll unload and leave. And we'll do it fast.'

'Sounds easy enough.'

The Hutu commander leaned into my face. Stale sweat smells dripping on to my skin. His eyes glaring. A sharp finger in my chest. 'And *you*. You will not take pictures of the soldiers.'

'Nope. Just people.'

And him leaning closer and spitting in my face. 'I don't care what you say! You lie! We are watching you! There are no soldiers here! Only refugees!'

Down behind the commander, a small Hutu dressed in black, grinning from ear to ear like a weasel.

'You will not take pictures of the soldiers! Only refugees!'

'Yeah . . . understood. Only refugees.'

Me and James climbed into the pick-up. Fritz got on to one of the trucks behind and the convoy moved slowly through the camp. Place was laid out like an African village. Straw huts and wood shacks along muddy lanes. Hutu sitting and waiting and baking in the brutal heat. And me taking careful shots of the faces watching us pass and seeing something in their eyes, something deadly. Behind us a mob gathered and began to follow. The something deadly felt closer.

'James, ever see *Night of the Living Dead*?'

'Rather odd question.'

'Yeah? Turn round. It's now playing at a theatre near you.'

And James looking back at the mob shuffling behind us. Thousands of dark eyes watching.

'Hmmm. Yeees.'

'I'm gonna swap tapes. I don't wanna lose the pictures of all these soldiers that ain't here.'

'Probably wise.'

I slid down into the pick-up and switched tapes. I stuffed the shot tape into the pouch of my flak-jacket next to a fat field bandage.

'James, hand me another blank out of the run bag. Think I'd better keep a spare on me as well.'

KABOOM! KABOOM! KABOOM!

Outgoing blasts of heavy guns. I jumped up, hit the roll button and waved the camera round in a wide circle. My eyes looking away from the lens like I had no idea what the hell was going on. Like I didn't even see the three giant 155mm guns in the middle of thirty thousand refugees. Nor the Hutu government soldiers shoving more rounds into the breech and blasting ninety-five pounds of high-explosive shells thirty-five kilometres across the sky into Kigali. I slid back down into the pick-up. Trying not to draw attention to the camera.

'Get anything?'

'Four or five seconds, maybe. Cock-eyed as shit. But if we slow down the shot we'll see the guns.'

'Unbelievable. An artillery base in the middle of a refugee camp.'

'You thinkin' what I'm thinkin'?'

'There may be a lot of Hutu militia hiding here as well.'

'And if all these bad guys know we've got their guns on tape, we're seriously fucked.'

'We may be seriously fucked anyway.'

'Huh?'

'Our photographer friend is still taking pictures like mad.'

'You're shittin' me.'

I looked back and saw Fritz hanging off the roof of the lorry snapping away at the guns. The mob pointing and watching him.

'Fuck me. Gotta switch tapes again.'

I opened the camera and hit the eject button just as the convoy stopped and backed up to the storehouse. The mob rushed ahead and surrounded the trucks.

'Not now, Jon. They're watching you.'

'Oh, swell.'

Hutu officers pushed through the crowd and shouted orders. Soldiers and men hauled boxes of protein biscuits from the trucks and carried them into the storehouse. One soldier stepped next to the pick-up. His eyes locked on me and the camera.

'I'm gonna duck into the storehouse and do the switch.'

'Then we have to hide them.'

'One step at a time, James.'

I jumped down and ran around shooting different angles waiting for the moment when suspicious eyes might turn away. A box fell and hundreds of biscuits splashed over the ground. Starving refugees scrambled for food till a dusty Mercedes skidded to a halt and the sweat-soaked Hutu commander climbed out of the car with the little weasel in black.

'Oh, fuck.'

'What is it?'

'Trouble.'

And me ducking into the storehouse and down behind a stack of boxes and pulling off the camera cover and hitting the eject button and hearing the tape wind off the heads and grabbing the blank in my flak-jacket.

'C'mon . . . faster.'

'You!'

Dirty boots marched into my eyeline. I switched off the camera and let the blank tape slide back into my flak-jacket. I looked up into the nasty glare of the Hutu commander.

'You!'

'Yeah?'

And stepping from behind the commander, the little weasel in black. A machete in his little weasel paws. His weasel face smiling with a tattle-tale grin.

'Come with us! Now!'

'OK, then.'

I followed them into a screaming mob. Roger and his two Ghanaian drivers overseeing the unloading and pretending not to notice James and Fritz against a wall, rifles pointing at their chests. Roger looked at me, his square-headed face saying, 'For God's sake, stay calm.' The little weasel in black slapped my flak-jacket with his machete and shoved me next to James. The Hutu commander leaned into us screaming in French for all the mob to hear. 'You filmed the guns!'

And James speaking French back in a calm voice. 'No, we didn't. We heard them and looked at them and turned away quickly. My camera-man, in fact, sat down so as not to appear to be taking any pictures. It's like you said. There are only refugees here.'

'You lie!'

And the mob howled. Edging closer.

The little weasel jumped in front of James. Machete blade ready to slice open James's throat.

'Who are you? Where are you from?'

'I'm a correspondent from—'

'*Belgique!*'

The mob howled again.

'No! I am British, Jon is American, and Fritz is . . . Fritz, what the hell are you again?'

'German.'

'Yes, of course. Fritz is German.'

'Lies! Lies!'

'Passports!'

The Hutu commander thumbed through the pages of our passports. Accusing tones with his staff. The little weasel in black grabbed the passports and waved them in our faces.

'Where are your Rwandan visas?' And waving them in the faces of the mob. 'They have no Rwandan visas!'

'Ahhh!'

'Hang on! We came in with the UN. Unfortunately there were no Rwandan officials at the airport to stamp our passports!'

'Spies! You are here to betray us!'

The mob crushed closer. Black hands reaching for our white skin. The soldiers pushed the mob back. But not too far.

'You will give us your film!'

Fritz rewound the roll in his camera and handed over a few rolls of film. I reached into the pouch of my body armour and felt the two cassettes. One shot full of soldiers that weren't really here, the other blank. My fingers going back and forth and back and forth till I pulled one out and handed it to James. And me looking at James and him knowing I was handing him the blank.

'And the one in the camera! Play it back! We want to see the pictures!'

'Just one moment. Jon, can we play the tape in your camera?'

And James looking at me and both of us knowing if they saw what was on the tape, we were dead.

'Nope. Not that kind of camera.'

'I see. I'm very sorry but we can't do that. It's not that kind of camera.'

'Lies! Lies!'

'I shall have my cameraman give you the tape from the camera. That's the best we can do.'

'*Les espions!*'

'Ahhh!'

And me and James whispering under the roar of the mob.

'We just gave 'em the bang-bangs.'

'We didn't have much of a choice. Still have the other one on you?'

'Yup, need to ditch it.'

'Indeed. Be careful.'

'*Les espions!*'

'*Non! Non! Écoutez!*'

James slipped into high-speed French with enough bluster and boff to focus the mob's attention. I stepped back just a bit. A Hutu soldier watched me lay the camera on the ground, then he turned away. I slipped back behind the lorry and ran up to the cab, pulled open the door and dug the shot tape out of my flak-jacket. I rolled it in a rag and stashed it behind the driver's seat. My mind spinning in a crash dive.

This is where it's gonna happen. Middle of fuckin' Africa.

And then grabbing a bottle of water off the seat and closing the door of the truck and looking straight into the death end of a .38 revolver. A young Hutu officer, his finger on the trigger, stepping closer and closer, till the muzzle touched the side of my head. I lifted the water-bottle to my lips and took a long slow sip, trying to think. Water dribbling down my face.

Middle of fuckin' Africa . . . Jesusfuckin'Christ.

I offered the bottle to the soldier. 'Drink?'

My hands were shaking.

He lowered the barrel and shoved it into my bulletproof chest. '*Allez.*'

The mob moving in closer. James still rattling away in French keeping the mob at bay. And then turning round to me in English. 'Christ. I can't keep this up all day, Jon. Have you . . . ?'

'Done it.'

'Oh. Well done.'

The little weasel in black shifted into full-tilt boogie. Stomping his feet and screaming curses in our faces and waving his machete above our heads. The mob grooving on the rush and howling for more, like a pack of hyenas.

'*Oui! Oui!*'

'*Tuez-les!*'

'*Tuez les espions!*'

The Hutu officers stood by nodding as if considering the cries of the people. Outside the trap, Roger and the Ghanaian drivers counted and recounted the food supplies as many times as they could, stalling for time. Hutu soldiers started pushing them back to their trucks. Roger pushed back and forced his way through the mob. 'Look, guys. They want us in our vehicles. They say we have to leave you here.'

'OK.'

'We'll wait as long as we can.'

'Thanks.'

'Whatever you do, stay calm. We're in this one together.'

'OK.'

A Hutu woman ran up to the little weasel in black. She babbled like a stoned-out witch and kept pointing towards my chest. A wide grin spreading across the little weasel's ugly face. He slithered close. 'This woman says she saw you with another cassette!'

'S'cuse me?'

My heart pounding.

'In your bulletproof vest! A cassette! Where is it?'

'Nope. No tape in my vest.' My legs feeling unsteady.

'She saw you at the truck! What were you doing? Hiding something?'

'It's hot. I was gettin' water. Here, want some?' Sweat dripping down my face.

'Liar!'

His weasel paws searched through my flak-jacket till he pulled out the field bandage. 'This is not a cassette!'

'Nope, it ain't. It's a bandage.'

'Where is it? Where is it?'

The witch woman wailed and shook her fists. The little weasel spat in my face. The Hutu commander raised his hands in the air. '*Assez!*'

Soldiers hauled the witch woman away and the commander grabbed the tape and film. He shouted orders to his troops and the soldiers disappeared into the mob. A ghostly sound began to swirl in the heat. Hutu voices chanting in weird rhythms and the sweat-soaked Hutu commander letting it sink into our heads. 'I am finished with you. You may leave . . .'

Hutu voices chanting louder.

'. . . if you can.'

'*Tuez les espions!*'

'Ahhh!'

'And what about all these people?'

'They are not my concern. Neither are you.'

He piled into his car with the little weasel in tow. The car looped round and drove by slowly. The commander laughing and the little weasel smiling through the window and tracing a finger across his throat. Two thousand Hutu crept forward with blood in their eyes.

'*Belgiques! Les espions!*'

'Fuck me. We been set up like horse thieves.'

'Yeees. Let's just try and move nice and easy.'

And me lifting the camera off the ground and us walking towards the trucks. Easy, easy. Hutu pushing us from side to side. Spit and shrieks and slaps in our faces. My eyes zooming through the angry crush. Clubs and machetes passing from hand to hand. Easy, easy. Fritz climbed into the back of one lorry. James and me kept walking to the lorry ahead, thinking it best to split up. The Hutu voices chanting louder and louder like weaving a spell.

'Back or front?'

'I don't think it really matters, Jon.'

'Well?'

'Well what?'

'Which one, then? Back or front?'

'Front.'

'OK, then.'

Reach for the door and ease it open.

'Ahhyaa!' The stoned-out witch woman jumped in front of us babbling words backwards and sideways and raising her hand in the air like an axe and chopping down on her neck, then howling with laughter and spinning away into the mob. Easy, easy. We climbed into the cab. Me next to a big Ghanaian driver and James next to the window.

'Hey. Mind if we come in?'

'Welcome, my friend.' The Ghanaian not smiling just looking straight ahead at the mob cutting off any way of escape. He slipped a two-sizes-too-small helmet on his big head. Hand-painted 'UN' on the side. The paint melting and dripping in the heat. His fingers touched a thirty-year-old carbine rifle next to the door. Twenty rounds, maybe.

'Thought you guys were unarmed.'

The big Ghanaian's head turned with a little-boy smile. 'This will be our secret, yes?'

'Guess it's somethin'.'

'Yeees. But not much good with this mob.'

The sun poured through the windshield like passing through a magnifying-glass. The hellish heat filled the cab and something grabbed my guts and squeezed. The fear monster sucking on the panic running through my brain. Outside, the witch woman still spinning and pulling her hair and pushing the men forward with mad shrieks and howls. Machetes sliced through the air in mock executions.

'Christ. If only I could get a picture of this.'

'Don't even think about it.'

'Ahhhh!'

'Don't s'pose we could just drive ahead.'

'Oh, no, my friends. They would chop us for sure.'

Bang!

A ghoulish old woman climbing up the lorry and swinging a club and hitting the bonnet over and over again. Her eyes flashing, her body writhing. Her head tossed back and a lusty moan oozing from her mouth. The moan seeping through the mob and rising and falling in vicious waves.

Next to James. A man's twisted black face pressing against the glass, his head tipping slowly to the side and a black hand chopping at his sweaty neck, up and down and up and down. A gurgling sound bubbling from his throat and his eyes rolling into his head. Rocks skimmed across the bonnet.

'Oh, shit.'

'Stay calm, Jon.'

'Just sayin' oh shit.'

'Try not to.'

'OK, then.'

And James and me trying not to make eye-contact with any one face in the mob. Our eyes zipping from here to there and back again. But mostly trying not to look afraid and all the time wondering when they were going to rip open the doors and drag us away.

'Look at their fuckin' faces.'

'Only gonna take one of them to start it.'

'Where's Tarzan when you fuckin' need him?'

Feet pounding in the dirt, and dust choking off the air, and everywhere, black hands chopping down on black necks like dancing before the feast. Thick tongues licking lips. Human beings no longer human but transformed into one hideous dead-eyed beast. Wanting release, wanting to fuck us good.

'*Tuez-les! Tuez-les!*'

'Ahhhhhh!'

The fear monster in my guts screaming for more and my brain spilling chemicals into my blood and the drugs washing my nerves with an ice-cold numbness. Shock twisting my head into dizzy little circles. Quick glance at James. Sweat dripping down his face.

'Fuck me.'

'Getting bad.'

'Just hope it's fuckin' quick.'

'I don't think it will be.'

'Maybe they'll go for our heads first.'

'God, I hope so. I don't want to see myself chopped apart.'

And James looking at me and me looking at him. Both of us melting in fear and sweat. Feeling it and seeing it in each other's eyes. Deathlike words and deathlike thoughts passing between us as comfort. Feeling ourselves slipping into darkness.

'My God. They're getting ready to do something.'

'Looks like it. Fuck me this is gonna hurt.'

'What about the tape?'

'Stashed in this truck.'

'You must tell me how you did that one day.'

'Yeah. Maybe when we get back to the lovely killing fields of Kigali.'

'That would be nice right now, wouldn't it?'

'Oh, yeah.'

And looking at the big Ghanaian. His eyes still staring straight ahead.

'If they drag us away . . . there's a tape behind your seat. Can you . . . get it back for us?' The words strangling my throat.

He pulled his gaze from the dead-eyed beast and smiled down on me. 'Don't worry, my friend. I will take care of it.' His voice like a whisper. His eyes red and wet and drowning in the screams of the mob.

'*Tuez-les! Tuez-les!*'

'What the fuck does "*tuez-les*" mean anyway?'

' "Kill them." '

'Yeah. Thought so.'

'Oh, shit, Jon.'

Black hands reaching through the window and clawing furiously, voices chanting and screaming and howling, hundreds of fists banging the lorry and the whole thing rocking on its wheels. And me looking through the windshield past the dead-eyed beast. A barren tree standing in a clearing. And me thinking that's where it'll happen. And seeing it in my mind. Dragged across the ground. Tied to the wide trunk. My guts spilling down my legs. Smelling my body rot in the African sun.

'You know, James . . .'

'Yes, I know.'

'Know what?'

'This is going to hurt.'

'Oh, God, yes, big-time.'

'Let's just get it over with.'

'Let's just hope it's quick.'

'I don't think it will be.'

'*Tuez-les! Tuez-les! Tuez-les!*'

Hands chopping faster and faster. Soon, very soon. Something long and sharp and dark poking through the fists and banging on the window . . .

'*Tuez-les!*'

'Jon.'

'James.'

'*Tuez-les!*'

'Good afternoon!'

. . . and there in the glass. Thick spectacles on a kindly black face. Some Hutu guy in a dusty black suit and skinny black tie and a black umbrella, shouting over the howls of the dead-eyed beast.

'The gentleman in the pick-up truck, he says you are from Moscow!'

'Yeah . . . what?'

'Moscow! I studied at Moscow University!'

Big smile across his kindly face. James rolled down the window.

'You don't say? I'm James Mates and this is Jon Steele. We both lived in Moscow. Well, I moved to London, but Jon is still there.'

'How nice! How do you do? You know, I heard the noise and thought I'd come down. I am a school-teacher! May I offer some assistance?'

And him holding on to the lorry, swaying from side to side.

'Well, yeah.'

He looked over the howling faces, shaking his head in disgust. 'I'm afraid these people are very ignorant! Where are the soldiers? They should have known this would happen to white strangers. Very dangerous times, these days.'

He climbed down and walked into the howls and screams waving his umbrella and shouting like a strict teacher to an unruly class. 'Listen to me! Listen! These people are our friends! They are here to help us!'

'*Belgiques! Espions!*'

'Ahhhh!'

'No! Listen! They are our friends! They are not Belgians! They have brought food! Would Belgians bring food to the Hutu? No! They are our friends! And if you kill them, there will be no more food, your children will starve! You know me! I do not lie! You must not kill them!'

And the teacher looking back with hurrying eyes and motioning the big Ghanaian to pull forward and the big Ghanaian pulling the two-sizes-too-small helmet down on his big head and turning over the engine and grinding the gears and slowly driving ahead.

'Move out of the way! They are our friends! Please do not kill them!'

The dead-eyed beast watched us pass . . . ready to pounce. But the teacher kept shouting and waving his umbrella and forcing the beast back and calling us forward inch by inch. Machetes and clubs and fists sank from the sky. Howls and screams dissolved into angry murmurs. And for a moment the beast was lulled to sleep.

The teacher jumped to the window, panic in his eyes. 'Listen to me. You must hurry! I will keep them occupied. But please, get out quickly! There are killers in the crowd. I am ashamed to say it. God help my poor country. Now please! Go quickly!'

We held our breath and drove ahead. Out the side window in the rear-view mirror, I saw the teacher behind us, still shouting and waving his umbrella, till the dead-eyed beast closed in around him, machetes rising into the air once more. The truck turned by the guns and the teacher disappeared from the glass. Out of the camp and up the dirt track and on to the jungle road. The big Ghanaian stopped a moment. He shuddered and shook with fear, then he rammed the lorry into gear and raced down the road.

'James . . . that guy back there, he fuckin' saved us.'

And James wiping his hands across his face. 'Yes, he did.'

'Who the hell was he?'

'I don't know, Jon.'

'James . . . when we left . . .'

'Yes, Jon, I know.'

We drove back to Kigali in silence.

I spent long hours in the dark of the Meridian Hotel, thinking about the kindly teacher who'd saved our lives . . . hoping he was OK . . . then trying to force him from my mind 'cause there wasn't a damn thing I could do about it.

'Hey, James.'

'Yes, Jon?'

'You believe in angels?'

His voice soft and quiet. 'Yes, Jon, I do. And after today, maybe you should too.'

'Yeah, maybe.'

And all through the night there was the taste of blood in my mouth, like it would never go away.

Afternoon matinée at Fort Apache. The Hutu guns from Camp Runda still lobbing heavy cannon shells into Kigali. Me and James and the WTN crew were hunkered down under the concrete ledge along the roof trying to get a shot of the damn things slammin' into something. So far no luck.

Shoosh . . . BOOM!

'Whack-a-what?'

'Whack-a-mole. Carnival game in the States. You got all these holes in a table and this little toy mole pops up outa one and you try and bang him on the head before he ducks back down. Hit him and you win a stuffed animal . . . poodle or a lion or somethin'.'

'And Kigali reminds you of whack-a-thing?'

'Sure does. Point the camera here, point the camera there. Always missin' the shot.'

Shoosh . . . BOOM!

'Got one!' called Jonathan, the WTN cameraman.

'Indeed!' cried James. 'Give the man a stuffed poodle.'

Black smoke rose over the city. Seemed the Hutu were trying to blow the Tutsi rebels out of the captured parliament building. The Hutu gunners had yet to hit it.

Shoosh . . . BOOM!

Then a now-hear-this voice shouting across the roof. 'Those fucking guys are wasting their goddam time!'

We turned round to an officer in a crisp uniform and blue beret standing alone in the middle of the roof. Sharp nose and a tough-as-nails chin. Narrow eyes, the kind that don't miss a thing. Perfectly trimmed moustache. Black insignia on green body armour, two now-see-this stars. Name on the breastplate, Lieutenant General Romeo Dallaire, commander of Fort Apache.

'Those RGF guys are so well dug in the Hutu are wasting their goddam ammunition! You know what the Tutsi do after a long day's march? They dig! Like fucking ants! They dig! Hutu can't touch them!'

His narrow eyes scanning the carnage below. His lips tight like he wanted to march down there and crack heads.

'Any of you know who invented modern tactical artillery warfare?'

And me and James looked at each other and then at the WTN crew. All of us wondering when the general was either going to get down or get killed. But Dallaire just stood with his hands on his hips, waiting for an answer from the dumbbell class of journos at his feet. No answer was offered.

'I'll tell you. Canadian general named Andrew McNaughton. Battle of Vimy Ridge. Ever hear of it? McNaughton sat across from the German front. The Germans were superior in number and dug in like hell. McNaughton knew he couldn't blast the enemy out of their bunkers so he divided the German encampment into grids and came up with a random sequence of targets and timings. Blasted the Germans for days and broke their will to fight.'

He looked down and took a breath and shook his head again, like knowing the mechanics of war. Like knowing in Kigali each shell meant more civilian slaughter.

'Artillery is as much a weapon of terror as a weapon of death. Look out there. No idea what the hell they're doing. Bastards are killing their own people.'

He marched forward and stood over me and James. 'You two over in Camp Runda yesterday?'

'Yes, General. Indeed we were,' said James.

'Heard you had a close shave. You all OK?'

'Bit spooky out there,' I said, 'but we're all right now.'

'You don't sound like a Brit.'

'No, sir. I'm a Yank. James is the Brit.'

'Well, that's OK too. Now, listen to me, this place is dangerous as hell. Watch your ass.'

'Yes, sir.'

He marched towards the steel door opening to the stairs. He spun round for another gaze over Kigali. Columns of smoke and pillars of fire. His hand rolling into a fist and tapping the steel door. Christ, would he like to crack heads.

'One more thing. I don't like anyone up here. There's a sniper picking away at this roof. Neither side will claim him. Shit keeps up I'm gonna come up here with a rifle and take out the son-of-a-bitch myself.'

He about-faced and marched down the stairs.

We saluted.

The shelling kept up through most of the night. Earlier, me and James and the WTN gang made a mad dash from Fort Apache back to the Meridian Hotel just before sundown. Tutsi rebels in the trenches blasting machine-guns into the trees as we screeched up to the parking lot. They held fire long enough for us to pass, then let the bullets rip one more time. Up in Room 317, we drank whisky and ate some cold MREs and drank more whisky and watched more of CNN's 'Crisis in

Rwanda'. News and endless promos talking about how we could only know what was going on in Rwanda by watching the 'World's Most Important Network'. More booze and another crawling expedition through the halls.

'Hey! CNN! You guys here yet?'

'Just the usual crowd of refugees.'

'We're fuckin' doomed without the World's Most Important Network here to tell us what the fuck is goin' on.'

'Indeed.'

Shell tracers cut across the dark sky and explosions flashed like dying stars. The Tutsi rebels were tightening their grip round Hutu throats, the Hutu lashing back like mad dogs. Me and Jonathan grabbed our cameras and we climbed on to the hotel roof for some night shots. We stayed up there a long time, watching and talking and thinking.

'Some job, isn't it?'

'Does have its moments.'

'Everywhere you go in this country it feels like somebody's out to kill you.'

'And every day we go out for more.'

'How do you explain your job to people?'

'I don't. I can't. Sometimes, I get around normal people and I feel kinda lost. Like I can't even fuckin' breathe.'

'Tell me about it.'

And the battle roared on.

I woke in the morning amid a weird calm. I crawled out of my sweat-soaked sleeping-bag and peeked over the balcony. Dawn's early light through a blue haze. The jungle chirped and whistled and croaked. Leaves like elephant ears hanging damp and heavy from the trees and a white mist drifting through the valleys. I pulled on the same sweat-soaked clothes from the day before and the day before that, and I remembered my dream. New York City. Midtown. Standing in a Jewish delicatessen. Bagels and lox, buttered rolls, coffee . . . white, no sugar. And this little Jewish waitress with one of those thick New Yak accents holding the coffee under my nose and saying, 'Gimme three hundred bucks.' And me saying, 'But I only got five dollars!' And her saying, 'Look, buster, don't stand there like a nudnik. You want coffee or not?'

'Please! I need coffee!'

'Jon, what are you talking about?'

'Nothin'. Just dreamin' 'bout coffee.'

'Oh, yes, please, make it two.'

'Not at three hundred bucks a cup.'

'Excuse me?'

We strapped ourselves into our flak-jackets and found our helmets and grabbed the camera kit and walked down the stairs through hundreds of Tutsi refugees. New arrivals from the terror in the streets.

'Place seems to be fillin' up.'

'Tourist season, you know.'

'You don't say?'

'Yeees. Come to Kigali and die.'

'Stick to reporting, James. Tourism ain't your bag.'

'I don't know. I think I'd be rather good at it.'

The Tunisian soldiers were cleaning their rifles down in the lobby. More *salam alekum*s and handshakes all round. Outside the shattered glass doors, Major Jean-Guy Laplante was huddled with a small Tutsi officer. The officer's eyes wide and angry. His hands waving up at the hotel and down towards the nearby rebel trenches. Tutsi rebels climbing out of the dirt in their flip-flop sandals and dusty clothes. AK47s still warm from last night's battle. The Tutsi officer stormed off and Jean-Guy strolled into the hotel.

'Good mornin', Major. What's up?'

'Our friend out there says you were on the roof last night. Taking pictures, *oui*?'

'Yup.'

'Well. He says if you do it again, they will kill you.'

And Jean-Guy refitted his cap and nodded like he was reporting last night's scores from the French Canadian Semi-Pro Baseball League. Quick pan out the doors, the rebels still standing with rifles in hand and the Tutsi officer pointing our way. James raised his shoulders and eyebrows as if addressing Parliament.

'Well. If that's going to be their selfish attitude you may tell them we shall just stay off their roof.'

'Yeah, me too.'

'Her Majesty's press, after all.'

'Yeah, me too.'

And Jean-Guy's head still nodding. 'You two guys are very weird.'

'You should have been with us in Siberia, Jean-Guy,' said James.

'What were you doing in Siberia?'

'Fifteen to twenty for killin' some waitress over a cup of coffee,' I said.

'Remind me not to ask you two clowns any more questions.'

'Well. If that's going to be your selfish attitude . . .'

'Yeah, me too.'

'Let's go.'

'Where?'

'Out there. The rebels took a village in the hills last night. They want us to see something.'

'See what?'

'Bodies.'

A long bumpy ride over jungle trails. Tutsi forces held the low ground with Hutu government troops up on the ridges firing down through the trees. Jean-Guy was driving right through the middle like a bat outa hell. A jeep full of hardcore rebels leading the way.

'So I 'ave convinced them to take us to this village. They were not happy about it but I told them if there was a massacre, then they must let the press see it. Like I said, I do not 'ave a lot of experience at this press stuff. I 'ope this was a good idea.'

'You're doin' fine, Major.'

'Indeed. A most pleasant tour of the countryside, Major.'

'How do I tell if you two clowns are being funny or not?'

'Easy. If we're scared shitless, then we're bein' funny.'

'So what about right now?'

'Laughin' our asses off.'

'Hear, hear.'

We pulled up to a heavily fortified line. Rebels rose from their positions and surrounded the jeeps. Local lingo back and forth in excited tones. The enemy was ready to counter-attack . . . hands signalling too dangerous to go on.

Jean-Guy cut in with his *québecois* and insisted we go ahead, and the rebels let us pass. The jeeps ploughing through the dirt and dashing across a wide clearing in plain sight of Hutu guns. Jean-Guy slammed the accelerator to the floor and we all held our breath till we slipped behind the trees of the next hill.

'OK. That went OK, I think.'

'Christ, Major, we're s'posed to be the weird ones.'

'Oh, you know. I mean we came all this way anyway.'

The trail narrowed into a jungle track. Ruts and holes making the going very slow. Then up along a ridge and stop at the edge of a dead quiet village. Tutsi rebels came out from the trees. Rifles moving this way and that, ready to kill. The jeeps backed into the trees out of the line of Hutu fire and we climbed out with the camera kit. The rebels gathered us in a circle and squatted us down in a pack.

The local commander rattled off the situation in a hushed voice. He said the rebels had come in at dawn after a long firefight. Hutu snipers still controlled the hills and were shooting anything that moved. Three rebels down already. There was only one way into the village, up along the main path. We had to stay low and quiet.

'*D'accord?*'

'*Oui.*'

'*Allez.*'

'Hang on.'

I pulled a small jar of Vicks VapoRub out of my flak-jacket and smeared a glob under my nose. I passed the jar around. Everyone smearing a glob under their nose.

'You've done this before, I take it.'

'Yup.'

'This stuff really help?'

'Better than nothin'.'

'Make a hell of an ad campaign for Vicks.'

'*Allez.*'

We walked near the treeline and followed a wood fence over a small hill. Huts and shacks spread out in a farming village, plots of tilled land silent and empty, cows cut open and rotting on the path. The rebels signalled us to move quickly through the next clearing in a group, no stragglers . . . moving one at a time would give Hutu snipers a sure-as-hell chance to kill someone. We ran till surrounded by a cluster of homes. Some made out of straw, the better ones made out of clay, a few with walled-in gardens. The air was humming with flies. Thousands of them. And not another sound of life.

'*Les Hutus ne peuvent pas nous voir ici.*'

'OK. We can move around in the village. They can't see us now.'

The pack moved ahead twenty metres. Me and James lingered back with the camera. Over in the tall green grass. A body sprawled under a rumble of flies. Rotting-meat smell rolling over the Vicks vapour and sliding down into my lungs. It swirled inside, washing every cell of my body with menthol-flavoured death. I moved along with the camera near the wood fence. A bloodied dress wrapped round a mass of bloodied flesh. A young girl, lashed and cut to pieces. Her hands lying in a nearby ditch.

'Yeees. We can't use much of this.'

'Nope. Ain't gonna be easy.'

'You have any more Vicks?'

'Yup.'

Everywhere, every step. Bodies chopped to hell, steaming and swollen in the heat. Over near a clay house, beyond the fence, a bloated black form shimmering in the midday sun. Flies hovering low over it like a small dark cloud. He lay face down in a bloodsoaked field. The field in which he'd planted vegetables to feed his family. The family was nearby, chopped to pieces and strewn across the dirt like garbage.

'Jesus.'

'You can see it happenin'.'

'How do you mean?'

'He's next to the house, the family's out in the field. They were probably hidin', then the bad guys broke in. Man told his family to run for it and he tried to hold the fuckers back. They dragged him out and sliced him open, then they chased the others down. Killed them one by one.'

'Bastards. Fucking bastards.'

'Makes you think how lucky we were the other day at Camp Runda.'

'Don't remind me.'

'Hard to forget.'

'Yes. It will be hard to forget any of this.'

'Trust me, James. You won't.'

I left James with his thoughts and walked alone through the slaughter. Hot wind blew up the path. Flesh rot and dust whipped round my head. Vomit rose in my throat and I gagged for air and sucked in a clump of flies. I staggered to the edge of the grass and spat and spat and wiped the dust from my eyes. And just below me, the body of a small child. Tiny hands clawing the ground. His head gone. My eyes panning with the flies and zooming in on something in the grass. A small round clump of blood-matted hair and two dead eyes staring back at me, like he was screaming for help ... and coming closer and coming closer.

'Oh, God!'

And me stumbling backwards and smashing down hard on my legs and shoulder. The camera crashing into the dirt.

'Goddam it!!'

Rebels spun round, weapons ready to blow me apart. James ran over and pulled me up on my butt. The rebels turned slowly back and walked on.

'Just what they need, Jon. A loudmouthed American with a weak stomach.'

'Fuck it, fuck it!'

He looked into my eyes like he could see the picture in my head.

'What is it?'

'Nothin', nothin'.'

Then a tingle on my arms and legs. Something warm and thick on my skin. Blood dripping down my arm. Hundreds of death-sucking flies crawling over my skin.

'Oh, shit. Get 'em off me.'

'Easy, Jon.'

James pulled out a pocket-knife and cut open the knees of my jeans. More blood and more flies. He pulled a field bandage out of his flak-jacket and ripped it open. We brushed away most of the flies and picked away the ones that wouldn't let go. They buzzed back to the rotting corpses in the grass.

'Nasty cuts.'

'I ain't havin' a good day.'

'I'd say you're doing all right.'

James poured water down my arms and knees and wrapped the cuts in thick bandages. I pulled the camera on my lap and checked it over ... the pistol grip was broken in half, the focus ring of the lens was bent and the eyepiece was hanging by a cable. I wrapped some gaffer-tape round the eyepiece and mounted it back on the camera. James pulled me to my feet.

'Everything OK?'

'May hobble a bit, but I can do it.'

'Not you, the camera. You are replaceable, the camera is the property of ITN.'

'Fuck off.'

'Just as I thought, you're good as new.'

Another courtyard. Seven more bodies hacked to pieces. Silence and horrible death smells. I framed the bodies through the grass and from behind bushes, trying to turn the hideous mounds of rotting flesh into pictures people would look at for a long time . . . all the time wishing I could cram the smell into the lens and broadcast it through every television in the world.

A rebel soldier touched my arm and motioned me to follow. I hobbled after him and pointed the camera down to his side. A thin brown hand clutching the black barrel of an automatic rifle. Pan up and follow the back of the rebel walking alongside a high fence then cutting through trees and bushes and into a small courtyard. The soldier turns to the lens and points away and the camera pans across a yard of rubbish and blood. And me thinking I would see a pile of death, till panning some more and seeing a frail old Tutsi man sitting in a rickety wooden chair.

'Fuck me. James, he's alive.'

'I don't believe it.'

The Tutsi rebel touched my arm and pulled me closer.

'*Les* Hutus killed dis village.'

'Why'd they leave him?'

'He sick and old. He not walk. His childs all dead.'

And me looking around at the slaughter and smelling the stench. 'Jesusfuckin'Christ.'

We moved close to him. A wood cane in his withered hands. A ragged straw hat on his ancient head. Pus oozing from his red, sick eyes and flies crawling over his face. James knelt close to him and touched the old man's hands. 'Sir, may I talk to you?'

A soft sound crept through the old man's parched lips like a last breath. The rebel bent low and spoke in the native tongue. The old man swallowed and nodded his ancient head.

'What is your name?'

'Karajesh.'

'Could you tell us what happened?'

The old man listened, then sat in silence as if trying to remember. James took his handkerchief and wiped the ooze from the old man's face, touching him like someone he loved. The old man raised a withered hand toward the trees and the nightmare returned once more.

'*Ils sont venus . . . sont venus.*'

They came, they came. The killings went on for days. Rape, torture, terrible screams. Chopping sounds and more terrible screams. They put him in this chair and he sat there unable to move. Just listening to the sounds of slaughter till there were no more screams, no more sounds. He sat there for days.

'I'm sorry to ask. We will tell your story to the world. I'm so sorry.'

And James touched the old man again and the two of them stayed motionless for a long time. Then the old man's ancient fingers touching James's face as he whispered, '*Merci. Merci.*'

'James. I need some more shots.'

'Yes . . . yes.'

James rested the old man's hands on his cane and walked away. I stepped back and set the camera on the ground and framed the old man at the long end of the lens. One old man sitting in the sun as if taking in the air of merciless death. Slow zoom into his face. The lens full with pain and grief and shock, the runny ooze dripping from his red sick eyes once more. Looked like tears.

'Jon.'

James standing at the opening of the old man's thatched hut. He nodded into the darkness.

'Bad?' I said.

'Just come see.'

I walked across the bloody yard, by the old man in the chair, and ducked under the low entrance of the hut. Down in the dirt on a straw mat, the old man's wife, lying under a thick wool blanket. Her skeleton-carved flesh shivering in the sweltering heat. All her hair fallen from her head on to the dirt. She was half dead.

'You gotta be kiddin' me. How the fuck could they just leave them like this?'

'Bastards. Fucking bastards.'

I moved close and pulled away the blanket. She lay in her own shit and piss and death sweat. Her skin hanging from her bones like a bag. I pulled the blanket over her shoulders and tucked it up under her chin. Down near her face, a glass of water and a few UN-issue high-protein biscuits on a broken plate.

'Jean-Guy left them.'

'Poor woman ain't long for the world.'

'I know.'

The woman's half-dead hand reached from under the blanket and crawled through the dirt. Broken and yellowed nails. Her hand opening and her skeleton fingers quivering, begging. I put one of the biscuits into her hand and her fingers closed round it and then let go. She was too weak to feed herself. I held her hand and lifted the biscuit to her mouth. She sucked on it like a baby.

'Jesusfuckin'Christ.'

I moved back and sat with the camera in my lap and focused into the woman's bald-headed face. Wet gums, blackened teeth . . . crunch, crunch, crunch. Her eyes, glazed with death and horror, always staring out there. Out there, where the children who grew in her womb and suckled at her breast lay slaughtered. She could smell them rotting in the hell-hot sun.

'Jon, Jean-Guy is calling us.'

'Should we take 'em back to Kigali? We can't just leave 'em.'

'Seems they want to stay here with their dead children. The rebels are taking care of them.'

Up to the edge of the village, rebels were digging trenches and lifting heavy machine-guns on to mounts and slapping in killer ammunition belts and taking aim across the valley towards Hutu-held Kigali. Tutsi fingers twitched at triggers and beaded talismans. Some fucker was gonna pay for this. Some fucker would pay.

'Over here!'

Rebels pushing against a huge gate. We ran over and gave a hand. Pushing and pushing till feeling something give way and the gate swinging wide and a blast of dead-flesh smells hitting us like a high-powered bullet.

'Oh, fuck.'

'Jesus.'

Bodies all down a hillside. Swollen and purple and cut to shreds. And all of us falling over and coughing up our guts. I dropped on to my bandaged knees and leaned against the gate and grabbed as many shots as I could without breathing. The stench stinging my eyes and slipping deeper down my lungs. Tasting it on my tongue and feeling it churn in my stomach. And trying to hold myself upright and frame shots of the bodies. A hand in the dirt, a leg in the weeds, a foot next to a lantern . . . blood, blood, blood. And then losing it and falling over and vomiting in the dirt.

We closed the gate and staggered away.

'Jesus.'

'Bastards. Fucking bastards.'

Rifles cracked from the high ridge and Tutsi guns began to return fire.

'We 'ave to go now. It will be dark soon. We do not want to be in the middle of this one.'

Back towards the jeeps. Passing the bloody lump of small-boy flesh in the grass. Blue shirt, blue trousers. Hands still clawing the ground.

Help me . . . please help me.

And then stopping cold in my tracks and shaking my head.

Please . . . help me.

'One second.'

And running back and kneeling in the grass.

'Jesus, Jon. Can you make that shot work?'

'Gonna try.'

Roll.

Tall green grass swaying in the wind. And through the grass a small blue shape steaming in the sun. Just a hint of blood. Tiny hands clawing at the ground. And me thinking of the people thousands of miles away looking at the picture on their TV screens and them seeing nothing but a small blue shape with a hint of blood . . . and not seeing *him*. Not knowing the small blue shape was once a little boy who laughed and dreamed. Not smelling his body rot in the dirt. Not seeing his blood-matted head, his still begging eyes.

Some fucker would pay.

Cut.

'Get what you need?' asked Jean-Guy.

'What I need is a fuckin' machine-gun.'

I was standing alone in the map room of Fort Apache, looking at

Rwanda and Uganda and Zaïre and Kenya and a whole bunch of other places I'd never heard of before. And I started to wonder how some place so small and so far from anywhere could be so fucked up. Corpses washing into Lake Victoria, bodies along the roads. No one with any idea of how many Tutsi had been slaughtered.

President of the United States Bill Clinton put out the word that Rwanda wasn't worth it. He implied that while the killings were disturbing, getting involved was not in the strategic interests of the United States. Scary thing was, most Americans probably thought the same thing. Bunch of ignorant Africans killing another bunch of ignorant Africans, right? Most of my fellow countrymen just like me, standing in front of a big map not knowing the difference between Burundi and Bujumbura.

'Can I help you?'

And turning round and seeing General Romeo Dallaire walking through the doorway looking his sharp, crisp self. A stack of papers tucked under his two-star arm.

'No, sir. 'Scuse me. I was just lookin' at the map tryin' to figure out the great unknown.'

A smile cut along the corners of his perfectly trimmed moustache. 'Hell of a place, isn't it?'

'Yes, sir.'

He dropped the papers on the table and stood next to me. The two of us considering the great unknown before us.

'Damn difficult place.'

'Yes, sir. Though kinda hard takin' a war seriously when you got one side called Tutsi and the other side called Hutu.'

'Till you get into the streets.'

'Yes, sir. Till you get into the streets. Well, thanks for your time, sir. I'll leave you alone.'

'No. No. You got some time? Then stick around.'

'OK, then. Mind if I ask you how a bunch of rebels in flip-flop sandals can overrun an established army in a matter of weeks?'

'That's a good question. The Rwandan Patriotic Front has one damn good commander. Guy called Paul Kagami – ever meet him?'

'No, sir.'

'Man knows how to fight.'

General Dallaire walked up to the map and moved his hands over the map, up and down and side to side.

'Son-of-a-bitch ran down from Uganda and fanned out in two lines. The RGF – you know who the hell the RGF is, don't you? Good. The RGF lost control of their supply lines and lines of communication. They've been falling back into the hills with no real plan. RPF has the city surrounded . . . here, here, and here. But if the RGF countered with fifteen hundred men through here and over here, well, hell, they could hold off Kagami's advance and buy time to regroup and maybe even blow Kagami's boys back to Uganda.'

'Doesn't seem like that's gonna happen.'

'No. It doesn't.'

'Ever feel like you wanna get in there?'

'How do you mean?'

'Other day on the roof, when we were all watchin' those shells hit Kigali, you looked like someone who wanted to get in the middle of it and crack heads.'

Another smile along the edge of his perfectly trimmed moustache. 'Well, you know. A soldier looks at battle as science. You analyse it and study it and try and learn from other people's mistakes. Sometimes I look at the RGF and wonder what the hell they're doing. And then I look at Kagami and think the man has guts. He instils that into his men with military discipline. God knows how long this will continue.'

His eyes roamed over the map, imagining different battles and counter-attacks.

'The Tutsi. How many killed so far, sir?'

His eyes fell from the map down to the floor. He shook his lieutenant-general head.

'Don't forget all the decent Hutu trying to save Tutsi lives. With all the reports coming in could be half a million. Probably more.'

'Jesusfuckin'Christ. 'Scuse me, sir.'

President of the United States . . . half a million human beings hacked to death . . . not in the strategic interests of the United States.

'How the hell could it happen, sir?'

'Let me tell you something. I warned the UN. I asked for more troops. I could have stopped this with five thousand well-armed troops.'

'You're kiddin' me?'

'Let me show you something.'

He dug through his papers and pulled out a two-page memo. 'I sent this to UN Headquarters months ago. We had cables and codices going back and forth. I warned them, I asked for more men. I told them we needed to just go in and seize all the militia's weapons. Yes, it would have been difficult and most probably messy, but look what's happened. We could have made a difference here.'

My eyes scanned over the document. Two pages. Official-looking headings and official-looking words directed to people with official-sounding titles at UN Headquarters in New York. Words about informants and plans by Hutu militias to slaughter Tutsi civilians. All in official UN-speak. Had a feeling of 'Warning!' and 'Help!' all over it.

General Dallaire slapped the document with his hand and stuffed it back into the stack of papers on the desk. 'I warned them.'

'What happened, sir?'

He just looked at me, not speaking, then he stared at the map. Cannon fire rumbled beyond the hills like a coming storm. General Dallaire leaned back on the table and listened to the sounds echo through the room.

'What you're not tellin' me, sir, is they didn't listen.'

'You know. It's a goddam tough situation out there. As it is now I've got enough men to protect the people under my command and run a few relief operations. Even that gets tougher by the day.'

'Yes, sir, s'pose it does.'

'Where you from?'

'Montana.'

'Beautiful country out there.'

'Yes, sir, sure is.'

Racing through the streets of Kigali again. Jean-Guy stomping on the gas and pulling his baseball cap snug on his head and turning hard and going faster, heading for the Red Cross hospital deep in Hutu-land. Me and James scrunched down in our seats holding on for dear life.

Kacrack! Kacrack! Zzzing!

Camera out the window spraying the air for pictures.

'Fuck me.'

'Oh, you know. I don't mind the shots but the cracks and zings make me nervous,' said Jean-Guy.

'Long as the fuckers don't go woopwoopwoop,' I said.

'Very unusual conversation up front.'

'Zing means the bullet already went by your head.'

'Oh, yes, I've heard this. Remind me about the "woopwoopwoop".'

'Means the bullet is pushin' the air away in front of you and you're 'bout to be hit.'

'Ah, I see.'

Kacrack! Zing!

'Let's hear it for all those cracks and zings then,' said James.

'Let's hope those fuckers are bad shots.'

'Listen, my friend. They don't even 'ave to be good shots, just lucky.'

'Say, Jean-Guy, you're in a cheery mood.'

'This place gets to me sometimes. You can never know who is shooting. Both sides would like us out of the way . . . *merde*. I will miss you two clowns. Sorry I 'ave to throw you out.'

'Well, I, for one, shall remove your name from my Christmas-card list.'

'Yeah, me too.'

'Don't worry. I'll be spending Christmas here anyway. But since you two 'ave been here, there are a hundred more journalists in Nairobi screaming for a turn. The general says we must rotate you guys out because he only wants four or six journalists at a time in this place. I hope this is OK.'

Kacrack! Crack! Zing!

'Now that you fuckin' mention it, it's swell.'

'Indeed.'

We crossed a series of Hutu checkpoints, vicious eyes watching us pass each and every time. My own eyes catching pictures through the town . . . burned-down houses, bloated corpses, well-fed dogs. Another checkpoint and then down a small mountain road where the jungle squeezed the daylight from the sky. Our voices quiet, our eyes searching. The road narrowed into a single dark lane surrounded by thick trees. Further down the road, firesmoke floating across the ground, then rocks and hubcaps and steel rails and stumps of trees blocking the road.

'Hmm. They 'ave a new checkpoint.'

Beyond the checkpoint, the road rolled down the hill to where a Red Cross flag hung from the trees. A hundred yards on, the Hutu were building another checkpoint. The Red Cross hospital was surrounded.

Government troops crept from the jungle and walked slowly towards our jeep. They raised automatic rifles to their sides and snapped bullets into the firing chambers. Hutu militia sat on the ground nearby, busily sharpening their machetes. Young boys watched intently as if learning the murderous trade.

'Christ. Nasty group.'

'I do not like the look of this place.'

'Welcome to fuckin' Checkpoint Zombie.'

A flat-faced Hutu leaned through the window, his breath reeking of alcohol and cooked meat. He snarled and turned the barrel of his pistol towards Jean-Guy's head.

'*Qu'est-ce que vous faites ici?*'

Jean-Guy pointed down towards the hospital.

'*On va à l'hôpital de la Croix Rouge.*'

'*Pourquoi?*'

Hutu hands reaching through the windows and searching through our bags.

'*De la nourriture! Donnez-nous à manger!*'

We handed over whatever provisions we had – biscuits, candy, chewing-gum, couple bottles of water. The flat-faced Hutu waved his fat black finger in Jean-Guy's face. His dark eyes flipping in his head as if sorting words in his drunken brain, then his slurry voice exploding. '*Nous savons ce que vous faites!*'

Behind him, Hutu militia rose like coming out of the grave. They shuffled towards us . . .

'*Nous savons ce que vous faites!*'

. . . till the flat-faced Hutu raised his hand in the air. The Hutu militia stopped as one and swayed from side to side, firesmoke wrapping round their legs. The flat-faced Hutu leaned closer to Jean-Guy and whispered, '*Nous savons ce que vous faites.*'

The goons stepped back and Jean-Guy drove ahead.

'Christ. Looked very familiar, didn't it?'

'No shit. Like one bad horror movie that keeps playin' over and over again.'

'These guys must 'ave been drinking since dawn.'

'Smokin' their brains out as well,' I said.

'Think so?'

'Trust me on that one, Jean-Guy.'

'Listen. We do not want to stay too long in this place, OK?'

'What the fuck was Captain Doom sayin' back there anyway?'

'Uh, let's see. "*Nous savons ce*" . . . *oui* . . . "We know what you are doing." '

Turn under the flag and drive through the trees up to the gates of the Red Cross hospital.

Nearby. A whistle . . . a flash . . . an explosion and molten metal cutting through the rush of burning heat. Three kids dragged to the emergency room. Blood splattered across the floor.

Kick on the camera and roll.

A little girl screams in pain as three nurses hold her down. Her right foot blown to pieces. Antiseptic and cotton touching the wound and the little girl screaming louder. The nurses' faces tighten and their hands bear down. The girl's screams surrender to murmurs of pain.

Pan right.

A tall boy bows his bloody head. His face contorted and twisted as latexed fingers squeeze together the gash in his skull. The boy's chest peppered with shrapnel. Tears pouring from his eyes and raising his hands and seeing nothing but his own blood.

Just to the left. Doors open into a makeshift operating theatre. Bright lights spotting down on a white table. A small black body motionless in the light as nurses wash the boy's skin with white liquid. A tray of sharp knives carried across the room. Back in the corner, a tall white man in a green smock tying a surgical mask round his face.

James poked his head inside. 'Excuse me, Doctor. Would you mind terribly if we filmed?'

'Well, hi there! No, come on in! Just shut the door behind you.'

'Thank you.'

'Hey! Don't mention it. Where you guys from?'

'British television.'

'Oh yeah? BBC or ITN?'

'ITN.'

'That's great. Careful you don't touch anything.'

A four-year-old boy lay under the lights. Fresh stitches holding his stomach together, left side of his face peeled away like a potato, a tiny ear dangling in clump.

'Is he gonna make it?'

'Hey! American. From the West, it sounds like.'

'Great Falls, Montana.'

'Is that right? I'm from just north across the Canadian border.'

'Is that right?'

'Sure is.'

He bent low studying the boy's blown-apart face. His doctor eyes focusing carefully into the wound. 'Stitched the little guy's stomach together already. It's pretty bad. You would not believe the size of the worm I pulled out of this kid's guts.'

'All right if we take pictures and talk while you work?'

'I suppose I can do that.'

'May I ask your name?'

'Sure. John Sundon.'

The nurses scurried around with cotton balls and liquids and bloody knives. John Sundon picked up a pair of tweezers and pulled the flap of skin across the boy's face this way and that, figuring how he was going to put it back together.

'Least this one got here alive. There's kind of a weird order of natural selection in Kigali. If you're not strong enough to make it to the hospital then you just die out there in the streets. Lots of times all I can do is finish the work of the bullets and bombs and slice off what's left of an arm or a leg.'

And John Sundon's hands still pulling at the skin and stretching it as far as it would go . . .

'I'd really like to put this kid's face back together but I may not have enough skin to do it. Suppose I could borrow some from somewhere else off his body. Don't think he'll miss it.'

. . . and then laying the brown skin down on the bloody face and picking up the shredded ear and holding it against the boy's head and checking it against the kid's other ear and then looking back and forth like a proud barber making sure everything was nice and even.

'You just do the best you can do,' he said.

And me walking round them in wide circles filming what felt like a small miracle under the lights.

'How'd you find your way here, Doc?'

'Can't really get this kind of practice back in Canada. Here it's kind of non-stop trauma. Twenty-four hours a day, seven days a week.'

John Sundon's eyes looked up from the boy into the lens. They reflected hope and sadness. Like it didn't matter that just now he was having one good moment sewing the kid back together. This place was a slaughterhouse and he'd seen too many children blown to pieces.

'Besides, what could I do? Sit in my comfy practice back in Canada and just watch this happen? I'm a doctor. I had to do something.'

'Thank you for your time, Doctor. Would it be OK if we looked around the hospital?'

'Go right ahead. Come back anytime.'

Dr John went back to work and we slipped outside and into the world of the armless and legless ones. Hutu and Tutsi children hopping and hobbling in clean hospital gowns. Boys showing off new one-legged tricks on crutches and girls giggling when the boys fell. Up the stairs and round a hedge there was a big walled-in garden packed with tents and wounded children. Crippled innocents seeking refuge in a place of shady trees and fragrant hibiscus. My mind couldn't connect the dots on this one. Just outside these flowered walls, madness and murder prowled the streets like the curse of Moses. But here, in Dr John's garden, the wounded children of Rwanda sang songs and laughed.

'You believe this, James?'

'Amazing.'

'Can't figure if it's wonderful or tragic.'

'I would say it's a bit of both. Look at them. So heartbreaking.'

There was a schoolhouse next to the garden. The classrooms now turned into hospital wards for the sick and wounded. Forgotten lessons still scribbled on slate, the chalk fading away. No one had thought to erase it. Under those forgotten lessons were the unforgettable lessons of war. A nurse bandaging all that was left of a young girl's leg, a black stump hanging from the knee. And a small boy waving his wrist in little circles before his eyes staring at the place where his hand used to be.

'Most of these children have no parents.'

A French nurse behind me. Her face drenched in sweat as she pulled her hair up and traced a damp cloth over the back of her neck.

'And most of them saw their parents slaughtered in front of them. Can you ever imagine such a thing?'

'Nope, I can't. I can't believe the kids are singin' up in the tents.'

'We try to distract them from the gunfire and bombs.'

'Seems to work.'

'*Oui*. Till the next bomb will fall into the hospital.'

Jungle sun streamed through red curtains and washed the room with bloodlike light. Nurses moved through the wounded children . . . some children crying, some sleeping, some frozen with shock . . . the lens panning over the room and hundreds of small dark eyes staring into the lens and into my mind.

Why are you here? Are you here to help us? Do something. Help us.

And I kept the camera rolling, feeding on their small dark eyes.

'Careful, Jon. You're about to step on a great shot.'

'Huh?'

Down between my filthy boots. A cardboard box the size of a case of beer. And inside, a green blanket wrapped round the tiniest black face. The face burned and scarred. Tiny black fingers poking from the blanket and curling into a fist and then a deep breath and the tiny face letting go with a glass-shattering screech.

'Shit. Didn't squash him, did I?'

'No, Jon, not yet.'

The French nurse reached down, picked up the wailing cardboard box and set it on a chair.

'*Pardon, s'il vous plaît.* We are running out of space. I'll just put him over here for now.'

'How old is he?'

'One month, that is all. Born in the middle of the killings. He is lucky to be alive, *non*?'

I focused the lens down and rolled a long, slow zoom into the infant's face. Coughs and screams and banging his fists in the air, closer and closer, till the scars and burns and tears filled the picture with pain.

'Oh, my. Look at that,' said Jean-Guy.

'Nice shot, ain't it?'

'Oh, you know.'

And Jean-Guy pulled a happy-snap camera out of his flak-jacket and flashed a quick shot of the baby. The baby screeched some more.

'Didn't know you were a photographer, Major.'

'Not like you. I just take pictures of things I see in this place. I want to make sure I never forget what happened here. We must never forget this place. That is what I think.'

He stood tall and quiet under his baseball cap, biting his lip, holding back his tears.

'Lemme tell you what I think, Jean-Guy. You're a hero. All of you from the general on down. You're all heroes.'

'I'm just a military policeman. It is my duty.'

'You're way beyond the call of duty, Jean-Guy. I get paid a hell of a lot of money to be here. You? You're runnin' around with us, riskin' your life tryin' to get the story of these poor people's misery out into the world 'cause you believe it to be the decent thing to do. Makes you a hero, sir.'

'I thought I 'ave told you to can it with that "sir" crap.'

'You sure did, sir.'

'Time to go.'

'Yes, sir.'

The boys at Checkpoint Zombie watched us pass through the haze of a drunken stupor. Round the bend Jean-Guy stomped on the gas one more time and raced towards the airport. Fast through the trees. Fast along the ridge. Fast round the mounds of rotting flesh.

'So maybe you two clowns would like to come back to this place?'

'Be our pleasure, Jean-Guy.'

'How 'bout those hundred journos in Nairobi?'

'Just get your names on the list.'

And he winked and refitted his cap and pushed down on the gas. I held the camera out the window and let it roll. Nearly Africa. Rifles blasting from the trees. Shells crashing in the hills. Dead-flesh smells in the air and the souls of half a million ghosts chasing close behind.

9

I CAME TO CASABLANCA FOR THE WATERS

16 May 1994

Happy fat-ass tourists mingled in the lobby of the Norfolk Hotel in Nairobi. Every last one of them in photographer's jackets and funny hats and cameras hanging from their necks. Getting set for another sunny day in Kenya's wild-game parks. Zebras and lions and giraffes and elephants.

'I wanna be like these folks. Go see an elephant. Come all the way to Africa, I wanna see a fuckin' elephant.'

My own camera was down by my feet while I was cramming food and medical supplies into my backpack . . . and trying real hard not to notice the clammy sweat running down my face. 'Fuck me. Don't think I feel well.'

ITN tape editor from London named Mike Turner sat nearby. He handed over bits of this and that and watched me stuff them in the pack. 'Ah, you know how it is, Jon. You're just a little nervous.'

'Yeah, maybe.'

James rounded the corner dressed in a very proper Oxford cloth shirt from Thomas Pink of London and torn-at-the-knee blue jeans. Grubby boots on his feet and that same beat-up briefcase in his hands. The man was ready for war.

'See you still got the briefcase, James.'

'See you still have your camera, Jon.'

The floor seemed to swell up and go down again. 'Oh, fuck.'

'Everything OK?'

'Don't know. Don't think I feel too good.'

'Oh, probably just a little nervous.'

'Yeah, maybe.'

Last couple of days the BBC managed to get into Kigali. But since the sun was shining in Kenya and the restaurant near the pool was good, I didn't give a damn. Besides, I was nursing the bruises and cuts on my arms and legs. Last thing I wanted to think about was 'Crisis in Rwanda'. News coming out suggested the story was calming down anyway. The Hutu militia were running out of people to kill and the Tutsi rebels and RGF had fought their way into a stand-off of sorts. Mess could go on for ever. ITN Foreign Desk suggested we might want to go back into Rwanda and shoot a special report for *News at Ten* on the kids we found at Kigali's Red Cross hospital. We didn't think about it much till the weather turned grey in Nairobi and it started to rain. So I ran down to the UN press office and presented a huge bouquet of flowers to the Nice Lady who made up the list of journalists trying to get into Kigali aboard the Canadian air-force relief flight.

'Oh, how lovely! Thank you!' And the Nice Lady scribbled our names at the top of the list. 'We can fit you in on tomorrow's flight.'

So here I was packing my backpack and feeling the hotel floor swell up and down one more time. 'I'm startin' to regret those fuckin' flowers.'

'Don't worry. You know how it is. Just a little nervous.'

'You guys got anythin' else to say or is that it?'

'Look, Jon. We go in, we shoot for two days, then we come out. Easy-peasy.'

Mike nodded his head like it was a swell idea. 'Yeah, that's it. In and out. Easy-peasy.'

'Yeah, maybe.'

'Listen up! We're going in for a landing! You know the drill! Suit up!'

Flak-jackets and helmets on. Sharp bank over the trees and a hard slam on to the runway. I peeked out the porthole. Kigali, just like I remembered it. Green and shimmering and full of evil little shits who kill people. Down the ramp and into the hell-hot heat once more.

'Allo! I am very glad to 'ave you guys here! We need help in this place!'

'Jean-Guy, you gave us this speech the last time.'

'Oh, that's right. We 'ave so many press people through here I feel like I am running a tour company. Let's get going.'

Into the jeep and a fast ride through the jungle. Soft evening light casting long shadows across the roads. The same roads with the same bodies lying just as dead as the last time we drove by. Few days in the sun had baked them into faceless blobs of purple flesh.

'Fuck me. Gettin' ripe out there, Jean-Guy.'

'You know, I wash out my nose day after day in this place but the smell never goes away.'

'Sometimes it grabs you when you least expect it. I was sittin' outside my hotel room yesterday watchin' the birds and lookin' at the flowers, and this breeze comes up and outa nowhere I could smell the bodies, like they were buried in my nose. Vomited my guts out on the grass.'

Jean-Guy nodded, like knowing the feeling too well. My eyes panned over the blur of green jungle racing by the window. Wind sounds whipping closer and closer. Hot sweat dripping down my back.

'Seems quiet enough.'

'Few bangs and a few passing bullets. But it isn't as bad as before.'

'That's good.'

'Well, actually it probably means the two armies are preparing for a major battle.'

'That's bad.'

'Who's here from the BBC, Jean-Guy?'

'Uh, let me remember those guys. Mark Doyle and Roger Hearing and a cameraman . . . uh, David somebody. Says he was in Moscow with you.'

'Guy with glasses? Nice guy. Always saw him in the streets.'

'I 'ave to say, they are not as much fun as you two clowns.'

'Well, you gotta remember, Jean-Guy, first thing you do when you join the Beeb is leave your sense of humour at the door.'

'They do take themselves *soooo* seriously at times.'

'I think they leave tomorrow anyway. And tomorrow we 'ave some stills guys and a team from Reuters TV coming in. Somebody named Julian Bedford.'

James sat upright like someone just dropped a mouse in his pants.

'Julian Bedford! My goodness! Why, he and I were at school together! Julian Bedford. We called him Nipple.'

The jeep cruised along in noticeable silence.

'James, lemme understand this clearly. You called some guy in school Nipple? What the hell for?'

'Good question. Let me think. I think it was because we called his older brother Tit.'

Jean-Guy pulled off his baseball cap and scratched the little hair he had left on the top of his head. 'Oh, you know. That makes a lot of sense.'

'Brits, Jean-Guy. They go into these weirdo schools as normal as me and you and come out like James and his old buddy Nipple.'

'Nonsense. You're just jealous of our superior form of education. Don't you forget the British gave both your countries the foundations of nationhood. Our schools reflect a sense of nobility and character. Honour and duty.'

'And what did your school buddies call you?'

'The name has been driven from my memory for ever.'

'Bad, was it?'

'Ghastly.'

The jeep ran along rebel lines and the slender shapes of Tutsi fighters rose from their foxholes and watched us pass. Gunsights of their AK47s following our heads just like old times. Quick turn through rebel bunkers and home sweet home, the Meridian Hotel. Tunisian soldiers still cleaning their rifles and refugees still cooking scraps of meat on little fires in the stairwells. Everyone welcomed us back like long-lost family.

Upstairs the BBC crew was packing up and getting out. They'd had enough. David was off in his room rolling up his sleeping-bag when I found him. His camera sitting in the corner, covered with dust.

'Hey, David.'

'Jon, I heard you were coming back.'

'And I heard you were leavin'.'

He looked away, like torn to hell inside.

'What's goin' on, David?'

'Yesterday we almost got killed. Mortar round just missed us.'

'Fuck me. That'll do it.'

'And I've got these two reporters here. They're fighting each other for airtime. Middle of all this shit and they're fighting each other for airtime.'

'Well, then, they're bein' assholes at the expense of your life.'

And he tied the sleeping-bag into a ball and sat staring at it. Rifles came alive just under the balcony. A small slash of gold colour floated into the room and spilled across the bullet-scarred walls. Our eyes turning to see the last shreds of sunset hanging above the jungle.

'Nice light.'

'Sure makes a good picture.'

'Jon, I just don't want anyone to think . . . you know.'

'David, you listen to me. Me and you worked side by side in Moscow. And when heads were gettin' bashed and bullets were flyin' you were always there. You never turned your back, not once. You can look anyone square in the eyes over this and fuck 'em if they don't like it.'

'You know I have a new daughter? She was just born.'

'Yeah? That's swell.'

'She means everything to me, Jon.'

'That's God's way of tellin' you there's somethin' in your life bigger than a minute forty-five on the evening news. Your daughter needs you a hell of a lot more than the fuckin' BBC. 'Less, of course, the Beeb is issuing spare daddies as part of their employee benefits package. Whole story in Kigali seems to be windin' down anyway.'

'Yeah, that's what my Foreign Desk says. Thanks, Jon.'

'You'd do the same for me. See you in the next shithole, after that daughter of yours grows a bit.'

'Good luck.'

'You too.'

Back in Room 317. James was on the satphone to his wife and kids in London, they missing him and he missing them. Lots of comforting words back and forth and James telling them not to worry . . . Things were quiet in Kigali and we'd be out in two days, he told them.

I spread out my sleeping-bag on the floor and lay down.

'Need to call anyone before I shut down the satphone, Jon?'

'Nope.'

And closing my eyes and feeling the room roll on the crest of a ten-foot wave. And me thinking how strange it was to be seasick in the middle of a fuckin' jungle.

It was not a good sunrise. One look at the Meals-Ready-to-Eat and I thought I'd vomit. Jean-Guy's speed trials through downtown Kigali adding to the horrible wobbling sensation in my stomach. He was taking us to the Rwandan government forces' headquarters deep in the centre of Hutu-occupied Kigali. General Romeo Dallaire led the way. Two Ghanaian jeeps with heavy machine-guns at the head and tail of the convoy.

'Nice thing about travelling with the general and a heavily armed convoy ready to blow anyone to hell that gets in the fuckin' way.'

'Yeah? What's that?'

'People get out of your way with a smile.'

'Funny how that works.'

Till we landed at Headquarters. The RGF's élite paratrooper unit had the building fortified with overturned cars and heavy lumber bunkers. We piled out of the trucks and felt the cold eyes of defeat drilling into us. Tutsi rebels had been kicking the shit out of these guys for days. The Hutu thought the UN, and anyone with them, was to blame. Especially white journalists telling all those white-man lies about the Hutu.

The Hutu commanding general seemed pleasant enough. He shook hands with General Dallaire and posed for pictures. The two men speaking in official diplomatic tones. Dallaire offering suggestions and the Hutu general brushing them away with polite gestures. They danced round each other for an hour or so. Dallaire then gently reminding the Hutu general that it was *his own Hutu people* starving in the streets of Kigali, and it was most unfortunate that some bastard was still shelling the runway and shooting at the UN relief flights because, as the Hutu general might imagine, the situation was making it quite impossible for the UN to bring food into the city and feed *his own fucking Hutu people*!

'Oh, mon général, ce seraient les Tutsi.'

And Dallaire gritting his teeth.

'You don't say?'

Dallaire marched out of the meeting and out of the door and paced around in the garden. Then he marched over to the UN pick-up truck at the point of the convoy and jumped up to the .50 calibre heavy machine-gun mounted in the back. His hands checking the ammunition belt and seeing everything was good to go. His narrow eyes focusing down the sight as he swung the gun from side to side. And me seeing that look in his eyes again. Like he wanted to crack heads, like he wanted to spin the fucking muzzle round and finish this shit once and for all.

'Looks in good order, men.'

'Thank you, sir.'

And he slapped his Ghanaian escort on the shoulders and walked back towards Hutu HQ. His reedy voice mumbling as he marched by. 'OK. Let's try this shit again.'

And he flashed a look at Jean-Guy. Photo-op was over. Jean-Guy herded us back towards his jeep.

'I think the general wants to 'ave some quality time with his hosts. We must swing by the airport and pick up the new journalists anyway. Then we can go to the Red Cross hospital for the pictures you two guys need.'

'Sounds good.'

Whistles and jeers back through Hutu-land. Felt ugly, like something bad coming down. Me and James looked at each other. His eyebrows curling into the top of his head. Jean-Guy stepped on it and manoeuvred fast through the dead streets. Every turn like a rollercoaster through my stomach.

'Jon, you seem to be turning a rather interesting shade of green.'

'I'm feelin' woozy as shit.'

'Oh, you know. That could be the heat,' said Jean-Guy.

'Yeah, maybe.'

Green light at Kigali airport. The Canadian Hercules on final approach. I grabbed the camera and rolled some shots of the giant plane scraping the trees and hitting the runway and rolling up to the blocks. The flight crew tossing off supplies and a handful of dazed journos. Me and Jean-Guy stood by while James reunited with his old school chum.

'Nipple! My dear chap! How are you?'

'Why, James Mates! You old Marlburian! How fabulous to find you here!'

'How fabulous indeed!'

And Jean-Guy looked at me and rolled his eyes, not knowing if he should stick around or give them some privacy.

A big Israeli cameraman from Reuters TV walked over with an American stills-shooter named Steve. We shook hands and talked. The Israeli was named Michael and he was just out of the Israeli air force. He told us how during the Gulf War he mounted nukes on to Israeli jets and if any of Saddam's incoming scuds'd been loaded with poison gas, then the Israelis were going to take out Baghdad.

'No shit?'

'No shit.'

Steve was another of those stills guys who dressed in black. Serious black hair hanging down over a face looking forever stoned. He stood there squeezing his eyes together like 'far out'. He was out of New York City and happy to be in the middle of Kigali. His cameras were clean and loaded and ready.

'Seen any bodies?'

'A few.'

'Hey, you guys!' Jean-Guy on the radio and waving us over. 'A squad of Ghanaian troops are downtown investigating a massacre. Do you want to go there?'

'Sure. Let's do it.'

'It's near that roadblock by the Red Cross hospital.'

'Checkpoint Zombie?'

'What's Checkpoint Zombie?' asked Steve.

'Lots and lots of bad guys.'

'ITN rides with me. Rest of you follow in the other jeep.'

The two UN jeeps roared down the airport road into town. Seemed every hundred yards a rifle ripped through the trees like some kind of mileage marker. Jean-Guy gunned the motor with each report and checked his rear-view mirror to make sure the rest of the gang was hot on our tail.

'I hope you do not mind if I keep you two clowns with me. I like your company on these roads. Takes my mind off all those damn guns.'

'And we enjoy yours as well, Jean-Guy.'

'I think I'm gonna be sick.'

'Now, now, Jon.'

'No, really. I think I'm gonna be sick.'

And me sticking my head out the window and feeling the hot wind in my face and getting a whiff of rotting flesh.

'Fuck me.'

'I'm sure it's the heat, my friend. It can make you feel very bad in this place.'

'Yeah, maybe.'

Just short of Checkpoint Zombie. Six UN soldiers moving up a dead-end road towards three or four houses tucked back under the trees. Gates and fences round the houses, some dog somewhere howling and barking like mad. Two UN soldiers jumped the fence and pounded on doors and windows. Four Hutu army regulars came out from the back gardens, rifles hanging from their shoulders. I switched on the camera and started grabbing pictures. So did all the other journos. The Hutu didn't like it one bit.

'*Qu'est-ce que vous faites ici?*'

'*On avait entendu qu'il y avait un massacre ici.*'

'*C'est privé ici. Vous devez partir!*'

And me whispering to James . . .

'What's up?'

. . . and him whispering back.

'Seems they don't want us around. They say it's private property.'

'You're shittin' me.'

Up from the main road. Firesmoke and the shuffle of feet. Ten or fifteen militia rounding the corner and watching us. Machetes behind their backs, waiting. The Hutu soldiers lit American cigarettes and sucked on slow drags of smoke.

'Sure as hell seems like we're bein' followed, James.'

'It certainly does.'

The Ghanaians spread out covering each other's backs, the Hutu soldiers kept waving them away.

'*C'est privé ici! Vous n'avez pas le droit d'être ici. Nous allons verifier chaque rumeur de morts.*'

The Hutu soldiers jumped the fence and banged on the door of one house. A hollow, booming sound, then listening to the silence. They turned and shrugged their shoulders.

'*Vous voyez? Il n'y a personne.*'

'Lemme guess. Nobody home.'

'Mmhmm.'

The Ghanaian squad leader shook his head and pointed to the door of the next house. He was going to open it with or without Hutu permission. The UN soldiers stepping closer and surrounding the Hutu. The Hutu whispered between themselves till one of them stepped back and reached down behind a small flower-pot and pulled up a set of keys. The Hutu walked to the gate.

'Now, how do you suppose those chaps knew where the keys might be?'

'Lucky guess, maybe?'

'You getting this on tape?'

'Yup.'

Tight shot. Hands fumble with the lock on the gate. None of the keys fit. The Hutu soldiers climb the fence and creep up to the door of the house. Zoom into a key sliding into the lock and Hutu hands turning the key this way and that. Pan down. A Hutu soldier's boot pushing the door back over yellow kitchen tile. Yellow kitchen tile smeared thick with fresh blood. The smell drifting out the door and across the ground. Then the door slams shut. The Hutu come back over the fence yelling and raising their weapons.

'*Non! Vous ne pouvez pas entrer dans la maison! C'est privé! Nous allons verifier chaque rumeur de morts!*'

And the Hutu soldiers shifted their eyes down the road. The militia still standing nearby, waiting for the nod to rush ahead with their machetes.

'*C'est dangereux pour vous ici.*'

Jean-Guy talked with the Ghanaians. They marked the house as a killing site. But whatever was in there was dead already and there was nothing the UN could do about it without starting a small war. Jean-Guy looked around and did some sums, just too many of the bastards. He led the UN troops up the hill to check out a few more houses. The journos followed. Me and James stayed back to shoot a stand-up in front of the killing site.

'We gotta do this fast,' I said.

'I have the words, let's go.'

I framed James against the house with the soldiers behind him, then the ground started to roll and I grabbed the tripod. The smell of blood churning in my guts. 'Oh, shit.'

'Come on, Jon. They're watching us.'

'I'm tryin', James. Just feelin' woozy again.'

One big Hutu soldier inhaling a deep drag and letting it go with a deep voice . . .

'C'est dangereux pour vous ici!'

. . . and my head buzzing on the deep voice and the blood smell sinking deeper into my guts and my high-school French finally catching up with me.

C'est dangereux pour vous ici! . . . It's dangerous for you here!

'Shit. I'm losin' it.'

'After the stand-up, please.'

And seeing James's face in the viewfinder and watching his lips flap up and down but not hearing a sound. Just this weird buzzing in my brain and feeling my stomach go up and down and up and down.

'Jon, the lens is moving around quite a bit.'

'Yeah, so's the whole fuckin' world just now.'

Six takes till I got one without James looking like he was tipping this way and that way. Trees rustled behind us as Jean-Guy and the rest of the press pack came back down the hill.

'OK. This seems like the only place where something happened. And looking at these guys all around us I would say we are making these soldiers very nervous.'

'We're makin' *them* nervous?'

'I know how these guys work. We'll make a report back at UN Headquarters. Let's just move over to the hospital and get away from this place. Are you feeling OK, Jon?'

'Comes and goes.'

'Let's get the hell out of here.'

We eased through Checkpoint Zombie. All the Hutu eyes watching us pass like memorizing our faces. An ice-cold burn on the back of my neck. I turned round and looked through the glass. My eyes doing a crash zoom into one man in the crowd, his hand and, rising to his sweaty throat, a single finger slicing from ear to ear. 'Swell. Fuckin' swell.'

'What is it, Jon?'

'Some asshole sayin', "Fuck you," in that special Hutu sorta way.'

'Excuse me?'

The jeeps turned up the drive and we all piled out. The new journos roamed around looking for stories. Me and James headed straight for the recovery ward looking for the wounded kids from our last trip. The room was packed with even more sad faces and more crippled lives. Dr John Sundon was making rounds when we walked in. 'Hi, guys! How are ya?'

'Fine. How's things with you, Doc?'

'Busy. But it's been pretty quiet for the last few days. No blast wounds today, thank God.'

'Seems to be fillin' up.'

'Well, you know. Even when they get better, what can you do? Can't really throw them out back into the streets. You can get killed out there.'

'No shit. Doc, you know what's goin' on down the road from here?'

'Jon, I don't like to think about it.'

'What shall you do with the children, Doctor?'

'You know, James, I've been thinking about that. I'm going to start a school. Right here! I mean, that's what this place was before, so why not?'

He was beaming like a proud daddy.

'So, Doc, there was this one baby in a cardboard box. Cut-up face.'

'Oh, yeah. We moved the little guy on to a cot. Let's see, he's somewhere around here. There he is, over by that young woman.'

A beautiful young brown woman with almond eyes. She was sitting on a chair, gazing down at the same tiniest black face still peeking from that same big green blanket. The healing burns and scars distorting his sleeping face.

Dr Sundon leaned close and whispered. 'That's the mother. Can you believe it?'

'Really?'

'Yeah. She got separated from her kids, came here to the hospital and found them all.'

'You mean the kids gettin' treated last week are related?'

'Yes indeed. All three of them. Amazing, isn't it?'

James smiled and rocked on his boot heels. 'Well, now. Looks like a story to me.'

'Sure does.'

James sat near the young mother with the almond eyes and listened to her story. She said the child's name was Jean-Baptiste, like the voice of one crying in the wilderness, she said. The little guy stirred and woke and rolled his tiny hands into fists and fussed some more till the mother opened her dress and suckled him at her breast.

'Jon, can we actually shoot an interview while she's nursing her child?'

'Sure. Great picture.'

'I just don't want some producer in London cutting it out because they find it offensive.'

'Middle of all this death and they're gonna find a woman with her baby offensive? Let 'em come out here into the middle of this shit and shoot it themselves if they don't like it.'

'Ah, you're feeling better. Good.'

'Like I said. Comes and goes.'

Then the little girl who had her foot blown apart last week hopped over on her good leg. Her mangled foot wrapped in a bandage the size of a football. Someone had given her a clean yellow dress. She sat with her mother, both of them with almond eyes. And she laid her head on her mother's shoulder and she stroked the head of the tiny Jean-Baptiste. The mother raised her almond eyes to the lens. 'My husband, he was killed by the militia. There was nowhere to run. Killers were everywhere. They waited in the streets for people to come out of their homes for food or water. Then the militia killed them. I don't understand what has happened to our world. I don't understand what has happened to my son.'

And tears rolled down her face.

Dr John took us to the bedside of the woman's son. The small boy lay as motionless as the day we first saw him on Dr John's operating table. Left side of his face heavily bandaged.

'Wasn't enough skin to do his face properly. He's going to have some terrible scars.'

'Still lucky to be alive, Doc.'

'I wish it was that simple. I thought I got it all. But there was one metal shard I didn't see. Wouldn't have got my hopes up if I'd seen it. The metal sliced into the boy's spine. He's going to be paralysed.'

Dr John reached down and touched the boy's bandages. 'Such a horrible injury in a place like this.'

'Poor fuckin' kid.'

The young mother crossed the room with her baby at her breast. She pulled up a chair and sat next to her crippled son. She talked in the softest tones. Her tender hands moving up and down the boy's dead legs. I sat down on a stool and framed the picture in the lens.

Roll.

A mother's hands trying to heal her crippled son with her mother's touch. Tears pouring from her almond-shaped eyes. The eyes looking into the lens. Pain and hopelessness ripping through the glass.

Why doesn't he move? Please. Why doesn't he move his legs?

And me letting the tears and pain and hopelessness pour into the camera till I couldn't take it any more.

Cut.

I stood up with the camera . . . and fell right down and out. Minute later I was looking up at James and Jean-Guy and Dr John. Their faces spinning and stretching like a bad cartoon.

'Jon, you are not well.'

'Told you so.'

Dr John felt my skin and pulled down my eyelids. 'You may have a virus. We can find room for you in here somewhere.'

James and Jean-Guy pulled me up and sat me on a cot. Someone handed me a bottle of water and I took a big gulp. It ran out my pores like a faucet. I looked round the hospital ward. Skeleton shapes on cots, a child in a coma, smells of urine and shit and sick. And then thinking about the killers just outside the hospital gates.

'No, thanks. Get me the fuck outa here.'

James grabbed the camera and pulled my arm round his shoulder and we stumbled out the door. Jean-Guy rounded up the rest of the journos and the entire tribe climbed into the jeeps. My green face hanging out the side window as we moved nice and easy through Checkpoint Zombie.

'I'm not sure who looks worse, Jon, you or those goons with the machetes.'

'I hope I puke all over these motherfuckers.'

'Oh, you know, I would appreciate it if you do not 'ave to do that.'

Racing through the streets again. Sun jabbing my eyes like needles. Hot air blowing over my face and the wobbles subsiding a bit. Jean-Guy telling James he was moving us into UN Headquarters.

'Hope you got a toilet that works 'cause I need to pray before the porcelain god, Jean-Guy.'

'I think you 'ave gone delirious, my friend. We 'ave big hole in the ground out back. But take your flak-jackets. Oh, take your helmets out there too. One of our soldiers was killed by a mortar while having a crap in this place.'

'Christ. What a way to go.'

'Jon, you think you can get through an interview with the general? That's all we need and this story is in the can.'

'Promise?'

'And a stand-up.'

'Oh, fuck.'

'Then we're finished and we'll get the first flight back to Nairobi.'

'Promise?'

'My dear chap, you have the word of an English gentleman.'

'Now I really am going to puke.'

And leaning out the window ready to lose it till rifles blasted from the jungle.

'Second thought, forget it.'

Turn through the barbed wire and sandbags and the Ghanaian soldiers still digging in the trenches.

'Oh, goody, Fort Apache. John Wayne home?'

'No, Jon. We're going to do an interview with General Dallaire.'

'Oh, that's right. Where are we again?'

'C'mon, I'll help you.'

James leaned me up next to a line of APCs. He set up the tripod and slapped the camera on top. 'Now all you have to do is push the button.'

'Swell.'

And me holding on to the tripod like a crutch while the world rolled from side to side. Rolling up one time, I saw Jean-Guy leading General Dallaire towards the camera. Blue beret, crisp uniform, green flak-jacket, tan Hush Puppies on his feet.

'Let's do this fast. I gotta head up the road and see what the hell's going on,' said the general.

'Yes, sir. Jon, are you ready?'

And me still looking down at the general's Hush Puppies.

'Jon?'

The general snapping with impatience. 'You feeling all right over there?'

'Sorry, sir. Just a little woozy.'

'Well, you look like shit. Can you do this or not?'

'Yes, sir.'

'Well, then, let's do it.'

James asked a few softballs to warm him up, then zoomed in on the safety of UN forces in Rwanda.

'Well, you're never safe in a war zone.'

Just outside the barbed-wire, rifles and machine-guns sounded off, but the general kept on talking.

'. . . ability to deploy troops . . .'

Shoosh . . . BOOM!

Me and James looked at each other then over to Jean-Guy. Jean-Guy shrugged his shoulders like no one tells a general it might be a good time to wrap it up.

'. . . monitor movements behind the lines . . .'

KACRACK! KACRACK! KACRACK!

Tunisian soldiers ran over to the far APC and pulled open the steel hatch. Ghanaian soldiers stomped around the perimeter and took positions with their rifles. Hutu and rebel guns popping in the jungle like the Fourth of July.

'. . . and the Security Council gave us a mandate to . . .'

The far APC growled to life with belching puffs of black smoke. General Dallaire spun round and threw his lieutenant-general arms in the air.

'Goddammit! Everybody just cut! Hold it! Just hold it!'

Absolute silence. No rifles, no bangs, no smoke, no nothing.

'Now, where the hell was I?' And the general finished his sentence when he was damn good and ready. He shook our hands and climbed into the waiting APC and tore out of Fort Apache. Jean-Guy waited for the dust to clear and stared into the jungle like he'd *heard* something. Something he didn't like.

'Listen, you two. I will go to the situation room and find out when the next flight is coming in. You will be OK out here?'

'Jon?'

'Oh yeah. I'll just keep holdin' on to the tripod through the stand-up.'

James grabbed the microphone and mumbled to himself the way all reporters mumble to themselves when they're thinking up a stand-up.

I focused the lens on his face and watched his eyes pan way over yonder as heavy rumbles rolled over the jungle.

'Sounds like it's coming from the airport.'

'Don't like the sound of it.'

'Yeees.'

Rifles picked up in the trees. Closer and closer.

'Should we be concerned about these guns?'

'Think we'll be all right here. Besides, little sound effects in the stand-up will make 'em love you back in London.'

'Oh, yes, please. I can duck and dive and look very brave.'

'Yeah. Lots of "Look at me, everyone! I'm in danger! Look at me! I'm in danger."'

'Never happens that way anyway, does it? Stand all day, waiting for something to go boom.'

He ran a few more words through his head then went for a take. Distant shells echoing under his words.

'. . . because there can be no excuse. All the world knew what was happening here. James Mates, *News at Ten*, Kigali, Rwanda.'

Shoosh . . . BOOM!

'Hey! And right on cue!'

'Not bad.'

And me leaning over the APC and yelling out over the barbed wire at the top of my lungs. 'Thank you! Everybody go home now!

Then the shit hit the fan.

Thousands of rounds ripped through the air and drilled us into the ground. The camera up on the tripod and rolling with bullets zinging by the lens and mortars crashing into the trees just beyond the barbed wire and me and James laughing our heads off.

'Maybe they didn't like your fuckin' script, James!'

'Nonsense! It was fucking brilliant!'

We stayed on the ground waiting for a lull. We waited a long time. We weren't laughing any more. We managed to collapse the tripod and pull the camera to the ground. Then heavy crossfire drilled us deeper into the dirt . . . then quiet. We scrambled along the sandbags and ducked into Fort Apache HQ as the guns exploded again. Jean-Guy walked out of the situation room. He wasn't laughing either. 'I 'ave bad news for you two. The rebels are moving into the city and there is a major offensive at the airport. Heavy shelling on the runway.'

'Any idea how long it will go on?'

'Who can know? All flights are grounded till it's over. We're cut off. I'm afraid this is the big one.'

And the floor started to roll and the room started to spin and my legs buckled under. 'Oh, shit . . . James.' And me grabbing James and feeling my body sink.

'Jon!'

And a little voice chirping in my head . . .

Whooopeee! Look at me! I'm in danger! Look at me!

It was like the Jonesing end of a four-day cocaine binge when there's no more blow and your nerves shake and burn and you're scraping over the floor snorting bits of white dirt hoping it's coke. Then you realize it's just dirt and junkie desperation twists you round and round like a dishrag, and bone-crushing pain crashes down like heavy shells. Christ! Listen to it! Every shell and every rifle round exploding in my head and the vibrations cutting through my guts like razors and me curled up inside my sweat-soaked flak-jacket trying to hide from the sounds. Oh, shit! Here it comes again! Then again and again. Then the sun comes up and the world really starts to sink. The shivers and shakes and the bone-crushing pain going on all night and into the next day and always the sounds of shells and blasts cutting deeper and deeper. And James fading in and out of the blasts and telling me to drink some water and then pulling the sleeping-bag over my shivering shoulders and putting my helmet over my head and then crawling out to the balcony during a lull and whispering down the satphone to London.

'We're trapped. Jon is pretty sick and it looks bad. No, there's no way out. We're cut off from the hospital, we're cut off from everything.'

And feeling the pain slam down again and grind me into the floor and then seeing James crawl back again with another cup of water and holding it to my mouth. Then the whole world sinking again and me grabbing my shoulders to keep from falling but feeling myself fall anyway and hoping I'd just smash into the ground so it could be over, for fucksake! But it wasn't over because the guns and the pain exploded again. Bullets and shrapnel screaming by the window louder than before and the shivers and shakes dragging me down through the bone-crushing pain and into that horrible rubbery room. Stretching and bending and going inside out and then seeing half a million dead-eyed faces coming out of the walls and floating over me. And feeling their dead-flesh smells crawl up my nose like thousands of ants digging into my brain and then someone grabbing my wrist . . . oh, shit! But it was only James with that fucking water again. Telling me to drink just a little more. And me tasting the water and it tasting like green slime and trying to swallow anyway and the water oozing through my skin and dripping down my face and the dead-eyed faces coming closer and closer like wanting to pull me down into the next horrible place. My voice whimpering with fear like the little boy from long ago and my drunken father coming out of the dead-eyed faces and laughing and screaming, 'YOU LITTLE SHIT! YOU WORTHLESS LITTLE SHIT! COME HERE! I'M GONNA FUCKING KILL YOU!' And my body shaking harder and harder and James holding the water to my lips and telling me to drink one more time. And then laying me back on the floor and pulling the sleeping-bag under my chin and him crawling over to a corner and sitting with his head in his hands while anti-aircraft artillery exploded just outside the window...

. . . then the roar of incoming shells smashing into Fort Apache.

KACRASH!! KACRASH!!

'Stop, Daddy! Please stop!!'

SHOOOOSH . . . KACRASH!!!

And James flying across the room and grabbing the shoulders of my flak-jacket and dragging me out of the horrible rubbery room into a blur of green uniforms. My mind trying to grasp what the fuck was happening. Ghanaian soldiers with helmets and rifles charging through the hall. James hauling me to my feet and us falling into the stampede.

'C'mon, Jon! Get up!'

SHOOOOSH . . . KACRASH!!!

'James . . . what . . .'

'Not now! We have to keep moving!'

Past a red fire bell hanging sideways off the wall and ringing its head off like *Alice in Wonderland*. Down the stairs into the dark lobby. Blue warning lights spinning in the dark and flashing across the blue helmets of the Ghanaian soldiers huddled on the floor with their rifles. Soldiers trained to defend themselves now sitting helpless in the sweaty dark. Their black faces staring out from under their helmets and the blue lights reflecting in their terrified eyes. James sat me against a wall and collapsed next to me. Someone killed the fire bell and the blue lights. And we all sat silently in the darkness listening to the killer shells hammer down. My hands digging into my skull trying to get a grip. My eyes adjusting to the dark and panning through the room. Smoke and shattered glass. Dust and sweat. Trapped and waiting for the end to come crashing through the roof in one flash of fire.

'James?'

'Yes?'

'This isn't good, is it?'

'No, I'm afraid not. I talked to Vicky Knighton on the Foreign Desk. She wants us out of here ASAP. She's terribly upset.'

'This ain't her fault.'

'One of the London-based cameramen let her have it.'

'What the hell for?'

'He told her it was a mistake to send you in here as a one-man band and it would be her fault.'

'Me? What the hell does this have to do with me? Hang on, what would be her fault?'

'He told her, "You have signed Jon Steele's death warrant." '

'Wh-what? Who the fuck would say somethin' like that?'

'You don't think I'd tell you, do you?'

'Who was it, James? I'm gonna fuckin' kill him!'

'Precisely.'

Jon Steele's death warrant . . . Jon Steele's death warrant.

Sounded like a curse. Like some son-of-a-bitch'd be happy to see me buy it in Kigali so he could say, 'I told you so.' Son-of-a- bitch! Fucking son-of-a-bitch! And me looking around the room at all the terrified faces looking back at me, and them seeing the face of the frightened little boy from long ago.

'No way, you fuckin' prick. No fuckin' way.'

I leaned my back into the wall and forced myself up from the floor.

'Jon?'

And wobbling round till I found my balance.

'Jon? What are you doing? Get the hell down!'

'I forgot my camera.'

'What the hell are you doing?'

And grabbing the handrail and pulling myself back up the stairs.
'Jon!'

'Death warrant, my ass.'

Roll, you motherfucker. Roll.

Faces and eyes and souls trapped in hell. Hands wringing tighter and tighter. The lens soaking them in and compressing them into two-dimensional images of fear. I shoved the lens close to the terrified faces, waiting for the faces to look into the glass so I could grab every shred of their fear and squeeze it for more . . . anyone's fear but my own. One Ghanaian, his head in his hands and his lips mumbling words of prayer or the names of his children, or maybe nothing at all. Good shot, now look for more. Somewhere in the dark a radio sparked with voices.

'Zulu Foxtrot Three! Zulu Foxtrot Three! What's the situation? Do you read?'

Spin the lens round and focus on a UN soldier yelling through the shellfire into a hand-held radio. 'Zulu Foxtrot Alpha Nine! This is Foxtrot Three! Shells hitting in and around Headquarters. Do not approach! Have report from Kigali hospital, one shell scored a direct hit. At least thirty dead!'

Quick pan round the room as everyone swallowed the words 'Direct hit! At least thirty dead!' And everyone wondering if they were next.

SHOOOSH . . . KACRASH!!!

The whole place rocking and rolling. Smoke filling the room, panic rising. Waiting for the next one, maybe the next one.

'Couple of men to recon outside! Now!'

Two Ghanaians secured their helmets, crawled over the shattered glass and out to the sandbags just beyond the door. They crouched under cover, waiting for a moment to sit up and see what the hell was going on. I crawled out and scrunched up next them.

'Hello, my friend.'

The big Ghanaian from Camp Runda staring down at me. His too-small helmet with the hand-painted 'UN' still wiggling atop his big head. Same way it did when the Hutu mob was screaming for our blood at Camp Runda.

'Hey, big guy! How come every time I see you it means trouble?'

'I was thinking the same thing, my friend.'

The big Ghanaian rose for a peek and I raised the camera behind his big head. Smoke and fire along the perimeter, wildfire bullets hunting for a kill. The soldiers' voices hushed now, quiet.

'We are in the middle of the battle.'

'Someone is targeting us too.'

'You guys know which side is doin' it?'

'Only the Almighty God Himself can tell you that, my friend.'

SHOOOSH . . . KACRASH!

The soldiers dived back through the doors and I lay on the ground and listened to the sounds of war crashing all round me. My heart pounding with the anti-aircraft guns. And smelling the cordite and firesmoke and closing my eyes and loving being alive right there in that one moment . . . sucking it in and holding my breath and feeling the adrenaline rush through my veins like a blast of high octane coke. Terrified and thrilled and grooving on the fix.

'Dear Lord. You sure made me one fucked-up cowboy.'

BANG BANG! BANG BANG! BANG BANG!

'Fine, then. Thy will be done.'

Jump back into the darkness. The big Ghanaian wiping the heat of the long afternoon from his face and looking into my eyes, knowing I was taking all these pictures in case one of those shells got lucky and we were all blown to hell . . . ain't that right, my friend? Yes, indeed, big guy, sure as hell is.

'Hey, James. Can you bring over the tripod?'

'How many times must I remind you to say "please"?'

He crawled over with the tripod and tucked up next to the door.

'May I ask what the hell you were doing out there?'

'Havin' a small moment in quiet prayer.'

'You? I don't think so. One minute you're practically dying, next you're running in and out of an artillery battle.'

'Yup. Weird, ain't it?'

I dragged the kit outside behind the sandbags and slapped the camera atop the tripod. Set the iris and focus, hit the roll button, jumped back through the doors and fell down next to James.

'Jon, what are you doing now?'

'Takin' a picture, what's it look like?'

Ghanaian soldiers leaned out from their hiding places, looked out the doors to the camera then over to me.

'Do you know what all these nice African soldiers are thinking just now?'

'Nope.'

'They are thinking that you, Jon Steele, are one very strange white man. And I think you may have a good deal to explain to the company accountants if that camera gets blown to bits.'

'Fuck 'em. It'll be a great fuckin' shot.'

'This is true.'

Then somewhere from the sky. A whistle and a roar and then feeling the sky slash open with heat and fire.

'Shit!'

'Down!'

KACRASH!!!

Rocks and dirt and glass flying through the doors. The ground vibrating and the walls shaking to kingdom come. Black smoke curling through the lobby and blanketing the room with terror. No one moving till the rumble faded away and the awareness of life passed from one fearful body to the next. Slowly, the soldiers pulled themselves off the floor, nervous sweat and grime dripping down their faces. I looked out the doors: the camera was still standing. 'Think I got that one.'

'Good. Now, go out there and retrieve that camera before I report you to the expenses department of ITN.'

'Yeah, yeah.'

I crawled out, grabbed the camera and rolled back through the doors to a safe corner. I rewound the tape and checked the shot through the eyepiece. Nice sunny day in Africa, just a bit of fire and smoke. Then the roaring sound of an incoming shell and a black streak cutting through the sky and something big slamming into Fort Apache . . . a flash of fire and smoke and rocks flying by the lens. Close, real close.

'Not fuckin' bad.'

'Really? Oh, let me see!' James grabbed the camera. His eyes wide with boyish glee. 'Oh, how lovely!'

Then the big Ghanaian crawled over and patted me on the shoulder. 'Me too?'

Rewind and play one more time. Then there was a whole line of me-toos waiting to see what almost killed us. Everyone slapping each other on the back and laughing at the picture and re-creating it with their hands and telling the story again and again. Outside, the shells faded away.

'Ah, recess.'

'Most probably the fuckers ran out of ammunition.'

'Does have that feel about it.'

'Certainly does.'

All clear, for now. General Dallaire and the gang raced back through the smoke and charged back to Fort Apache. I ran out with the camera for his arrival. The press pack dashed into the building as the general strolled round the sandbags with Jean-Guy in tow.

'You back already?'

'Never left, sir.'

'Goddam.'

He marched towards the doors and stopped. He turned round real slow and took careful reconnaissance of my grubby face. His mouth stretching tight under his perfectly trimmed moustache. 'Mr Steele, may I loan you a razor?'

'Actually, sir, I never shave in a war zone.'

The general's eyes squeezing together . . .

'Excuse me?'

. . . and Jean-Guy refitting his baseball cap in oh-shit fashion. My words sounding very close to disobeying the direct command of a two-star general, for Godsake! Dallaire's back went straight like a man of military discipline who had no place in his command for sloppy. Sloppy meant dead, goddammit!

'Would you care to explain yourself, Mr Steele?'

'It's kind of a superstition, sir. I never shave around guys with guns.'

'Uh-huh.'

And I held up the camera, trying to change the subject. 'Sir, would you like to see a shell just missing Fort Apache?'

'Fort *what*?'

And I rolled back the tape and played the shot. General Dallaire grabbed the eyepiece and held it to his eyes.

'Goddam! How 'bout that! Goddam!'

He looked over the grubbiness of my face one more time. 'You ever been hit?'

'No, sir . . .'

And me rubbing the stubble on my chin.

'. . . not yet.'

He tapped my arm with his fist. 'You can keep the fuzz.'

'Thank you, sir.'

He nodded and about-faced and marched through the shattered doors of his beat-up command. Jean-Guy took a long breath and winked and followed the leader, his voice chuckling as he went by. 'All I 'ave to say is, he must like you.'

'Yeah? Think so?'

'Yeah.'

Inside.

'Attention!'

'As you were.'

General Dallaire listened to his second-in-command report the situation. James pointed toward Dallaire and rolled his finger. 'Good stuff!' I kicked on the camera and zoomed into the general's face as he listened intently and looked around the room at all the lives under his command. And there was that crack-some-heads look in his eyes again like he knew, he goddam knew. Some son-of-a-bitch out there wanted his people dead so the same son-of-a-bitch could blame it on the other guys. And if he found out who the son-of-a-bitch was, well, by God he was going to blow that little shit to hell and back. The second-in-command saluted and walked away. General Dallaire stood with his hands on his hips, his eyes looking down at the beige Hush Puppies on his feet. The man was thinking, till he realized every set of eyeballs in the place was watching him think.

'Listen up!' he commanded.

The room fell silent to his voice.

'This is no time for bullshit. You know and I know this situation is not going to get any easier. Our troops out at the airport are underground in their bunkers. They're getting shot at, we've been shot at, and you've been shot at too. This is just going to get nastier. Be careful! Don't be stupid! Stay off the balconies and away from the windows! Anyone without his flak-jacket will be outside filling five sandbags! And I mean anyone! I'd rather you fill five sandbags with dirt rather than us filling five sandbags with bits and pieces of you!'

He bowed his head and listened to the rumble of faraway guns. The battle pounding in another corner of the jungle. General Dallaire knew it would be coming back soon enough. And he knew there was a time to hunker down and a time to keep the troops moving. Get 'em off their butts and back to work, anything to keep the fear from strangling the throats of his soldiers.

'Now, it's a beautiful day outside. The sun is shining and there's still a few birds singing in the trees out there.'

Everyone letting go with nervous laughter.

'Carry on and resume your duties.'

'Yes, sir!'

Me and James went up to our room and crawled out on to the balcony and set the satphone on the concrete ledge. I mounted the camera on the tripod and focused out into the evening sky and the red tracers flying across the red horizon. Tutsi rebels parked an anti-aircraft gun just under the balcony and let the fucker rip into the surrounding trees. The balcony shook with every round. I sat under the camera with my helmet on my head, holding the tripod steady through the shakier explosions and listening to bullets ricochet off the walls of Fort Apache. James hunkered down with the satphone and filed reports for every broadcast organization in the world. Even the World's Most Important Network, CNN, called in begging for news.

'James, ask them when the fuck they're gonna get here!'

'Sssh, Jon. I'm going on the air!'

'And tell 'em to bring some dope!'

A pile of MREs lay near the door. I opened some sort of casserole in a tin and scooped out a bit with my filthy fingers. Wasn't bad. I started shovelling it in like ice cream.

James finished his report, crawled over and watched my pig-out. 'Well, I have addressed the world.'

'Good for you. Seems you got this story by the balls, it's all yours.'

'Now if we could just get some of your pictures out.'

'Yeah, well, one of these fuckin' days.'

And James watching me pig-out some more. 'You feeling better?'

And me wiping the grub from my face. 'S'pose I am. Weak but better.'

'Strange, isn't it? Survival instinct as instant cure.'

'Kind of an adrenaline and shit-brown-shorts cure.'

'My goodness, what a day.'

'James, thanks for gettin' me through it.'

He looked down at the MREs and dug through the tins. 'Yeees. Now, where are you hiding all those yummy protein biscuits?'

Sneaking up to the roof before dawn, hoping the general wouldn't notice. Out of the stairwell and dash across the roof into the elevator shaft. Three walls of solid concrete round me, safe enough. I smashed out a small window, stuck the lens through the hole and rolled some pictures. Dim blue light through a steamy jungle haze, a rooster crying at the first rays of sunlight, shells rumbling in the hills. It was going to be another hot day in Kigali.

Kick in the lens doubler and zoom into the airport. Place sure was taking a beating. Busted glass and blast holes in the tower, columns of smoke along the runway, shell fire in the nearby trees. Pan down into the streets of Kigali. Junk and trash and packs of wild dogs. One woman running from behind a tree and dashing from hiding place to hiding place. Always looking behind her and always running faster. A UN APC racing down a jungle road. Rifles open up from the trees and the APC lunges forward and crashes through an abandoned roadblock before turning into Fort Apache.

I checked my watch, six thirty. General Dallaire would be marching through the halls soon. Time to go. I grabbed the camera and peeked out the elevator shaft. Looked fine. I jumped up and ran back towards the stairwell. Rounding the steel door a high-powered bullet ripped past my head. I dropped to the ground and waited. Another bullet, then nothing. I crawled across the roof and down the stairs.

'Fuck me. That would've been hard to explain.'

Back in the room. James sat under the balcony wall with the sat-phone to his ear again talking to ITN foreign editor Vicky Knighton. She was issuing specific orders to stay put and not leave the UN compound. So we sat like caged bears, listening to the battle come and go. We crawled around the floor and dug out some MREs and mixed up weird combinations of food. Beef stew and chocolate, orange drink powder with chicken mush. Then we twiddled our thumbs and listened to the battle some more. We made stupid calls on the sat-phone. Me trying to order a pizza from Italy and James wanting to call a few sex-chat numbers in France and discuss something he called the 'euro'. Can't say I had a clue what the man was talking about, but I kept noddin' with serious concern anyway ... yeah, euro bad, euro bad. We made lists of ITN management and rated them according to our own scale. Absolute asshole, dickhead, nice but dim, top-class. Then we'd sit around and twiddle our thumbs again. All through the day the rebel anti-aircraft gun circled round Fort Apache like some annoying neighbourhood ice-cream truck. It let off six or eight rounds, then pulled back down the road. Hutu kept lobbing heavy mortars our way trying to nail the damn thing. Back and forth and back and forth, all fucking day.

'Piggy-in-the-middle, isn't it?'

''Scuse me?'

'You Americans have Whack-a-mole, we British have Piggy-in-the-middle.'

'James, you lost your fuckin' mind?'

'You remember telling me about Whack-a-mole?'

'Yup.'

'Well?'

'Well what?'

'God, you Americans. Pay attention. Outside soldiers are dropping bombs and shells all around us.'

'Yup.'

'And both sides are spraying the jungle with machine-gun fire. Now, if you add all that to the fact neither side is going to give two coconuts to help us, then you have something akin to Piggy-in-the-middle.'

'OK, got it. But that's not really the rules of Whack-a-mole.'

'You're telling me there are rules to Whack-a-mole?'

''Course there are. You got all these holes on a table and this little mole keeps poppin' up its head from different holes, and you try and smash the critter with a hammer before it ducks down.'

'And is this a real mole?'

'Nope. But I know some guys who tried it that way once. Made a big fuckin' mess outa their mom's kitchen table.'

'Hmmm.'

''Nother high-protein biscuit?'

'Thank you.'

Heavy shells sailed down the hills closer and closer to Fort Apache. We moved to the furthest corner from the balcony and spent another hour listening to the explosions and feeling the world rattle till the next reload cycle.

'Hard to know, really, which side to cheer for. The ones who want to kill you or the ones who don't care if you're killed.'

'We're never gonna get that fuckin' pizza.'

'Yeees. I sometimes think we should have been on that plane to Nairobi.'

'Sounds like a scene from *Casablanca*.'

'Oh, wonderful movie, isn't it?'

'Can you believe fuckin' Ted Turner had it colourized?'

'Cretin. I shall not be asking him round to my club.'

'Me neither.'

'Jon. You don't have a club.'

And the guns pounded to life once more. Pound, pound, pound, pound.

'I fear we might be here for ever.'

' "The plane to Lisbon, Rick. I have often wondered why you were not on that plane" . . . great fuckin' script.'

'Oh, the best. "Did you steal the church funds? Run off with a senator's wife? I like to think that you killed a man . . ." '

'. . . "It's the romantic in me." '

' "Why, I came to Casablanca for the waters." '

' "Water? There is no water in Casablanca. We're in the middle of the desert." '

'"I was misinformed." '

GTTTTRRRRUUUPPTT! CRACK! ZING!

'No shit misinformed!'

And us starting to laugh.

SHOOOSH . . . KACRASH!!

'Fuckin' bombs in Casablanca, Rick!'

KACRASH!!

'Nice fuckin' waters, Rick!'

'We are two misinformed assholes, Rick!'

BANG BANG! BANG BANG! BANG BANG!

'But we'll always have Kigali!'

And howling our heads off and kicking our legs and laughing and crawling over to the balcony and screaming like kids.

'So fuck you, Rick!'

SHOOOSH . . . KACRASH!!

'And fuck you guys too!'

And screaming and laughing louder till we looked behind us and saw Major Jean-Guy Laplante on his hands and knees, peeking round the doorway.

'What the heck are you two clowns up to?'

'Hiding, what's it look like?'

Then a huge explosion knocking us back and into the room. Fort Apache swayed from side to side and thick smoke poured in through the balcony door. The sound rumbled and echoed and faded away. It was quiet before we noticed we were flat out on the floor with Jean-Guy between us like Piggy-in-the-middle. He refitted his baseball cap and looked at James, then at me, then straight up to the ceiling. 'OK. I think that went OK.'

'So what brings you to our humble *pied-à-terre*, Jean-Guy?'

'Let me remember. Sometimes the bombs make you forget what you are thinking. Ah, *oui*. I 'ave a message from the general. He says the rebels are making the big push for the airport. And if they pull it off it will be the end for the Hutu government in this place. The RGF could regroup in the centre of Kigali but they would not hold it for long.'

'How long does the general think it will take?'

'Not sure. Days, weeks. What he does know is that none of this is good for the UN troops. First, we're trapped between them. Second, whoever loses is sure to blame the UN. Things could get very messy for all of us. And that means you too.'

'Not us, Jean-Guy. We're leavin' Fort Apache on the next plane to Lisbon.'

'Pardon?'

'Never mind, Jean-Guy. Jon is a bit stir-crazy.'

'Perhaps I can help you with that. The general is going out to the airport to inspect conditions of the UN troops out there. The Hutu still 'ave three divisions at the Kanombe barracks near the airport. So the general is very concerned for the safety of his men if this gets worse. He says he may 'ave to pull his men out of harm's way.'

'*Aaand?*'

'I suggested we take the press along and he has agreed. I hope that is OK.'

'But we were havin' so much fun here in our own little world.'

'So I noticed. I think you two clowns need some fresh air. We'll travel in APCs because, as you may have noticed, there is a war going on out there.'

Steve and Michael crawled through the doorway with their cameras dangling round their necks. Their eyes focusing on the three of us squashed together on the floor.

'Hey.'

'Whatchuguyzdoin'?' said Steve.

Jean-Guy shrugged his shoulders.

''Aving the press briefing. What does it look like?'

Steve stared like he was trying to grasp the time of day. 'Huh?'

'Let's get to the APCs before the general shoves off without us.'

The steel hatch slammed shut in my face and it was dark and hot. Little squares of light streamed through the bulletproof windows up front. A Tunisian gunner secured the turret hatch, hit the driver on the shoulder, and the APC tore out of Fort Apache and into the war. Me and James and Steve and the big Israeli Michael and the rest of the press pack sitting on benches in the rear. All of us bouncing round like bowling balls in a steel can.

'Damn good thing we're wearin' helmets!'

'Certainly is!'

The Tunisian driver ripped through the streets and cut fast round sharp corners, the engine growling loud as a jet plane. The press gang rolling from side to side and hanging on for the ride. Steve smiling like it was all far out.

'Jeeze. He's really cruisin'.'

A saucer-sized porthole on the hatch. I held the lens to the light and tied to grab a picture. Everything was a blur.

'He's sure cruisin' all right.'

Small round plate under the porthole. I pushed it aside. Little tunnel to the outside world. Just enough for the barrel of a rifle. The gears wound down and the APC slowed to a stop.

'Everyone out!'

Me and Steve kicked open the hatch with our boots and found ourselves staring at one blown-to-hell airport. Shattered glass and twisted steel and chunks of concrete everywhere we looked. The main terminal building and flight tower looking like the Leaning Tower of Pisa.

'Jeeze.'

'Fuckin' hell.'

'You Americans have such a way with words,' said James. 'Brief, but graceful. I must incorporate such colourful expressions into my script.'

Another Tunisian APC pulled up amid the rubble and stopped nearby. General Dallaire climbed out with Jean-Guy and a few staff officers. The Ghanaian company commander for the airport stepped up, saluted sharply and stood by in silence while Dallaire stared at the building. I switched on the camera and framed the general's face in the lens, watching for that crack-some-heads expression in his eyes, but this time seeing a man who knew all his efforts at peace were going up in clouds of cordite smoke.

'Shit.'

'Sir.'

'Goddam shit.'

'Sir.'

'How many direct hits?'

'Four, sir.'

'Shit.'

'Sir.'

Shells exploded on the far end of the runway. Dallaire turned his head and listened, measuring the sounds.

'Sounds like .82 mil.'

'Yes, sir.'

'Shit.'

'Sir.'

And he marched through the rubble and the twisted steel of the shattered doors and into the terminal. He stood before mounds of shattered glass the length of the building.

'Goddam.'

'Sir.'

'They blew out every goddam window in the place.'

'Yes, sir.'

He reached out and tapped a huge piece of jagged glass still hanging from the frame. It crashed down a mere toe chop from his Hush Puppies.

'Goddam.'

'Sir.'

'Where are the fucking guns?'

'Sir. They move after every few rounds, sir.'

Dallaire looked up through the gaping holes in the ceiling. Blue sky and flash marks. Shrapnel scars splattered all down the walls.

'I want to see the men.'

'Yes, sir.'

The Ghanaian company commander heeled round and led the way at a quick march. General Dallaire followed with determined steps. I dropped the camera at his heels and let the lens follow him through the rubble and the glass and the chunks of concrete, thinking how the man never walked, he only marched. He kicked aside a broken door and chunks of debris. Then, above our heads, a whistle and a roar and a huge crash and the building shaking with the blast of an incoming shell. The camera jiggled in my hands, but the general marched ahead without missing a step. Down behind a two-metre wall of sandbags, down a blast-worn stairwell, into a dark, airless cellar. Hundred Ghanaian soldiers crammed together in fear-soaked sweat.

'What the hell's going on in here?'

The faces turn amazed and stunned.

'You guys still smiling?'

'Yes, sir!'

General Dallaire had words with this soldier and that soldier. Each one of them looking up to the Old Man with respect and honour. Each one of them knowing their general had crossed through some serious bullshit just to check up on them. Each one of them smiling and shaking his hand. Then he marched back up the stairs and out of the building. He climbed on to his APC and looked out over the runway.

'Goddam.'

'Sir.'

James leaned near the camera, whispering, 'Stick with him. He's good stuff.'

'You bet, 'specially when he's standin' in plain sight of anyone with a high-powered rifle.'

Dallaire climbed down the APC and pointed across the runway. 'Let's take a run to the other side. Got a hundred more men over there.'

'Sir.'

Back into the APC. Camera behind the Tunisian crew's heads looking like silhouettes against the patches of square light coming through the bulletproof windows. They drove fast round the blast holes and unexploded shells lying in the runway. They pointed to columns of black smoke rising along the tarmac. The runway was under fire again. Steve and Michael pressed up behind me checking the shot.

'What's it look like out there?'

'Sorta like racin' across a bull's eye in the middle of target practice.'

'In Israel we call that the West Bank.'

'Swell.'

The APC swerved off the runway, raced along a dirt track, then hit the brakes. We kicked open the hatch, poured out of the APC and chased after the general. He was walking along the ridge above his troops. The wide Ghanaian faces looking up from their holes in the earth surprised as hell.

'You guys still smiling down there?'

'Yes, sir!'

'Thought so. Just keep your heads down when the shit starts.'

'Sir.'

'Go for cover and stay happy.'

'Yes, sir.'

Dallaire marched through a field of tall grass and stood atop a small hill. He pressed a set of binoculars to his eyes and panned across the trees trying to make out which guys were doing a better job of killing the other guys. Rifles snapped and echoed across the tarmac. Shells started to hammer down into the centre of Kigali. Dallaire didn't budge. He just kept looking and studying the battle. Like nothing I'd ever seen.

'Great fuckin' pictures, James.'

'He's good, isn't he? Can we make a story out of him?'

'We can make a fuckin' movie. I mean, look at the guy. He's John Wayne, ain't he?'

Dallaire lowered the binoculars and considered the scene, waving his hands like drawing a map of what the hell was going on, then shaking his head. Whatever it was he saw, it was fucked. He looked down the hill then turned to his staff. Something had caught his eye.

'You men stay here.'

And he marched off alone. I took off after him with the camera rolling. His Hush Puppies kicking through the tall grass and the lens rising above his bulletproof vest and the picture opening to a battered

Hutu garrison in a low clearing. Hutu soldiers with their rifles pointing at General Dallaire. He stopped fifteen yards from the barrels of
their guns. Close enough to feel the anger and hatred in their eyes, like
all this shit was the fault of the white man standing before them. All the
Hutu faces tired and hungry and beaten to hell. Pan the lens round and
zoom into Dallaire's face. His lips pressed tight and his teeth biting
down hard as he inspected the miserable state of the Hutu soldiers.

'Goddam.'

'Sir,' I said, thinking it was the polite thing to do so as not to let the
general think he was mumbling to himself, and thinking that's why
everyone else did the same thing around him anyway.

He stood in silence watching Hutu soldiers. After a time he raised
his arm in sharp salute, his voice calling in French, '*Courage!*'

The Hutu lowered their rifles and nodded. Dallaire spun round,
marched back to the APCs and gathered his officers round him. A few
enlisted men came out of their trenches just to be near the Old Man
and hear his words.

'This is all bullshit.'

'Sir.'

'The way this is going most of those Hutu soldiers will be dead in a
matter of hours.'

'Sir.'

'And we are in the middle. Gentlemen, this *is* bullshit.'

'Sir!'

'And if it keeps up we'll pull the hell out.'

'Sir.'

'If the battalion was here and it was mechanized we could defend
the airport. But two hundred guys? No goddam way, no goddam
way.'

'Sir.'

'We'll let them fight it out and if they want to give it to us, then we'll
take it.'

'Sir.'

'Then we'll fucking defend it!'

'Sir!'

'Goddam right!'

And he grabbed the binoculars for one more gaze over the runway
and the jungle and the heavy shells falling into a smoking Kigali. A

skinny young Ghanaian soldier moved near the camera. He stood as close as my shadow.

'Hello, Mr Cameraman.'

'Howdy.'

'You are from Nairobi?'

'Sort of.'

'Oh, very nice. When you go back to Nairobi?'

'Hard to tell. Kinda stuck out here with all you guys just now.'

'When you go back, you would send some AA batteries for our radios?'

'S'pose so. What's your name?'

A smile spread wide over his white teeth. 'Oh, you would not remember it, but do not worry.'

Another Ghanaian pressed forward with another friendly smile. 'And some film. We have no film for our cameras.'

Then another . . .

'And some of these kinds of batteries for our cameras and . . .'

. . . the shopping queue growing longer and more requesting. And me taking notes trying to get it all down.

'. . . some pencils and paper, so we can write to our families.'

'Yeah, OK. But who do I send it to?'

And they all laughed and smiled. The skinny Ghanaian soldier taking my hand and holding it and swinging it back and forth like we were old pals from some African village.

'Oh, it does not matter. We will all share!'

And them all laughing again and the skinny soldier still holding my hand and swinging it back and forth and back and forth. Automatic rifle in one hand, my swinging hand in the other. Back and forth some more and a polite British public-school cough behind me.

'Uh, Jon. Do you realize you are holding hands with a soldier?'

'Yup, James. I do.'

'Might I ask why?'

Back and forth and back and forth.

'Ain't really sure, but he won't let go.'

More wide, toothy smiles all round.

'And he's got a fuckin' rifle, James. Any man with a loaded rifle wants to hold my hand and grin all day, it's fine by me.'

'Wait till this gets back to London.'

'James, right now me and this soldier are best pals. One word from me and he's gonna blow your fuckin' head off – ain't that right, my friend?'

More toothy smiles from my Ghanaian pals. 'Oh, yes, yes.'

'Right, Jon, you just stand there and hold hands to your heart's content.'

'Thought you'd be seein' it my way.'

'My dear chap.'

A low whistle and a swoosh and an incoming shell crashed three hundred yards away. The general gave orders for the soldiers to get underground and the rest of us to get our butts into the APCs. The steel cans roared back across the bull's-eyed runway and slammed to a quick stop. The hatch pulled open and Jean-Guy poked his head into our APC. 'The general wants to 'ave a word with the company commander. You guys stay put.'

The Tunisian driver eased back the throttle and the gunner opened the top hatch and the steel can filled with bright sun and damp air. We sat and waited, listening to shells slam down on the runway. Then the sound of something falling hard and close.

'Seal it up! Now!'

And the darkness squeezed tight once more. Muffled explosions outside the steel shell, like Muhammad Ali pounding a sack of potatoes.

'Fuck me. Gettin' busy out there.'

'Yeah, but we have to be safe in here.'

'I should think so.'

Boom boom! Boom boom!

'This shit happens all the time in southern Lebanon.'

'See, listen to Michael. He's from Israel, does this all the time. We could survive a direct hit, couldn't we, Michael?'

'No. Not really.'

'Jeeze.'

And the shells fell harder and the sound cut sharper. I peeked out the porthole. Smoke and fire rising from the terminal.

'Fuckin' hell. Place is gettin' hit!'

'You don't suppose they're trying for us?'

And a powerful blast and all kinds of shit hitting the sides of the APC.

'Looks like it.'

'Jeeze.'

The gunner reached over and threw open the hatch.

'You run inside. We wait here.'

Me and James and Steve and Michael grabbed our cameras and jumped out of the APC and ran into the terminal just as another shell smashed into the roof above our heads.

KACRASH!

'Fuck me!'

'Now, this we don't get a lot of in southern Lebanon.'

Then two shells in the same breath hitting hard and the building rocking, shaking from head to toe. Glass and steel and concrete skidding across the floor as General Dallaire marched out of the smoke. 'What the hell you guys doing in here?'

'Nothin', sir. Just kinda thought we'd get in and out of the APC a few more times.'

'Just kind of thought you'd be safer in here.'

'Uh, that too.'

'Bullshit!'

'Sir.'

Then a howling roar and . . .

SHOOSH . . . KACRASH!!!

Dallaire marched to the edge of the shattered doors and looked round the corner. Black smoke rolling through the blue sky.

'Right! That's it! We're leaving! Get out and get in the APCs quick!'

We grabbed our kits and charged out the door into the smoke, Dallaire's voice yelling after us: 'And watch for small-arms fire out there!'

And James's voice following me: 'Now he tells us.'

Rifles cracking and bullets ripping in the air. Our boots hitting the ground like a herd of cattle gone mad. Steel hatches swinging open and the Tunisian gunner hauling us in. Engines revving up, ready to break away.

'All accounted for!'

'Slam it shut and lock it down!'

'Got it!'

'Go! Go!'

The APC bucked and reared. Steel tracks digging in the dirt and charging ahead and me swinging the camera up into the bulletproof windows. The driver crunching the gears trying to make the fuckin' thing go faster and the whole steel can sliding round a corner. And through the growling engines, the ceaseless report of booms and blasts.

'They're shooting at us!'

'Sounds like it!'

'Jeeze!'

Faster and faster. The gunner holding on to the top hatch ready to pop it open and blast our way through if need be. The APC's gears grinding harder and the tracks digging in deeper. And then the sound of a hundred jack-hammers drilling into the roof of the APC.

'Fuck me!'

'What the hell is that?'

'That what I think it is?'

'Can't fuckin' believe it!'

'What?'

And me laughing and giggling to myself and feeling my heart pound to the sound of machine-gun rounds ricocheting off the steel plates just above our heads.

21 May 1994

James was holding the satphone at arm's length from his head. His face grimacing like a kid caught with his hands in Momma's cookie jar. Vicky Knighton's voice screaming down the line from London: 'You did what?'

'But, Vicky, we didn't know they were going to attack and we were in an armoured vehicle and—'

'I don't care! I told you to stay in the UN compound! We've sent someone to the Ugandan border on a Lear jet. They're going to wait for you to get out. All you have to do is get to the border!'

'That might be a little difficult.'

'It's there if you can make it! But for God's sake! Stay in the compound! Under no circumstances are you to venture into the streets!'

So we sat like caged bears again.

'Mad, huh?'

'You might say that.'

'She can't really expect us to stay in here all day.'

'She's just worried. Didn't have the heart to tell her there's practically no chance of driving out of here.'

'You can make that NFW.'

'Excuse me?'

'No fuckin' way.'

'Ah.'

'I was walking along the perimeter and bumped into that Tutsi rebel liaison guy.'

'That would be "officer", but do go on.'

'Yeah, whatever. Guy looks like a fuckin' Boy Scout. Anyway, I asked him about the road towards Uganda. He said the rebels got the whole road locked down and'll destroy anything on it that moves.'

'How nice.'

'So I asked him if we could get a rebel escort. He said, "No. I am afraid not." So then I asked him if we could get permission to drive ourselves and he said, "No. I am afraid not." So then I asked why and he said, "Because we will kill you." '

'Yeees.'

'So I finished the conversation with "Thank you, you little prick." '

'Ever the diplomat. And what did he say?'

'He bowed and said, "Not at all." '

'Would be nice if we could get a picture story out of here. So far it's a great radio story.'

'Lemme tell you, it ain't much fun sittin' on ten shot tapes and hidin' in Fort Apache and wearin' full body armour day after day. Soon as this siege breaks and everyone else gets in here with their cameras, my pictures'll be half the price of week-old horseshit. Still, we're here and we ain't workin' in a bank and . . . I forgot what I was sayin'.'

'What an interesting and logical argument. Full marks for your brain.'

'My brain should be workin' fine. Haven't had a fuckin' joint in two weeks.'

'Sure about that? No sneaking off into the jungle for a quick one?'

'Nope.'

'Cross your heart?'

'Yup.'

Jean-Guy popped his head into the room. 'I don't know if this is a good idea, but since it's relatively quiet in this place today . . .'

'Yes! Thank you, Jesus! And your boredom shall come unto an end!'

'Pardon?'

'Gospel 'cording to somebody.'

'Never mind, Jean-Guy. Whatever it is, let's go!'

The jeeps raced through the ghostly streets of Kigali heading for an orphanage on the edge of the city. Been some time since any food had made it through the machetes and the killings and all the evil stuff falling down through the skies. But just now the skies were calm and blue and the air was cool through the trees. My heart beating in relaxed rhythms.

'What do you say about the state of your life when drivin' through Kigali seems normal?'

'Yeees. If one's idea of normal is driving through a place with rotting corpses in the road.'

'But a lot of 'em have been dragged away by the dogs. Even the dead smell isn't as bad as before.'

'Or perhaps you just don't notice it any more.'

'S'pose.'

Groups of Hutu soldiers stood on the edge of the roads at sparsely positioned roadblocks. Then over a bridge, Hutu boy soldiers, ten and twelve years old, armed with grenades and rifles. They lowered their rifles and held out their hands, begging for food. We tossed out some MREs and they let us pass. Down in the ravines more Hutu regulars sat round a fire. They looked as hungry and worn as the boy soldiers on the bridge.

'Looks like the rough end of the war, Jean-Guy.'

'Oh, you know. These guys 'ave been taking such a pounding. One day we'll drive along here and they will be gone.'

'Or dead.'

'That is what I mean.'

'How long you been out here, Major?'

'Six months. Seeing the same terrible things day after day. And now the general wants me to stay on for another six months. I want to see my wife and my house, but what can I do? If I turn my back from this place, I do not think I would ever forgive myself.'

We cruised round scrub and trees blasted on to the road. Our heads out the windows looking for unexploded shells. Then the road was clear and Jean-Guy stepped down on the gas.

'Well, who knows, Jean-Guy? Stick around another year and you'll probably make colonel.'

'Oh, not me. I do not 'ave the college for the senior ranks.'

'You're jokin'?'

'That's the army. Then again, I am only a military policeman. But I will get potato chips.'

And me looking at James and James looking at me and the both of us thinking Major Laplante had been in the jungle far too long already.

'I was just thinking of what I really miss after six months in this place, potato chips.'

'Potato chips,' I said, seeking confirmation.

'Well, I, for one, Jean-Guy, would not be craving crisps after a year in the jungle. I'm afraid it would be something more in the line of—'

'Ohyeahohyeah. I miss that too. And I love my wife but I don't dream about her, I 'ave these dreams about potato chips.' And he re-fitted his baseball cap and licked his lips. 'Nice and salty. And not that crap that comes in those tubes.'

'Pringles and that Ruffles shit. Fuckin' garbage, Jean-Guy.'

'I hate them too! No, I dream of the real thing. Open the bag and smell them. Mmmm.'

'Can we dream of some beer while we're at it?'

'Oh, yes, potato chips and beer. Mmmm.'

The sun beat down hot. We drove along a dirt road and turned into a small village where Hutu civilians sat in patches of shade waiting for the end of one more dreadful day. A gang of kids ran after us, clapping their hands and laughing, their bare feet whipping up little cyclones of red dust. We pulled through a gate and were surrounded by all kinds of Rwandan faces. Light brown skin, narrow noses. Black skin, flat faces. Hutu and Tutsi orphans all jumbled together inside a tumble-down fence.

'We find them wandering the streets or sitting next to their dead parents, so we bring them here. At least here they 'ave some kind of home.'

'They safe out here?'

'As safe as anyone can be in this place.'

Kids with snotty noses and dirty hands mugged for the camera and danced round like any other kids in the world seeing a TV camera.

Those were the ones who'd been here a while. The new arrivals stood off by themselves . . . quiet and distant, as if still hearing the screams in their heads. Inside the big house, ten-year-old boys washed huge pots twice as big as themselves. Other boys were busy cooking up buckets of rice and beans. And out in the garden, young Tutsi girls washed torn clothes and laid them on bushes to dry in the sun. UN soldiers kicked a football across the dirt while a pack of boys tumbled over it, laughing and yelling and begging for more.

A wood fence ran along the garden and turned a corner under a clump of trees. A hundred Hutu children from the next village gazed through the wood slats, every one of their faces drawn with hunger. One of the Ghanaian soldiers carried over a box of high-protein biscuits and handed packs over the fence to the kids. Things broke into a small riot when it was clear there wasn't going to be enough to go round.

I pushed the lens up to the fence and framed the begging faces and begging hands. Biscuits flying through the air, hungry voices screaming, little black hands reaching into the sky. Down in the crush of bodies a small boy, four or five years old. Fat tears rolling down his face as the bigger children stepped over him and pushed his face into the dirt. And me thinking I should reach over and help the kid out of the dirt, but just zooming into his fat tears instead.

'C'mon, give me a shot.'

The little guy grabbed hold of the fence and pulled himself up through the crush, fighting his way to the top till he got his little hands round a pack of biscuits.

'Yes! Gotcha!'

And I looked into all the other begging faces. Their hands still reaching, their voices still crying for food. I drew them closer into the lens and let their hungry voices scream some more. Letting the pictures roll for a long time, then shutting off the camera and turning away. And hating myself for turning away but loving the pictures and knowing they were good. Good enough to hit people watching TV thousands of miles away. Hit them hard enough to make them feel something. Maybe, please, God, maybe.

Jean-Guy waved me over to the house. 'Something you should see inside.'

'Any other cameras in there?'

'No. Do you want me to get them?'

'Nope. Let's go.'

We went in through the kitchen and down a narrow hallway towards a beam of soft light pouring through opaque glass. Jean-Guy stopped at the door of a small room and tipped his baseball cap back on his head. He nodded into the room. Just around the door, a Hutu boy sat on a bed with his arm round a young Tutsi boy. The Hutu with a lost look in his eyes. The Tutsi no more than a sack of bones . . . his skin wrinkled and scarred, his body twisted like a broken doll. I panned the lens up from the boy's twisted feet, over his skeleton legs and his protruding ribs, his bony arms hanging lifeless from his shoulders. I zoomed into his death-mask face. Huge dark welts swollen out the top of his smashed skull and his eyes rolling in unconscious circles.

'Fuck me. What the hell happened?'

'No one knows. They came here last week and 'ave been sitting like this ever since.'

James came into the room and took a deep breath. 'My God.'

'You fuckin' believe it? Kid's skull is smashed in four places. He shouldn't even be alive.'

The Hutu boy looked up from his lost place and started speaking in his native language.

'What's he sayin'?'

'I'll get somebody who speaks the lingo.'

And Jean-Guy dashed down the hall as the Hutu boy kept talking in words we couldn't understand. His voice barely more than a whisper. James sat next to the Hutu boy, listening and nodding as if we understood the words just to keep him talking. Few minutes later Jean-Guy returned with a teenage Hutu girl and she translated the boy's whispers. 'I found him in a ditch. The militia killed his family. His mother, his father and all his sisters. Then they tried to kill him with a hammer. I saw it, I saw it.'

The Hutu boy softly touched the swollen welts on the boy's skull. The broken boy's eyes rolled towards the touch as if remembering gentleness.

'They kept hitting him on the head till they thought he was dead. And when they left, I went to him. He was still breathing so I carried him here. I will take care of him.'

None of us moved. There was only the sound of the tape rolling in the camera. And then the sounds of faraway shells. The Hutu boy looked into the soft opaque light coming through the window.

'What is the name of your friend?'

'I do not know his name. I do not know who he is. I found him in a ditch. I saw it. I must take care of him.'

'Why?'

'Because I am Hutu and he is Tutsi.'

Then the lost look came over his eyes once more and he slid back into silence. His Hutu hands caressing the Tutsi boy's shattered skull and resting it close to his neck. Jean-Guy's radio sparked with military-speak. Shelling was getting heavy in Kigali. Everyone was ordered to get back to base ASAP.

'Everybody to the jeeps!'

Hutu forces were dropping shells into the centre of Kigali trying to break up the rebel advance. Fort Apache sitting smack in the middle again. Me and Michael and Steve decided to sneak past General Dallaire's office and get up to the roof for some pictures. Top of the stairs we pushed open the steel door for a wide view of the city. 'Seems OK.'

'I want to go down to the far end of the roof. How about you guys?'

'I've got a bunch of those shots already, Michael. Think I'll just sit here and wait till something comes real close. How 'bout you, Steve?'

'Jeeze. I'll just wait here too. So far it's only good for TV.'

'Just be careful, Michael. There's been a sniper out there working the roof.'

'Hutu or Tutsi?'

'Hell knows.'

Michael crawled over the waterpipes and ductwork and set up along the edge of the roof. I set my tripod on the steps of the stairwell and let the camera roll on autopilot. Steve snapped a few shots then settled down to polishing his lenses.

'Jeeze. I really wanna get with the rebels comin' into Kigali. That's where the pictures are.'

'Hard trick from this side.'

'Yeah.'

'You hear somethin'?'

'Like a zing?'

'Yup.'

I reached for the camera and heard another round rip through the sky, then a growling hum and a loud crash against the steel door and the door slamming into our faces and throwing us down the stairs.

'Shit!'

'Jeeze!'

'Fuckers got us in their sights.'

'Not us. Michael.'

'Shit!'

We crawled up the stairs, opened the steel door and looked down the roof. Michael was laid out like a pancake, camera in his hands.

'Michael?'

'Someone is fucking shooting at me!'

'You hit?'

'Not yet.'

Another shot and a cloud of dust and chipped concrete just above Michael's head.

'Shit! I don't need this! I can go back to Israel and have the Palestinians shoot at me!'

'Fuck me. The general ain't gonna like this shit.'

'Whatta we do?'

'Talk him back.'

'Good idea.'

And we leaned over the top step with the steel door covering our backs.

'Listen, Michael! Follow our voices and don't look up!'

'This is like being on the West Bank!'

'Go left!'

'Now go right, under the pipes.'

He crawled and ate dirt for an hour working his way back towards the steel door. All the time bullets ripping inches above his head. He edged his way closer and closer till me and Steve reached out and grabbed hold of his bulletproof vest and hauled him inside just as another high-powered round smashed into the steel door. We tumbled back with Michael on top of us. His face was filthy and he was breathing fast.

'Jeeze.'

'Shit!'

'You look like you been rode hard and put up wet.'

'Thanks. Huh?'

'Just some cowboy talk. Wish there was a bar in this town, I'd buy you a drink.'

Then three incoming shells rocked Fort Apache and the bells started ringing and the blue lights started flashing and we tore down the stairs. The Ghanaian troops and Canadian officers were scrunched into the lobby for another round of Piggy-in-the-middle. Smoke and dust swirling through the dark. We got down in a corner near James and waited for the bombs to pass us by.

'And where have you naughty boys been?'

'On the roof.'

'Anything happen?'

'Almost.'

Couple of Ghanaian soldiers carried a desk into the lobby. Another soldier brought a chair and a battery-powered lamp. General Dallaire followed with an armload of paperwork and sat himself down in the middle of the dark room to attend to it. Shells slammed down round Fort Apache for hours and we all sat entertained by the sight of the general scribbling away in the middle of a battle. Sweat curled through the room on whiffs of cordite, the building shook like an earthquake. But General Dallaire kept reading and writing like he was home in his study. All the man needed was a pipe and a good old dog at his feet.

'You suppose this is for the benefit of the men?'

'Fuckin' works for me.'

'Yeees.'

The general spotted the Tutsi liaison officer through the dark and called him over. The guy looked even more like a Boy Scout standing next to Dallaire and saluting upwards as the general towered over him by a half-metre.

'That the guy who said the Tutsi would kill us if we tried to leave?'

'Yup.'

I wandered over with the camera, framed them up and watched the general bite his lip while the Tutsi officer expressed his deep and profound shock that the general could think the Tutsi rebels might be in any way deliberately targeting the UN mission or using the UN compound as battlefield cover. The Boy Scout poured on the bullshit and Dallaire just stood with his hands on his hips.

SHOOOSH . . .

'Hit it!'

. . . KACRASH!!

Everyone hit the floor and covered their heads and waited for the aftershocks to pass. And when they all looked up, Lieutenant General Romeo Dallaire was still standing there with his hands on his hips. Looking down on the Tutsi officer cowering on the floor. The general rocking back and forth on his Hush Puppies, waiting for this Tutsi liaison Boy Scout son-of-a-bitch to say something interesting.

'You were saying, Captain?'

Every UN soldier in the dark room nodded with pride. They nudged each other in the ribs. 'You see the Old Man? Didn't even flinch. Not one bit.'

And James crawling up next to me. 'You're right. This is a movie and he is John fucking Wayne.'

'Told you so.'

The battle faded back into the hills. Me and James ran up to our room and spent the rest of the day pinned to the floor, acting like we were in some war movie yelling, 'Fuck you!' and 'Fuck you too!' over the balcony as the shells pounded back down the hills towards Fort Apache then back into the hills again. The neighbourhood rebel APC pulled up under Fort Apache and started blasting into the trees over and over again as well.

'Fuck you too!'

'Christ. Is there more to this script or is this it?'

'It's the problem with action movies, ain't it? Not enough fuckin' character development.'

KACRASH!!

'Fuck you!'

'And fuck you too!'

'We wanna go home!'

BANG BANG! BANG BANG! BANG BANG!

Close in rifles sprayed the jungle in every direction. Bullets skimmed off the walls of Fort Apache.

'Enough already!'

'Yeah! Fuck you!'

BANG BANG! BANG BANG!

'And fuck you too!'

Jean-Guy crawled into the room and on to the balcony.

'I 'ave a message from the general!'

'Is that in the script right now, Jon?'

'I ain't sure. Don't think we're supposed to get a message from the general till Clint Eastwood shows up with Tom Cruise.'

'I thought we were expecting Bruce Willis.'

'You two clowns are losing it fast.'

'Not much else to do round here just now, other than feelin' your brain rattle in your head.'

'Let's go inside for the press briefing.'

'You mean you really *do* have a message from the general?'

'Yes.'

'For us?'

'Yes.'

'Ain't lookin' for volunteers, is he?'

'Come on.'

We crawled back into the room and assumed the usual position of the three of us lying on the floor staring up at the ceiling. Jean-Guy between us fiddling with his baseball cap.

'OK. Intelligence is reporting to the general that things are moving very fast out there. There doesn't seems to be any counter-attack by the government troops. He doesn't understand it but that's what's happening. The whole thing could be a trap by the Hutu. Either way we are heading for the final showdown.'

'Holy shit.'

'So here's what I'm going to do. I 'ave my radio here tuned to the frequency of our boys in the airport bunkers. That way you will hear what is going on. But please don't tell anyone, OK?'

'Of course, Major.'

'OK.'

And he pulled his walkie-talkie out of his body armour and dropped it on the floor. He jumped up on to all fours and crawled out the door.

'Wouldn't you care to stay for tea, Major?'

'Yeah, we're gonna pretend we're in some other movie now.'

'Uh, no, thanks. I seem to 'ave lost my radio. Now, where did I leave the damn thing?' And he crawled out the door.

'Guess it's time to go to work, huh?'

'Yeees.'

'Fuck me. Up and down and up and down. Like bein' on a fuckin' roller-coaster.'

'That young boy. The one whose head was crushed with a hammer.'

'Don't, James. That picture is gonna give me nightmares for a long time.'

'Me too.'

'You hear that?'

'I certainly do.'

You could feel it come to life. Like a demon unleashed upon the earth. Killing and killing and killing some more. Red tracers howling through the darkness and glowing with fire. Flashes and explosions and huge clouds of smoke rolling above the jungle billowy and blood-like. Chunks of metal screaming by the balcony. James huddled with the satphone reporting the story to the world and me under the camera holding the tripod steady and letting the demon dance in the lens all through the night.

I leaned into the corner and felt the explosions roll through my body. And I watched the jungle burn into the killer night, thinking it was the most beautiful thing I'd ever seen. I kept watching till a weird numbness came over me. And I remembered the Tutsi boy at the orphanage, his smashed skull and his eyes rolling round in his head. And I wondered if he, too, could see this beautiful demon dancing in the firelight sky. Then amid the roar of battle, I fell asleep.

22 May 1994

Five a.m. Dozing against the wall. Voices crackling over Jean-Guy's radio. 'RPF troops sighted at airport perimeter. Heading towards the runway and meeting little or no resistance. Repeat: RPF troops heading towards the runway. Meeting little or no resistance.'

And me and James jumping like startled rabbits.

'Fuck me.'

'It can't be.'

Command voices sounding just as startled: 'Zulu Foxtrot Four. Repeat transmission. Repeat transmission.'

'Rebel forces coming over the fences and heading towards the runway. Meeting little or no resistance.'

James grabbing the satphone to call London, and me grabbing the camera and the tripod and running up the stairs to the roof.

'Fuckin' hell!'

'It can't be!'

Top of the stairs, kick open the steel door and run across the roof into the elevator shaft. Set up the tripod and zoom out over the smoking jungle towards the airport. The tower blown to hell even more, nobody in sight. Pan left. Early-morning mist already boiling in the oncoming heat, the black runway shimmering in little waves.

'OK, then. Come out, come out, wherever you are.'

There! In the bush. Something moving. Focus deep. A tall slender shape with a rifle probing the edge of the jungle. Moving left then right, then squatting down in the mist and waiting. Scanning the runway with his rifle and waiting some more. Then he steps catlike out of the bush and on to the runway. He fans his weapon from side to side then sinks to his knees. He turns to the jungle and signals with silent hands. Then slowly, very slowly . . . a long line of Tutsi rebels coming out of the bush with the same catlike steps. Twenty-five men with AK47s and heavy machine-guns and rocket-propelled grenade launchers, all taking position across the runway. Waiting for any sign of resistance. There was none. Just like Jean-Guy's radio said.

The steel door scraped open again and General Dallaire marched on to the roof. Binoculars in one hand, a steaming cup of something in the other. He stood next to the elevator shaft, screwed the binoculars to his face and took a long, unbelieving gaze on to the runway. I stood by in silence hoping he might go away. He didn't budge.

'Uh, mornin', General.'

He jumped round the elevator shaft and glared inside. 'What the hell are you doing up here?'

'Thought the general might want to see the first contingent of rebels taking the runway . . . sir.'

'No shit?'

'Yes, sir, no shit. I've got this long lens and—'

'Let me have a look.'

He marched into the elevator shaft in serious step-aside manner and grabbed the camera with his lieutenant-general hands. He zoomed and panned and twisted the eyepiece and bent the tripod and ground the lens gears into sawdust.

'Am I doing this right?'

'Oh, yes, sir. Just fine, sir.'

'Goddam. Look at that. Goddam.'

He squeezed his eyes together taking close inspection of the picture. Then he stepped back from the camera like something was seriously out of uniform. 'Why the hell isn't this thing in colour?'

'Colour is radiation, sir. Professionals spend a lotta time on the eyepiece and colour would burn their eyes out. Black and white is better for the eyes, sir.'

'No shit? Huh.'

And he glued his face to the camera and stared through the lens a long time, shaking his head and biting his lip like he couldn't believe his eyes.

'Goddam. Goddam.'

'Sir.'

And then panning the camera wide over the jungle.

'I can't understand these sons-of-bitches. Where the hell is the Hutu army? Where the hell is the counter-attack? Every time the Hutu have an opportunity to hit back they just fall apart. Christ, these Tutsi rebels know how to fight a fucking war. Goddam. Goddam.'

The general stood back and took another long reconnaissance of my grubby face. And me knowing I looked considerably worse for wear than the last time he checked me over. 'You do look like shit.'

'Yes, sir. S'pose I do.'

And he held out the steaming cup in his hands. It smelt good.

'Have a sip.'

'Thank you, sir, don't mind if I do.'

Hot tea with a dash of milk, no sugar.

'Now, get your ass off my roof.'

'Yes, sir.'

Running down the stairs into James and Steve and Michael.

'Jon! There you are! Jean-Guy is taking us out there!'

'I saw it, James! I got the shot! First group of rebels coming on to the runway! They've fuckin' done it!'

'It can't be!'

The jeeps screeched out of Fort Apache towards the airport, racing by the now empty Hutu army roadblocks. Everywhere we looked, huge blast holes in the road, twisted bits of shrapnel, chunks of jungle tossed about in giant clumps.

'Christ, they had one hell of a bang out here.'

'Looks like King Kong sneezed, don't it?'

'Where the hell is everybody? Just the same old rotting corpses.'

'Yeah, well, the one down here's pointing that way.'

'So?'

'Maybe, we should just go that way . . . maybe.'

'OK, then.'

Down a small road and round an intersection and smack into a squad of front-line Tutsi rebels. Their rifles pointing our way.

'Bingo!'

Jean-Guy pulled up and greeted them. They stood silently with serious looks on their brown faces. Their battle fatigues dirty and sweat-soaked like they'd just marched through hell. One stepped forward and shook Jean-Guy's hand. 'We take de airport.'

'Double bingo.'

'We take dis village.'

'I am Major Jean-Guy Laplante and these people are from the international press. May we come with you?'

The rebel commander looked us over and nodded.

'Please, but no touch. Mines and booby traps everywhere.'

Like a ghost town. Puffs of firesmoke blowing through the sun and the heat and over the bodies of dead Hutu soldiers. Lots of 'em. They lay in doorways and behind concrete blocks, along the sides of wood huts and under wide trees. I lowered the camera near the ground and let the lens walk between the bodies and the thick pools of blood sinking into the African earth. Soon the flies would come, then the dogs, then the rotting smells would fill the smoky air.

The road led to the edge of the runway. The rebels set themselves in defensive formation and looked across the Tarmac. All around them, more bodies and more blood. Another squad of rebels was already sorting through the abandoned cases of bullets and grenades and mortar rounds. None of it would go to waste. They arranged the bits of Hutu ammo into small piles. Each rebel would carry some to the next battle and kill the Hutu with their own bullets.

'We capture some people too.'

'Where are they?'

'We give to de UN across de runway.'

'Jean-Guy?'

'Let's go.'

The jeeps raced on to the runway, swerving round blast holes and unexploded shells. A couple of UN APCs sat in the high grass across the Tarmac. I could see the blue helmets of the Ghanaian troops gleaming in the sun as they stood guard over a mass of Hutu civilians kneeling before them.

'Holy shit!'

'It can't be!'

'There's over a thousand of 'em.'

'Mostly women and kids it looks like.'

'It can't be!'

Women and children and old men all huddled in panic and sweat. Tutsi rebels moved slowly through the crowd. The Hutu looking down as the rebels walked by, hoping the Tutsi would not stop before them.

Out on the runway. Hundreds more Hutu coming out of the heat haze like a mirage. Bundles on their heads, children at their breasts or strapped to their backs. I rolled for a minute then raced on to the runway for some close-ups, jumping over a dead Hutu soldier and round a live mortar round. The Hutu saw me coming and stopped in their tracks. The women screaming as if I was gonna kill them. They turned to run away.

'No! No! It's OK! OK!'

They fell to their knees crying and holding out their hands begging for mercy. I knelt near them trying to calm them down.

'It's OK, c'mon. *Allez. Allez.*'

And I walked towards the UN troops with two hundred terrified Hutu following behind. James stood at the edge of the runway watching the faces go by. 'Ah, Jon Steele captures a battalion of Hutu. How very Jon Steele.'

'Just some terrified civilians. Look at 'em, they're all shittin' themselves with fear.'

'Don't think Jean-Guy thinks they're just civilians.'

Over by the APCs, Ghanaian soldiers patting down each of the prisoners, Jean-Guy ripping machetes from bundles and pistols from baby blankets. I followed him round the back of the APC. He opened the hatch and tossed ten machetes on to a pile of pistols and clubs and even more machetes, hundreds of them. He slammed the hatch shut and looked over the Hutu. 'They're out there, you know. The killers are hiding with them.'

'Seems impossible. I mean, look at 'em.'

A rebel soldier stood nearby. He was watching the Hutu as well. 'You do not understand Rwanda. It is not just de men. Women and de children too. Many of dis people have killed.'

And me gazing over the faces and seeing nothing but fear and hearing nothing but infants screaming in the hot sun. James came over and made notes of the weapons in the APC and introduced himself to the Tutsi rebel. 'What will you do with these people?'

'We question dem.'

'But are they not under the control of the UN?'

'We will find de killers.'

'Will the killings stop if you win the war?'

'We win de war. We take Camp Kanombe.'

'What?'

'We take Camp Kanombe.'

'Fuckin' hell. S'posed to be three divisions of Hutu soldiers out there.'

'No. Dey gone.'

'It can't be.'

'We gotta get over there.'

'Jean-Guy?'

'Why not?'

Race off the runway and roar ten kilometres into the jungle on dusty roads rising and falling through the hills. Thick green trees opening to fields of tall brown grass blowing in the wind, then back into the canopy shade of the jungle. And all down the roads, long lines of Tutsi rebels. The victorious flip-flop army still running with RPGs and heavy machine-guns and cases of ammunition balanced on their heads. Looked like some sort of weird circus parade. Further down the road, rebels were digging trenches and building wood fortifications. Long bursts of automatic rifle fire echoed from deep in the jungle. The rebels stopped and listened, then started digging again.

We skidded to a halt in the centre of Camp Kanombe. Place was quiet as Sunday morning. Not a Hutu soldier around, not a drop of blood, not one sign of fighting. Artillery and shells still mounted on trucks, thousands of unused bullets scattered in the dirt, the Rwandan army regimental flag torn to shreds.

'It's like everybody just disappeared.'

'Oh, you know. Unless this is some kind of trap, the Rwandan government is finished. Three divisions run away rather than fight, unbelievable.'

'You tellin' me they let their own men die at the airport so they could run away?'

'Looks like it.'

'And they left their women and children to fend for themselves.'

The rebel commander shook his head and traced circles in the dirt with his flip-flop sandals.

'No. Not all of dem. Come with me.'

Back out the camp to a dirt crossroads. Rubbish and junk and bodies. Hundreds and hundreds of bodies.

'Oh, shit.'

'Civilians.'

'Hutu.'

'What the fuck?'

We climbed out of the jeeps and stood amid the dead. Men and women and children, slaughtered and left to rot in the sun. A young man draped over a bicycle with his head blown apart. A woman and a man close together in the tall grass, their skulls seeming to float in pools of blood. My eyes going back and forth and back and forth, then scanning over all the bodies in the road.

'Fuck me. They all got it in back of the head. Looks like close range.'

'Yes. I was just thinking the same thing, Jon.'

'Damn. All of 'em carryin' all the stuff they owned, headin' away from the camp.'

'Jean-Guy, do you think these people have been executed?'

'*Oui.* And judging by the blood and the smell, they 'ave been dead for at least eight hours. That means they were killed by their own troops.'

'No Tutsi left to kill, so they kill their own people for doing nothing more than running for their lives.'

'Fuckin' monsters, fuckin' monsters.'

I walked along the road, the dead smell baking up in the sun and filling my lungs. A gentle breeze combed through the tall grass and I watched the grass bend and sway over the bodies. An old couple almost holding hands, both their skulls blown apart. Across the road, a small boy in a red sweater, flat on his back. His arms curled up his sides, a finger on his lip, his unmoving eyes seeming to stare at the clouds floating through the sky above.

Jean-Guy's radio broke the silence. A stern voice giving orders.

'Orders from General Dallaire for Major Laplante. You are to return with the press corps, at once!'

'Oh, oh.'

'Doesn't sound good.'

Back at Fort Apache. Me and James sitting in a small room wondering what the hell was going on.

'Didn't sound as if the general was very pleased.'

'Nope. But we gotta get back to those bodies and do some pictures, James. Fucksake. Hutu killin' their own people.'

'I know, I know.'

The door flew open and General Dallaire marched in. Me and James jumped to our feet. Jean-Guy eased in behind the general looking like he'd had a serious dressing-down.

'Sit down! Goddammit! I want you two to listen and listen hard. I got three divisions of pissed-off Hutu running around Kigali. I got one highly annoyed Hutu presidential guard looking for someone to blame. And to top it off, Kigali is still crawling with Hutu militia who love nothing more than killing people. Now, if any of these groups happen to hear that my UN soldiers took a bunch of western press types for a slow waltz round Kigali airport and Camp Kanombe, well, shit! They will not be happy! You read me?'

'Yes, sir.'

'I know you want to get on your satphone and tell the world about all this, but for now, I need you to keep your mouths shut for the next twenty-four hours! You are in my command and I am giving you a direct order. You will *not* say one fucking word about your UN guided tour till I get a handle on what the hell is going on out there! And I don't want to hear any bullshit about censorship, this is about safety. Your safety, the safety of my troops and the lives of whatever innocent civilians are left in the streets. Make no mistake about the situation, gentlemen. At this very moment, every one of us is in danger of getting killed! Understood?'

'Understood.'

'Sir.'

He spun round and marched through the open door. Jean-Guy slumped against the wall and refitted his baseball cap a few times.

'He pissed off at you for taking us out there, Jean-Guy?'

'Oh, you know. Let's just say I will not sit down for a week. He gave me a real kick right up the butt.'

'Damn good thing the Old Man wears Hush Puppies 'stead of army-issue boots.'

'Oh, yeah. There is that.'

A long silence. And me looking at James and James looking at me. Scratching our heads wondering who was going to say it first. Then both of us speaking at once.

'Jean-Guy—'

'Listen, Jean-Guy—'

'I am not going to like this, am I?'

'We must get back to those bodies.'

'There's just a couple of hours of light left in the day. Shit breaks out and the bodies disappear and we got no proof of what happened out there.'

And Jean-Guy grimacing, like he had a bad toothache.

'Only to the crossroads, Jean-Guy.'

'Yeah. I mean, it ain't really in the camp. Not even the airport . . . really.'

He took a deep breath. 'You two clowns want me to go back to the general and ask him to let me take you back out there?'

'Yup.'

'It's important, Jean-Guy.'

'Dammit! I 'ave been in the middle of this slaughterhouse from the beginning! I know what is important!' He pulled his cap down on his head and walked out the door . . . 'Dammit! You two!' . . . and he slammed the door behind him.

We sat for a few minutes and decided it was no-go, so we wandered into the lobby and met up with the rest of the press pack. Everyone with a long face and everyone listening to the odd mortar round coming down near Fort Apache. Michael and Steve measuring the sounds for distance and accuracy.

'Counter-attack?'

'Too soon.'

'What about the bodies?'

'We're tryin'.'

'Jeeze.'

'You're not planning to sneak out there yourselves?'

'Nope. We're all in this one together.'

'Jean-Guy got the brunt of the general's anger.'

'We should go easy on him. He's been great to all of us.'

Heavy guns banged in the city. Fort Apache wiggled a bit.

'Ain't over yet, is it?'

'Be another long night.'

'Yeees.'

'Maybe Kanombe was a trap.'

'And if the army breaks through and comes our way.'

'We're fucked.'

Jean-Guy came into the lobby. We made room for him amid our navel-gazing session.

'Hey, Major.'

'Hi, Major.'

'Sorry we landed you in the shit, Major.'

'You've really been great to us.'

'Can the bullshit!' And he rubbed his chin and nodded his round head up and down. 'I 'ave asked the general about taking you out to the bodies. He says you can 'ave one hour. One hour. But you're still under orders to keep your mouths shut for the next twenty-four hours or till he gives you the go-ahead. I hope this is OK.'

We grabbed our cameras and ran for the jeeps.

Soft afternoon light. Long shadows across the road and a gentle breeze cutting through the trees and it was almost cool in the shade. The rebels had gone and the rifles in the jungle were quiet for now. Only sounds were birds and tree frogs and journalists' boots walking through the killing ground.

I was looking down on a man's body slumped in the dirt. Blood and brains baked like stew on the back of his head. The sun had been hot, very hot. Over in the grass the body of the small boy in the red jumper. His arms still curled up to his sides, finger still on his lip. His dead eyes still gazing at the clouds. His family all round him. Skulls blown to pieces and their bodies lying in grotesque shapes, twisted and bent.

I laid the camera in the dirt and tried to frame the shots with all the horror I could see. And as the pictures rolled through the lens I could imagine these people running through the downpour of shells last night. Terrified and panicked and running for their lives. Maybe not seeing the Hutu killers waiting on the road with their rifles and pistols ready. And even if they had seen them, they wouldn't have worried: they were all Hutu.

In the middle of the road. A man lay with all his possessions scattered round him. His head a bloody mass. I filled the lens with his bare feet, the out-of-focus bodies beyond him in the frame. Wanting the picture to tell another story of terror and murder. One man carrying all he owned, walking point-blank into the barrel of a gun. The bastards blew off his head then took his shoes.

On the side of the road in a drainage ditch. A huge bundle in the grass. I walked closer and looked down. A woman sitting in the ditch and leaning back against the bundle. A red scarf wrapped round her head, the scarf holding her skull together. Some bastard pressed a gun to her temple and sent a bullet into her brain, blowing her eyes out. She wore a purple dress and her arms were wrapped round a small bundle. No, not a bundle. A baby. A small baby with half its head blown away.

I stood a long time, unable to turn away, not believing the picture before me. A baby, a *baby*, for Godsake. My mind started spinning. And then I could see it playing in my head like a movie. She was running away with the rest of them. She had the baby in her arms and the bundle on her back. She was slower than the rest but struggled to keep up. She saw the muzzles flash ahead and she heard the bullets explode. She jumped into the drainage ditch to hide. Pulling the baby close to her breasts and whispering softly, 'Don't cry, my little one, don't cry!' Then she heard the voices and the boots coming closer. Her heart pounding in terror as the monsters stood over her. She would pull the baby closer. 'Please. Not my baby! Don't hurt my baby!' And she would feel something hot and deadly against the side of her head, her eyes catching the glimpse of a dark steel tube.

'Please! I beg you! Not my baby! Not my ba—'

She wouldn't hear the explosion. She wouldn't hear her baby scream in terror. She wouldn't see the muzzle move towards her baby's head. Her dead arms unable to comfort her child before the monsters pulled the trigger one more time.

James walked up next to me and looked down into the ditch. 'My God.'

'I want this picture, James.'

'Tough one to put on the screen.'

'Fuck it. We should show it like it is.'

'You know how it is, Jon.'

'Yeah, I know how it is. We only show acceptable versions of war and death. Put this shit on the air and let 'em see what's goin' on. Fuckin' hell, James, that's a baby down there!'

'Easy, Jon.'

'Fuckin' bastards! Fuckin' bastards!'

'Jon. If you want the shot, then make it work. C'mon, now.'

'Fuckin' bastards!'

I grabbed the tripod and jumped into the ditch. Shit and piss and blood splashing up my legs and sinking into my boots.

'Christ! It's a sewer! They died in a fuckin' sewer!'

I set up the tripod in the muck and slapped the camera on top. I bent down trying to get just under the blown-apart faces for the angle to make the shot work. The shit and the piss and the blood rising into my lungs and vomit churning in my throat and me bending down even lower towards the slop till the shot was right.

Roll.

Warm and gold light. Soft greens and cool shade. A woman in a purple dress sitting in the tall grass for a rest, leaning back and looking to the sky. A sleeping baby in her arms, the small face nuzzled near his mother's heart. In the eyepiece there was no blood, no stench, no death. Just a mother and child forever sleeping in the African sun.

Cut.

'James, could you help me outa here . . . please.'

'Of course.'

He pulled me up and I coughed and spat the death from my guts.

'Tough one, wasn't it?'

'Yeah, but I got it. I fuckin' got it. Please, God, just get us outa here so we can ram the picture down the world's throat. Fuckin' bastards.'

'Don't worry. It will happen.'

'Yeah, maybe.'

The sun slipped into the jungle. Guns echoed from the city. The evening bullshit was coming down. Jean-Guy checked his watch. 'OK. Let's wrap it up and get back to HQ!'

'Hey! I think this one's still alive!'

A UN soldier pointing down into the grass.

'I think his eyes just moved!'

We dashed up the road. I pulled the camera on my shoulder and focused down on the bodies.

'Which one?'

'Over there.'

Pan left and see the little boy in the red sweater, still as death.

'Nope. He's dead. I saw him before.'

Then in the eyepiece, the dead eyes blinked.

'Holy shit!'

Pull wide. No blood behind his head. Just a horrible wound on his left leg. His thigh muscle blown away. The blood jellied and congealed over the wound. And his eyes focused down from the clouds to the gaggle of stunned faces looking down at him.

'My God. They left him to bleed to death.'

'Poor little fucker's terrified.'

Jean-Guy pulled his radio from his flak-jacket. 'Foxtrot Four. Foxtrot Four. We are near the airport and have found a small boy. Badly wounded but still alive. We will try to get him to the Red Cross hospital in Kigali.'

'Negative. Repeat: negative. Heavy fighting in the centre of town. UN vehicles being fired upon. We'll have a Red Cross medical unit meet you at the airport and take the boy from there. Copy that?'

'Copy.'

James kept looking down to the boy and then up to me . . .

'It can't be.'

. . . then down to the boy and up to me.

'James. You been sayin' that all day.'

'I know. But this boy has been out here all last night and all through the day in this horrendous heat. So, it can't be.'

Out of the bush. A squad of Tutsi rebels with their rifles on their hips and pointing our way . . .

'Qu'est-ce que vous faites ici?'

... and Jean-Guy stepping between the soldiers and the boy in the grass.

'Ce petit garçon est blessé. On doit l'amener à l'hôpital.'

'Non! Il est Hutu! Vous devez le laisser!'

The boy's eyes reflected fear. His little chest heaving with quick breaths.

'What's the fuck's goin' on, James?'

'They are ordering us to leave him.'

'What? Little guy's startin' to freak out.'

'Yeees.'

'Hell with it?'

'Hell with it.'

Steve and Michael nodding in agreement.

'Hell with it.'

'You wanna keep rollin', Michael, in case these guys decide to get nasty?'

'Fine.'

Me and James knelt down to the boy. The rebels moved closer.

'Arrêtez! Qu'est-ce que vous faites?'

'Let's lift his sweater.'

'Nice and easy.'

No blood, no wounds. We reached under and felt his back, all clear.

'Leg looks really bad.'

'How can you tell? All I see is a big hole full of bugs and flies and blood.'

'Yes, Jon. Like I said.'

The boy's eyes watched our white faces. His eyes turning to the rifles then back to us over and over again, fear and panic rising.

'Christ. His mouth's dry as sand. Anyone got anythin' to drink?'

Steve passed down a bottle of water and the kid guzzled it down.

'Easy, easy. Slowly, slowly.'

'This is one tough son-of-a-bitch.'

'Indeed, thirsty too.'

The rebels were babbling down their radios. Jean-Guy knelt close to us and whispered, 'Look. These guys are not happy. They say this kid could be a killer.'

'He's fuckin' five or six years old! Shot by his own people, for fucksake!'

'Well, they're calling for more troops. They want to take him from us. We may 'ave a bit of an incident on our hands.'

'Then let's try and move him. We need a stretcher.'

'James, gimme one of the ceramic plates from your body armour.'

And I pulled the front plate from my own flak-jacket and we eased the two plates under the boy's back and legs. His face twisted in pain. 'Aaah!'

'Yeah, we know, but we gotta get you outa here.'

We covered the boy with a plastic sheet and grabbed hold of the bulletproof plates. The Tutsi soldiers moved in and surrounded us. Rifles at our backs.

'It's OK, little guy, it's OK.'

'*Non! Vous devez le laisser! Il est Hutu!*'

More rebels came out of the bush. Ten rebels ready to open fire on a pack of journos and one wounded boy.

'Great. More pricks with guns.'

'I thought these were the good guys.'

'Here beginneth the lesson,' said James.

'*Vous devez le laisser!* Hutu! Hutu!'

'Yeees. Here beginneth the lesson.'

'Major, it's your call.'

Jean-Guy pulled off his baseball cap and scratched his head. Then he pulled the cap down low and took a deep breath. 'Fuck these guys. Let's go!'

Up.

'Aaaah!'

'Kid's got a set of lungs on him, don't he?'

And we stepped out of the bush and pushed through the rebels. Michael rolled his tape and Steve flashed his stills. The rebels saw the cameras and stepped back. We laid the boy in the back of the jeep and tore down the road. The Red Cross ambulance was waiting. We each took a turn patting the kid on the head and saying goodbye. Off under a tree, Jean-Guy standing alone, staring deep into the darkening sky. I walked over and stared with him for a time.

'You OK, Major?'

'Jesus Christ. We passed that little guy once, didn't we?'

'Yup, we sure did.'

'What if we 'ad not gone back out there?'

'Yeah, but we did. And you took us back out there. You saved that kid's life, Jean-Guy.'

He turned away and kicked his boots into the dirt. 'Jesus Christ, Jesus Christ. There is so much death in this place.'

Last night it was like the dance of the demon. Tonight it was like the gates of hell had blasted open into the African sky. Explosions and fire tore through the dark and reached into the stars. Me and James and Michael and Steve suited up in flak-jackets and helmets and watched the show from the roof of Fort Apache. The battle was centred round the airport so it was relatively safe, just a few stray bullets screaming by our heads. And hell, if General Romeo Dallaire was going to stand there with his binoculars glued to his face and not budge, so were we.

'Jeeze. Look at it.'

'Fuck me. Like one of those cartoons where Wyle E. Coyote gets the shit beat out of him by that big sheep dog.'

'I love those Warner Brothers cartoons, especially the Road Runner.'

'What are you Americans talking about?'

'That out there. Looks like Wyle E. Coyote gettin' the shit kicked out of him by the big sheep dog.'

'Ah, of course it does. Sorry I asked.'

The fires howled and screamed. Explosions churning up waves of heat, swirling into hellish winds and blowing over the jungle past our faces.

'Could fry an egg up here.'

'It is remarkable.'

'You know last night I was thinkin' it was alive. Now it's like somethin' else.'

'Like something dying a horrible death.'

'Scary thought.'

'It's a scary place.'

'Maybe they hit the ammunition stores.'

'Poor fuckers in the middle of that must be terrified.'

'Jeeze. Look at it.'

'Remarkable.'

I walked over near the general and leaned over the ledge of the roof. Down below, some of the Canadian officers were hanging their army-issue socks out to dry in the red-hot glow of the battle fires. And me thinking how weird it was that life could go on in such a scary place, then looking up into the sky and watching the flames climb higher, and hearing all the dead of Rwanda screaming in one terrible voice, *My God, my God, why hast thou forsaken me?*

'Major Laplante tells me you and Mr Mates want to get to Nairobi fast as you can.' The general still watching the explosions through his binoculars, aware of my presence, but not taking his eyes off the battle, not for a second.

'Yes, sir, General. We think we got one hell of a story 'bout this place. But it ain't gonna do you nor your men any good sittin' here. We need to get it on the air before the rest of the world gets here with their cameras.'

'That right?'

'Yes, sir.'

'Well, let's see how this goes tonight. Maybe we can help you out.'

'Thank you, sir.'

'And remember to bring a razor with you next time.'

'Yes, sir. I'll remember.'

23 May 1994

I rolled over in my sleeping-bag and listened. Quiet. I walked out on to the balcony for a look around. Sun coming up through the dawn, the sky pale blue and endless, the jungle green and cool.

'Anything happening out there?' James sitting up and scratching his head.

'Nope. Seems like it's over.'

'How do you mean?'

'Listen to it. Not a sound, not a faraway gun. Rebels must've held on.'

'Yeees.'

'James, it's time to get the fuck outa Dodge.'

'I know.'

And we munched through the MREs and considered our options. There were none. I threw on my bulletproof vest and walked down the stairs and out the building. The big Ghanaian soldier from our adventure in Camp Runda was bent over the engine of his UN truck, tinkering away with the fan-belt.

'Mornin', big guy.'

'Ah, hello, my friend. What will you be doin' today?'

'Just tryin' to get home. I got this shoppin' list from the guys at the airport. You want anything?'

'Oh, no, my friend. We will all share.'

'So I been told.'

'But some spaghetti sauce would be very good.'

'OK then.'

'I like the Paul Newman's Spaghetti Sauce, Sockarooni.'

'Yeah? Me too. Gotta bit of a kick to it, don't it?'

Outside the gate and across the road. A Tutsi foot patrol came out of the rubble and sat in the tall grass. They looked relaxed and easy. A jeep full of Tutsi officers wound up the road and stopped near the rebels. Their laughter drifting across the road into Fort Apache. I wandered through the sandbags and barbed wire and headed for the jeep. The Tutsi liaison Boy Scout was riding shotgun.

'Mornin'.'

'Good morning.'

'Seems quiet.'

'Yes, it does.'

'Look, me and my partner have all these pictures and a great story to get out to the world. All 'bout you and the suffering of your people and the way you seem to be winnin' the war.'

'How nice.'

'Yeah, well. We really need to get the hell out of here and get the story on the air. We have somebody waitin' for us with a jet on the Ugandan border. So I'd like to ask you again if we could get an escort out of town?'

'Oh, no. I am afraid not.'

'Why not?'

'Because we will kill you.'

'You said that the last time.'

'Yes. I am afraid I did.'

'Well, thanks anyway.'

'Please, do not mention it.'

I walked back into the compound and down the back of the building. Place looked like it was tilting a bit to the left, but it was still standing. Christ, what a battle. Razor chunks of steel crashing into walls, high-powered rounds blasting through windows, fire and scorchmarks all down the side of Fort Apache. And me standing there hearing the sounds and seeing the explosions and feeling all of it deep in my guts.

I dragged my boots over pieces of shrapnel in the dirt. I knelt down and picked up one blob of metal. It was jagged and sharp and vicious. I tossed it from hand to hand, thinking I'd take it back to my flat in Moscow and set it on a table and look at it. Impress people, maybe.

The more I held it the heavier it felt. Then it was vibrating and growing hot and it burned my skin. I held on to it and squeezed tighter, the sharp edges cutting into my hand and burning more and more till it burned like hell and I let it fall . . . a dull thud, like something dead hitting the ground. I stepped down and smashed the killing thing into the dirt.

'And fuck you too.'

Back in the room, James was reading some book the size of Johannes Gutenberg's Bible. I lay down on the floor and tried to make out the title. Looked like *An Analysis of Fifteenth-Century Stuffnobodycaresaboutanymore*. Had far too many letters. I gave up. So I sat around and twiddled my thumbs thinking, any moment, some reporter guy in a photographer's vest was going to fly through the door with a live hook-up to CNN, where some other guy with nice hair and nice suit would be sitting at a desk in Atlanta, creaming his pants and barking, 'THE FIRST PICTURES FROM BESIEGED KIGALI, ONLY ON CNN!' And this reporter guy in the photographer's vest would be standing over me with the rest of the world's press corps and they'd all be wearing photographer's vests as well and everybody'd be laughing till the cows came home. And this reporter guy would point down at me and yell accusingly, '*Ha!* We told you so! *We* are the World's Most Important Network!'

And I'd yell, 'Oh, yeah?'

And he'd yell, 'Yes, you news worm! So double *ha!*'

And I'd yell, 'Oh, yeah?'

'Jon. To whom are you speaking?'

'Huh?'

'You just keep mumbling, "Oh, yeah?"'

'I do?'

'Yes. Are you aware that, besides you and me, there is no one else in the room?'

'Yeah, yeah. Just wanna get the fuck out of here.'

'Nothing we can do about it.'

'Yeah, yeah.'

'If you're that bored we could take a run over to the Red Cross hospital and see our young friend from yesterday.'

'The kid from the roadside?'

'Yes. If the battle is over then it should be safe out there.'

'We been sayin' that for two fuckin' weeks.'

'Indeed we have. But to tell you the truth, I'm bored as hell as well and this book is absolute crap. Don't really know why I read this junk. C'mon, wouldn't you like to see him? After all, we dragged him out of a ditch.'

'Yeah, maybe. Could use the shot, I s'pose.'

Jean-Guy was in Operations listening to the latest broadcast on Radio Milles Collines. The Hutu government was saying it was all over. The Tutsi rebels were coming into Kigali and everyone should run for their lives.

'Seems like the exodus has begun.'

'God knows where the hell they'll end up.'

'Some place they fuckin' deserve, I hope.'

'Not terribly charitable, Jon.'

'Nope.'

'Anyway, what do you think, Jean-Guy? Red Cross hospital?'

'Oh, you know. The roads should be OK. No reports of anything bad in this place today.'

'Any chance of a plane comin' in?'

'That would take a miracle.'

Steve grabbed his stills cameras and jumped into the back of the jeep with James, I rode shotgun next to Jean-Guy. We tore out of Fort Apache and headed to the centre of town. The streets were empty. Just rubbish and junk and unmanned roadblocks. Jean-Guy eased up on the gas and tapped the steering-wheel, his eyes scanning the road.

'I 'ave to say, it is very quiet.'

'Don't start. Any time anyone says that, it's trouble.'

'Now, Jon, not every part of your life works like a movie.'

And Steve cleaning his lenses and watching the jungle pass by. 'Jeeze. Isn't this where they shot at us the last time?'

'Yup.'

'But it sure is quiet.'

'Don't say th—'

KACRACK! ZING! KACRACK!

Automatic rifles, bullets hitting the road ahead.

'Shit!'

'Fuckin' told you so!'

Jean-Guy swerving and stomping on the gas and flying across the ridge.

'What are they doing?!'

'Shootin' at us!'

'From the hill!'

'You see them?'

'Fifty yards, max!'

'Shit!'

Jean-Guy ripped off his baseball cap and slapped on his helmet and scrunched down in the seat and spun the wheel hard. The jeep rounded the top of the ridge out of the line of fire, then raced down a narrow jungle lane towards the Red Cross hospital.

'First time I've seen you with a tin can on your head, Jean-Guy.'

'Well. Better safe than – oh, shit.'

'Jeeze.'

Dead ahead, Checkpoint Zombie. Two hundred Hutu militia standing round campfires. Logs and junk spread across the road. Not a Hutu soldier in sight. We sank low in our seats.

'This was a big mistake.'

'What the fuck are these guys still doin' here?'

'And with all their new friends.'

'Lots of new friends.'

And me sinking down lower.

'Fuck me. Should we turn around?'

'Too late. If we look like we are running away they will come after us.'

Angry and vicious eyes watched us approach. Some hands reached for machetes, other hands reached for clubs. And as Jean-Guy crept up to the roadblock, the mob crushed in round the jeep.

'I 'ave not seen many of these guys before. This is not good.'

Jean-Guy rolled down his window and held out his hand.

'Ça va, mes amis?'

The voices shouted back and spat in his face.

'Qu'est-ce que vous faites là?'

Some of the Hutu started pushing the jeep and banging on the windshield. Then, out of the firesmoke, a massive Hutu staggering towards us. Half military, half civilian. Full-dress Head Goon with a machete in his belt and .38 revolver in his hand. He waved his weapon in the air and the mob fell back.

'Allez! Allez!'

'Fuck me. This guy is seriously fucked up.'

'How can you tell?'

'His eyes.'

'Bad?'

'Gone.'

'Shit.'

'That's only half of it, all these fuckers are jacked to the moon.'

The Head Goon stood near the jeep and spat. Globs of wet dripping from his mouth. He staggered again and leaned through Jean-Guy's window. He smelt like death.

'Qui êtes-vous?'

'Nous sommes de la mission de la ONU de Rwanda. Ces hommes font partie de la corps de presse de la ONU.'

Jean-Guy speaking soft and slow. The Head Goon moved closer to Jean-Guy. His freaked-out eyes locking on Jean-Guy's throat as if transfixed with the sight of the major's Adam's apple going up and down and up and down. A wicked smile spread over the Head Goon's stoned face.

'Ah, la ONU.'

Jean-Guy told him we wanted to go to the hospital . . .

'Ah, l'hôpital.'

. . . there was a young Hutu boy there. We saved him and wanted to tell the world about him . . .

'Ah, le petit garçon.'

. . . we found him yesterday near the airport.

'L'aéroport! L'aéroport!'

The Hutu screaming like a madman and the scream rushing through the mob and hitting their blood like mainline smack.

'Aaah!'

'*Pourquoi est-ce que vous étiez à l'aéroport? Pourquoi?*'

'*Espions!*'

'*Vous nous avez trahi!*'

Hands pounded the jeep. Faces contorted with rage.

'They think we betrayed them.'

'I'm gettin' that feelin'.'

'Jeeze.'

'Big mistake.'

The Head Goon waved his pistol in the air and the mob settled back again. He ordered the way clear and pointed down the hill to the hospital.

'*S'il vous plaît. Continuez, nous vous attendrons.*'

Jean-Guy eased ahead. We all took a long breath.

'Jeeze. What the hell was that about?'

'He says they will wait for us.'

''Nother way out of here, Major?'

'*Non*, we 'ave to go back the same way.'

'Fuck me. That's why he let us through.'

'Probably sending for more of his friends as we speak.'

'Shit.'

Jean-Guy turned the jeep into the hospital and shut down the motor.

'Look. Ten minutes. No more.'

'How 'bout five?'

'Even better.'

We ran into the trauma ward and found the young Hutu boy on a bed under the window. The light flowing through a red curtain and resting on his face. His eyes looking above as if watching the clouds still. A finger still touching his lips. His wounded leg wrapped in a thick bandage. A nurse was arranging a blanket over him.

'He gonna be OK?'

'Oh, he will recover from the wound. Difficult to know about his mind. We don't even know his name and he doesn't speak. He screamed through the night with nightmares.'

Me and Steve took our shots and looked around for anything more.

'Think that's it for me.'

'Yup.'

I knelt close to the boy. I wanted to say something. But the fear monster was screaming in my head about all the goons waiting to party down the road and I just wanted the hell out of there. 'See ya round, kid. Stay tough.'

Out the ward and through the one-legged kids on their crutches and the young ones up on the hill in their tents, still singing their happy songs. Jean-Guy and James waiting by the door. 'Finished?'

'More than finished.'

'OK. We will go back down the road nice and easy. Everyone must stay calm. No pictures and no fear. OK?'

'How about mild forms of panic?'

'Should we call for some back-up?'

'*Non*, look around at these kids. The longer we stay inside this place the more danger these kids are in. Those men at the roadblock are waiting for us. We don't want them coming in here. Those men are killers.'

'Shit.'

'We have no choice. *Allez.*'

Fear and sweat.

Hearts pounding in overdrive.

Blood rushing fast.

Slowly, back up the hill to Checkpoint Zombie.

The hungry mob was waiting on the road. The Head Goon at the point, still grinning with that whacked-out look on his face. Just a little more intense, like he'd pumped another hit of mainline death into his veins. The jeep crawled forward and the mob closed in.

'Fuckin' *déjà vu*, James.'

'When are we ever going to fucking learn?'

Voices chanting and the mob coming closer . . .

'*Trahison!*'

'*Espions!*'

'*Vengeance!*'

. . . hands pounding the windows.

My eyes zoomed through the mob. Coming down a dirt path through the trees, a whole shitload of Hutu rushing towards us. Clubs and machetes swinging in the air.

'Company's comin', Jean-Guy!'

'Oh, shit.'

'*Trahison!*'

'*Espions!*'

'Oh, fuck.'

'Everyone stay calm.'

'Just sayin' oh fuck.'

And the voices screaming and the air getting hot and all of us feeling all the madness of this murderous place crushing down for the kill. The Head Goon watching us squirm and rubbing his cock in time with the screams.

'*Vengeance!*'

'*Espions!*'

'Jeeze. Look at them.'

'James, they got that fuckin' look in their eyes.'

'This was a big fucking mistake.'

A whisper next to me.

'I said never again.'

Then I saw Jean-Guy's shoulders rise slow and easy. I knew the move. The move of a gunslinger. Never watch the eyes or the hands because by then it was too late. The shoulders told you the time had come. My eyes panned down and crash-zoomed into the holster on Jean-Guy's belt. His hand pulling at the stock of his .45, thumb flipping off the safety, finger on the trigger. Weapon ready, slug in the chamber. A slow pull and the weapon rising to the window. Jean-Guy's eyes dead ahead, not giving it away.

'Dear God. I said never again.'

A slow glance my way and half a smile . . . the message loud and clear in his gunslinger eyes. Before these bastards slit our throats, Jean-Guy was going to blast that Head Goon's motherfucking face all over the jungle.

'*Vengeance!*'

'*Oui!*'

'*Espions!*'

'*Oui!*'

'*Tuez-les!*'

And the mob rushing forward and grabbing the doors, machetes swinging for our heads.

'Never again!'

Jean-Guy smashed down on the gas and the jeep lurched forward knocking a bunch of Hutu militia down on to the road.

'*Arrêtez-les! Arrêtez-les!*'

'*Tuez-les! Tuez-les!*'

'What the fuck's that one mean?'

'Kill them, Jon.'

'Oh, yeah, I remember.'

And both of us leaning out our windows and screaming, 'Not today, motherfuckers!'

'And fuck you too!'

One more dash through Hutu-land. Shots ripping along the ridge, bullets hitting the side of the road just under the jeep and me and James holding our flak-jackets up to the windows. Jean-Guy scrunched down behind the wheel like a midget, pounding his boots on the gas trying to make the jeep go faster.

'See the flashes in those trees?'

'We're heading right for them!'

'Hang on!'

'Those fucking bastards! Those fucking bastards!'

'Whatchuknow, this is where they shot at us before!'

'So you keep reminding us, Steve!'

'A hundred metres and we're OK!'

Jean-Guy cutting the jeep left and right and zigzagging between the hillside and the long drop down the side of the mountain . . .

'We're going to make it!'

. . . and the radio crackling from Jean-Guy's bulletproof vest.

'Zulu Foxtrot Three! Zulu Foxtrot Three!'

'Fuckin' hell, now what?'

'I read you, go ahead!'

'Do you have the ITN crew with you?'

'Affirmative!'

'Be advised a plane is arriving at Kigali airport in fifteen minutes!'

'Fuck me!'

'Did he say a plane?'

'He sure as hell did!'

'My God! Imagine hearing that message while having one's legs cut off!'

'Holy shit, James! Holy shit!'

And speeding down off the ridge and over the bridge and into rebel-controlled Kigali. Jean-Guy eased off the gas, sat up in the seat and wiped his face with the back of his hand. He flipped on the safety of his revolver and slid the weapon back into the holster. 'I don't mind telling you, I was scared back there.'

'You weren't alone, Major. Three of us were ridin' on the edge of your life back there.'

'Fucking bastards!'

He tapped the steering-wheel, took off his helmet and refitted his baseball cap down on his round head. I kept watching him as he manoeuvred the jeep through the jungle. Hearing his voice in that one moment, 'Never again. Never again.'

'Hey, Jean-Guy. When we were back at the roadblock . . .'

'Mmmm?'

And then remembering some questions should never be asked of a soldier.

'Never mind.'

'OK.'

Into Fort Apache. James on the satphone telling London we were getting out and me packing up the kit and hauling it downstairs and stuffing it into the jeep. UN troops ran over to say goodbye and add a few more items to the shopping list. I spotted the big Ghanaian and gave him a hug. 'Thanks for everything, big guy.'

'Remember, my friend, spaghetti sauce.'

'Yup, Paul Newman's Sockarooni.'

'Yes, my friend. Sockarooni.'

Into the jeep and race to the airport. The Canadian air-force Hercules swooped in just above the trees and did a low pass over the runway, checking for unexploded shells. Steve and Michael went to work taking pictures of the first relief flight coming into Kigali since the siege began. I waved farewell. Jean-Guy helped us pull our gear out of the jeep.

'Now, listen, you two clowns! You 'ave to be fast. They are taking some shots from the ground! They are going to taxi along the runway and throw some supplies off the rear, then you must jump in!'

'What?'

'Jump on board!'

'On to a moving Hercules?'

'Oui. It is easy!'

The Hercules hit the runway and slowed to a crawl. The rear cargo hatch coming down and the flight sergeant signalling to Jean-Guy.

'Right! Three slats coming off. Then you must run like hell!'

'Swell.'

We crouched down in the backwash of the massive engines. One slat packed with supplies down the ramp and on to the tarmac, then another, then another. Then the flight sergeant calling us over with furious waves.

'Now! Go! Go!' yelled Jean-Guy.

'Not the goodbye we planned, Major!'

'No time for that crap! Go!'

I grabbed his hand and held on tight. 'Thanks, Major. You're a damn good man.'

'Just don't ever forget this place.'

'No way, Major. No matter how much I'm gonna want to.'

'Yes, I know. Me too.'

He raised his hand to his baseball cap, snapped a salute and ran off the tarmac.

'Plane is moving, Jon!'

'Oh, shit! Jumpin' on to a moving plane! Here we go!'

We tore after the Hercules. It was moving away faster and faster. The flight sergeant and the rest of the payload crew waving us on like watching a horse-race.

'C'mon! C'mon! We got to get off the ground!'

'Move it!'

And running harder and tossing the gear on to the cargo deck and the crew grabbing the backs of our flak-jackets and hauling us on board.

'Get forward and strap yourselves in! C'mon, move!'

The Hercules raced to the end of the runway. The pilot spun it round, slammed down the throttle and the green giant of a plane ripped ahead. Me and James leaped into the jump seats along the fuselage and held on for the ride.

'My dear chap! Quite the exit, don't you think?'

The pilot pulled back hard on the controls and the Hercules roared higher and higher into the African sky.

'Fooled the fuckin' devil again, James. Fooled the fuckin' devil again.'

10

TWO CUPS OF TEA

Moscow, June

From up here it was OK. Late-afternoon light poured through the tall windows above Taganka Square and it felt warm behind the glass. I'd been there most of the day watching the light move over Moscow. Bureau sounds and bureau voices drifted in from the newsroom round the corner and mixed with kitchen smells of onions and garlic and fried meat.

'Uh, well . . . Jonka. You are hiding again.'

Oleg Nikolaevich shuffling in next to me. Two cups of tea in his hands.

'No. Just goin' over some paperwork.'

'*Da*. In the storage room away from your friends.'

'OK, then. Just thinkin'.'

'Here is *chai*. Drink.'

'*Spasibo*.'

He peeked over the rims of his glasses and watched me sip from a chipped cup.

'Uh, well . . . Katrina the cook is very worried.'

'*Pochyemu?*'

'She says you do not eat enough of her delicious lunches and that you are growing too thin.'

'What is it with Russian women and food?'

'Actually, she is Georgian. This makes it much worse.'

'Ah.'

'And Ilena thinks you are too glum.'

'The cleaning woman? I've upset the cleaning woman?'

'She wishes to know why you have stopped meeting her for secret hugs and kisses.'

'What?'

'*Da*. But she is a very young and beautiful cleaning woman and . . . well, this is Russia, and as the poet once wrote, "The winter ice in the northern city of Arkhangelsk warms the blood of every virgin and her lips . . ."

'Oleg. Besides the fact you're talkin' bullshit, is there anything you don't know 'bout my life?'

'Uh, well . . . let me think. You have not been living with your wife for some time. Your relationship with Bridget is like one of your Hollywood movies in which the whole world weeps. You seem to be drinking and smoking dope and whatever else far too much. You look like a prisoner of the gulag and your temper is worse than ever.'

'Thank you.'

'*Pozhaluista*.'

We watched the sun slide towards the sharp towers of Stalin's sky-scrapers. We sipped tea and sat quiet-like for a long time.

'Uh, well . . . Jonka. I am worried about you as well.'

'What is it, comrade? Just fuckin' say it.'

'The way you go up and down. The way you explode. It is as if there is something horrible in your brain. You have changed, Jonka.'

'I'm fine, comrade.'

'Are you, Jonka?'

I was a mess. Holding on to the threads of other people's lives try-ing to stay above the something horrible in my brain. Getting messier all the time. Kate and Bridget, Bridget and Kate. Wandering between their lives letting each of them think it might work out 'cause I was just too damn afraid to let go of anyone or I'd be swallowed up by the something-horrible in my brain that came for me every night in my dreams. The faces, the screams and the sweat-soaked fear in the night. So, come the Moscow nights, I ran away from the dreams. Getting wasted on dope and heading down the road to that place of booze and gorgeous Russian girls dancing in the spinning lights. And the lovely Natasha, always there, always waiting for me, always wanting to take away the pain. Her killer grey eyes drawing me deeper and deeper into her web of star-skimming drugs and blood-rushing sex.

No nightmares in heaven, my darling. Let me take you.

Yes, baby, take me . . . take me.

'Jonka?'

'Yeah. Sorry, Oleg. I'm OK.'

'Why don't you come to my home for dinner tonight? Nadya and Anya would love to see you. It has been a long time. We'll drink vodka and laugh. Anya's Mozart is quite good these days. She has been studying very hard in school and Nadya has been cooking all day thinking you might—'

' 'Nother time, Oleg. I got some other plans tonight.'

'Jonka, please. You could always talk to me. Where have you gone?'

'Oleg, I . . . Hell. 'Nother time, Oleg. OK?'

'*Da.* Another time.'

And he collected the teacups and he shuffled out the door.

Crashing down days later. Phone ringing me out of a druggy fog.

'Yeah?'

'Jon, it's the Foreign Desk in London. We want you to go back to Africa.'

'What?'

'Bobby Moore and his team are already there but we want you and Julian Manyon to travel from Moscow and get there as soon as possible. It's cholera. Cholera has broken out and it looks very bad. It could turn into a massive epidemic. Jon? Can you hear me, Jon?'

'Yeah, I hear you. So where's this place exactly?'

11

GOMA

July, 1994

My boots sank between the bodies. I braced the camera on my shoulder, leaned over and looked down through the lens. My fingers turning the focus ring till the blurred image in the eyepiece became sharp and clear. Till a dead black face stared up through the glass and into my eyes. Let the tape roll a long time . . . then pull the zoom slow. Another dead face. Then another.

The sun hot and sweaty down my back and a yellow dust sliding deep into my lungs. A stinking yellow vomit dust. Pull the picture wider and pan left and pull the picture wider still, till thousands of bodies filled the frame. Some wrapped in dirty sheets, others wrapped in straw, most of them just left dead and exposed to the baking sun and the yellow dust. Hold the shot for twenty seconds and pan the camera up the hill and into the sun. The yellow vomit dust floating heavy and thick in the light. Then I heard sounds. Retching coughs, heaving chests, vomit spilling from dying mouths. You see, they weren't all dead, not yet. Some would die in the next minute, others would lie almost dead for hours more, suffering in the boiling heat, waiting for the cholera to kill them. And through that long hot afternoon, I watched them die.

Look at it. It's the wrath of God, fuckin' wrath of God.

Words running through my head like a firewall between my eyes and my brain, trying to protect myself from the ghastly world around me. Wasn't working much.

Fuckin' wrath of God.

Then again, maybe I just didn't give a shit about these people. Maybe they were just pictures and nothing more. Maybe I hated their fuckin' guts for what happened in Kigali. The war in Rwanda was over. The Hutu on the run for weeks now . . . fear of Tutsi vengeance fast on their heels. A fear created by Hutu Radio Milles Collines to empty Rwanda of people and deny the Tutsi any real victory. Also gave the mass killers in the Hutu army and militia deep cover. Kick up an exodus of a few million people, then hide amid the chaos.

'Run away! The Tutsi will kill you! Run away!'

The fear spread through the villages like brush fire. Terrified Hutu strapped their children to their backs and piled huge bundles on their heads and followed the exodus west into Zaïre. The Hutu prophets on the radio whipping them on with crazed panic.

'Hurry! The Tutsi are coming to kill you! Run away!'

Dusty steps, boiling heat, merciless sun. On and on till they crossed the Rwandan border with Zaïre and collapsed on to fields of black and razorlike rocks. They were dying of thirst and searched the barren landscape for a stream or a river, only to find small pools of fetid water already poisoned with the human faeces of the exodus come before them. They drank deep anyway. They built small twig fires against the darkness, ate what little food they had left and watched as tens of thousands more Hutu followed in their footsteps. An endless swell of weary souls looking for a place to rest. And when the sun rose the next day, the Hutu nation beheld the vision of its murdering prophets. Hundreds of thousands of Hutu spread over the black and razorlike rocks. Cholera killing them one by one. The town nearby was called Goma.

Christ, look at it. Wrath of God. It's the fuckin' wrath of God.

One body next to a pile of Hutu dead. His head resting on a leg sticking out of the pile. I leaned down near the dead face and looked off into the direction of his eyes, wanting to see the last picture in his head. Arms and legs and mounds of dead black shapes wound together like tumbleweed. I lowered the camera and grabbed the picture as he would have seen it. A death dump of human beings.

Pan round slow.

A frail arm rising from the dead, a woman's arm, reaching at the sun then falling down on to her death-mask face. Her teeth chattering like freezing, yellow drool dripping from her mouth. Then she was gone.

Fuckin' wrath of God.

Out in the middle of the death dump there was a small boy sitting quietly. His fingers touching the hand of someone nearby. Just sitting, waiting for the someone nearby to wake up and take him home. I stepped closer and set the camera for close-ups. Panning the lens down from the boy to the someone nearby ... dead. The small boy didn't know it yet, didn't know he'd been left alone in a field of corpses. Hold the shot. Ten seconds, twenty. Cut.

Few metres away a red umbrella popped open in the air. A small circle of shade falling over two elderly shapes. I stood a moment wondering about the weirdness of it all. Then careful steps and leaning this way and that way trying not to fall into the bodies. All the faces staring up at me as I passed by. All the faces with curious death-mask expressions as if they, too, were wondering about the weirdness of it all.

How can this happen so fast? Tell me, Mr Cameraman. How could we all die like this?

Wrath of God, pal, fuckin' wrath of God.

I waded on through the bodies. Felt like thick mud sucking at my boots. The elderly woman under the red umbrella cradled an old man in her lap. His breathing quick and shallow, he was going fast. The old woman looked up into the lens. Her eyes yellow and sick and cursing the white man come to watch them die. She pulled a blanket across the frame and hid them both from the lens.

Pan left up the hill into the hard sun. Three silhouettes moving through the light. Two men dragging a young man between them. The young man falls to his knees and pukes down his legs. The men pull him up and carry him to the edge of the death dump. I hustled up the hill. The men watched me coming, probably thought I was coming to help, right up to the moment I crouched down and stuck the camera in the young man's face and hit the roll button just in time to watch him slide to his knees again. Dizzy and mindless and sinking into death. His friends or his brothers, or the plain strangers who'd found him on the road, set the young man on the jagged black rocks and just let him go. He fell in a lump. Cholera spittle on his lips, choking sounds deep in his throat. Pan up. The men watching then looking at each other, then wiping their hands on their dirty trousers and walking away. They didn't look back, not once. I pulled away from the camera and looked down into the dying boy's face. His unfocused eyes staring into the sky. And all around him, all the bodies staring into the sky. Thousands and thousands of dead eyes staring into the yellow dust sky.

'Careful what you touch here.'

I turned round to a black face wrapped in a filthy mask, bloodshot eyes caked with yellow dust.

'Death is everywhere, my brother.'

'I was just wonderin' why all these people were on their backs. Like they were lookin' into the sky. Seen a lot of that all over the world, dead people lookin' up into the sky. Never could figure it out.'

His yellow dust eyes looked down at the bodies, his head nodding slowly. 'Ah, yes. And does this seem strange to you, my brother?'

'Does make a curious man wonder.'

'Perhaps this way they can look into the eyes of God when they die.'

'Christ. Imagine that. All these faces lookin' up at the Good Lord wonderin' what the hell's goin' on.'

'Yes. The Good Lord is very busy, I think.'

'You an aid worker?'

'I suppose. If that is what you call this work.'

And him wiping his arm across his eyes. Streaks of sweat and yellow dust across his face. 'We tried to separate them at first. Put the dead on one side and the sick on the other.'

'What happened?'

'They all began to die. Can you imagine that? Thousands and thousands of people falling dead, all at once.'

'Shit. Fuckin' place is full of weird imaginations.'

'Now we be harvesters of the dead. We collect the bodies and take them out beyond the airport.'

And him coughing hard and hitting his chest and spitting up into the filthy mask wrapped round his face.

'We make a big hole in the earth and we throw them in.'

'How many today?'

'Who knows this? Thousands, thousands. You may come see with your camera.'

'I'll do that. Sounds like a good shot.'

'Shot? Ah, yes. A photograph. I know in some places people believe the photograph steals the soul like a thief. I think you are collecting many souls in your camera today.'

'Not really. Most of these folks are already dead and gone.'

'You think so?'

And him glancing over his shoulder like something was following him. He leaned close to my face, his bloodshot eyes squinting tight.

'They are here, my brother. All of them. They are all around us. We take the bodies, but I think you must take the souls. Be careful what you touch. Death is everywhere, my brother.'

He turned and forged a path through the bodies. Choking sounds drifting round my head. Like dying voices begging for help.

'What about the live ones? Still a few of them out here.'

He turned and called through the yellow dust, 'Yes. They will die soon. They will all die. Then you will have so many souls for your camera. Be careful what you touch.'

'Yeah, yeah. Death is everywhere.'

'Yes, my brother, everywhere.'

And he walked into the yellow dust haze to join a tribe of men in masks. They'd been working since before dawn, wandering through the thousands of bodies, searching for just the right corpse, or maybe just making sure the body they picked was actually dead. They reached into the tangled mass of bodies, pulling at arms and legs till the chosen one could be yanked free. The head falling back and bouncing from side to side as the men in masks carried the chosen one to a small truck and tossed him in. A truck already stuffed with corpses.

Stinking air blew across my face. The smell wrapping round my head and making me dizzy. I closed my eyes. Just for a moment. I wanted to keep working. I didn't want to stop. So many pictures. So many unbelievable pictures.

Wrath of God.

Another truck pulled up to the edge of the death dump. Big thing with high wood railings round an open back. And another tribe of men in masks began sorting through the bodies. Pulling and tugging and dragging the dead to the big truck and lifting them over the wood railings and letting the bodies fall with heavy dull thuds. Then again and again, till there are no more thuds. Just the slapping sounds of flesh on flesh as the dead tumbled on to one another.

I snapped the camera off the tripod and followed the men in masks up to the truck and got low as they lifted another body into the sun. Looked like a dark cloud passing through a bright sky. I shoved the camera at one of the men in masks. 'Hold this a second, pal.'

'Pardon?'

And I climbed up the wood railings and on to the truck cab.

'OK. Pass it up.'

The aid worker lifted it up and I saw his hands. His death-soaked hands wrapped round the camera. 'Oh, take it now, please. So heavy, like one of the dead.'

'Yeah. Sorry 'bout that.'

'Do not fall into the bodies.'

'No. Fuck, no.'

Focus and roll.

A heavy lump carried inside a soiled sheet of yellow daisies and blue flowers. The men in masks struggle with the clumsy weight. They stop and lean against the wheels to catch their breath, then heave the load atop the railings. The sheet catches on a scrap of metal and the men try to shake it loose, once and twice, till the yellow daisies and blue flowers split apart and a bloated body falls onto the pile of dead. Quick sums in the lens. Five or six bodies deep, thirty bodies across, one hundred and fifty Hutu dead in one truck. Took all of ten minutes.

Cut.

Fuckin' wrath of God.

I looked up into the sun. Straight into the white light till it burned. I wiped the sweat from my face and saw the yellow dust on my palms. The smell twisting my guts in tiny corkscrew circles like I was stoned on bad acid. Down in the truck, a jumble of dead faces watched me choke.

You see, Mr Cameraman. This is what it is like to die in Goma.

I spat bits of vomit from my mouth and forced the stinking air in and out of my lungs, till my body settled into a steady rhythm.

Yeah. Well, right now, dickhead, I'm alive and you're not. So fuck off.

I jumped off the truck and headed towards the tripod. The camera heavy on my shoulder, like maybe the aid worker with the bloodshot eyes was right and the lens *was* sucking up the souls of the dead . . .

They are all around us, my brother.

No way. No fuckin' way.

. . . and then me wondering how many souls it would take to drag me down.

'Oh, Jon! There you are! Good! I've been looking for you!'

My head snapped back to see Julian Manyon making his way through the bodies. He'd been up on the high ground where Médecins sans Frontières had a small emergency treatment station.

'Listen, Jon. There's a French nurse up on the hill who speaks quite good English and I'd like to—'

Julian stopped in his tracks and gaped down at a body at his feet. He bent over for a better look. 'Hang on a minute, this one's not moving.'

'That's 'cause he's dead.'

'I beg your pardon.'

'They're all dead round here, mostly.'

Julian's head did a quick pan all round him. 'Good Lord. Fucking incredible.'

'Yup, death is everywhere.'

'I beg your pardon?'

'That's what the man says.'

'Which man?'

'Man out there.'

I threw the camera on the tripod and rolled a few more shots of the men in masks harvesting through the death dump and tossing more bodies into the back of the truck. The truck sinking heavy and low on its axle. The men in masks climbed atop the bodies and pulled the filthy bits of cloth from their faces and lit up a round of smokes. The death-crazed aid worker with the bloodshot eyes slid behind the steering-wheel and turned the ignition. The truck sputtered and pulled away.

'My God. It's incredible.'

'Great pictures here, Julian. Lots and lots of great fuckin' pictures.'

'Yes, right. Listen, I want to get some shots of the French nurse before we lose her.' He pointed towards the tent. 'She's over there. I think you can pick her out easily enough.'

She was tall and slender. Long blonde hair held back in a leather slide. Blue jeans and docksider shoes, no socks. A dirty white smock over a dirty white T-shirt and latex gloves on her hands. Her name was Katrina Lefèvre. She was screaming at an old Hutu woman and her two small children. '*Momma! Allez! Allez!*'

Momma sat next to her dying husband. He lay there vomiting on to the rocks, his eyes rolling in his skull. The children watching with fearful faces. Cloth bundles and stacks of pots and pans surrounding them like a fortress. Momma thought that would make it OK.

'Momma, please! You do not understand! It is dangerous here!'

But Momma just kept wiping vomit from the lips of her dying man. '*Merde!*'

Katrina grabbed an African aidworker and dragged him over to Momma. 'You must tell her to leave! She will die and so will the children!'

The African barked the words to Momma in the tribal lingo but Momma just kept wiping vomit from her dying man's lips. She wasn't going to budge. A radio on Katrina's hip blared with a garbled voice.

'Oh, now what?'

And she grabbed the radio like she didn't have time for this shit. Some voice from base asking about the situation and what was needed.

'What do we need? What do we need? We need water!'

She raised her arm and wiped sweat from her face, careful to keep the cholera-stained glove from her mouth and eyes. Her voice pleading into the radio. 'Please! This is an emergency! We have nothing!'

Katrina clipped the radio back on her belt and turned to Momma. She reached down and pulled Momma's arms away from the dying man. I moved in with the camera and Katrina looked into the lens. 'They drink whatever water they can find, but it is all infected with the cholera. We are trying to send away the people who are not sick. If they stay in this place they will have the cholera as well. They do not understand how contagious it is! It moves from one to another so quickly! They will all die!'

And she walked away waving her hands before her eyes. 'This is the biggest catastrophe I have ever seen in my life. We need water! Water! We will all die without water!'

Pan down the side of the hill. Thousands of bodies, thousands of dead and dying. And Katrina Lefèvre still waving her hands before her eyes as if wanting them all to disappear.

Goma airport. A battalion of the French army had taken over the place and turned it into a base camp for relief operations. They secured the runway and co-ordinated rescue flights in and out of the cholera zone. Zaïrian government officials just got out of the way, knowing somewhere down the line there'd be plenty of goodies to steal from the starving refugees. Members of the press were allowed to plant tents on a patch of grass next to the perimeter fence along the main road. A thin strip of criss-cross mesh and razor wire was all that separated us from the rotting corpses on the road and the thousands more Hutu filling up the rocky field nearby. Curious Hutu stood at the fence, their fingers curled through the razor wire, their sickly eyes watching us work. I was helping Dick Donnelly and Angela Frier sort out a campsite. Donnelly was one of ITN's best tape editors and Angela was one of ITN's best producers-in-bullshit-places. It was a good team on limited means.

'One tent, we have one tent.'

'So where are the others?'

'Robert Moore's crew is using one for editing and another for storage.'

'Hang on, you guys. Aren't they sleepin' down at the hotel? Can't they keep their stuff down there?'

'Jon, you know how it is. It's the usual turf war. Bobby and his team don't want us here. They feel we're moving in on their story.'

'What's the problem? We're in the same fuckin' company and they got the lead every night. We're just here for a couple of specials, ain't we?'

'I know. And the Foreign Desk is massaging Bobby's ego every five minutes, but it isn't enough.'

'Excuse me? What's all this? What is happening?'

'Hello, Julian. Seems Bobby and his team aren't happy.'

'Why not?'

'Turf war.'

'It gets worse,' said Angela. 'Bobby has suggested to London we do a story on airport security.'

'You're fuckin' jokin'. Airport security in the middle of this shit?'

'No, I'm afraid not.'

Julian boiled with outrage and made ready for battle. Nobody was going to bully Julian Manyon out of a story. Especially a story Julian Manyon had deemed worthy of Julian Manyon's talents. Julian's voice booming through the camp like a bloodhound.

'Absolutely not! I have learned there is a British woman of Irish descent working in a relief camp forty or fifty kilometres from here. *That* shall be our first story! Airport security, indeed!'

'What will Bobby think?'

'I do not care. How about you, Jon? Do you care?'

'Nope. Seems to be plenty of dead people to go round.'

A noticeable silence.

'Yes, well. Quite.'

Julian stormed off to settle the matter on his own terms. He was good at that. Angela chased after him to make sure Julian and Bobby settled things in a professional matter, or to pick up the pieces, whichever came first. She was good at that.

Dick Donnelly and I watched them march off towards the un-suspecting enemy. 'Should be interesting,' Donnelly mused.

'Ever notice how reporters go nuts on big disaster stories? Like they smell awards in the stench or somethin'.'

'Unlike cameramen, of course.'

'Course. Everyone knows cameramen are only in it for the free beer.'

'Sure they are. Here, take this, Jonny boy . . .' He handed me a fat roll of power cable to unravel. '. . . and don't tell anyone, but I swapped power generators with Bobby's crew.'

'You did what?'

'I don't think they'll notice. And I've been borrowing bits and pieces of stuff we need as well. Have to get our team up and running somehow.'

I peeked into the tent. Floor to ceiling with borrowed video contraband.

'Looks like the bridge of the *Starship Enterprise* in there.'

'They don't call me Dodgy for nothing.'

'Guess not. So where we gonna sleep, Mr Dodgy?'

'On the ground.'

I looked round up to the perimeter fence. Gaunt and whacked-out Hutu faces still gaping through the wire.

'We'll stack up the empty cases round here, see, and make a little wall between us and our friends staring through the fence.'

'Just saw some old woman down the road tryin' the same trick. Didn't seem to be workin' too well.'

'Probably not. All this dust will kill us anyway. Or at least the edit gear, which is more important to the company than our sorry asses anyway. But it's the best we can do. Just have to be sure we don't fall asleep with our sleeping-bags over our heads.'

'Why's that?'

Dodgy glanced up to the road. A line of trucks from the death dump rumbling through the fading light. The men in masks floating ghost-like atop mounds of corpses.

'Those guys might think we're just two more bodies along the road and toss us in the back of one of their meat wagons. Next thing you know we'll be waking up at the bottom of a big truck with a few hundred bodies on top of us.'

He winked.

'So, Jon, your reporters kiss and make up?'

'Sorta.'

'Meaning Julian gets what he wants . . .'

'. . . and Bobby Moore accepts it as the consummate professional.'

'Yup. Julian even managed to grab some floor space down at the hotel with Bobby Moore and his crew.'

'What? Leave here and miss all this luxury?'

'Isn't much better down there. Whole town is awash with bodies.'

Sitting round a Primus stove with a few of the guys from Britain's Channel Four News. Drinking whisky and watching the satellite transmission tent glow blue and red and green in the night. Pictures from Goma blasting up into space and around the planet. Hutu faces still hanging on the fence, straining for a look at the images on the TV monitors.

'Christ. Watchin' yourself die live on TV.'

'Doesn't get more awful than that, does it?'

'What do you suppose they make of all this?'

'God only knows.'

'Damn strange seein' the Hutu die like this. Can't really feel sorry for them after Kigali.'

'Fairly fucked in Kigali, was it, Jon?'

'Like I said . . . can't really feel sorry for them.'

The runway roaring and flashing as huge transport planes landed one after the other and off-loaded tonnes of supplies. Food, water, medicines, more and more TV crews from all over the world.

'CNN will be arriving tomorrow, I'm told.'

'Well, I suppose that means we now qualify as a genuine news event.'

'Hear, hear.'

'Get any shots today?'

'More than enough. Unbelievable out there, isn't it?'

'Anyone got anything for the nose?'

'Got some Vicks VapoRub. Works wonders.'

'The dust is a killer. I can't even breathe any more.'

'My edit pack crashed.'

'Fifteen thousand dead so far.'

'Jesus.'

Next day. Me and Julian and Angela stuck on a narrow road jammed with corpse-laden trucks and beat-up cars and buses and horse-drawn carts and thousands of half-crazed Hutu refugees. Horns and sirens and desperate voices. Down in a ditch, fresh bodies from last night's cholera kill, waiting for collection by the men in masks. Refugees on the road didn't take any notice of them, they were too busy dying themselves.

'Place gets weirder and weirder, don't it?'

'We really must get a move on.'

'Do we need any more pictures of these bodies, Jon?'

'Got plenty for now. All we need's a story.'

'Yes. The clock is ticking. We've got ten hours till the programme.'

'Hope your British nurse of Irish descent is out here, Julian. You sure that French nurse from yesterday won't do?'

'Jon, may I remind you we work for *British* Television?'

'Oh, yeah.'

'Damn. We really must get a move on. What *is* happening?'

'Fuck it. I'll go find out.'

I jumped out of the jeep and pushed through the refugees. They fell aside like worn-out weeds. Vomit smells dripping in the air and yellow dust forming a sour lump in my mouth. I wrapped a bandana round my face and pushed ahead. Round the trucks jammed with corpses, the beat-up cars and buses, then stopping cold in my tracks. Dead ahead, two minivans side by side in the middle of the road. The occupants laughing and chatting away the morning like long-lost pals. My eyes zoomed through the windshields and focused on the combat uniforms, the black berets with blue ensign. Hutu soldiers of the glorious Rwandan army.

'Swell. Fuckin' swell.'

Their eyes turned on me as dark faces edged up from the rear seats. Civilians with that dead-eyed gaze. Hutu militia.

'Oh, double fuckin' swell.'

I stood watching them watching me, fear jabbing my skin sharp and needlelike, a voice screaming in my head.

Killers! Killers!

I turned and ran, smashing through the refugees till I slammed into something brittle and weak. It fell back into the road almost breaking into pieces. It was a girl, a young Hutu girl. A half-dead infant rolled out of her arms and tumbled over the burning-hot asphalt. The baby didn't cry, didn't make a sound. I just stood there staring at them.

The young Hutu girl gazed past me with unfocused eyes. She was already dying and there wasn't a damn thing I could do to help her, not a damn thing. Slowly, she staggered to her feet and gathered up the child as if it was a sack of mislaid, forgotten things. A few faltering steps and she was lost in the dusty haze of the walking dead. I turned back to the Hutu soldiers. Evil smiles and evil laughter coming my way, enjoying the sight of the white man pissing himself with fear. Pictures rewound and rolled through my eyes. Bodies hacked to pieces, heads blown apart. *Killers*. Rivers of blood, rotting flesh. *Fuckin' goddam killers*. Madness rising inside me and my feet moving towards them, the soldiers still laughing.

'Howdy.'

'*Oui? Pardon?*'

'Sorry. I don't speak a whole lotta French and just now I got all these voices in my head. Most of 'em tellin' me to get the fuck out of here, the rest of 'em tellin' me to do somethin' real stupid like rippin' your fuckin' face off. But I've been doin' a lot of drugs lately and I'm not sure what the hell's goin' on or why the hell I'm standin' here. *Parlez* any English?'

Confused looks. Confused looks that didn't like the tone of my voice.

'OK, then. Any of you guys from Kigali?'

'*Comment?*'

'You know. A million people, all of 'em slaughtered. Lots of laughs. And let's not forget the poor fuckin' Hutu at Camp Kanombe. Lots of dead people there too. My particular favourite was the woman and the baby in the sewer ditch with the back of their heads blown off. Good trick, that one. Don't know 'bout you guys but I keep seein' that one over and over again in my head. Took some manly balls. One of you guys do that?'

'*Comment?* Kanombe? *De quoi parlez-vous?*'

'Yeah, you're right. What the hell? Let's let bygones be bygones. After all what's a million dead Tutsi between cowards like us. Tell you what, just move your vans, please. You're blockin' the road for miles.'

'*En français?*'

That same killer smirk and me feeling as if my nightmares had broken the bounds of sleep and were staring me down in the middle of a jungle road. Madness rushed into my blood. I was stoned on rage. I rammed my fist into the door of the van. 'Move your fuckin' vehicle, you fuckin' prick!' And hitting the door again. 'Move!'

'*Va te faire foutre!*'

'Yeah, whatever! You see those trucks? Look at 'em. Stuffed with bodies! Your own fuckin' people! That's your fault! You did this, you assholes! And with a little luck you'll fuckin' choke to death your-selves! And when it happens I wanna be there so I can shove my camera in your face and watch you die, you fuckin' prick! In the mean-time, *s'il vous plaît* your fuckin' ass and *allez!*'

A senior officer leaned from the shadows of the far minivan. He bowed with grace and charm.

'Oh, *pardon, Docteur. On ne veut pas vous empêcher de travailler.*'

And me staring at him, trying to unravel the words. '*Travailler*' ... 'work'. '*Docteur*' ... easy enough. Shit, bandana over my white face and no camera to give me away. Fucking idiot thought I was a doctor. The Hutu officer ordered the vehicles on and he bowed again.

'*Pardon, Docteur.*'

I walked back through the staggering refugees and jumped into the jeep with Julian and Angela. Diesel fumes belched as the traffic jam loosened up.

'Ah, good. We're moving. What was the problem up there, Jon?' said Julian.

'Nothin'.'

I pulled the bandana off my face and closed my eyes. Hard thuds beating in my chest and the sour lump of dust in my mouth tasting like something dead and me sliding my shaking hands under the camera.

Death is everywhere.

Help us! Help us!

How could this happen?

Don't leave us here!'

Death is everywhere.

Fuck you. Ain't me. It's the wrath of God.

'Judas Priest. Angela, Jon. Look over there, see that? Soldiers, hundreds of soldiers.'

'Hutu.'

'Are you quite sure, Jon? How can you tell from here?'

'Trust me. They're fuckin' Hutu.'

The road curved round high jungle mountains, then fell into another volcanic valley of black rock and bone-dry earth. Men hacked the few branches from the few trees left standing. Children gathered wood scraps for fires. Women dipped buckets into mucky ponds of brown water. Water that would give them cholera and kill them. We slowed as a group of men in masks dragged bodies across the road. The dead smell infested the jeep and slid into our lungs and followed us all the way to the far end of the cholera zone, where a single white tent from Médecins sans Frontières sat on a sun-scorched ridge. Place was surrounded by thirty-five thousand refugees. Looked like Noah's Ark floating atop a flood of sick and dying Hutu.

'Jesus wept.'

'Better than yesterday.'

'How's that?'

'Bunch of 'em here are still alive.'

'We're still a long way from the tent.'

'Shall we leg it?'

'Yup.'

We climbed out of the jeep, grabbed the camera kit and hiked into the camp through rings of sickness. Each step taking us deeper into the plague. Here, cholera just beginning to claw at throats. Deeper inside, coughing and vomiting and sick bodies collapsing. By the time we reached the tent, the Hutu were dying all over the ground.

Christ Almighty. Look at the pictures!

The tent flap snapped open and a stout woman with white skin and a gentle face closed her eyes against the bright sun. She waited a moment and then drew a breath. She opened her eyes once more and whispered, with an Irish lilt, 'Oh, God, there are so many.'

'Guess that's her, Julian.'

'Right. Seven hours till the programme, two hours back to Goma.'

'Three.'

'Depending on the roads. And I need at least four hours to edit. Leaves you with two hours to shoot.'

'One. But it's all I need. I'm just gonna follow her and see what happens.'

'Might I suggest . . .'

'Nope.'

'. . . introducing ourselves first.'

'OK. But make it quick.'

Her name was Cresta Hook and whatever we wanted to do was fine. 'This is going to be on tonight? I wish I could call my relatives back home.'

'We would be happy to call them for you and tell them,' offered Angela.

'No, perhaps not. I look like hell and my voice is going in this dust and heat. Excuse me.'

A group of men carried an unconscious man to the tent. A screaming woman behind them. Cresta pointed to the ground. 'Here! Put him here!'

She dashed in and out of the tent. A bag of IV fluids in one hand, rubber tubing and a long needle in the other. She knelt on the ground and lashed the bag to the side of the tent, she found a vein in the man's arm and jammed in the needle. She opened the sick man's eyes and checked his pulse. She taped the needle on to the man's arm and placed the screaming woman's hand on top of the tape. The woman pulled away like it was some kind of evil voodoo. Cresta grabbed the woman's hand and yelled through the woman's superstitions. 'Listen to me! The needle must stay in!'

The lens follows her every move. Her eyes searching through the sick for the most desperate, the one who would die in the next second if she didn't do something, anything. She dashes into the tent again and emerges with a small plastic cup of water, careful not to spill a drop. Sweat pours down her face and her fair Irish skin burns in the blistering sun. She kneels down between the sick and raises one old woman's head to the cup. 'Easy, dear, just a little.'

'Uhhh.'

'Easy, easy.'

And she lays the woman's head back on the ground.

'Water. We need water,' she whispers.

Again Cresta steps through the bodies, looking for those who may live. She stops, reaches down and carefully unwraps a dead woman's grip from around her boy. She checks the boy's pulse then grabs his arms and drags him over the rocks towards the tent. 'Come on, little one. Hold on,' she says to the silent child.

Into the shade of the tent and grabbing another IV bag and needle. Cresta touches the half-conscious boy's face – he's almost dead. 'Hold on. Just hold on.'

Hutu women stagger into the shot. A man stumbling and sagging between them. Cresta sees them out of the corner of an eye. 'Here! Put him here!'

The Hutu women lay the man in the shade of the tent next to the small boy and Cresta sets another IV drip in the man's vein. 'This is all we can do. It's the only thing that can save them. Get fluids back into their sick bodies.'

Her Irish eyes looking at all the thousands dying round her. 'Oh, God, there are just so many.'

Julian crouched down near the camera. 'How is it, Jon?'

'You'll fuckin' love it. Great pictures.'

Another frail body falls to the ground. Cresta runs to help.

'Listen, Jon, we shall need an interview at some point.'

'Do it now.'

'Not while she's giving treatment.'

'Why not? Be a great shot.'

Zoom in. Roll.

Cresta's hands sliding a needle into a thin black arm. Pan up slow to the beautiful face of young black girl and pull wide as Cresta draws a long tired breath. Julian moved in. 'Is she going to live?'

'She might.'

'All these people. Are you sure it's cholera?'

'Severe diarrhoea, vomiting, sudden collapse, death within hours. It's cholera.'

'And how do you feel seeing all this?'

'Desperate. Once we knew a million people were coming, we knew it would happen.'

Cresta stands and sighs as the camera pans over the multitude for pictures. A listless woman with glassy eyes, already drooling from her mouth, rocking back and forth, moaning and gagging. And the child in her lap, sucking at a ragged tin cup, filthy brown water dripping down his face. Another man, crawling through the bodies as if knowing that when he stops he'll die. Finally, he can go no further and vomit spills from his mouth, his face hanging above the stinking wet and turning to the lens and staring into the glass. And as I hold him in my eyes, I feel him gasp for air. Pan back to Cresta Hook . . . She sighs again. Years of experience telling her that even with all this before her, the real flood of the dead was yet to come. She coughed and tried to clear the death from her throat.

Cut.

'Did you folks bring any water with you?'

'Only one litre bottle.'

'Oh, please . . .'

Her voice desperate and dry as sand.

'. . . anything would help.'

'Let me go and get it,' said Angela.

'Oh, thank you.'

Few metres away a woman screamed as her man fell to the ground. She called his name and wailed and called his name again. The two infants strapped to her back screeching at the sound of their mother's cries. Cresta ploughed through the bodies and tried to calm the woman with her soft Irish voice. Another IV solution, another needle. I switched on the camera and zoomed into the faces of the babies. Dirty faces and the traces of a thousand tears. Cresta calmed the mother and touched the babies and looked into their eyes for signs of cholera. 'Your babies. Any vomiting, any diarrhoea?'

A Hutu man nearby translated the words to the woman. The woman shook her head, no, not yet. Cresta lowered her eyes. 'Oh, thank God,' she said.

Angela found her way back to us. A bottle of clean water in her hands. Cresta's eyes jumped and she grabbed the bottle. 'Thank you. Oh, thank you.'

She raised it to her lips and drank with fat gulps.

Angela leaned close to me. 'Jon, they're starting to fall down everywhere.'

'Looks that way. And Julian's nurse of British descent ain't far behind.'

Cresta pulled her mouth from the bottle and gasped for air. 'My first drink of water since this morning,' she said.

'You don't have any water for yourself?'

'No, we ran out long ago.'

'Good Lord,' said Julian.

'Too bad he ain't here,' I said. 'He could do his wedding-at-Cana trick.'

Cresta gulped some more water then drew another long breath. 'Thank you, so much.'

'How do you keep from catching cholera yourself?' I said.

She smiled and looked at the men and women and children at her feet, all of them dying. 'Who knows? I might already have it.' And she offered the water-bottle to me.

'Drink?'

'Nope. That's OK.'

'Good. I can use it then.'

Cresta roamed through the sick, pouring drops of water from the bottle on to the lips of screaming babies and delirious women and whomever else she spotted on the verge of falling into a coma, till all the drops were gone. Then she moved through the maze of IV lines along the tent checking the flow of fluids. She knelt among the bodies feeling for pulses and looking for unmoving eyes. Behind her, a man with a grey blanket tucked under his chin. Cresta looked down on his ravaged black face. Fixed pupils, no pulse. One more body for the flood.

I spun round the lens looking for more pictures. I *needed* more pictures. Cresta Hook might be a saint and it might be my job to paint her that way . . . but I was here to watch the Hutu die, one by one. Down the ridge at the backside of the tent, a man walking with a small bundle in his arms. My eyes zoomed into the way he was carrying it, cradling the thing as if something delicate.

I ran over and switched on the camera and held the lens low next to the man's hands. The hands of a father carrying his dead baby through the camp. The child floating in the lens, angel-like over the bodies below. Then on a patch of grass, a stone's throw from the tent, the grieving man lays the baby on the ground. Three months old, not much more. Then there was an old woman, then there was a young boy, then there were thirty-nine bodies side by side on the ground. All of them dead in the last few minutes.

Look at the pictures. Look at the pictures. Fuckin' hell, fuckin' hell.

'Jon!'

Julian calling from the ridge top and pointing towards the tent. Cresta was trying to drag a sick boy to it. One of those wide-angle shots that said it all. Dead bodies in the foreground, dying people all over the ground below, Cresta up on the ridge trying to save one more life while on the verge of collapse herself. But it was too far without a tripod. I needed something solid and steady. I looked around for an open patch of ground, but there was only bodies. My eyes shot towards Cresta again, falling to the ground under the strain. She took a deep breath and pulled the arms of the sick youth round her neck.

'Dammit!'

I dropped to my knees . . .

'Sorry 'bout this, pal.'

. . . and I laid the camera across the back of one of the dead. I steadied the camera and zoomed in for the shot.

Roll.

Cresta pulls hard and rises from the ground only to fall again. Horrible strain on her face and breathing deep as she reaches under the boy and drags him over the rest of the sick and lays him in the shade of the tent. She slumps down next to him and wipes the exhaustion from her face. Another deep breath and Cresta Hook goes back to work saving as many lives as she can before the deluge washes them all away.

Cut.

Then faint steps behind me. A weak voice. I turned round to just about the oldest man I ever saw, dragging his ancient wife over the rocks. She was barely conscious and sinking fast. The old man babbled with toothless gums, tears streaming down his face. He was shattered with fear and his voice ached with pain. Mumbo-jumbo words pleading for help.

'Not me. I'm only a cameraman. Up there's help,' I said.

The old man's filthy hands grabbed my arm. His toothless gums slapping together again and his voice pleading some more. The old woman's legs covered in shit. Death smells reeking from both of them.

'Listen. Over there. Not me.'

Then the old man wept, babbling like a lost child. My mind zoomed into his eyes and the sounds of his voice as if I could understand his mumbo-jumbo words . . .

She is my wife and she is all I have. Sixty years, please. Help me, please. She is my wife.

'Goddammit!'

And I threw the camera over my shoulder, pulled the old man's arms round my neck, grabbed his ancient wife round her waist and struggled up the hill with both of them. The old man's voice crying and wailing with each step.

'What the fuck is it with you people? You think I'm some kinda doctor? I'm a goddam cameraman. I take pictures, for fucksake.'

The old woman vomited. Cholera-soaked puke splashing on my lower leg.

'Shit . . . shit!'

I pulled harder and hauled them over the bodies. My hand feeling the sweat of the old woman's dying skin. Hot and squishy, like she was melting in my hands. And the old man still babbling and weeping, then gagging and coughing.

'Oh, swell. Now you too!'

The tent seemed to slip further away with every step. The old man clawed at my chest, afraid I might let him fall.

'Fuckin' hell. Fuckin goddam hell!'

And I collapsed next to the tent. An African nurse walked by and I grabbed her wrist and pulled her to the ground.

'Hey! This woman needs help.'

'Oh, yes, yes. Very bad, very bad.' The nurse checked the old woman's pulse. 'Very bad, very bad.'

'So you keep sayin'. They're all yours now.'

I got up and tried to brush off their stinking smells. The old man reached for me again. More tears dripping down his face. And me holding him down and looking into his eyes. 'Look! I told you once. I'm a cameraman, I take pictures. You and your woman and everyone round here. You're just fuckin' pictures! I don't give a shit! Don't touch me! Don't ever fuckin' touch me!'

And I threw the camera on to my shoulder and stuck the lens in his face. His face crying and his toothless gums gnawing together and his voice howling with pain. The picture was crap but I kept rolling, trying to cram him into the lens and out of my life. But I knew he was already there, for ever.

I switched off the camera and walked away. The old couple's foul smells drifting after me like one more nightmare. And me stomping my boots over the ground shaking off the puke and looking at my hands, streaks of sick and sweat and melting death on my skin.

'Bastards! Fuckin' murderin' bastards!'

I knelt on a bare patch of ground between the bodies and rubbed my hands in the dirt till they felt raw.

The water fell cool and sweet. Showering down on my face and rolling down my chest. And I scrubbed and scrubbed at my hands like Macbeth's mad wife. Harder and harder till stinking pus bled from my pores. I held out my hands and watched it curl down the drain. Then it stuck to my feet, molasses-like, and something started pulling at my legs and I could feel myself spinning down into blackness and . . .

'Shit!'

. . . I bolted up in the dark night, clutching the hood of my sleeping-bag round my head.

'Only a dream! Shit! Only a dream!'

The hands of my watch glowed in the night. Three thirty. I tucked my knees under my chin and looked up to the fence and the death camp across the road. Quiet. Like all the refugees were either sleeping or dead. Maybe they were all dead by now. Then I could get the hell out of this place and go home.

Fuck me, home. What a fuckin' joke.

I remembered a wife and a lover and a son. But I couldn't see their faces any more. They were pictures long faded. I'd even spoken to them once or twice over the satphone from this hellhole. Their voices distant far beyond the miles. Truth was, I had nothing to say to them. All I wanted was to take pictures, the most cruel and face-slapping pictures I could find. There was no room in my life for the living.

What the hell's happenin'?

A lightheaded weirdness spinning in my head. Round and round. And then knowing the darker truth. Amid the dust and the stinking smells and the corpses, hearing their thoughts and feeling their souls, I *was* home.

Christ, what's happenin' to me?

Whhhrrrrrhhhrrrrhhhhhrrrrrrrrrhhhhhhhhrrrrrr.

'What the hell?'

I opened my eyes to dawn's early light thinking Dick Donnelly was snoring like a water-buffalo again. But he was curled up in his sleeping-bag like a baby. Then up the hill near a new patch of press tents just inside the fence. I rubbed my eyes and looked around to see if anyone else was seeing it too. Maybe it was just another druggy dream.

'Dodgy, wake up. You gotta see this.'

'Huh?'

'You gotta see this.'

'What?'

Whhhrrrhhhhrrrr.

'Up there.'

'Hmmm. Now there's something you don't see every day.'

Waving a hair-dryer and fluffing her long black hair and shaping it this way and that way was CNN's Christianne Amanpour. The hair-dryer loud enough to wake the dead.

Whhhhrrrrhhhhhrrrr.

A small crowd of Hutu refugees gawking through the fence as she bent over and brushed her hair down then threw her head back like some advert for a brand new, full-bodied shampoo.

'Think the refugees know what a big TV star she is?'

'Jonny boy, they've probably never seen a fucking hair-dryer before.'

Whhhrrrhhhrrr.

'I should get the camera.'

'Not even you could be that cruel.'

'Nope. S'pose not.'

I crawled out of my sleeping-bag and lit the small Primus stove and boiled up some water for tea and opened one of the French army's MREs. The eyes of the refugees turned to me now. I had food and water, hell of a lot more meaningful than some white woman doing weird magic with her hair. I turned my back on their hungry eyes and stuffed my face. Dodgy stretched his way over to the fire.

'Ah, tea. Good one, Jonny boy.'

'Hard with all those faces starin' at ya.'

'Poor fuckers.'

'One day they're gonna rip down that fence and slit our throats for our food.'

'That reminds me. I want to move down to the hotel with Julian and the rest of the Bobby Moore gang.'

'I was jokin', Dodgy, least I think I was.'

'No, it's not that. Couldn't blame those poor fuckers if they did. I can't work here in that fucking tent. The noise and the dust is too much for the gear, not to mention my brains. Julian and I were cramped in there for hours yesterday. And now we have these new orders from London.'

'What new orders?'

'You haven't heard? ITN is launching a national appeal on Monday night to raise money for the aid agencies working in Goma. They have movie stars and politicians all lined up for this mega-broadcast. Julian and I are supposed to cut ten minutes for the lead. Some epic piece explaining this terrible mess. The ITN gods have decreed it better be good.'

'Nothin' like pressure from the suits in the middle of a tough assignment.'

'Yeah, well, don't forget you have to shoot it.'

'Oh, right.'

'You need to find me some gut-wrenching pictures, Jonny boy.'

'No problem. Can't fuckin' miss out there.'

We packed up the edit kit, shoved into the jeep and headed into Goma. Wandering refugees, dead bodies and dust all along the way.

First time Dodgy had been out of the press camp since we arrived. His eyes stupefied with the everywhere death.

'My God. It's unbelievable. I can't even count them all.'

'Look at the ones wrapped in straw. Those are the ones that get me.'

'Why's that?'

'Dunno. Just does.'

'How the hell do we get all this into ten minutes?'

'All we really gotta do is find the worst place there is out there. The darkest corner in all this hell. It's somewhere. Just gotta find it.'

Round a corner in the centre of town and down a dirt road. Crowds of misshapen locals pressing against any conveyance with white faces inside. Beggars without arms or legs still trying to make a goo-goo from all the foreigners in town. We eased ahead near the high stone walls of the Bougainvillaea Hotel and hauled the edit gear inside.

'Nice change, ain't it?'

'I should say so.'

One of those quaint colonial era places left over by the Belgians. Bungalows and canopied walkways. Polite young African boys to do one's laundry and sweep the floors. An open-air restaurant with a fine view of the garden. Trimmed lawns, fragrant flowers.

'Almost enough to forget about the rotting corpses just over the walls.'

'Long as the wind keeps blowin' the other way.'

Julian sauntered down the walk in a freshly laundered shirt. Tasteful monogrammed initials on the breast pocket. 'Ah, Jon. Good news. I've spoken with the owner of the hotel. There are no more rooms but he is happy to let you set up your tent in the garden.'

'No, that's OK. I'll stay down at the camp.'

'Jon, that makes no sense. In fact, it is stupid and unhealthy.'

'Yeah. But I'm there and if there's a food riot or somethin' I'm there.'

'You are making no sense. Are you quite all right, mate? You seem to be acting a bit strange these days.'

And me looking at him trying to figure a way to explain I *liked* it down in the death camps. Falling asleep and waking with the smells and dust in my brain. The only buzz in town. Fucksake, I *liked* it.

'I'm fine. Just better I stay where I am.'

'Well, then, how about some lunch? The food is quite edible here.'

'OK, then.'

Chicken and chips and beer. All served by another set of polite young African boys. Decided then and there I'd be taking my meals at the hotel from now on, fuck the French MREs. I might be warped beyond all repair and want to hang out with the dying and the dead, but the living made for better dinner company. Especially when there was plenty of beer to smooth off the sharper edges of any more nightmares. Me and Julian and Angela and Dodgy talked over the Monday night programme and what we were going to do. We decided the only thing we could do was go out there and shoot the hell out of the place and hope we found something killer enough to shake millions of goo-goos from teary-eyed viewers. Julian coughed and cleared his throat, letting us know luncheon was finished.

'Right. Let's go then.'

'Where to first?' I burped.

'The Hutu army camp we passed yesterday.'

'Oh, swell.'

The sun hammered down hard and a shadowless white light burned the blue out of the sky. Refugees shuffled in the heat trying to stay alive one more day. We drove slow and easy through the sweltering mob. Just ahead of us, hunched backs glistening with sweat, bare feet trudging over hot asphalt. Grunts and groans as a tribe of men in masks pulled an oxcart weighed down with corpses. High wood spokes turned by our windows, arms and legs dangling from the cart, swinging like broken metronomes.

'Jesus wept. It's like the Middle Ages.'

'All they need is some guy in a hooded robe ringin' a bell – "Bring out your dead! Bring out your dead!"'

A few rickety kiosks had sprung up along the roadside. Four poles and a chunk of tin roof. A lean-to of straw probably taken off some rotting corpse. A couple of crooked tables with scraps of foul meat and rotting fruit lying out in the baking sun, for sale at black-market prices. Hutu soldiers stepped over the dead bodies in the road and strolled along sampling the bits of food on display. They made lazy choices. An old Hutu woman on the ground reached up and begged for crumbs. The soldiers kicked her aside and walked on.

'Look at those fuckin' bastards. Won't even help their own people.'

' 'Twas ever thus.' Angela sighed. 'I suppose we could have brought some food from the hotel.'

'I'm afraid that would start a bloody riot.'

'I know. It just breaks your heart to see them suffer.'

'Wrath of God, fuckin' wrath of God.'

'You don't care for them much, do you, Jon?'

'Stone-cold killers out there, Angela, everywhere you look.'

Julian turned and stared with disbelief. 'Jon. There are women and children out there too.'

'Don't care. I saw what these fuckers did in Kigali.'

Down under a patch of wide trees. A rundown shack in the shade. Woodsmoke drifting through the trees and hundreds of Hutu soldiers walking up and down the path to the main road. And me brushing yellow dust off the camera and wondering why we couldn't just turn round and go back to that nice colonial hotel with the fragrant garden. Find some comfy chairs under a tree and get drunk and forget the pictures playing in my head. All the bloodlust Hutu faces, machetes crashing down, rotting corpses in the streets of Kigali.

Fuckin' hell, Kigali. Weeks ago. What the fuck am I doin' here?

'Jon, are you all right?'

'Yeah. Let's park the jeep on the main road.'

'Why should we do that?'

'Just park the jeep up on the road away from the Hutu soldiers' camp.'

'I don't think we'll have a problem, Jon,' said Julian.

'And don't tell anyone I was in Kigali.'

'Jon, I think you're being far too cautious.'

'Listen, these bastards scare the shit out of me and they should scare the shit out of you. Trust me on this, *these* are the bad guys.'

I climbed out of the jeep and threw the camera on my shoulder. Dust and woodsmoke rolling into my lungs and something evil coming up behind me, a sweaty stench. I turned round slow and looked into the darkest eyes, a black face with a black beret atop his head, a few of his black-beret buddies leaning over his shoulders for a sniff.

'*Belgique?*'

'Swell. Right on cue. Killers 'R' Us.'

'*Comment?*'

'*Pardon. Américain. Je suis américain. Ils sont anglais.*'

They leaned closer for a better sniff, just to make sure. They glared at the camera and circled round, hunting for a reason to pounce.

Yeah, yeah. It's me. I was there, you fuckin' bastards. I know all about you.

'Jon! Let's move on!'

'I'm comin'! Pardon, guys. Gotta go.'

I eased past them and walked slowly away. Wanting to run as fast as I could but walking slower still, hoping they couldn't smell the Kigali fear dripping down my back.

Murdering bastards. Let 'em die. Let 'em all die.

'What did those fellows want?' said Julian.

'Wanted to know if we were Belgians.'

'Good Lord, why?'

'Long story. Lead the way, *bwana*.'

I hid behind Julian's tall frame and we marched into the camp. Julian walking with stout chest and firm chin as if daring anyone so much as to touch a subject of the British Crown. He barked to one grungy Hutu soldier, '*Excusez moi! Où est votre commandant?*'

'*Qui êtes-vous?*'

'*Je suis Julian Manyon d'ITN!*'

And me losing the rest of Julian's French but thinking it sounded awfully like 'Take me to your leader, you smelly little man!' And the smelly little man about-faced on his heels and quick-marched through the camp. Julian raised his chin a bit higher in the air and walked ahead. Me and Angela looked at each other, shrugged our shoulders and followed on, our boots crackling in the dirt. Defeated and angry Hutu eyes turned towards us and followed our steps. The Kigali fear ran colder down my back. Ice-cold claws scratching at my skin.

'Fuckin' hell.'

'What is it, Jon?'

'Nothing. Just keep movin'.'

'I don't think anyone here would remember you.'

'Doesn't matter, Angela, I remember them.'

Let 'em all fuckin' die.

'Jon! Angela! Over here!'

Julian managed to round up the senior officer in the camp. A skinny colonel in crisp Rwandan army uniform. A group of young officers stood behind him, their uniforms just as crisp. Boots blacked and shining in the dust. I switched on the camera and framed them all in the lens. Julian started chatting in oh-so-polite French and the colonel bowed and replied in wheezing but deferential tones. I zoomed in for a closer look. Watery and unfocused eyes, a rough cough. Seems *le commandant* wasn't feeling terribly well.

'*Oh, oui*, there were massacres in Rwanda. But these were in response to Tutsi massacres.'

The colonel's aides all nodded, like they were believing the lie themselves.

'And you feel you have no responsibility for the thousands of people? Your own people dying from cholera just outside your camp?'

'*Mais non!*'

His body rattled with another cough while all around him, and all through the camp, smug, well-fed Hutu soldiers stared us down with the same message: 'Tutsi bad. Hutu good. So fuck off, white man.'

Pan over the camp. Entire families sleeping in rusting cars and broken-down trucks. Blankets stretched between wheels and bumpers. Children peeking out from makeshift homes. Kettles boiling over, wood fires and steam flowing through the camp. Then four Hutu soldiers carrying a mattress over the rocks. A lifeless hand falls and swings from the mattress.

'Shit. Back in a flash, Julian.'

'Excuse me?'

'Keep him talkin'.'

I ran round the cars and the makeshift homes and closed in on the soldiers carrying the mattress. Zoom in and roll. A yellow foam mattress. A soiled sheet. The body of a dead Hutu soldier. Vomit still wet down his army uniform. The soldiers slide the mattress on to the bed of a pick-up truck and the dead face falls to the side looking into the lens. A face twisted with horrible sickness and death.

Just beyond the truck in a patch of weeds, a stinking haze floated through the yellow dust. Ten more dead soldiers lying out in the weeds, melting in the sun. Small bits of filthy rag over their faces as a final salute from their comrades in arms. I moved through the weeds and around the bodies, set the camera on the ground and pulled the lens wide as for ever. The foreground full with the dead and the weeds blowing from side to side in the stinking wind. And above the weeds the remnants of the glorious Rwandan Hutu army, living rough and looking the other way. I touched the roll button and let the lens suck on the picture. My eyes searching the frame, looking for some-thing. Thirty seconds. Forty. Cut.

I switched off the camera. It wasn't this picture I was thinking about. It was another picture. A small boy in weeds just like these. His body hacked to pieces, his head kicked away like a toy. Christ, how many times had I seen that picture in my head since Kigali? Hundreds, thousands. Him and all the others. Fear and nightmares, every fucking night.

I reached over the bodies and pulled one of the filthy bits of rag from a dead soldier's face. I watched flies crawl over his mouth and nose and eyes. I wanted to see him dead. I wanted to memorize the look on his face. And I felt revenge race through my blood like high-octane drugs. It wasn't the picture I was feeling, it was hate. And it felt *good*. I leaned close to the dead soldier. The flies buzzing in my face. And I whispered my prayer of revenge.

'Rot in hell, you motherfucker.'

I tossed the rag back on to the soldier's face. Hung there sorta half-mast. One dead eye locked on to me, like he was thinking about my words. Tearful sounds caught my ear. A Hutu boy sitting on a rock near the dead soldiers. He wiped dribbles from his nose, his eyes glassy and wet. Maybe he was feeling the heat, maybe he was sick, maybe he was crying for the dead. I didn't know, I didn't care. Back in the camp Julian was still chatting up the Hutu colonel. He signalled to me to grab another bit of oh-so-polite conversation.

'And will you ever make peace with the Tutsi and return to Rwanda?'

'*Mais non*. We shall never return to Rwanda with the Tutsi in control.'

'Even though here your men may die from cholera?'

'*Oui. C'est vrai*. Some of us will die. But not all of us will die.'

And *le commandant* coughed and wheezed and wavered in the heat. I watched him through the lens. Zooming slowly into his sickly face.

There's always hopin,' fucker.

The restaurant of the Bougainvillaea Hotel was packed with drunken journalists and relief-agency types. Not the doctors or nurses. They were still sweating away in the death camps. These were the managerial and public-relations types with the cushy expense accounts, just like us journos. A pleasant mix of world travellers who knew how to have a good time in the midst of one more shithole. Polite young African boys hustled trays of food and booze between noisy tables. Cigarette smoke and tropical flowers scenting the death stench from beyond the garden walls.

'Fuckin' bizarre, ain't it?'

I was sitting at a table in the corner with Angela. Me babbling on about the weirdness of it all and Angela listening patiently. She didn't say a word. Her hands just turned the stem of her wine-glass in slow circles. The wine in the glass seeming to be still, only the glass turning.

'You know, a short time ago, the Hutu slaughtered almost a million Tutsi. And what happened? Not much. Then the Tutsi rebels charge into Rwanda and chase the Hutu into Zaïre where they start droppin' dead from cholera, and bingo! The whole world bleeds for the poor, suffering Hutu. I mean, for Christ's sake, the dogs in Rwanda are still gettin' fat off the bones of the Tutsi. And now we're doin' a story to raise millions of bucks for the Hutu. Now, does any of this seem weird to you?'

I took a long swallow of cold beer. So cold, little drops of ice ran down the bottle and over my fingers. Angela looked at me then down to her glass and turned the stem of her wine-glass again.

'There are killers out there, Angela. We're makin' the world feel sorry for cold-blooded killers.'

Peals of laughter circled the room like another round of drinks.

'What the fuck are we doin' here, anyway?'

'Our job, Jon. We are doing our job. None of us here are saints. We're journalists and this is the job we do. Sometimes we can make a difference, most times we can't. That's just the way it is.'

I looked into her eyes, blue and soft and kind. For all her legendary toughness, Angela Frier was a woman of honesty and decency.

'Jon, not everyone out there is a killer.'

I wanted to believe her but I was stoned on revenge and hate and nightmares, and it all felt better each time I thought about it. Decency choked in my throat.

'Wrath of God. I need another beer.'

'Listen to me, Jon. I don't know what's wrong with you but listen to me. Those children out there, those Hutu children, they do not deserve to die from cholera.'

'Fuck 'em. Let 'em all die.'

*

'You see that?'

'What?'

'Something over there. Big rat or something running into the camp from the road.'

Sitting around another Primus stove with the Channel Four mob polishing off a bit more whisky. They too had dined at the hotel but were back at the press camp with the dust and the death smells and the ghostly shadows of dying refugees up on the road.

'Anybody try the showers the French soldiers set up at the other end of the camp?'

'Good, isn't it? Zip up in a bag. Hot water and soap and Bob's your uncle.'

'Place'll be in the *Michelin Guide* soon.'

'How many bodies you count on the roads today?'

'Gave up counting.'

'Hey! There's another one. You see it?'

We peered through the fire flame, nothing.

'Think you're losing it, mate.'

'I'm telling you, something is out there.'

'What shots you get today?'

'Found some lovely fellows from Radio Milles Collines. They're still broadcasting that charming "Kill the Tutsi" shit.'

'You surprised?'

'Not really.'

'I saw some of the Hutu militia in the camps. They've taken over the distribution of supplies from the relief agencies.'

'Most likely hoarding them for themselves and their army buddies.'

'No shit.'

'No one said these guys weren't organized.'

'This mess'll never fuckin' end. Everybody wants to kill everybody else.'

'Over and over again.'

'Put a fence round the place, let God sort 'em out.'

'Jon, that sounds terribly American.'

'Stupid, you mean.'

'Well, yes. But full of macho vigour as well.'

'Y'all are jealous. Empire envy. Plain and simple.'

'How did this Yank sneak into our fine British club, anyway?'

'Let's toss him to the Hutu.'

'Hear, hear!'

'Cheers!'

Clink. Slurp.

'Look, lads, something is definitely out there.'

I rolled over and saw one of the somethings run through the gate and down the road. 'There's somethin' out there all right.'

'I told you.'

Then three more.

'I think we're being invaded.'

'Quick. Hide the whisky.'

A couple of French soldiers hustled through the gate and called behind them for two more somethings to hurry up. Zip. Zip. Then the soldiers sealed the gate on the heels of tiny black feet. The band of somethings scampered through the shadows on to a patch of grass. The soldiers arranged them in a tight circle and waved their hands to make them sit down. They sat.

'Kids. Little Hutu kids.'

'I'll be damned.'

I picked up my camera and wandered over to the invasion site. Eight little kids, maybe five or six years old, wolfing down protein biscuits and guzzling water at the speed of light. The kids looked nervously into the lens. The French soldiers talked to them in soothing tones. The kids smiled and wolfed and guzzled some more. One of the soldiers opened a new box of biscuits and passed them around.

'On trouve les enfants pendant la nuit.'

'Sorry. I don't speak French.'

'Ah, oui. We find them on the road at night and we bring them inside for the food and water.'

'Who are they?'

'Orphans, lost.' And him rolling his fingers trying to knit the words together. 'Their mothers leave them at the gate and go away.'

'Abandoned?'

'Oui. Abandoned.'

'Their mothers just leave 'em?'

'What can the mother do? She is dying from the cholera. She tells the child to wait at the gate for food. Then she goes out into the field to die.'

'Huh. What'll happen to these kids?'

'They will go to the orphanage. But it is *très mal* . . . uh, very bad.'

He pulled another water-bottle from thin air like a magician. Sixteen dirty hands shot into the air.

'*Non. Vous devez partager. Vous prenez ceci et en suite donnez-les aux autres.*'

And the bottle was passed from thirsty mouth to thirsty mouth.

'So, how long you been here?'

'From the beginning. I help collect the bodies.'

'That's gotta be hard.'

'*Oui.* It is so . . . so . . .'

But he couldn't find the words this time. He just stood lost in his own private nightmare.

'So tell me somethin'. How do I find this orphanage?'

The sun rose over faraway hills. Big orange blob hanging in a grey sky of dead air. I climbed into the back of a UNHCR truck packed with abandoned Hutu kids. They looked at me and I looked at them. None of us with any idea where the hell we were going. The truck pulled through the airport gate and honked and twisted its way down the road towards Goma. Firesmoke curled low to the ground and the withered bodies of the Hutu refugees seemed to float in a haze of funereal incense.

Men and women touching members of their families to see who was sleeping and who was dead. The dead ones grabbed by the ankles and dragged through the dirt and over the black rocks towards a pile of corpses along the side of the road. Maybe the men in masks would collect them today, maybe not.

Out in a stony ravine, French army bulldozers shovelling hundreds of bodies into a pit. No gravestones, no markers of any kind. Just one man dumping bags of lime over the dead before the bulldozers sealed the pit for ever. Was gonna be a busy day. Just past dawn and two more trucks stuffed with corpses already waiting to dump their load. I panned over the faces of the abandoned Hutu kids. Every pair of young eyes transfixed by the bodies tumbling down. Arms and legs flapping and a blur of black skin falling rainlike into the ground. Round a bend and the Hutu kids' eyes turned back to me. So I looked at them some more.

Further down the road. A long building with arched roof and a wooden cross atop a forlorn steeple. Catholic church named after some long-gone saint. I looked at my watch trying to figure the days. Saturday? No, Sunday. The Day of Rest. That's what the good nuns and priests taught me once upon a time. And on that day I would go to church and light candles and fall on my altar-boy knees and thank God for all his kindnesses. Always prodded by the good nuns to remember the starving babies of Africa. So I'd rush through a few extra Hail Marys, thinking the angels would carry my words across the seas to save the suffering unfortunates. Another pan across the abandoned Hutu kids. The starving babies of Africa were staring me in the face.

Dear Lord, you are seriously outa touch.

Out through town and alongside more trucks *en route* to the burial pits. The men in masks sitting above the bodies and passing us with expressionless faces. Quick sums in my brain. Three trucks at the dump site, two trucks on the road. Maybe five hundred dead Hutu already. Sunlight broke through the haze and streamed down on the road ahead catching a cloud of dust and setting it alight with fiery colour. The cloud spun round and round, towered into the sky and whipped down a dirt road. I watched it fade away, thinking it was just another of those weird things in this very weird place, till the truck downshifted and headed down the same dirt road, as if the firecloud was leading us in procession. Bumps and turns and the Hutu kids holding on to each other and looking scared as hell when we hit the end of the line.

The back gate dropped and voices called for us to climb out. The Hutu kids shook with fear. I pulled the camera strap over my shoulder, climbed over the kids and jumped off the back of the truck. A couple of African aid workers held out their arms coaxing the kids with soft words. 'Ça va bien, mes petits. Ça va bien.'

'They all seem pretty scared,' I said.

'You cannot blame them. Can you imagine what their lives are like now? We want to keep these children on this side of the hill. It is very bad over there.'

My eyes followed the dirt road up a small rise. Woodsmoke coming over the horizon, cries and whimpers hanging in the haze.

'That the way to the orphanage?'

'Oui. Take care. There is much cholera over there.'

'I'll be all right.'

'You think so?'

'Yup, just gonna take a few pictures.'

I headed up the road. My boots kicking up a powder-fine dust. The kind that gets into your lungs and you spend the rest of your life coughing up. I wrapped a bandana round my face and walked on towards the cries and whimpers. The stench of death drifting closer in the woodsmoke. Round some razor-sharp rocks and onto the rise.

Holy shit.

Thousands of Hutu children. Like small black forms from another planet. Some in rags, some naked. Some walking, some lying in the dirt, all of them baking in the African sun. I took a deep breath and felt a buzz running through my blood. Without even looking through the lens, I knew I'd found the darkest corner of hell. I switched on the camera and went to work.

Holy shit!

Roll.

A young boy sitting on the hot ground, his skin sagging over his ribs. Delirious and drooling and singing a song to himself to chase the bad things away. I knelt down close and pulled the lens wide. The boy's shrivelled body dominating the frame, his yellow eyes flipping from side to side not wanting to see the sick and dying around him. For a moment the boy stops singing and his eyes focus on a small girl nearby. She's on the ground with her mouth in the dirt, flies and bugs crawling over her face. She doesn't have the strength to brush them away, she's just waiting to die. The boy's eyes glass over again and he slips back into his sing-song madness where the bad things do not dwell.

Cut.

I kept watching the boy, listening to his voice. Slow and mournful and vibrating through me. Then there was another voice and another, then thousands of voices. The kids, all these kids. Their tiny voices so frail and weak on their own, all blending together into an unearthly sound.

Forget it, fuckin' forget it.

Roll.

Out through the wiggly waves of heat. A boy tugs and pulls at the arms of someone bigger, trying to drag him through the dirt. The boy reaches down and tries to lift the unconscious form but it's too heavy and they both fall to the ground. A small cloud of dust twirls above them then blows away. The boys do not move again.

Pan left.

A girl stumbling in smaller and smaller circles, arms out from her sides like she's learning to walk. A shred of dirty cloth hanging from her shoulders. The remnants of the little girl's dress, all she has left in the world, fluttering after her. She's beyond feeling, beyond seeing. Her feet are bleeding in the dirt. But something inside her drives her faster and faster till her knees buckle and she tumbles down like a broken doll. She looks barely eight years old.

Pan left again.

Four or five African women run through the children washing sick from the young bodies and collecting infants lying in the sun and telling the older children to help with the little ones. Under a wooden shed a huge cauldron boils with a gooey grey soup. Streaks of steam curl from the bubbles and spread over a long queue of hungry children. Tiny dirt-caked hands holding plastic bowls of every colour in the rainbow. Greens and blues and purples and reds. One of the women stirs the soup and sees the faces of the children and wipes tears from her own eyes. 'There is not enough. There is just not enough. Everyone must take less. Every day everyone must take less. Oh, Jesus, what will we do?'

And me walking round the kids looking for hunger and fear and pain. I needed to get it all on tape. I needed these pictures, I needed 'em *bad*. Through the legs of the queue. Children on the ground, too weak to stand. Children with begging and dying eyes, their tiny black fingers scraping empty bowls hoping someone would remember them.

Christ, what pictures. What fuckin' pictures.

Deeper into the camp. Tents stuffed with sick Hutu children. Piss and shit and vomit stench. And that same unearthly sound of tiny voices. I jumped out of the tent and tried to breathe. Sweat rolling down my face and my heart beating fast. And hearing the tiny voices again and again till my ears were ready to burst.

What's goin' on? What the hell's goin' on?

Down in the shade of the tent. An African man hunched over a tiny infant covered in dust and yellow drool. The man holds a small cup of water to the infant's lips. She tastes and swallows. Her tiny eyes opening for a moment. The man's voice cracks . . .

'Jesus. I thought she was dead. I was going to leave her in the dirt.'

. . . and he holds the cup to the child's lips again. Another sip, another swallow.

'See, a little water and they come back to life. That's all it takes. It's like a miracle.'

Kofi Obay. He had a real job somewhere in the world but when he saw the children of Africa dying on his TV, he rushed to Goma. He rolled up his sleeves and searched through the bodies picking up all the bits and pieces of life he could find. He was desperately trying to organize another orphanage a few kilometres away.

'I mean, look around. Two days ago we had fifty children in this place. Now, thousands. And the children are getting weaker and weaker. We could only give them the bare minimum, but now with all this sickness, there just isn't enough.'

'They all seem to be sinkin' fast.'

Kofi Obay set the infant on a piece of cloth and touched her face. 'What can you say? When adults go to war this is what you get. Innocent children suffering.'

'You gonna take this little one with you?'

'She'll only die here. They are dying faster and faster now. We had our first cholera death on Friday. Now they carry them away by the truckload. This isn't an orphanage any more, it's a death camp.'

Up on a bare hill a hundred metres away. A tin-roofed shack surrounded by hundreds of tiny black shapes.

'What's that place up there?'

'The clinic.'

'Doesn't look good.'

'It's terrible. Every time you see it, you die a little.'

'Well. Good luck to you.'

'And you.'

And once more my boots sank between the bodies. Tiny bodies, naked bodies. Sick and dying Hutu children sprawled over the rocks and in the dirt. Arms and hands stretching and reaching.

Crawling, fucksake. They're trying to crawl.

Three steps up to the tin-covered porch. The floorboards covered with dead children. Fifty, sixty, more. And all their arms and hands like the kids in the dirt. Like they died crawling over each other. I stepped through tiny bodies following the reaching hands, then round a corner. The darkness of an open door and a dead air flowing from the darkness. Then it hit me. The door, the hands. I spun around.

Oh, fuck me.

They *were* crawling. All of them. Fanned out across the ground and crawling to get to this place, this door. Hundreds and hundreds of dying children clawing at the dirt trying to make it to the clinic.

Fucksake, Jon! Put down the goddam camera! They're all dying! Help them!

A body quivered next to my leg. A small child crawling over my boots. Yellow froth gushing from his mouth, then nothing. Just a dead child wrapped round my leg. Cold chills in the heat. I shivered like a wet dog and fumbled with the camera.

Pictures. Get the pictures!

And I looked out over the hellish ground. They were coming, all of them, all the children, crawling closer and closer. Like grabbing hold of my skin and pushing me back through the door and into the sickening dark.

At first there were only the smells. Soiled flesh . . . death. The stink ripped the air from my lungs and I gagged till a rush of vomit spewed from my guts. I fell back through the dark and hit a wall and crumpled in a heap, gasping for air, any air. Even the dead air stinging my face and hands and all down my back.

Where the hell am I?

Cold chills again, coming down hard like a junkie nightmare. My eyes searching the darkness for a way out. I pulled the eyepiece to my face and hit the roll button. Then emerging from the dark, slowly, very slowly. Hundreds of tiny yellow eyes floating in the blackness.

Holy shit.

A small windowless room. Blistering heat. Heat made damp from sweat and sick. Wall-to-wall wood bunks crammed with children. Six to ten in one bed. No mattresses. Black skin scraped with wood-worn sores.

Sweat pours into the eyepiece and the picture fogs into a translucent mist. I got to my feet and walked down a dark narrow path between the tangled limbs and tortured bodies, the desperately sick coughing and vomiting over the living and the dead.

A connecting hall opening into a bigger room. More wall-to-wall bunks stuffed with dying and dead children. And down on the floor in the sick and slop, young bodies spread over every inch of space. A stream of blue light slips through the dark and falls like saving grace over the body of one young girl, naked and still on the floor. Her hands curled under her chin like she was fast asleep. Her young body was just beginning to change. Curves on her hips and small mounds on her chest. A pool of wet flowing from under her as all her life, and all the life that would flow from her, dies.

Sweet Jesus. Sweet Jesus, look at this!

Pan up slow.

A tiny child close to the lens. He coughs and spits, his ribs rattling like bones in a bag. He spits again and the spray splats on my face. His death smell sinking into my skin.

Fuckin' hell! Keep rolling!

Steps behind me. An African nurse in a cholera-stained dress. Her hands extended and holding the tiniest infant in her palms. Tiny arms dangling through her fingers. Motionless, lifeless. The nurse shuffles by me, unnoticing and ghostly. The lens follows her down the hall and into another windowless room. She turns here and there, unable to find her way through the hideous maze. Dead children at her feet, dead children all round her. She looks at the dead infant in the palms of her hands then turns to the camera. Tears gush from her eyes and she mumbles mad sounds. And she steps towards me.

Please, there is no more room . . .

And closer.

. . . what shall I do with this child?

And slowly raising the dead baby to the lens.

This isn't happening.

Please take this child, there is no room.

No fuckin' way.

Like an offering to the camera.

Agnus Dei . . .

The child floating in the lens, the nurse weeping, death smells wrenching my guts, death spit on my lips.

. . . qui tollis peccata mundi . . .'

And I backed away down the hall, trying not to trip over the bodies on the floor. Falling into walls and bunks. Tiny hands reaching and begging from piles of bodies. Vomit dripping down the beds and horrible screams and choking and all the yellow eyes closing in round me.

... *miserere nobis.*

'No! No!'

Out the door and into the searing light. Stumbling over the dead bodies on the porch and down into the dirt covered with the Hutu children still crawling to their death. Cold chills racked my body and I spat and spat and spat. And then the weird unearthly sounds came again. The cries and whimpers of the dying Hutu children calling . . .

Mercy! Please have mercy on us!

Then dizzy and weak and floating like a dead child and falling into a dark pit of rotting corpses.

'Easy, take it easy.'

Some still photographer holding me up on my knees. His accent German or Scandinavian or something. His sunburned face wrapped in a white bandana. Leica cameras hanging round his neck. Yellow dust-crusted eyes.

'You are passing out. Hold my arm.'

'What have I done?'

'What? Take it easy. You need water. I have some in my bag.'

'No. I gotta go.'

'You are not well. You need water.'

'No. Gotta go.'

He held me steady till I found my breath. I got to my feet and cradled the camera in my arms and staggered away. The photographer's voice calling after me . . .

'It is hard, seeing all this. Like the end of the world.'

. . . and me stumbling in circles, like one more dying child.

12

FLASH FRAME

Flat out on the floor of the dark room.

Can't move.

Can't sleep.

Can't even close my eyes.

Can't stop remembering.

Got it bad this time . . .

. . . not enough booze . . .

. . . not enough dope . . .

. . . maybe too much.

Fuck it.

Need more.

Swig it down and light it up and suck it in and let the dope seep into my brain. Letter from the ITN bossman crumpled on the floor. Bossman thinks I'm great. Thinks I'm brave. Thinks I'm the best cameraman there is. Fuckin' hell, bossman should see me now. Not quite the ITN poster boy any more. Got back to Moscow, headed straight for Natasha and her killer grey eyes. Her killer voice whispering through candlelight and dope smoke and hypodermic needles.

'No monsters in heaven, my sad darling. No monsters in heaven. I can take you to such a place.'

'Yeah? How you gonna do that, baby?'

'Watch, my darling.'

And Natasha pushing the needle into her arm . . .

'*Da*, so beautiful.'

. . . and her skin glowing warm as the drugs rushed through her veins. I stared into her killer grey eyes. Higher and higher. Racing like a comet to Never-Never Land.

'Let me take you, my sad darling. I know you want it too.'

13

LAST SHOT

Bosnia, 20 August 1994

One more job. Just gotta get through one more job.

Sarajevo. Place still fucked up beyond all recognition. Just like the last time I was here. Snipers working the streets and war-weary Bosnians running from one hole to another. Came this time with a couple of ITN guys out of London; Terry Lloyd was the reporter. He took one look at me and rolled his eyes. 'Christ, Steele. You look like something the cat dragged in.'

'Gee, thanks, Terry. Nice to see you too.'

'I wonder if it's too late to get another cameraman. Chris Squires. Yeah, that's who we need. He's a great cameraman.'

Didn't sound like he was joking much. Think he thought I was looking a bit ragged round the edges. Didn't help myself by hanging out the windows of the Holiday Inn screaming at the Serb snipers across the Drina river. 'Grow up, you fuckin' assholes!'

'You know, Steele, it's going to be pretty fucking difficult explaining to ITN management how you were shot sticking your head out of the window under sniper fire.'

'Yeah, well, listen to him shoot. Taptap, taptaptap, taptaptaptap, taptap. Every night. Sounds like the drums from *Let's Go*. You know? The

Ventures back in the sixties? Fuckin' sniper thinks he's a goddam drummer.'

'That's it. Somebody get me Squires' number. Steele's gone loopy.'

'Mean you don't hear it?'

The rest of the crew listened for a moment . . .

'Not really.'

. . . then opened another bottle of wine. Not a lot to do in Sarajevo after the sun went down but drink and drink some more till you got hungry enough to head downstairs for the Holiday Inn *menu du siège*.

Taptap, taptaptap, taptaptaptap, taptap.

'Oh, just fuckin' grow up!'

'Are you deliberately trying to get yourself killed, Steele?'

'Nope. Just havin' some laughs.'

I jumped back into the room and babbled non-stop about nothing till the hotel generators kicked on and the television flickered with fuzzy pictures of some terribly hip Irish rock band wailing about all the injustices of life. Gave me the opportunity to babble about MTV being the future of television and how it proved we were all doomed by reducing our attention span to the length of a mouse fart. Terry Lloyd and the crew just kept drinking and staring at me, like I *was* loopy.

'Aren't you supposed to go on holiday after this job, Steele?'

'Yup. Why?'

'You need it.'

'Yeah, maybe. S'posed to go to the States. My wife has this family wedding and my son has this play opening in New York and then I'm gonna head out to Montana or maybe I'll go to Paris. Caribbean might be good too.'

'Doesn't sound like you know what the hell you're doing.'

'Yeah, maybe.'

'I heard you broke up with your wife.'

'I heard you broke up with Bridget.'

'I heard you've lost it completely.'

'Yeah, maybe.'

'Well, you've had a helluva run this year. Awards coming out your ass, and that's great, Steele, but believe me, it takes its toll. You need to get away from all this war shit before you really do lose it.'

'Well, this is gonna be my last job for a while. One more shoot. Go out on a good one.'

'Pretty quiet round here, these days, except for the day-to-day run-of-the-mill murder in the streets.'

'Never know, Terry. May get lucky.'

'We'll go see the Bosnian army tomorrow. See if we can find some action to calm you down.'

The boys opened a bottle of whisky and I headed to my room. I'd copped some good Bosnian dope and wanted to get wasted solo style. Dream of Natasha and her killer grey eyes and fly away. Through the dark stairwells and dim halls along the river-view side of the Holiday Inn. Rooms at this end of the hotel sat smack over Sniper Alley. Heavy plastic sheets and cardboard signs tacked over the door frames . . . 'KEEP OUT!!!' Serb snipers hunkered down a few hundred metres away across the river, just itching for something to kill. I pulled back the plastic sheet and ducked in. Bullet scars on the walls, lighting fixtures and bits of ceiling hanging from overhead, lumber and sandbags stuffed where the windows used to be. Lots of nights Bosnian soldiers would sneak into these rooms and fire back across the river. Tonight it was just a loopy cameraman. I crawled under the barricades and lit up a joint and gazed out into the killer dark. And I sat listening to the Serb sniper fire his deadly rounds all through the night . . .

Taptap, taptaptap, taptaptaptap, taptap.

. . . he never missed a beat.

Sunny afternoon. Cruising through a maze of Sarajevo back-streets to Third Army HQ in the centre of town. Trying to convince the Bosnians to take us to an active front. Round the Muslim graveyard and down a narrow street of high-walled buildings two hundred metres off Sniper Alley. Kids running in mad circles playing kid games and laughing like they were in another place, not here.

'HQ is just over there by those children.'

'Always nice to plant your army in the middle of a quiet neighbourhood packed with kids, isn't it?'

Terry was up front with Sandy MacIntyre, the ITN producer on this trip. I was bouncing around in the back of the armoured car with my camera and the flak-jackets and helmets.

'Why the hell can't we get some decent seats in the rear of these armoured jeeps? Like the BBC and CBS and all those other guys.'

'Because, Steele, comfy chairs are for wimps and we're trying to make a man of you yet.'

'Chris Squires wouldn't complain, would he?'

'Never.'

'Fuck off. I'm goin' on vacation soon.'

'Thank God.'

The truck stopped and I grabbed the camera, pushed open the rear door and jumped out. Fifteen dirty-faced Bosnian kids rushed round me like street rats. Holding out their paws and grabbing at my pockets hunting for treasure.

'*Bonbon! Bonbon!*'

'Anyone ever tell you kids candy'll rot your teeth?' I said.

'*Bonbon! Bonbon!*'

'Yeah, yeah. OKOK.'

'OKOKOKOK!'

And I dug through my pockets and pulled out a handful of candies and held them high over their little heads.

'OK, who gets it?'

'OKOKOKOK!'

The kids jumped up and down, giggling and reaching into the sky. I let the candies fall and the kids snatched them in mid-air. Not one bonbon hit the ground.

'OK, gotta go.'

'*Ne! Yosh bonbon!*'

'More? I told ya. Candy'll rot your teeth.'

'*Yosh! Molim! Yosh!*'

And down in the laughing faces, one little girl. The brightest of them all. Her eyes sparkling with laughter, her tiny hands holding my fingers and squeezing tight. She was swinging her head from side to side and her long blonde hair was moving like it was caught in the wind. She was having the most fun in the world just now. My eyes watched her in slow motion. She made me smile from somewhere long ago.

'What you think, sweetie? Give 'em more? *Yosh bonbon?*'

'*Da! Da! Moooliiim!*'

Her eyes brighter and brighter and her tiny hands squeezing my fingers tighter and tighter. I started pointing and gesturing and waving my arms in the international sign language understood by every kid in the world.

'OK, tell you what. I gotta go in there and I'll be back in ten minutes. Wait here and I'll get *yosh bonbon* from the truck. OK?'

'OKOKOKOK!'

'*Yosh bonbon!*'

The little girl let go of my hand and wrapped her arms round my waist and gave me a big hug.

'I'll be back, sweetie. I promise. You just wait here.'

I joined Terry and Sandy in a small office just inside the doors of Third Army HQ. We sat around and drank coffee and waited for someone to process our request. The kids' laughter coming through the opaque windows.

'Nice to know you can still make a few friends, Steele, even if you have to bribe them,' said Terry.

'See that one little girl with the blonde hair? What a heartbreaker.'

'You got that right. The kids are like that all over Bosnia. You just want to stuff them in your suitcase and get them out of here.'

A junior officer came into the room, shook our hands, and explained the numerous impossibilities involved in taking us to the front at the present moment. We sipped our coffee and nodded respectfully while listening to his various lines of bullshit. Outside, shots from an AK47 snapped from the rooftops.

'Hallo.'

'Sounds like a Bosnian shooting across the river.'

'Little early in the day, ain't it?'

Another outgoing round.

'Keeps it up he's going to wake up the Serbs.'

'Can't believe he's shootin' with children around.'

'Just another form of battlefield cover to these guys.'

Then three more automatic rounds. We sat listening to the sounds of the children's voices still laughing and giggling outside the window.

'Must be OK.'

The junior officer cleared his throat and returned to his line of bullshit. 'As I was saying, gentlemen . . .'

KACRACK! ZING! CRACK!

Silence.

'What the hell was that?'

'Incoming. Fuckin' monster bullet. Sounds like it ricocheted off the building.'

'Or the street.'

'Or both.'

Sandy MacIntyre looked me dead in the eyes. 'You don't suppose . . .'

Then a woman's screams cut through the glass.

'Marina! Marina! *Ne! Allaha mu ne!* Marina!'

I bolted for the camera and tore out the door and into the street.
Empty, like everyone just vanished into thin air.

'Marina! *Allaha mu ne!*'

Across the road, an old woman cowering in a doorway, her hands
clutching her breasts and her horrified eyes staring down at the street.
I ran round the armoured jeep and into the middle of the road. The
little girl with the brightest face and the laughing eyes was lying in a
pool of blood.

'Marina! *Moya* Marina!'

Three men rushed into the street and knelt round her. I chased after
them and switched on the camera and hit the roll button. The desperate men calling to the little girl . . .

'Marina! *Molim!* Marina!'

. . . and touching the girl's face and holding a cloth to her neck. The
bullet had caught her in the throat. Blood pumping in spurts through
the men's fingers. Marina's eyes seeing us.

'Jon! Jon!' Terry and Sandy at the back of the armoured pulling out
flak-jackets and tossing one into the street. 'Jon! He can see you! The
fucking sniper can see you!'

'Get on a vest!'

A small car screeched round the corner, the rear door swinging
open. The men lifted Marina off the street and threw her across
the back seat. Their voices full of panic and fear but trying to comfort
her. Marina's eyes still seeing, like she could hear their voices.
The cloth round her neck floating in blood. Gurgling sounds in her
throat.

Arms and backs crossed in the lens blocking the shot. I grabbed one
shoulder and pulled hard and shoved in the camera. And there, in the
viewfinder, Marina's eyes looking into the lens. Her head turning to
the side just for a second, like any curious child. Then her eyes losing
focus and rolling away. The car door slammed shut and the driver
raced up the street and round the corner. I raced after it till it was gone

. . . stopping over the pool of innocent blood in the street and panning down and rolling the picture for a long time.

'*Ne! Ne!*'

Behind me. A young man standing in the middle of the street, smashing his fists into his face and staggering towards Sniper Alley.

'*Ne! Ne! Zashto ubiyete destsu? Zashto?*'

His screaming voice questioning and pleading.

'*Zashto? Zashto?*'

'Jon! Get out of the fucking road!'

Terry and Sandy still pinned down against a concrete wall and pointing towards the river.

'Get down, for fucksake!'

I jumped behind a Lada and locked the lens on the screaming man. Fat tears pouring down his face, his hands ripping open his shirt, exposing his heart to the unseen killer.

'*Putsi omenhe! Nehu detsu! Ubey meh!*'

And falling to his knees, his arms stretched wide. He was begging to die.

'*Ubey meh! Molim te ubey meh!*'

Christ. He's gonna get it. He's gonna fuckin' get it.

Watching, waiting.

I held him in the lens. Like another pair of eyes somewhere across the Drina river. A pair of cold eyes looking down another lens. A lens mounted on a Draganov sniper rifle. A calm finger on the trigger. Another 7.69mm high-powered bullet in the firing chamber, ready to rip.

Watching, waiting.

Blood pulsing. Me and a Serb sniper, sharing the same heartbeat, breathing in the same rhythm. Two sharpshooters waiting for the kill.

'Anton! Anton!'

Men dashed from a doorway and dragged the grief-crazed man from the line of fire.

'*Ne! Ne! Ubey meh!*'

Doors slammed and the street was quiet again. I ran across the road and dropped next to Terry and Sandy.

'They got her in the neck.'

'How bad?'

'Real bad. Blood everywhere.'

'Oh, shit.'

'That guy was begging the sniper to kill him.'

'Yeah. Thought he was gonna get it, for sure.'

'Poor man, Jesus.'

'They were calling a name, Marina.'

'Must be her.'

'Should we get to the hospital?'

'Yeah.'

Into the armoured truck again and racing through the back-streets towards the western hills of Sarajevo. A big yellow Soviet-style hospital. Looked like a battered fortress on the losing side. Sandbags and scorchmarks all down the walls. We ran inside and found two hospital workers in bloodstained smocks smoking cigarettes and drinking Turkish coffee.

'You gotta little girl – what's her name, Terry?'

'Marina. Shot in the neck?'

And Terry pointing along the side of his throat.

'Ah. *Mala devoychesta*. Marina, OK. OK.'

'She's OK? Thankfuckin'God.'

'May we see her? Photograph?'

'*Slikaj*. Photograph, *da*.'

And one of the workers waved us in and led us up some stairs and down an empty hall.

'Let me tell you, Steele, it's a fucking miracle if she survived.'

'What they said, ain't it? Said she was OK. Must be in the operating room.'

'God, I hope so.'

The hospital worker stopped suddenly before a steel door. He yanked hard on a rusty handle and pulled the door wide. Death smells slapped our faces. The worker wiped his hands on his bloody smock and drew a long drag from his smoke and stepped into the dark, tiptoeing over something on the floor. He hit a switch and a fluorescent lamp buzzed and flickered and flooded the room with sickening light. Down on the floor. A small figure covered in a bloodied sheet, long blonde hair poking out from underneath.

'Oh, shit.'

'Oh, dear God.'

A few more drags off the cigarette, clouds of smoke drifting through the fluorescent light. Then the hospital worker bent over and pulled away the sheet. A beautiful little girl, naked and dead in the sickening light. Dried blood and yellow antiseptic all down the front of her body, a horrible gash across her throat. The sniper's bullet had slaughtered her like a lamb.

'You photograph?'

The hospital worker waiting for me to photograph the naked body.

'What?'

'*Slikaj?* You photograph?'

'Jon?'

'No. Cover her up, just cover her up.'

He tossed the sheet down and shrugged his shoulders. He switched off the lights, stepped across the body and slammed closed the steel door. Little Marina was locked away in the forever dark.

'Jesusfuckin'Christ.'

'You OK, Steele?'

'I don't know. Somethin'. I thought she was gonna be OK.'

'Come on. We should do the story. It's all we can do now.'

'Yeah. I s'pose.'

Outside the hospital Terry and Sandy talked out the plan. I opened the rear of the armoured vehicle and tossed in the camera, looking at the front of the lens and brushing off the dust in slow circles, till an ice-cold chill ran down my spine. The voices around me fading away. My eyes staring at the reflection in the front of the lens, *and seeing*.

'I'll go to the TV station and get whatever tapes are around.'

'Good. Steele and I will drive back to that street.'

Oh, fuck.

'What do you think, Jon?'

Oh God, please, no.

'Jon?'

'Sniper Alley.'

'What? Why?'

'I wanna go to Sniper Alley . . . by Romeo and Juliet Bridge. I need some shots.'

'What kind of shots? That's the most dangerous part of town.'

'You all right, Jon?'

'No, I ain't all right. I'm fuckin' loopy, remember? And that little girl in there's dead.'

Jesus, it fuckin' can't be.

'It's not your fault, Jon, it's Sarajevo.'

'Look. I wanna go to Sniper Alley. Now.'

'OK, Steele. But you're going to wear a fucking flak-jacket this time.'

'Fine, then. Let's go.'

Terry jumped behind the wheel and I jumped into the back. I pulled the bulletproof ceramic plates out of the flak-jacket and slid the empty shell over my shoulders. There'd be nothing but blue cloth and a thin kevlar mesh between me and a high-powered bullet. I rested the camera on my knees and I stared into the reflected light of the lens again.

You fuckin' bastard. You goddam fuckin' bastard.

We drove through the city in silence. The ice-cold chill flowing through every street and round every corner like a river. All leading me down to one place, Romeo and Juliet Bridge, the heart of Sniper Alley. Place where once upon a time two lovers lay rotting for days after they were gunned down by sniper fire. Sarajevo was a good place to die. Terry pulled up on to the pavement and tucked the truck under a high building. I looked through the bulletproof glass and saw Bosnian civilians peeking out from behind concrete walls and narrow doorways, then dashing across the intersection as fast as they could run. A small traffic island in the middle of the intersection with a couple of bullet-riddled trees. Half-way mark through the killing zone. Catch your breath and tear out into the open once more. Every step of the way in plain sight of Serb snipers.

'Listen, Steele. I don't know what you're up to but you damn well better be careful. Don't do anything stupid.'

'I'm gonna run with 'em.'

'You're going to what?'

'I'm gonna fuckin' run with 'em!'

'The hell you are!'

'It's OK, Terry. Everyone dies in Sarajevo.'

I kicked open the rear door, jumped out and threw the camera on my shoulder. 'See you around, Terry.'

'Jon!'

And I ran into the intersection rolling on the terrified faces around me. The men, the women, the children. All of them racing across the road and jumping behind trees then running out into the open again.

All of them sweating fear and praying to make it to the other side before a sniper's bullet cut them down. All of them except one.

'*Yosh bonbon!*'

Breathing hard and fast.

I'll be back, sweetie . . .

Heart pounding like rapid-fire bullets.

. . . you just wait here.

'Jon! Enough, Jon!'

And then into the street again.

'For fucksake, Steele! That's enough!'

Come on, do it! Somebody, please do it!

Down behind the trees. Legs feeling shaky. Soon, comin' soon. Keep running, just keep running. And looking down into the reflection of the lens once more and seeing my own face and *knowing . . .*

'Steele! Fucksake! Come back here!'

. . . that the last thing little Marina saw in her ten-year-old life was her own face reflected mirrorlike in the lens of my camera. The camera I shoved in her face as she lay choking on her own blood. Her little eyes watching, then turning like any curious child . . . then she watched herself die.

C'mon! Just pull the fuckin' trigger and kill me! Just fuckin' kill me!

14

THE COLOUR TEMPERATURE OF LIGHT

London, 23 August 1994

There was a clock in the corner. I could hear it ticking. Soft metal taps but that was all. Heavy drapes and thick carpets swallowed the sounds of Marylebone Road and the outside world. Blue light glowed round the edges of the drapes. Blue summer light that faded quickly in the dim room.

Ticktock, ticktock.

'Jon, I'm very concerned about your state of mind.'

And there was this voice coming from across the room. A young woman, a doctor, couldn't remember her name but she was watching me, watching my hands. My always shaking hands.

'Can you try and talk a little?'

There was a lamp in the corner and it was bright. Too bright when I stared into it. It hurt my eyes. But I watched the light hit the wall and spill out through the room like warm mist, and then it was OK.

'You're hurting, Jon. You're hurting very badly.'

'I was in Sarajevo, then I was at the airport goin' somewhere and I ca– I can't sleep.'

'I know. I want to help you.'

Help us!

'Ain't me. Not me. The others.'

'Who, Jon?'

'All of them. The ones I hurt.'

'Whom did you hurt, Jon?'

'Everyone. I hurt everyone.'

My voice circled through the room but I didn't recognize it when it came back to me. Sounded like it was someone else in the room and not me.

'I think you should admit yourself into the hospital, Jon.'

'Wha– ?'

'We can put you on medication. Sedatives to help you get back into a regular sleep cycle. You cannot go on like this. You need to rest.'

Faces flashing before my eyes.

'No! I ca– I can't.'

'Why not?'

Horrible dead faces.

'Because they'll find me.'

'Who, Jon? Who would come for you?'

'All of them . . . all of them.'

'Is there anyone we could contact for you?'

'No. Nobody. There's no one left.'

'There must be someone who can care for you.'

'No! They're all gone. Just as dead as everyone else . . . or me. Maybe it's me. I ca– I can't tell any more. It's like I'm not . . . oh, Jesus. I gotta get out of here.'

'Try to relax. You're under so much stress.'

Don't leave us!

'Stress? Fucksake, you callin' this stress?'

'Yes, Jon. And you're in terrible pain. Whatever has happened, whatever you've seen, it's tearing you apart. You must try to let us help you.'

'I ca– I can't. You can't see it. It's . . . oh, God. I gotta get out of here.'

'This isn't fair to you. All you're feeling. Can you try to let me help you?'

'I . . . I . . .'

Then tears washing through my eyes and me tasting water and salt and vomit and death. Feeling them coming again.

Oh, Jesus, not again!

And seeing all the corpses float out of the walls and me smelling their rotting flesh and feeling their skeleton hands touching my skin.

'Christ! They won't leave me alone!'

'Who, Jon? What is it?'

Run! Fuckin' run, dammit!

'If you come into the hospital we'll help you sleep for a few days. Then we can get you into therapy. We can help you through all the other things you've been through when you're feeling stronger emotionally.'

And the young doctor still looking at my always shaking hands.

Shit! She's one of them! It's a trap! Stop shaking!

'I have to go. I have to go.'

'Listen, Jon, you're confused and shattered and in a great deal of pain.'

'Fuckin' hell. It's not my pain that matters.'

They're all dying!

'Jon. I know you've seen some terrible things, too many terrible things.'

'It's just I ca– can't sleep.'

'And you feel you've abandoned people you love. Your entire world is in turmoil.'

'I don't love anyone . . . never could love . . . anyone.'

'We can help you.'

'It's too late. They're dead . . . all of 'em . . . her.'

'Who, Jon? Who is she?'

'She's fuckin' dead. God, she was only a child and I . . . I . . . I did something terrible.'

'Do you want to talk about it?'

'No . . . no.'

'Sooner or later you must deal with your feelings about the things you've seen. You are in danger . . .'

'No!'

'. . . of hurting yourself. You need help.'

'I can't! I have to go.'

'Why, Jon?'

''Cause . . .'

And then the endless tears. Flooding through the room and washing up round the chair and the ticktock of the clock growing louder and louder . . .

Oh, God, no! Not the drowning dream! Please not the drowning dream!

Ticktock. Ticktock.

. . . and me grabbing the arms of the chair but feeling the water rise up my legs and over my body and round my face.

'Jon, you are suffering from acute post-traumatic stress syndrome. You need sleep.'

Then the dead hands reaching from the deep and me shaking my head and my face going under the water . . .

'I'm gonna die . . . I'll die.'

. . . and the dead hands wrapping round my legs and pulling me under the waves.

'Jon? What's happening?'

No! No!

TICKTOCK! TICKTOCK!

'You'll die if you go to sleep?'

And me nodding under the water and holding my breath and the rotting corpses squeezing my chest trying to force the air from my lungs and hearing the clock blasting like killer shells and the dead hands tearing me from the chair and pulling me deeper and deeper into the forever dark.

'Why will you die, Jon?'

And seeing all the dead eyes circling round me and rotting corpses squeezing tighter and tighter . . .

Let me go! Let me go!

'Why, Jon? Can you tell me?'

. . . and then crashing through the surface and gasping for air and thousands of dead hands clawing at my legs . . .

Help us!

'Because I fuckin' deserve it!'

'Why, Jon? Why do you deserve to die?'

No! It's only a dream! It's only a dream!

'Because . . . because . . . they're all dead!'

'And you couldn't save them, could you?'

Put down the fuckin' camera! They're all dying!

'Yes! No! Shit! Christ . . . I didn't even fuckin' try!'

'And you think you should have helped?'

'Don't you understand? Can't you see it? I let them die! I stuck my camera in their faces and I let them all die!'

'Jon, it isn't your fault.'

'For fucksake! It is my fault! Can't you fuckin' understand? It *is* my fault! I wanted to see it! I wanted those pictures! I needed all of them to suffer! I needed them to die!'

'Why would you need people to die, Jon?'

No! No!

'Why, Jon?'

. . . and a child's terrified scream ripping through my brain . . .

'So . . . so people would think I was brave! So people wouldn't know I been afraid my whole fuckin' life! So I could be some kind of fuckin' hero!'

. . . then there was only the sound of the clock.

The soft metal taps of the clock in the corner.

Moscow, dawn, 17 September 1994

The Moscow river was grey and it lapped up the grey stone steps and crested just under the soles of my boots. I tapped down and watched tiny ripples drift back out into the current where the Kremlin Palace and the cathedral towers reflected yellow and gold in the river. Been sitting on the stone steps most of the night. Vodka bottle in one hand, empty notebook in the other. And me trying to think of some words, or trying to drink. Couldn't remember which came first. But just now the vodka was almost gone and the notebook was empty and my brain was numb. Still, thought I should write something to mark the day. It was my birthday.

'The sun rose over the grey river and there was a cobalt sky and fire-bird clouds. And the tired sun said, "What a long strange trip it's been."' I put those words down in the notebook and that was that, couldn't think of anything else. So I had another swig of vodka and watched the wiggly Kremlin some more. That's the way I lived, these days. Watching and drinking and roaming the Moscow streets. More glorious vodka, more mind-spinning dope, more 'I love you' lies from the lips of Russian whores. I bagged out of the hospital in London. Just no way I was ready to face all the pictures in my head. So I said to hell with it and flew back to Moscow. Hide among the brooding souls of

Russia. Pretend everything was fine and nobody would know, till I walked into the ITN Moscow bureau over on Taganka Square. Oleg was waiting with his tousled hair and his down-on-the-point-of-his-nose spectacles.

'Uh, well,' he said.

Tears filled my eyes.

Oleg held out his arms when I started to shake. 'Oh, Jonka, *moi* Jonka.'

And I walked out. Same way I walked out of countless lives. I just turned round and walked. I never looked back. So much for hiding back in Moscow. Then the nightmares started again. Technicolor terror in my head.

Another swig of vodka. It burned. A delicious burn all the way down into my blood. I waited for that warm tingle as a few more brain cells turned to sludge. Then another swig and another. I poured a swig of vodka into the river. It floated like oil for a moment then disappeared beneath the waves. I laid the bottle down on the grey stones and gave it a *spinnnnnn*. The bottle clanked and clinked and spat till it stopped and pointed thataway. So that's the way I walked.

Across Kamennyi Bridge and under the ramparts of the Kremlin. Guards at Borovitskaya Tower watched me lean against a lamp-post and lower my zipper and drain forth like any decent drunken Russian. I raised both my hands in gymnastic triumph.

'Hey, look, Boris! No hands!'

My amusement was not shared by the guards.

'Oh, fuck off if you can't take a fuckin' joke.'

Zip.

'Oops.'

Steaming piss on my boots.

'Bound to happen sooner or later, I s'pose.'

Round Alexander's Garden and up the uneven cobblestones towards Red Square. And me trying to remember the first time I walked over these stones. Early morning, 1990. Red Army soldiers rushed around me and ordered me to follow them and marched me into the square. Soldiers on either side of me doing that weird kick-march thing. I thought I was under arrest for some heinous crime against the Soviet State. Turned out I was just first in line to visit

Lenin's tomb. Guards pulled open the mausoleum doors and pointed the way down to the Great Dead Man.

That was a lifetime ago. When it was all new and good.

Now, Christ. What the hell'd happened?

I wandered into the middle of Red Square. Not a living soul around. I stood quiet and still. Another autumn in Mother Russia. Wind slipped up from the river and it was chilly in the dawn shade. Then sunlight cut through the shadows and sparkled over the candy-coloured domes of St Basil's Cathedral. Perfect gravestone for the fool saint buried deep beneath the cathedral's red-brick walls. Fool was actually a nice word for raving loony. Guy used to roam Moscow in rags and scream about wickedness and doom and the end of the world. Holy Mother Russia made Basil a saint anyway. My eyes panned round the scene. Three nutters alone on Red Square. The Great Dead Man, a Raving Loony Saint, one Burnt-out Cameraman. Best pals. I fumbled through my pockets and found my notebook and I scribbled some more words, 'My best pals are dead.' Then the autumn wind came up from the river again and everything was quiet and still once more.

'Right. Any you dead guys want coffee?'

My voice bouncing off the Kremlin walls. No takers. So I went alone. That's when the tears started again. Staring down into a ten-dollar cup of coffee at the Metropole Hotel. Happened like that. One minute I was fine, then the next minute I was terrified and crying, then I got drunk and stoned and whacked out till I was fine, then over and over and over. I stirred the coffee and drank it down. I tried to read my fortune in the wet grains at the bottom of the cup. Gooey and brown was all I could make out.

Ah, fuck it.

I tripped out on to the street and stumbled through a whirling blur of early-bird Russians. No one noticing me, no one touching me . . .

'*Urah*, comrades!'

. . . like I wasn't there any more.

'Look at me! I'm dead too!'

Then the weariness came down hard. Weeks without sleep. Couldn't sleep 'cause the nightmares lived there. Then the nightmares were everywhere. Day and night. Chasing me through the streets till I couldn't run any more. I just wanted to lie down. All the way down where I could sleep for ever. And I knew how to get there.

I can take you there, my sad darling.

And I was ready. Finally fuckin' ready.

I steered a ragged course for Mayakovskaya Ploshad and my favourite Russian whore, Natasha. The one with the killer grey eyes and all the magic drugs. Been avoiding her for a while, waiting till the time was right. She'd be having breakfast at the American Café with all the other hookers and vampires crawling in from the Moscow night. She'd taken me to the edge a dozen times. She'd nibble the veins in my arm and dig her teeth into my flesh till she could taste blood. And every time I looked into her killer grey eyes, I knew she wanted to finish me off. Whole thing was a game for her.

No more sadness, my darling. Just a wonderful place.

One wonderful rush to Never-Never Land. Just load the needle with a little extra whack and never come back. Christ, I was so damn ready.

Back through the street-markets of old Moscow and down a small street of autumn trees. Crumbling buildings of pale greens and blues and yellows. Stone statues above the doorways. A child's face watching me from behind window lace. I wanted to remember everything along the way. Wind snapped through the trees and leaves tumbled down round my head. I tried to catch one as it fell and I remembered myself as a little boy, running through the woods chasing the falling leaves. And I remembered how I always felt so wonderfully alive in the season of dead and dying leaves. But that was a long time ago. And now it was time to sleep. I rolled a fat joint and lit up. Long pull, then another.

No more sadness . . .

Take me, baby, please, just take me.

And wanting Natasha to push the needle into my arm.

. . . a wonderful place.

Then fade to black.

Thud . . . boom.

What the hell?

My eyes panned up to the sound. Up above the autumn trees. The tower of a small Russian church. A shrunken shape in black robes climbing a ladder into a spider's web of ropes in the tower. An Orthodox priest with a scraggly grey beard, black cap atop his long grey hair. He wrapped the ropes round his hands and he bowed slowly to the morning sun rising in the east.

Gong. Gong. Gong.

Low deep tones vibrating into the early-morning sky and the priest pulled more ropes and high-pitched bells chased after the deep-throated bells. Then pulling all the ropes at once and the air was full of noise. Bells and bells and more bells. Big ones, little ones. Clanging and ringing, bangs and gongs. And me standing there watching the bell-ringer priest pull faster and faster. Twisting like some mad wizard, mixing the bells into one cacophonous voice singing to the Russian skies. The sounds pulsing and vibrating all through me. Louder and louder till the priest let the ropes fly from his hands and there was only the deep-throated bell humming through the trees.

Gong. Gong. Gong.

Then fading away into the autumn wind. The priest bowed to the morning sun once more.

'Bravo! Bravo!'

The priest looked down from his bell-tower.

'Bravo! Hell, Quasimodo deserves a drink.' I searched through my coat for the vodka bottle till I remembered I'd left it back by the river. 'Oh, shit. Sorry, padre. Don't have any vodka but how 'bout a toke of some ass-kicking gra—?'

But when I looked up the bell-ringer priest was gone.

Then the whole world went wobbly. The joint fell from my hands.

Fuck me. Come on, keep movin'.

I stumbled in circles trying to remember which way was thataway. Round and round till I stumbled into a heavy wooden door. My fingers feeling gnarls of old wood rubbed smooth with time and touch. I pushed hard against the door and fell into another world.

Smoke and incense and darkness. Then pools of warm light glowing all round me. I wobbled from side to side trying to focus my stoned eyes. Candles. Hundreds and hundreds of candles flaming in the dark. And old Russian women moving between the pools of light, tending the flames. Their voices calling to each other in prayerful rhythm. Frail Russian voices, ancient Russian prayers.

I eased through the dark over a stone floor towards a pool of light. Candles flickering atop a tall brass stand. One old woman with an old woollen scarf over her hair and her face tinted with firelight. She was peeling away the melting wax and praying over the flames as if comforting them against the dark. And my eyes staring at the flames and following curls of candlesmoke higher and higher to the icons of prophets and saints painted on stone. The suffering Madonna. The murdered Christ.

'Damn, Toto, don't think we're in Kansas any more.'

Then other pictures flashed from the walls. Tortured bodies and dead faces hanging in the candlesmoke and incense. And a little girl emerging from the forever dark. Blood flowing from her neck and falling like rain. Her little dead hands reaching for me.

'No! Leave me the fuck alone!'

I spun round and stood face to face with the bell-ringer priest. His ancient blue eyes looking deep into mine. Silently watching, searching.

'*Chto ty delayesh?*'

'Sorry, padre. Didn't mean to disgrace your church.'

'*Kolokola priveli tebya syuda.*'

'I got somethin' about bells, but you gotta believe me, man, I am way too fucked up to understand a word you're sayin'. I'll be goin'.'

'*Chto s toboi sluchilos? Podozhdi.*'

''Scuse me?'

'*Podozhdi. Kuda ty idyosh?*'

'Nowhere. Wasn't goin' nowhere. I was just passin' through and got a bit lost.'

And he raised his rope-worn hands. A long candle between his fingers. Thin and yellow. A hopeless sliver of wax.

'*Vot. Vozmi etu svechku.*'

'No. Not for me.'

'*Pochemu nyet?*'

And he reached over just over my heart. Then closing his eyes and touching my chest softly. Once, twice, three times. Then looking into my eyes and searching still. He opened my hands and laid the candle across my palms.

'*Vozmi eto.*'

'No. Not for me.'

'*Pozhaluista.*'

'Pl-please. Just let me go.'

'*Pochyemu nyet?*'

Then the tears coming again. The bell-ringer priest searching deeper into my eyes.

'Look, trust me ... I'm the last fuckin' person you want in this place.'

And the tears poured down my face. My voice choking on words the bell-ringer priest couldn't even understand.

'I don't belong here. I ...'

And all the pictures and all the dead faces and all the nightmare crashing down at once.

'I ca– I can't take it any more.'

Thousands and thousands of pictures. Twenty-four frames per second, racing through my eyes. I could see them. All of them. But this time they weren't pictures. They were real. They were alive.

'I didn't know what I was doin'. I thought they were only pictures! I mean, I knew ... but I had to make them nothin' but pictures. I c– I couldn't let 'em be real. It was just too much to see ... oh, God.'

The bell-ringer priest still holding my hands. His lips quivering and tears in his ancient blue eyes as if he could see all the souls dying in my eyes over and over again.

'I'm so sorry. Oh, God. I'm so sorry. How do I tell them? I let them die and I never told them.'

And I wept. My tears falling over the stone floor. My sobs echoing through the candlesmoke. Sacred icons looking down.

'Oh, Jesus. I'm so sorry. I'm so sorry they suffered. I'm so sorry they died. I'm so sorry!'

The bell-ringer priest squeezed my hands and drew me close. My sobs fading to whimpers. Whimpers fading to silence. He raised his rope-worn hands and made the sign of the Orthodox cross over my head. He kissed my cheek and he walked away.

And I stood alone at the edge of the shadows near a pool of warm light for a long time. Amid the ancient Russian prayers and incense and candlesmoke. Waiting for the feelings to come. Feelings that would hit hard and roll through me till the end of my days.

I reached out and held the candle to the flames.

The wick blackened and flashed and firelight exploded in my eyes.

EPILOGUE: THE WAY OF SORROWS

Arab East Jerusalem, December, 2000

Fire in the streets. Arabs and Jews going at it again. Been like this all over the West Bank and Gaza for ten bloody weeks now. Three hundred Palestinians and nearly fifty Israelis killed so far. Arabs calling it martyrdom, Jews calling it murder. Arabs thinking they're fighting for freedom, Jews thinking they're protecting innocent lives from terrorism. All of them children of the Prophet Abraham. Brothers slaying brothers while praying to the same God. What a fuckin' mess. People call this place the Holy Land. Seems more like an unholy maze of hate and vengeance.

Lion's Gate in the Old City of Jerusalem during the Muslim holy month of Ramadan. I was pinned down in the middle of one more battle. Started at high noon just after Friday prayers. Palestinian boys known as the Shabab charged out through the green doors of Al-Aqsa Mosque throwing stones and Molotov cocktails towards waiting Israeli troops. The Israelis answered with stun grenades and rubber bullets. Back and forth and back and forth all day. And me running between the stones and the bullets cramming pictures into the lens. Shabab with their faces wrapped in *koufiyahs*, eyes ablaze with sacred purpose, slings loaded with stones. And just ahead under a low stone archway Israeli soldiers in bulletproof vests, sweat dripping down their faces, rifles loaded with bullets. Between them lay a narrow cobblestone path called the Via Dolorosa, the Way of Sorrows. Two thousand years ago a man named Jesus walked down this same path on his way to crucifixion. Lying there amid the fire and smoke of present-day battle, my mind was spinning with wonder.

Then something through the smoke ... shadows racing across the low winter sun, then falling down atop the roofs of Arab houses ... *Shit!* Israeli snipers taking positions above the Way of Sorrows. I looked back at the Shabab still winding their slings like windmills and letting another wave of stones fly, their voices crying ...

'Allah Akhbar! Allah Akhbar!'

... and I knew it was gonna happen again. Someone was gonna die. *Please, Lord, don't let it be me. I ain't ready to die just yet.*

The Israeli soldiers charged and the Shabab turned to run away. That's when the Israeli snipers opened up and bullets ripped through the air. My eyes zoomed through the chaos till I saw one Palestinian boy in a white shirt. He could've jumped over a nearby ledge and got clean away. *Mush mushlika, en bayah,* no problem. But he dashed across the courtyard and started climbing up a stone wall when an Israeli bullet sparked against the stone and his head snapped back and he sank to the ground. A ricochet got him in the throat.

Boots of Israeli soldiers rushed over me and into the lens. Zoom in. Two of the soldiers fall near the boy, tear open a field bandage and start wrapping it round the boy's throat. I jumped up and ran towards them, pulled the zoom lens wide, the camera still rolling. Fifty heavily armed Israelis hunkered down behind stone pillars and aimed their rifles towards the high walls surrounding Al-Aqsa Mosque and Temple Mount. And up on the walls, the Shabab letting go with an avalanche of stones. Pan down and zoom in. The soldiers still wrapping bandages round the Palestinian boy's neck. The boy's chest motionless, he was already dead. But the soldiers struggled to stop the flow of blood anyway. Maybe they didn't know the boy was gone, maybe they thought they could bring him back to life. I didn't know. I just couldn't take my eyes off the vision before me. Israeli soldiers, their hands drenched in blood, leaning over a dead Palestinian boy as if trying to protect him from the falling stones.

The battle went on for hours till the sun sank beyond the Jerusalem hills. The Israeli troops withdrew and the Shabab went home. I wandered over the empty battleground looking for pictures. On the spot where the boy was killed there was a pool of blood. Someone'd dipped their fingers into it and scrawled a message across the stone wall: '*Allah Akhbar*' . . . 'God is Great.'

I made my way to ITN's Jerusalem office and watched the pictures hit the satellite to London. I cried some more. A colleague of mine who'd seen the pictures came into my edit suite and told me to look at the shot one more time. Seems there was something I'd missed. I rolled the tape and fell back in a chair. The last round out of the sniper's rifle hitting the ground inches from the lens, inches from my head. Rewind and watch it again, rewind and watch it again.

'Fuck me.'

'You are very, very lucky, Jon.'

Please, Lord, don't let it be me. I ain't ready to die just yet.

The night turned cold and rain fell through the darkness. I bought a small bunch of daisies and walked back to Lion's Gate. The pool of blood and the message on the wall now washed away in the rain. I laid the flowers on the ground where the boy was gunned down. Wasn't condemning the Israelis, wasn't cheering for the Palestinians. I was just the last person to see one young boy alive. I needed to remember what I'd seen and how it felt. I prayed for his soul. I prayed for all the souls murdered in this unholy war. And I stood there a long time, feeling the pain that comes with the job of surviving such events in such a place.

I'd done a lot of that over the last few years. Through Chechnya and Afghanistan, East Timor and Kosovo, India and Pakistan, now the Middle East. There were wars and famines. Earthquakes and floods. There was suffering and death, lots of it. And at the end of each day I'd walk off somewhere and take a moment to think about the things I'd seen and how I felt about them. Sometimes I'd shed tears for the dead. Sometimes I'd shed tears for myself. I was always grateful to have survived.

Someone once told me I was quite the adventurer. Thought about it over the years and decided it wasn't quite true. Adventurers have another sort of life. They plan things out, then charge ahead with compass in hand, dreaming about making it into the history books.

No, I decided I'd been a wanderer most of my life. A body of constant motion unable to settle down. Wasn't really looking for anything. Just had to keep running away from wherever I might be at the time . . . I was that unhappy with who I was. Price of the voyage seemed cheap enough, just leave my emotions and feelings, my entire life, by the side of the road. Took a few affairs of the heart to realize how lonely that could be. Took a few more affairs of the heart to learn I couldn't use other people to fill the loneliness. For a time it didn't matter, I was an emotional hobo travellin' light.

Somewhere along the road I picked up a camera. Gave my wanderings a bit of direction and a few laughs till I wandered into the fog of war. More war than I was ready for. Whole scene went down like good drugs. Walking through the valley of death and coming to the other side over and over again. Man, what a rush. Dig it . . . I was invincible, I was cool . . . I was somebody else, not that frightened kid from the Montana sticks, too ashamed to keep his own name. I was in total control, master of the fuckin' world. Till all those feelings and emotions I'd left by the side of the road caught up with me that one terrible day in Sarajevo.

After my crack-up at Heathrow Airport in 1994, after turning away from the lovely Natasha and her killer grey eyes and all the drugs I needed to die, after lighting a candle in a Russian church, things changed. Wasn't like I was cured. Wasn't like I was any more fearful than before, wasn't like I was fearful any less. I just tried going from day to day thinking, *I ain't ready to die just yet*. Doesn't sound like much but, hell, it was all I had in the moment. Besides, it's hard to find any twelve-step programmes for war junkies. I found a shrink in Moscow and started talking. I pulled out some paper and started writing. And the more I talked and the more I wrote, the more I came to terms with living my life through the looking-glass. I started feeling the pictures coming through the lens. And that saved my life.

I've seen the heroes of this world, though I couldn't tell you their names. They're the innocent ones caught in the vainglory of power. They lose everything, they suffer beyond measure, they die the most terrible deaths. It's the innocent ones who carry the true nobility of humanity. I've seen them all over the world. Men and women protecting the last shreds of their families when all else is lost, finding the courage to make it through one more day of starvation and war, leaving the bodies of loved ones in the dirt and walking on because there was no other choice.

Thousands and thousands of innocent men, women and children died in my eyes. Lots of bad guys too. I still see all of them in my dreams, but I don't run any more. Every once in a while I wake with memories and I know it's gonna be one of those nights when the pictures play endlessly through my head. I get up and make a cup of tea, sit in the dark and wait. And the pictures come one by one, each of them with a story. And I sit in the dark and listen . . .

'. . . they burned down my house.'

'. . . my baby has no food.'

'. . . we've nowhere to hide.'

'. . . he's dead, he's dead.'

'. . . please, help us.'

. . . and I wait till each story is finished.

All these people I've seen, all these precious lives wandering through my eyes. All of them so easily forgotten by the world after the pictures fade. But I won't forget. I can't forget. Their stories are heart-breaking and true and need to be told. Maybe all us war cameramen know that in our hearts. We're a cynical bunch, but corner any one of us in a bar after a day like today and you'll find we do it because we believe it must be done. Even if no one else listens, even if no one else cares. The innocent ones whose lives we've captured have no voice, they have no protection. When they see us coming with our cameras, they hope we can help 'cause often when we show up there's no one else. Maybe that's why we risk our lives finding their stories, maybe that's why we risk our lives telling them. Maybe that's why I'm stand-ing in front of this stone wall in the Old City of Jerusalem just now, saying a silent prayer for all the souls that wandered through the camera lens and into my life. Telling their stories gave me a reason to stay alive.

The cold rain kept falling at Lion's Gate. I was soaked to the bone. The daisies on the ground looking like they might float away and follow the ghost of Jesus down the Way of Sorrows. I looked at my watch. It was late . . . and tomorrow was gonna be another bad day in the Holy Land. More people would die, more families would be torn asunder, more suffering voices would rise unto the merciless heavens. .

And me in the middle, grabbing pictures and shoving them down the world's throat.

If I make it through the day, I'll be grateful.